Global History

Global History

Interactions Between the Universal and the Local

Edited by

A. G. HOPKINS

First published 2006 by
PALGRAVE MACMILLAN
Houndmills, Basingstoke, Hampshire RG21 6XS and
175 Fifth Avenue, New York, N. Y. 10010
Companies and representatives throughout the world

PALGRAVE MACMILLAN is the global academic imprint of the Palgrave
Macmillan division of St. Martin's Press, LLC and of Palgrave Macmillan Ltd.
Macmillan® is a registered trademark in the United States, United Kingdom
and other countries. Palgrave is a registered trademark in the European
Union and other countries.

ISBN-13: 978–1–4039–8792–1 hardback
ISBN-10: 1–4039–8792–0   hardback
ISBN-13: 978–1–4039–8793–8 paperback
ISBN-10: 1–4039–8793–9   paperback

This book is printed on paper suitable for recycling and made from fully
managed and sustained forest sources.

A catalogue record for this book is available from the British Library.

A catalog record for this book is available from the Library of Congress.

10   9   8   7   6   5   4   3   2   1
15   14   13   12   11   10   09   08   07   06

Printed in China

Contents

List of Illustrations and Maps

Illustrations

Maps

Preface

Globalization has become big business for scholars as well as for corporations. During the past decade, economists, political scientists, and sociologists have generated a huge literature on all aspects of a process that now envelops much of the world. A spirited debate has arisen about the novelty of globalization and the extent to which its roots can be traced to a distant past. As yet, however, few historians have engaged with this literature and its accompanying controversies. The purpose of this book is twofold: to encourage historians to add their expertise to the discussion; and to contribute to the way history is taught in an age in which national histories have ceased to capture some of the most important developments of our time.

We have tried to meet the first aim by exploring one of the principal themes to have emerged from the recent literature: the realization that globalization produces diversity as well as uniformity. This perception is captured in our sub-title: the relationship between universal ideas and policies and the varied outcomes that follow from applying them in different places and at different times. The resulting interactions are traced in the Introduction, which offers an explanation of the varied outcomes, and in the subsequent chapters, which show that historians can remain faithful to their training in mobilizing documentary evidence and incorporating fieldwork into detailed research while also contributing to the much larger issues raised by the process of globalization. We have not attempted to produce a study that is comprehensive; such an undertaking would require many volumes. It has also to be said that the regions and themes covered here are unlikely to coincide with the priorities of all readers. In our judgment, however, what matters is how effectively we have treated the historical examples we have selected. We hope that we have been able to show how themes arising from the study of globalization can be linked to detailed cases that otherwise appear to have nothing in common. By choosing illustrations from economic, political, diplomatic, social, and intellectual history, we think that we have also shown how the literature on globalization can appeal to all branches of the discipline.

Our approach to the second aim is unusual to the extent that all contributors, except one, are from the Department of History at the University of Texas at Austin. Since globalization is a new subject for historians, there was little prospect of drawing on a wide range of scholars who were already familiar with the relevant literature, and still less chance of ensuring that the resulting volume would amount to more than a set of largely unrelated studies. We judged that every sizeable university department of history ought to contain the necessary range and level of expertise to support an enterprise of this kind, and that a sustained, collective effort would produce results in a new field of enquiry that one brief meeting or conference would not. Our collegial endeavor has involved four workshops, hundreds of e-mails, and innumerable conversations extending over three years. The commitment of my younger colleagues, who are responsible for the greater part of the book, has enabled the study as a whole to achieve a degree of coherence that otherwise it would not have attained, though we are aware that the result remains exploratory rather than definitive. We hope, too, that our book demonstrates that other departments of history can do what we have done, and perhaps improve on our efforts. Both the writing and the teaching of world history are changing as historians begin to grapple with the academic implications of globalization in the new century. Textbooks will have to be rethought; teaching may require greater teamwork. Our study can plant only a small signpost, but we think that it points in the right direction.

The one exception to the Austin-based team is William McNeill, the distinguished pioneer of world history. We felt that we needed an outside check on our intense but largely internal deliberations, and we are very grateful to Professor McNeill for agreeing to contribute an Afterword that comments on our work and sets it in a context that extends beyond the two centuries we have covered. We would also like to express our appreciation of the valuable comments made by three anonymous referees, who provided a further test of our desire to confirm our favored arguments. The enterprise as a whole has benefited from the collegial ethos of the Department of History and from the support of the Chair, Alan Tully, whose interest in the work helped to ensure that we stayed on course, if not exactly on time.

A. G. Hopkins
Austin, Texas
May 2006

Acknowledgements

It is a pleasure to acknowledge the financial assistance of the Walter Prescott Webb endowment, which met the cost of our four workshops. Webb is a celebrated name among American historians; he also remains a famous figure in the Department of History at the University of Texas at Austin, which he served for 30 years. His spacious historical interests continue to be represented in the work of current members of the Department; we hope that the present study, too, carries forward the spirit of his enquiries into the moving frontiers of history. Finally, we should also like to acknowledge the support given by the staff of the Department of History, who responded to the demands of our in-house co-operative with their customary resilience, efficiency and good humor.

Every effort has been made to trace the copyright holders of quoted or displayed material, but if any have been inadvertently overlooked the publishers will be pleased to make the necessary arrangement at the first opportunity.

Notes on the Contributors

Erika Marie Bsumek is Assistant Professor of History at the University of Texas at Austin, where she teaches courses in Western history, Native American history and environmental history. She received her PhD from Rutgers University and has held fellowships from the Geraldine R. Dodge Foundation, the Tanner Humanities Center, and the Huntington Library. She is currently completing a book entitled *Indian-made: The Production and Consumption of Navajo-ness, 1868–1940* (forthcoming from the University Press of Kansas), and is working on a second book, *The Concrete West: Engineering Society and Culture in the Arid West, 1900–1975*. She has published articles and chapters on the history of ethnology, consumerism and American Indian culture.

Roger Hart is Assistant Professor in the Department of History at the University of Texas at Austin. His areas of research include Chinese history, the history of science, and critical theory. He earned a BS from MIT and an MS from Stanford, both in mathematics, and a PhD in history from UCLA. He is the recipient of an American Council of Learned Societies Fellowship (2004–05), and a National Endowment for the Humanities Fellowship at the School of Historical Studies, Institute for Advanced Study, Princeton (1999–2000). He is the author of numerous articles, and is currently completing a book entitled *Western Learning in Seventeenth-Century China: A Microhistorical Approach to World History*, while also working on a second book, *The Early History of Linear Algebra: Chinese Sources*.

Mark Atwood Lawrence is Associate Professor of History at the University of Texas at Austin. He holds a PhD from Yale University and held a John M. Olin Postdoctoral Fellowship in International Security Studies at Yale in 1999–2000. He is author of *Assuming the Burden: Europe and the American Commitment to War in Vietnam* (University of California Press, 2005). He is now working on a study of US policy-making toward the Third World during the 1960s. His other projects include a co-edited volume of essays (with Fredrik Logevall) entitled *The First Vietnam War: Colonial Conflict and Cold War Crisis*, forthcoming from Harvard University Press in 2007. He has also published several articles and chapters on US policy-making toward Asia and Latin America. In 2004, he won the President's Associates Award for Teaching Excellence from the University of Texas.

Tracie Matysik is Assistant Professor in the Department of History at the University of Texas at Austin. She received a PhD in European Intellectual History from Cornell University, after which she spent a year as a Mellon Postdoctoral Fellow in the German Studies Department at Cornell University (2001–02), and a further year at the Center for European Studies at Harvard University (2002–03). She has published articles on the history of psychoanalysis and on the history of sexuality. At present she is finishing a manuscript entitled *A Cultural History of Ethics: Between Nietzsche and Freud,* and is beginning a project on the reception of Spinoza in nineteenth-century Germany.

William McNeill is Robert A. Milikin Distinguished Service Professor Emeritus at the University of Chicago, and a past president of the American Historical Association. His PhD from Cornell has been followed by honorary degrees from universities in the United States and elsewhere. He has long been recognized as an outstanding pioneer of world history, a position attained in 1963 with the publication of *The Rise of the West: A History of the Human Community* (2nd ed. 1991), and confirmed by many subsequent publications, including *Plagues and Peoples* (1976), *The Pursuit of Power: Technology, Armed Force and Society Since A.D. 1000* (1982), and *Keeping Together in Time: Dance and Drill in History* (1995). His autobiography, *The Pursuit of Truth: A Historian's Memoir,* was published in 2005.

Mark Metzler is Assistant Professor of History and Asian Studies at the University of Texas at Austin. He holds a PhD from the University of California at Berkeley, and specializes in Japanese history and international political economy. His publications include *Lever of Empire: The International Gold Standard and the Crisis of Liberalism in Prewar Japan* (University of California Press, 2006) and "Woman's Place in Japan's Great Depression: Reflections on the Moral Economy of Deflation," *Journal of Japanese Studies,* 30 (2004). He is now writing a book on postwar Japan, to be called *Stabilizing Japanese Capitalism: Japanese and American Visions, 1945–1960.*

Karl Hagstrom Miller is Assistant Professor at the University of Texas at Austin, where he teaches in the History Department and the School of Music. He holds a PhD from New York University. His book, *Segregating Sound: The Transformation of Southern Music, 1888–1935* (forthcoming from Duke University Press) examines vernacular music within the context of Jim Crow segregation, intellectual history and the globalization of the phonograph industry.

Geoffrey D. Schad was Visiting Lecturer in the Department of History at the University of Texas at Austin in 2002–03, and is currently Assistant Professor of History at Albright College, Reading, PA. He received an AM in Regional Studies (Middle East) from Harvard University, and a PhD in History from the University of Pennsylvania. He specializes in the modern social history of the Arab Middle East, with a concentration on Syria during the French Mandate. His publications include "Colonial Corporatism in the French Mandated States: Labor, Capital, the Mandatory Power, and the 1935 Syrian Law of Associations," *Revue des mondes musulmans et de la Méditerranée*, 105–6 (2005), which won the Syrian Studies Association's Best Article Prize in 2005. He is currently revising his dissertation, *Colonialists, Industrialists, and Politicians: The Political Economy of Industrialization in Syria, 1920–1954*, for publication.

Philip L. White is Emeritus Professor of American History in the Department of History at the University of Texas at Austin. He received his PhD from Columbia University. His publications include *The Beekmans of New York in Politics and Commerce, 1647–1877* (1956), and *Beekmantown, New York: Forest Frontier to Farm Community* (1979). His long-standing interest in the origins of American national identity found expression in "The Americanization of George Washington," *History of European Ideas*, 15 (1991). His wider interests in the history of nationalism are expressed in his current research for a book tentatively entitled *The Civic Heritage: Multi-Ethnic Identities in World History*.

1

Introduction: Interactions Between the Universal and the Local

A. G. Hopkins

Prologue

Presidential elections are not the first examples that come to mind in considering the history of globalization. Since World War II, however, national elections have increasingly reflected global as well as local issues. The re-election of President Bush in 2004 is a case in point. The campaigns of both candidates centered on the powerful universal and local forces that are the subject of this book, though the President, it might be said, was more successful in appealing to both in equal measure. The universal dimension was forcefully publicized in the commitment to prosecute the "war on terror," to eliminate evil, and to spread freedom and democracy throughout the world. The local aspect was clearly delineated in representations of the folksy man of the people who could be counted on to uphold small-town values. This image remained strong in part because the President's patriotism had not been compromised by any special affiliation with the imperfectly understood but self-evidently dangerous world beyond America's shores.[1] From one perspective, the President of the United States is now closer to being the ruler of the world than any previous claimant to the office; from another, his re-election was decided ultimately by voters in a few districts in two or three swing states in one country.

At first sight, the universal and the local appear in this example as antonyms: the universal stands apart from and above the local and spreads its influence far beyond its centre of origin; the local, in many pluralities, is impinged upon and reshaped by superior forces. This characterization is not wholly mistaken; if it were, the terms "universal" and "local" would lose their meaning and it would be impossible to order our thinking about the world to reflect asymmetrical relationships of size, structure, and power. For these reasons it makes an appropriate appearance in the pages that follow. Nevertheless, to formulate the connection in this fashion leads readily to the view that the world order is the product of challenge and response, of actors and reactors, and of victors and victims. Everything we now know about the history of the non-Western world suggests that these dualisms are at best inadequate and at worst misleading. Additionally, everything we have come to understand about the West suggests that it displays attributes that used to be assigned to other, supposedly less advanced peoples. The resurgence of ethnic claims and the accompanying advance of separatist movements in parts of Western Europe is one striking example; equally telling, if less dramatic, are the ways in which custom and connections exert powerful influences on societies that are supposed to exemplify modern principles of rationality and merit.

The re-election of President Bush shows how readily reality crosses these divides. The universal and the local, though formally opposites, combined purposefully in November 2004 to produce a more powerful electoral force than either could have done on its own. Moreover, on close inspection, the universals promoted by the United States reveal the depth of their local roots. Definitions of terror and evil, like concepts of democracy and free-dom, are not self-evident, free-standing notions; they acquire meaning only when they have been given specific content, which is provided by the beliefs and interests of the power that promotes them. Other nations configure the same generic terms differently. Similarly, what is conventionally designated as "local" may to some degree be the product of supra-regional and supra-national influences. The creation of localities by these means can be seen in the migrations that brought settlers, and ultimately voters, from Europe to the United States. They appear, too, in the priorities of the locality, as expressed, for example, in the swing state of Ohio, where in 2004 a number of important industries depended on world demand for their products.

The intermingling of universal and local may also blur their separate identities. Influences coming from one direction can be absorbed, reprocessed and even re-exported to the center of origin. They may be presented as if they were trade marks of a set of universal principles or patents of local identity, but they are often hybrids. The artifacts of American culture – from apple pie to Southern music – are home-grown in one sense but also transplants in another, less direct sense because their distant origins include ingredients from abroad.[2] The botanical metaphor serves the analysis of globalization particularly well: Linnaeus devised his celebrated classification of plants, set out in his *Species Plantarum* (1753), from evidence that enabled him to discern relationships among flora whose seeds had been transmitted across the continents, irrespective of political or other barriers.[3] This silent but momentous act of globalization created difference out of commonality, species from genus, local from universal.

This prologue introduces, in the most compressed form, the main subject matter of this study. The commentary that follows unpacks these summary remarks and examines them under four headings: historiography, analysis, history, and application.

Historiography

The study of history develops in two ways. One impulse derives from revisions proposed by the scholarly body itself as a result of dissatisfaction with dominant approaches and interpretations; the other reflects the influence of events in the wider world, which help to give each generation of historians its priorities and distinctive character. When the two influences are brought together, conditions are set for fundamental historiographical change. We are now at such a moment. Two interlocking developments have opened the way for fresh approaches to the past. Postmodernism, the main stimulus to fresh historical thinking for a decade or more, has now been assimilated; its limitations have also become apparent.[4] At the same time, the dramatic assault on the Twin Towers in 2001 and the subsequent "war on terror" redirected scholarly attention to material forces, geo-politics, and the long historical roots of contemporary discontents. This combination of internal skepticism and external trauma has begun to shift the focus of historical research and, by implication, has raised questions about the way history should be taught in the twenty-first century.

If there is one concept that captures both the spirit and the content of the trend that is beginning to appear, it is globalization.[5] This subject has been debated among social scientists for more than a decade, but the events of what has become known as Nine Eleven gave it greater visibility and urgency, and also brought it to the attention of historians. Globalization involves the extension, intensification and quickening velocity of flows of people, products and ideas that shape the world. It integrates regions and continents; it compresses time and space; it prompts imitation and resistance. The results alter and may even transform relationships within and among states and societies across the globe. Evidently, globalization is a capacious concept that requires careful unpacking. A full consideration of its definitions and diversity cannot be pursued here, nor is it necessary to do so because accessible discussions of both are now readily available.[6]

What matters for present purposes is that the literature on globalization presents historians with new opportunities. It offers the prospect of rehabilitating branches of history, such as economic history, that have fallen out of favor in recent years while also presenting considerable scope for political, social and cultural historians. The research agenda offered by globalization ought therefore to eliminate the familiar contest between the sub-specialisms of historical study. The themes captured by globalization also respond to a developing need, expressed by students in universities throughout the Western world, for courses and research topics that rise above the national epic. These students include the next generation of professional historians. Irrespective of their occupations, they are all citizens, and increasingly citizens of the world. The study of history will be remiss if it does not adjust to this fact – and teaching cannot change until new history books have been written.[7]

Until now, what might be called supra-national history has been dealt with in two ways. One, termed international history, is long established; the other, world history, is a more recent development – at least as far as teaching is concerned.[8] International history covers relations between states, principally during the modern era, and in practice has concentrated chiefly on diplomatic and economic relations. World history, on the other hand, is by definition comprehensive. It seeks not only to understand other societies but also to place them in a schema that makes sense of the whole.[9] The problem is how to make this noble goal operational. The burden of information is daunting; the organizing principle is not easily found. In skilled hands, the study of world history can turn admirable intentions into substantial achievements. In less capable hands it can fall victim to two temptations. One reduces the subject to loosely linked encyclopedia entries; the other reformulates the evidence to produce a disguised version of the Rise of the West, and its luckless accompanist – the Fall of the Rest.

It should be said at once that the literature on globalization does not provide a ready-made solution to these problems.[10] Globalization is not a general theory in the sense that modernization theory, the dependency thesis and Marxism are general theories because it lacks a central proposition that is capable of embracing the constituent social sciences. Globalization is better thought of as a process or set of processes requiring exploration rather than as a hypothesis awaiting refutation. Accordingly, we refer here to the literature on globalization in general and to theories of globalization in the plural. The literature is huge; the theories are disconnected. Economists debate the merits of free trade; political scientists discuss the future of the nation state; sociologists examine the consequences of increased information flows. Like ships that pass in the night, they sail in parallel lanes but rarely see one another.

Nevertheless, the history of globalization has the potential to overcome the limits of existing approaches to supra-national history. It is more comprehensive than international history because it seeks to capture all supra-national connections and encompasses themes such as environmental change, the movement of ideas, and the spread of disease that have little or no place in traditional studies of international relations. It offers new analytical starting points to world historians because it draws upon a substantial body of existing social science literature that has already generated a range of organizing principles.[11] The fact that the literature has produced clusters of testable hypotheses attached to different facets of the process of globalization rather than one overarching theory should make it attractive to historians because it enables them to formulate arguments that relate more readily to case studies. As yet, few historians have engaged with this daunting literature, though an increasing number are now inserting the term "globalization" into the titles of books and articles. Using the term catches the eye but does not necessarily enlarge the analysis. The present work hopes to make a firmer and more explicit connection between the literature on globalization and the study of history by demonstrating how themes derived from the former can be connected to detailed research of the latter.

A previous volume, *Globalization in World History*, also edited by the present writer, attempted to show how historians could both use this literature and contribute to it. As this was the first book on the subject to be written entirely by historians, it seemed appropriate to discuss a wide range of general issues relating to globalization and to offer an agenda for future historical research.[12] The book reached two main conclusions. One established the antiquity of globalization and put forward a set of categories and sequences to explain its character and evolution. The other demonstrated that, historically, globalization was a multi-centered phenomenon and that, even today, it can be understood fully only by recognizing that it is not simply the result of a dominant center activating lesser peripheries, but is jointly produced by all parties to the process. The present volume incorporates these findings but has a new and more specific focus, which is expressed in the sub-title. Exploring interactions between the universal and the local enables historians to join the discussion of globalization at the point it has now reached. It also shows that historians, whose training is embedded in local case studies, do not have to distort or desert their discipline in order to join their research to the very wide issues raised by the process of globalization.

The debate on globalization has moved through two broad, overlapping phases. In the early 1990s, when serious discussion of the subject began, it was widely assumed that the global trend was towards uniformity. Free trade would deliver economic development; democracy would bring freedom and peace. The eventual result was thought to be a happy homogeneity, as measured, variously, by the withering away of competing ideologies, the rise of a common consumer culture, and the decline of international conflict. This confident and optimistic view of the coming world order was encouraged by the spirit of triumphalism that followed the collapse of the Soviet Union in 1991, and by the economic boom of the late 1990s. These events also reinforced the long-standing assumption that standardization would take place as other societies assimilated themselves to Western ways. This was a comfortable and comforting thought for those who happened to live in the West: other values and habits would have to change but not those of the dominant minority; benign expansion would uplift and mold the rest of the world while simultaneously benefiting the major powers. These presuppositions were very similar to those espoused by the advocates of free trade in Britain in the mid-nineteenth century and by the proponents of modernization theory in the 1950s and 1960s. These precursors attracted little attention in the 1990s, which may help to explain why the commentators of the time failed to see the limitations of their own vision.

Globalization does indeed have homogenizing tendencies, and these have been well documented. However, from the close of the 1990s the literature began increasingly to emphasize the heterogeneous consequences of globalization as it became apparent that, under certain circumstances, the process reinforced rather than destroyed local affiliations, and that local influences could be recycled in ways that shaped the originating and supposedly universal impulse.[13] In retrospect, the shift of emphasis is readily explained. The decolonized empire demonstrated that it could strike back, as it did on Nine Eleven, by turning the weapons of globalization against its advocates. The subsequent "war on terror" drew a dark and immobile cloud across international skies. The collapse of the "dot.com" boom shook confidence in the economic power of the West. At the same time, it became evident that the recipients of globalization did not always gain from the process and might even resist it. The mood of triumphalism faded; history, in the sense of competing ideologies, refused to come to an end. Difference dominated, whether in the supposed "clash of civilizations," in the sharp contrast between the rich in the West and the multitudinous poor among the Rest, or in the disjunction between growing economic integration and resurgent forms of nationalism. We are therefore joining the debate at an apposite moment. As the universalizing ambitions of the day break on the sharp rocks of reality, historians, who have a special interest in micro-studies, are especially well placed to examine the pieces.

Analysis

Historians generally use the terms "universal" and "local" in a broad, commonsense manner that appears to need little definition. The use of the terms in this book, however, calls for further explanation because they are key words in the analysis of globalization.[14]

"Universal" is a weighty term with a long history. It can be traced back to Plato's concept of timeless, ideal types and it remains a central concern in philosophy today. A consideration of universals also enters theology, psychology, linguistics, law, and aesthetics, and is found in one guise or another in many other disciplines including, as noted earlier, botany.[15] Each of these subjects employs the term in ways that have created distinct lines of enquiry. For present purposes, however, the term has one general meaning that is found in all applications: the concept of commonality. This idea refers to processes that are held to be applicable to the world as a whole, whether they involve ideas, institutions, or people, or all of these combined. According to this view, commonality exists because human beings have shared dispositions. In Kant's formulation, for example, man is endowed with reason and enjoys rights; the two create a single moral community. Kant expected that this community would eventually take political shape through the creation of a league of states spanning the world. Today, the concept of human rights enshrined in the Charter of the United Nations is based on related assumptions about commonality.[16] The International Criminal Court exemplifies the belief that there are rules of justice that apply throughout the world and take precedence over state law.[17] Globalization can be regarded as a manifestation of universal principles to the extent that, whether by intention or result, it realizes commonality by increasing homogeneity and reducing diversity. The phrase "the global village" refers not only to ways in which the world is becoming smaller, but also to ways in which it is becoming more uniform.

This formulation allows two further refinements to be made. The first is a distinction between universal and global. It is evident from what has been said so far that the term "universal" means more than the totality of things found in the world, even if they interact at various points. A universal, that is to say, has to be global, but global phenomena are not necessarily universal because interactions among them may not be expressions of commonality. This distinction draws attention to the fact that universals carry normative connotations: if commonalities exist, they ought to be realized.

In Aristotle's illustration, it is only when acorns become oaks that universal "oakness" is achieved. As formulated by philosophers and commentators in the eighteenth century, universal principles found popular expression in the language of natural rights, such as liberty, equality, fraternity, and the pursuit of happiness. These ideas were carried forward in the nineteenth century and represented in various notions of progress or, in the language of the day, "improvement." Similar normative aspirations are attached to the discussion of globalization. Those who favor globalization, like those who oppose it, hope for a world that will realize human potential by expanding political freedom and raising living standards. Their disagreements concern means rather than ends.

The second refinement is expressed in the term "cosmopolitan." This term, too, has a classical, Western ancestry and varied uses. Historians of the modern world often use it as a synonym for universal, both in the very general sense and in the specific sense of commonality (with its attendant moral imperatives). There is impressive support for this position, which runs in a wavy line from the Stoics to Augustine and on to Erasmus and Kant. However, there is an additional meaning of "cosmopolitan" that distinguishes it from the definition of "universal" employed here. Universalism, the search for commonality, implies exclusivity: the local and the particular are to be transformed into a higher, more advanced state, whether by persuasion, conversion, or conquest. Cosmopolitanism, on the other hand, may also involve a willingness to respect diversity.[18] From this perspective, a cosmopolitan would support multi-culturalism rather than assimilation and would be inclined to favor relativism over a universalism that seeks to spread a common set of supposedly superior values.

These positions are not always as clearly separated as this stark formulation suggests. Kant's hope that commonality would be realized politically through the creation of a league of states fell short of the unified world government advocated by others in the nineteenth and twentieth centuries.[19] Accordingly, we have adopted the term "universal" in this study to avoid confusion with the second meaning of "cosmopolitanism." However, the second meaning is valuable if it is used to refer to movements that extend beyond a society or state and interact with different localities while respecting their differences.[20] Diasporas are interesting examples of this type of cosmopolitanism because they are not created by universalist impulses. Indeed, as ethnic groups in dispersal they can be thought of as mobile regional or even global localities that interact with host societies without seeking to impose their own sense of commonality on them.[21]

Our treatment of the local takes its cue from the preceding discussion of universals. In this context "local" appears as an antonym, the particular, which has accompanied the discussion of universals from classical times to the present and gained particular impetus following the growth of liberalism in the nineteenth century. It appears in philosophy in various types of nominalism and individualism, and in the emphasis placed in historical studies on singular case studies, on individual actions, and on a denial of various forms of historicism. The principle is clear; the practice, as with universalism, is less so. Locality, like centrality, is partly a matter of degree and partly a matter of perspective. The degree depends on relativities of size and power. Perspective is important because what one observer regards as a locality or a periphery may be, for an inhabitant, a center – even the center.

The definition of localities, like the identification of universals, therefore includes a subjective element. To the extent that the exercise can be made objective, the outcome may be decided by power as well as by inclination. That is to say, a designated locality may have a view of the cosmos – its cosmos – that could well be exportable but is confined by the lack of material means of doing so. Conversely, where localities or peripheries acquire the means of expansion and thereby become centers in their own eyes and in the regard of others, they invariably promote universals that are then projected on the wider world in the shape of free-standing, self-evident truths. States and nations exhibit this tendency; empires epitomize it.[22]

The diverse strands of thought relating universals and particulars come together in the assorted concepts of modernity that have influenced Western thought so profoundly from the eighteenth century down to today.[23] Amidst their many differences, Enlightenment thinkers agreed on the need to apply reason to human affairs so that universal good of one kind or another could be realized. This enterprise was linked to a new emphasis on empirical enquiry that fostered the counting, mapping and classifying world that emerged in the nineteenth and twentieth centuries. These influences have left their imprint on all the important surges of development thinking during the last two centuries.[24] Each school of thought elaborated its own holistic imagery linked to concepts of progressive stages of growth that ran from Smith to Marx and on to the modernization theorists of the mid-twentieth century.[25] Imagery of this kind gained popularity during the first half of the twentieth century as a result of the growing penetrative power of technology, which made greater integration possible, and the crises of two world wars, which seemed to make it necessary.[26] The threat of chaos spurs the creation of new grand designs for creating world order, and sometimes of a new Leviathan to preside over it. When Francis Fukuyama advanced his claim that liberal democracy constitutes the final form (or, as Lenin might have said, the highest stage) of human government, he was writing against the background of the collapse of the Soviet empire.[27] Fukuyama was also influenced by Hegel's theory of historical development, which in turn was rooted in Christian conceptions of a providential order.[28] On this interpretation, the United States is the fifth and last of the divinely ordained world empires. Modernity, it seems, has very ancient roots.

It is true that theories of globalization also incorporate influences from schools of thought that claim, in one form or another, to be postmodern, but elements of postmodernism have been traced to the nineteenth century, and therefore mark less of a break with the past than is often supposed.[29] The antiquity of the origins of globalization theories, though rarely emphasized in the standard texts, suggests that, while they may be distinctive, they are not entirely new. As Roger Hart observes in his discussion of Hegel,[30] every major contribution to development thinking claims to be both superior and universal, yet turns out to be historically more specific and intellectually more parochial than its advocates imagine. The claims and especially the errors of the past now seem transparent; those of the present often remain opaque until they become history. An awareness of historiography can help to distinguish between what is new and what has been carried forward, and thus between the issue of the day and the riddle of the ages.

There is merit, then, in placing the literature on globalization in the context of previous attempts to devise development policies of universal application. This exercise provides a congenial way for historians to approach the subject of globalization. It also it fashions a specific intellectual framework for the substantive chapters of this book, all of which deal with the nineteenth and twentieth centuries, and so fall within the period covered by the Enlightenment and theories of globalization.

In making this connection, however, it is equally important to avoid creating an unhistorical great chain of intellectual being leading from low-level beginnings to the latest summit – on which we stand.[31] This judgment requires us to move beyond over-generalized and historically detached representations of the Enlightenment that have gained popularity in some academic circles in recent years. Enlightenment thinkers advanced universalist doctrines, but in doing so engaged with localism and explored relativism, not least because they were concerned to find anchors for individual rights.[32] Locke and Rousseau spanned the many prominent thinkers who grappled with the problem of providing a universal foundation for individual liberties in an age of divine right and absolutism. D'Alembert tried to find ways of reconciling the universal and the local.[33] Eminent historians of the period complemented his endeavor by adopting a cosmopolitan (rather than a universalist) approach to national history.[34] Diderot began by exploring universal claims but decided that they were ethnocentric and therefore relative.[35] His conclusion followed a long-running debate on relativism initiated by Montaigne, who asked why cannibalism was morally wrong and why, dogmatic injunctions apart, Frenchmen did not (and should not) eat one another.[36] Recognizing the diversity and subtlety of Enlightenment thinkers makes it possible to draw legitimate connections between their agenda and that of subsequent schools of thought that have wrestled with the problem of modernity – including, today, theories of globalization.

History

The assessment of historiography at the outset of this chapter showed that the subject has developed to the point where globalization is now seen to produce diversity as well as uniformity. The discussion of analytical issues that followed suggested how key terms can be defined and then combined in the debate over modernity so that they, too, encompass both diversity and uniformity. The next task is to draw these findings together and make them operational by investigating the historical forms taken by the interaction of universal and local forces. The number and range of the possibilities are so large that it is tempting to settle immediately for a conclusion that emphasizes the formidable complexities of the case. To do so, however, would be to surrender too readily to uncertainty, albeit of a judicious, scholarly kind. The chapters that follow recognize complexity but avoid adopting it as the default position. Instead, they identify and trace specific ways in which the universal and the local have interacted.

The relationships that emerge extend over two centuries, span different parts of the world and deal with a variety of historical themes. The ensuing chapters demonstrate that all branches of historical study can be connected to wide-ranging literature on globalization. Accordingly, the contributions made here cover political, diplomatic, economic, social, cultural, and intellectual history. In the spirit of globalization, the contributors pursue ideas across academic borders; in accordance with historical practice they present detailed research whose underpinnings of source and method can be recognized by other historians, even if they are unfamiliar with the subject matter.[37] At the same time, we readily acknowledge that the topics treated here are less than comprehensive. Large parts of the world have been omitted; a number of important themes, such as gender, science, and the environment, have been deferred for future treatment. Comprehensiveness, however, is not the goal. The idea is to make a start on a new subject by showing how the literature on globalization can be used to connect historical topics as diverse as Navajo weaving and Japanese political economy, thus elevating them above the national and regional frameworks that conventionally contain them.

The discussion that follows begins by identifying the fictive and applied forms of universalism that appear in the case studies that ensue. Fictive forms of universalism are found in claims that are held to be unbounded, eternal truths. These claims are produced by specific historical actors in particular places. Once launched, however, they orbit the world as apparent abstractions and acquire a dynamism of their own that is removed from their origins. The most widely publicized of these ideas today, such as freedom and democracy, achieve the status of honorary concepts that are accepted unquestioningly – at least by the society that promotes them. Wherever they land, however, universal claims assume a material presence and are applied through official policies and informal influences that aim to translate ideals into realities. It is at this point, as we shall see, that gaps appear between the proclaimed universality of a principle and the stubborn facts of time, place, and alternative ways of organizing the world.

Although the majority of the universals considered in this study originate in Europe and the United States, our collective story is far from being another version of an old tale, the rise of that imagined entity, the West. The universals referred to here did not act alone or in isolation but in competition with other claimants. Far from imprinting themselves on inanimate localities, they were accepted selectively, reshaped and sometimes recycled with the result that it is now hard to distinguish source from recipient. We hope that this approach will provide a fresh and fully global perspective on some familiar and conventional themes.

Every chapter gives prominence to a weighty universal, whether fictive or applied or both. Erika Marie Bsumek shows how the Navajo, having avoided Spanish expansionism in the sixteenth and seventeenth centuries, became caught up in the "manifest destiny" of the United States in the second half of the nineteenth century, when the moving frontiers of commercial capitalism and cultural supremacy threatened to roll over them. Roger Hart's re-examination of Hegel's *Philosophy of History* deals with a universal in its idealist form, the concept of 'spirit," whose purpose was to attain freedom – in the special sense of realizing the identity and self-sufficiency of individuals within a modern, that is rational, state. Mark Metzler looks at the reception of Western economics in Japan by focusing on the less publicized branch associated with Friedrich List rather than, more conventionally, on Smithian free-trade doctrines. Tracie Matysik's examination of the Universal Races Congress of 1911 shows how the delegates wrestled with the problem of creating what, today, would be called a global civic consciousness by trying to work out ways of defining and underpinning human rights.[38] Karl Miller traces the globalization of the music industry at the start of the twentieth century following the rise of the large firm, which had the ability to stretch across the world, and the advance of technology, which produced the magic of the phonograph. Geoffrey Schad assesses the consequences of applying the universal principle of self-determination to the Middle East (and to Syria in particular) following World War I. Mark Lawrence sees the Cold War and its expression in Vietnam as a phase in the history of globalization that was driven by a renewed effort to assert universal liberal values after 1945. Philip White's wide-ranging survey traces the use and abuse of the term "nation state" and relates its shifting meaning to different phases of European history.

All of these universal principles, including Hegel's seemingly abstract "spirit," acted on or were closely related to specific localities. But some of them also had to engage with powerful competitors. Mark Metzler's account of Japan's economic "miracle" following the Meiji restoration in 1868 is a case in point. Metzler gives refreshing prominence to the ideas of Friedrich List, who opposed what he termed the "cosmopolitical" school of liberal economics with his own brand of national economics. List's alternative path has had universal and lasting appeal. It influenced economic policy in the United States as well as in Germany and France in the nineteenth century. It resurfaced in the twentieth century in the neo-mercantilist policies adopted during the 1930s and later on by many newly independent states in the ex-colonial world. It entered the thinking of dependency theorists in Latin America after World War II, and it is present today (though largely unrecognized) in the arguments of the anti-globalization lobby.

The dispute undoubtedly opened up a huge gap in Western development thinking. Yet the relationship between the two streams of thought is more complicated and more creative than this summary suggests. Smith did not deal with industrialization or the nation state because both were still on the horizon when he published *The Wealth of Nations* in 1776.[39] List was writing more than half a century later, when the problem, as he saw it, was to promote industrialization in "late-start" countries that were also struggling to become modern states. List thought that national unity was the best means of overcoming backwardness: as state boundaries consolidated the nation, so too they improved the prospects for applying protectionist economic policies. In formulating his theory, List, like Hegel, had the unity of the German states in mind, though his main work does not refer to Hegel or to "spirit." However, List also believed that protectionism was a stage that would eventually give way to universal free trade. To this extent, it can be said that he and Smith were ultimately in accord. In historical terms, however, the difference between them was considerable and it continues to the present day.

Lawrence, writing of a much later period, also gives prominence to

competing universals – in this case Western liberalism and Soviet communism – that had common roots in European thought. Marx, like List,
dissented from Adam Smith in fundamental ways but drew on his thought
too, just as he transformed Hegel's dialectic and, in effect, grounded 'spirit"
in class. Yet, it need hardly be said, the disagreements were profound: they
acquired powerful political shape after the Russian Revolution in 1917 and
became more assertively international after World War II. Lawrence picks
up the story after the turmoil of war, when the United States was trying to
put in place a peace settlement that would install the universal liberal values
of free trade and self-determination. The closest parallel here is with the
development plans devised by the British after 1815.[40] Britain, too, designed
a postwar settlement that moved towards free trade while also supporting
liberal, that is progressive but not radical, governments throughout the
world. Both countries were reacting not only to the upheaval brought about
by devastating wars but also to a period of protectionism that both preceded
and accompanied them. Adam Smith dismembered mercantilism in his
work, but it lived on during his life and was extended during the long wars
with France. In the same way, the United States tried to change course after
1945 by moving the world away from the protectionist policies that had
initiated a period of what has been called deglobalization during the 1930s.[41]
The main difference was that, after 1815, Britain was unchallenged, whereas
after 1945 the United States had to deal with a powerful ex-ally and new
rival, the Soviet Union.

There was a moment in 1945 when the United States seemed to be willing to support Cordell Hull's universalist blueprint for the United Nations.
However, when Truman replaced Roosevelt, military interests persuaded
the administration to adopt a more nationalist stance towards international
issues.[42] The onset of the Cold War confirmed that there would be no single
world order. Lawrence recasts the contest in terms of a struggle between
two competing universals that carried the combatants to hitherto remote
parts of the world and in this way extended globalization, albeit in plural
forms. One of the unanticipated consequences of the Vietnam War, as he
points out, was to increase civic consciousness about global issues. In the
Western-dominated part of the world globalization spread through the
resumption of world trade, the rise of trans-national companies, the increase
in governmental and non-governmental international organizations, and the
acquisition of self-government by colonial and quasi-colonial states.[43]

This economic and political program received comprehensive ideological backing from modernization theory, which aimed at pulling traditional
societies, as they were called, into the modern world. Elements of modernization theory had already appeared in the Age of Manifest Destiny, which

had encompassed the Navajo, in the Spanish-American war, and in the person of President Wilson, but they reached their highest stage in the 1950s and 1960s in the context of the Cold War. Modernization theory was based on an elaborate panoply of antonyms and abstractions that supported a mountain of empirical research and a plenitude of impressive footnotes. In the end, however, the antonyms turned out to be false and the empirical research was shown to be mainly an exercise in remaking the world in the image of the United States.[44] The universal assumptions of the West could accommodate neither the Soviet Union nor Vietnamese nationalism. The ironic and tragic result was that the attempt to achieve perpetual peace created tensions that appeared to be leading to perpetual conflict. The subsequent retreat from this type of foreign policy idealism in the 1970s and 1980s was followed by its revival in the 1990s and its expression in Iraq after Nine Eleven. These oscillations in American foreign policy have a long and well documented history, though this is a case where knowledge appears not to affect practice.[45]

Schad's chapter on the Middle East deals with a competing universal of an entirely different kind: the world of Islam. This engagement has received considerable publicity recently in the shape of a titanic "clash of civilizations," in which the progressive and universal values of the West are opposed to the illiberal and resolutely conservative traditions of the Islamic world.[46] Modernization theory, it would appear, had not died but was simply awaiting resuscitation. As Schad demonstrates, the "clash of civilizations" is a gross and misleading formulation. The Middle East can be understood only if the issues of the present are placed in a historical perspective that sees the region as having long engaged with globalizing processes and as responding in ways that have tried to balance adaptation with the maintenance of core values. In the eighteenth century the bureaucratic-agrarian empire of the Ottomans was strong enough to contain pressures for change.[47] In the nineteenth century the empire responded to external demands with much the same mixture of resistance and cooperation that characterized other parts of the world. The universal principles promoted by the French Revolution and imposed by British free-trading liberalism involved the region in far-reaching political and economic reforms.[48] Ottoman reformers sought to adapt secular ideas of modernization to an alternative ideology that reflected indigenous traditions in the hope of promoting changes that would also limit Western penetration.[49] At the turn of the twentieth century, the Young Turks constructed an Islamic tradition of constitutionalism to give their reform program popular appeal.[50] The "self-strengthening" movement in China had a similar purpose in seeking to incorporate Western ideas into a vision of a new Chinese-designed world order.[51] Japan, as Metzler shows, was engaged in the same exercise after the Meiji restoration in 1868.[52] On this evidence alone, it is hard to sustain a case for Ottoman or Muslim "exceptionalism."

The net result of the reforms in the Middle East (and in China too, though not in Japan) was to introduce destabilizing elements that weakened Ottoman independence.[53] The empire was dismembered after World War I and its component parts, as we shall see later, were made into new localities in the interests of nation-building.[54] For immediate purposes it is sufficient to conclude that Europe and the Middle East were already too entwined by 1918 for the stark contrasts contained in the "clash of civilizations" thesis to represent reality. The corollary is that the most commonly observed problems of the Middle East today are joint products of the interaction of the two regions and not the responsibility of one alone.[55]

The competing universals considered so far were tangible and combative, so it is worth inserting some remarks on what might be called unreported universals. The illustration offered here refers to China and serves as a reminder that future work on the history of globalization needs to move further from its Western centre.[56] Hart's chapter shows how dismissive Hegel was of China's history and achievements. Hegel was reacting partly to the sinophilia that had captured Enlightenment thinkers earlier in the eighteenth century, but he was mainly concerned to show that "spirit," having hovered briefly over China, had long since departed and was winging its way towards the German states. Hegel's metaphysical leaps and bounds enabled him to skip over Chinese history without giving it serious consideration. The Macartney mission, which Hegel was familiar with, might have caused him to reconsider his basic assumption about the nature and location of "spirit." Macartney's attempt to open trade with China in 1793 failed. In doing so, it exposed a conflict between two imperial systems, each with "universalistic pretensions" that were supported by "complex metaphysical systems."[57] Had Hegel discarded his verificatory procedure and examined the literature available to him with greater objectivity, he might have been obliged to recognize the possibility of an alternative Chinese universal.[58]

We also know that elements of this Chinese universal were exported to Europe by Jesuit agents in the seventeenth century and attracted the attention of political economists in the eighteenth century. Confucian ideas of the natural order and how to realize it had a particular influence on the physiocrats, who were concerned to revive the prosperity of French agriculture. Exactly how far Confucian thought penetrated European ideas of political economy in Europe remains speculative. It is clear that physiocracy (literally the "rule of nature") was well developed in China itself. Heavy emphasis was placed on the centrality of agriculture in the economy and on its self-regulating character.[59] Trade was highly controlled, as it was in mercantilist France, but ideas of what has been called "nascent economic liberalism" had also emerged by the eighteenth century.[60] Quesnay himself acknowledged his debt to Chinese sources, so much so that he was known to contemporaries as the "Confucius of Europe."[61] It has even been argued that the concept of *wu-wei* ("action by non-action") inspired Quesnay to formulate the principle of *laissez-faire*, which in turn influenced Adam Smith.[62] This particular claim is insufficiently documented to be treated as more than a suggestive idea, but there is no doubt of the general influence of Chinese thought on the political economists of the day.

The story does not end there. Confucian conceptions of the universal natural order gained ascendancy in Japan in the eighteenth century at the same time as Confucian ideas were being warmly received by Enlightenment philosophers in Europe.[63] A fresh set of policies for dealing with mercantilist issues (such as the balance of trade) was also being developed in Japan in the eighteenth century.[64] The discussion and experimentation of the time contributed to indigenous principles of political economy that could be applied to both mercantilism and free markets. Mercantilist principles included a vision of a state-controlled economy as part of a program of national economic development, as formulated by Sato Nobuhiro (1769–1850), who prepared the first economic development plan for the Satsuma domain in 1830. Market principles included the idea, in line with Confucian thought, that freedom of trade imparted order and harmony to human society – an invisible hand, it might be said.[65] When List's *National System* was translated at the start of the Meiji era, its message fitted into an indigenous tradition of thought that favored state intervention and the creation of a national economy. When Japanese scholars translated Adam Smith's *The Wealth of Nations* at about the same time, they were making available liberal ideas of political economy that already had a place in their own tradition of economic thought.

All the universals featured here, whether acting independently or in conjunction, interacted with localities of very different shapes and sizes. The requirement that comparisons should match like with like cannot be met where the Navajo stand at one end of the spectrum and Japan at the other. But it is possible to identify different types of interaction and their varied outcomes, which range from cases where universal impulses helped to sustain localities to those where they undermined them. Similarities can be pointed out, too, even though they may not pass the most rigorous tests of comparative history.

Bsumek's chapter deals with the ways in which the Navajo have held on to their social cohesion and cultural identity without seeking to retreat from the globalizing world that now embraces them. Bsumek follows this process through the history of weaving, which remains a major Navajo industry today, as it has been for centuries. The Navajo acquired sheep (and thereby wool) from Spanish agencies in the seventeenth century while also managing to avoid direct Spanish rule. Subsequently, they built up a substantial weaving industry, which included exports to neighboring peoples and those further afield. The most serious challenge to their independence came in the second half of the nineteenth century, when they were threatened by Euro-American settlement, which encroached on their land, and by assimilationist policies, which imperiled their culture.

The Navajo responded in ways that were similar to the reactions of other native American peoples as well as to societies elsewhere in the world where indigenous peoples were confronted with the prospect of colonial rule. Militant resistance, the first line of defense, ended in 1868, though small, sporadic rebellions occurred down to 1913. Pacific resistance, which lasted longer and was more successful, took various forms, including a sustained commitment to cultural symbols and artifacts. As the Navajo became incorporated into the United States, weaving acquired additional significance as part of what might be called a cultural resistance movement. The value of weaving, as Bsumek emphasizes, already extended beyond the market price of cloth and rugs because the act of manufacture was also an expression of cultural identity. The craft was intimately linked with Navajo myths of origin; weaving rugs was a symbolic way of weaving the social order so that the parts cohered and the patterns pleased. The Navajo attempted to sustain their culture and economy by engaging with the wider world. Their weaving captured the attention of a new generation of American consumers who were keen to buy "native" products before they died out. Expanded demand led to the codification of Navajo rugs and cloth to safeguard the interests of both purchasers and producers. Today, the export of Navajo rugs has become so successful that they have generated the sincerest form of flattery: imitation. Navajo products have been copied and indigenized elsewhere, notably among the Zapotec, with the result that their authenticity has been called into question.

The history of the Navajo suggests two general conclusions. The first is that the universal impulses represented by the spread of US commerce and culture promoted Navajo weaving throughout the twentieth century. This benign outcome carries no guarantees. The Navajo might have been overrun by assimilationist policies in the late nineteenth century; their weaving industry might be jeopardized in the present century by cheaper copies made elsewhere. The second conclusion is that to attribute this outcome to the success of free trade in opening up backward economies is to fail to give proper weight to the antiquity of Navajo entrepreneurship and its continuing dynamism today. Moreover, to cast the encounter solely in terms of economics is to miss the vital cultural component that underpins Navajo enterprise. In this respect, as in many others, the story of the Navajo can be generalized well beyond their borders.[66]

The local was also sustained, and indeed enhanced, when the American music industry began its global expansion at the start of the twentieth century.[67] Initially, as Miller shows in his chapter, the industry aimed to make Western music the universal idiom. The combination of enterprise and technology, in the shape of the large firm and the phonograph, appeared to be irresistible.[68] Soon after the turn of the century, the industry embarked on a program of "cultural uplift" that was designed to convert listeners to the supposedly superior sound of the classics. Cultural assimilation was seen to be partner to national unity. Consumers in the Northern states faced the commercial counterpart of the assimilationist policies that the Navajo confronted in the South-west. The strategy failed, and the limited market for classical music was soon saturated.

In these circumstances the music industry was forced to explore markets overseas. While still trying to promote classical music, the industry's agents stumbled upon local music. They disdained what they took to be its primitive form, just as they looked down on popular music in the United States. But they were obliged to develop it because the market for Beethoven (or even Gilbert and Sullivan) was even more limited in Bengal than it was in Illinois. The wholly unintended result was that the industry preserved and popularized local music across large parts of the world. In improving their balance sheets, the record companies inadvertently assisted the rising cause of colonial nationalism by adding to the store of indigenous cultural traditions. A recent study of India has explored the process by which Northern and Southern music became differentiated in the first half of the twentieth century and shown how indigenous musical forms were codified, thus greatly improving their ability to represent distinctive traditions in the regions concerned.[69] The music industry's experience overseas was then relayed to the United States, where it was used to create a market for home-grown local music, beginning by responding to demand in the immigrant communities and later extending to marketing music from the Southern states.

Miller's analysis places the origins of the globalization of the music industry at the beginning of the twentieth century instead of towards its end, as is conventional.[70] Consequently, any attempt to link these developments with "late capitalism" or the postmodern era is misplaced: they were there, at the creation of the industry, one hundred years ago. From the perspective of this study, Miller shows that trans-national enterprise sustained local cultural forms, which in turn provided vital support for their own enterprise. The weavers of the Navajo and the musicians of the Carnatic have in common the fact that globalization promoted their activities.[71] They may now share a local burger too because MacDonald's has responded to cultural differences by adapting the universal burger: local varieties now contain regional ingredients.

The example of Japan also shows how an idea with universal claims, in this case in the field of economic policy, was adopted in ways that added to existing policy options and strengthened the economy. However, as Metzler unravels the relationship between List's thought and that of one of his most prominent advocates in Japan, Takahashi Korekiyo (1854–1936), it becomes evident that this was far from being a simple case of a happy meeting of otherwise wholly different minds. List's own mind was formed far more by the university of life than within the ivory tower.[72] His considerable knowledge of the German states outside his native Württemberg was acquired largely while on the run from conservative rulers who were angered by his numerous and well publicized proposals for reform. He arrived in the United States as a refugee but soon caught the eye and patronage of President Jackson, who eventually returned him to Europe in an official capacity. List's "national system" therefore had cosmopolitan origins, and his recommendations acquired universal pretensions partly because of his wide knowledge of the predicament of late-start countries that were attempting simultaneously to develop their economies and create strong modern states.[73]

It is equally clear that Takahashi was not sitting quietly at home waiting to be uplifted by superior Western knowledge. He grew up at a time of intellectual ferment, when Western ideas of all stripes were entering Japan and mingling with existing modes of thought. Takahashi himself traveled widely: he learned English in California and observed the operation of protectionism in the United States. As Metzler shows, Takahashi was advocating a type of "national system" in Japan before List's work was known there, and his views were also influenced by Japanese theories of political economy that were first formulated in the eighteenth century.[74] In this instance, universal and local had cosmopolitan origins that merged to produce national policies.

List adopted the common assumption among his contemporaries, including Adam Smith and Karl Marx, that development would take place across the world in stages. This was undeniably a universal proposition, and it influenced development studies, including modernization theory, in the twentieth century. List's principal interest was in the developing states of Western and Central Europe and the United States, which were trying to catch up with Britain. Although his theories later appealed to countries outside the Western world too, List himself said very little about these regions and what he did say was unflattering, though in line with other post-Enlightenment views of his time. The rest of the world, in List's judgment, was far from the stage where protectionist policies were appropriate. Turkey was a "corpse"; the remainder of Asia was "mouldering."[75] Their regeneration required a long period of "care and tutelage" through an infusion of "European vital power."[76] Backward regions like these should be opened to free trade so that they could begin the development process by exporting agricultural products. "Wild and uninhabited" countries elsewhere needed a stiff dose of European colonial rule.[77] As a prediction of the shape of things to come, List's prescription was not far off the mark, but his Eurocentric view of what was later called the Third World also helped to perpetuate misconceptions that hampered the development he wished to see.

The final illustration of how a universal idea melded with, and was realized in, the particular returns us, briefly, to Hegel. In Hegel's view, history was the means by which spirit developed increasing self-consciousness. This process occurred in successive stages and was driven by a dialectic that gave prominence to different parts of the world at different times. Hart shows how spirit, which in principle could be lodged anywhere, was in practice to be found in the Protestant, Germanic nations. To accomplish this feat, Hegel was obliged to discount the history of much of the rest of the world, including China. This was a congenial task. Hegel was keen to elevate the German states because he wanted to see them regrouped and strengthened after the upheaval of the Napoleonic wars. He was also reacting to the sinophilia of Leibniz, Voltaire and others, who saw in Confucianism ways of grounding ethics without relying on religious injunctions, and thus support for their own universalizing moral and political programs.[78] However, Hart's analysis moves beyond the question of how Hegel transformed the local into a false universal. His more important concern is to alert us to the insularity and subjectivity inherent in the exercise of devising and promoting principles that are held to be universal. The lesson is one to be carried forward: what we can now see in Hegel might also apply to current, enveloping claims about the merits of globalization.

The remaining four chapters deal with cases in which the universal undermined the local or at least proved unable to support it. The clearest example of the latter is the Universal Races Congress (URC), which Matysik examines in her chapter. In the broadest historical context, the

URC reminds us of the continuing presence, in an age of rampant nationalism and imperialism, of strands of humanitarian internationalism that reach far back into the nineteenth century to the anti-slavery movement and to Cobden's brand of liberal, free-trading cosmopolitanism. In the context of contemporary globalization, the URC stands as an early example of what are now called international non-governmental organizations. The aim of the Congress, which met in 1911, was to promote international understanding and cooperation and in particular to find common ground amidst racial differences. The delegates were driven by two conflicting forces: heightened tension among the great powers, which threatened war, and rapid advances in communications, which held out the promise of greater integration, and – so it was hoped – peace.

In the event, the URC's good intentions could not bridge the gap between advancing universal ideals and respecting local differences. When it came to practicalities, the URC struggled to find alternative models to the nation state, which entrenched difference at the expense of commonality, and to colonial rule, which dispensed inequality. It is interesting to note that one of the prominent participants, Paul Reinsch, later played a part in helping to devise the mandate and trusteeship system, which he saw as means of managing the transition from colonial rule to independence.[79] At one level, the URC can be regarded as the vehicle of a group of liberal progressives whose moderation prevented them from stepping outside the system they wished to change. At another level, however, they can be seen, as Matysik sees them, to have grappled with a problem that stands before us today in a world in which universal human rights jostle with multiple cultural differences – still within the framework of the nation state.

More generally still, it is possible to fit the URC into the development of the social sciences in the United States in the late nineteenth century. A central theme of the day was the need to devise a set of universally valid rules of social conduct at a time of rapid economic change and energetic nation-building. The anthropologist, Franz Boas, who was a prominent participant in the URC, played a major role in this endeavor.[80] Thinking of this kind tends to conflate the ideal and the real. The rules that were devised were founded on "universalistic abstraction" and accompanied by ahistorical approaches, which in turn can be traced to founding assumptions about American exceptionalism.[81] To the extent that the URC was part of this process, it pointed the way towards the abstractions of the future, but it should also be credited with recognizing that diverse realities impeded the application of lofty ideals. A less modest stance was taken by President Wilson, when he proclaimed in 1918 that freedom and democracy were American principles that were also principles of mankind and could and should transform the world.[82] Not for the last time, universal ideals collided with immovable realities, and rarely more tragically than in the Middle East and Vietnam, as Schad and Lawrence show in their respective chapters.

As we have seen, the Ottoman Empire had long struggled to work out an accommodation with acquisitive foreign powers, notably Britain, France, Germany, Austria and Russia. By 1914 the experiment had undermined Ottoman finances and eroded the empire's political authority. The "sick man of Europe" died during World War I, and was cut into pieces at the peace settlement that followed.[83] The Middle East was then reordered to fit the universalist ideals of President Wilson and the material interests of Britain and France.[84] The victors set in motion a new phase of compulsory experimentation with Western ideals in the shape of an ambitious program of nation-building that has consumed much of the energy of the region ever since. Schad's analysis of this long and draining experiment shows how it cut across existing affiliations both to the old Ottoman Empire and to the vibrant force of Islam. The Ottomans had ruled by recognizing local differences. Until the late nineteenth century, Muslims had lived largely peaceably alongside Christians in the Balkans and Jews in Constantinople. The new Arab states, however, required uniformity. But they also lacked legitimacy and ethno-linguistic homogeneity. In these unpromising circumstances, self-determination, the new prescription, was guaranteed to handicap them at birth. The attempt to develop national affiliations produced authoritarian central governments with close ties to the military while also retarding the development of a commercial middle class whose interests lay in markets beyond the national boundaries. The alternative strategy was to develop pan Arab nationalism and pan-Islamic affiliations, which drew upon long-established ties but also ran counter to the demands of the new "nation" states.

When viewed from this angle, it is evident that the experiment with nation-building in the Middle East had little chance of success. The principle of self-determination can be applied only by creating localities and giving them borders. But this exercise runs the risk, and perhaps courts the certainty, of installing governments and ideologies that respect neither minorities within their borders nor commonalities above and beyond them. The URC pondered this issue; the attempt to install democracy to Iraq is entangled with the same problems today. Indeed, one of many ironies in the current situation is that the constitution planned for the new Iraq will transfer power back to three provinces of the old Ottoman Empire. This, it might be said, is nation-building in reverse. All that remains is to revive the Ottoman Empire itself to oversee regional defense and free trade. This revanchist solution is now out of time, but it is worth noting, if not too wistfully, that under other circumstances Ottoman cosmopolitanism would have been well suited to the needs of globalization, and that the world of Islam is also one that rises above mere territorial boundaries.

Schad's analysis of the Middle East is complemented by Mark Lawrence's reappraisal of Vietnam. Both regions were occupied by contending universals; both were sites of experimental nation-building following the upheaval caused by world wars that felled imperial overlords. The main difference was one brought about by the passage of time: the victors of 1918 had to remake long-established affiliations; the victors of 1945 had to deal with the newer demands of colonial nationalism. In neither case, it seems fair to say, did the dominant foreign powers understand or even recognize the forces that confronted them. In these circumstances the recipients were blamed rather than the plan – a miscalculation that can be traced to the ease with which policy-makers merge abstract ideals with their own experience, thus leaving little room for the experiences of others and less still for their aspirations.[85]

Lawrence's chapter centers on interactions between the universal claims of the leading protagonists in the Cold War and the ambitions of the two branches of the nationalist movement in Vietnam led by Ho Chi Minh and Bao Dai respectively. Seen from the outside and from the standpoint of diplomatic relations, the contest is usually portrayed as a struggle to win hearts and minds. The rhetoric of universal principles validated the mission and fortified its agents while also advancing pragmatic goals. Seen from the inside and from local perspectives, the question was how to harness external forces to the nationalist cause. The two nationalist leaders selected and recycled the idealist principles pressed upon them by the major powers. They added their own contributions, too, from their cosmopolitan experience of travel in Europe and the United States, as did the Japanese statesman, Takahashi Korekiyo, referred to earlier. Ho worked in Paris; Bao Dai played there. One absorbed the universal principles that underpinned anti-colonial nationalist movements everywhere; the other acquired a taste for the high life associated with the most affluent reaches of Western consumer culture. Ho died in Hanoi in 1969; Bao Dai died in Paris in 1997, where he had lived for nearly half a century.

Unsurprisingly, Ho Chi Minh was more adept than Bao Dai at co-operating with the protagonists in the Cold War while also giving assurances that registered with his political base at home. More important, Ho's program appealed to local people and their values, and his organization was effective in harnessing peasant villages to the political and military cause.[86] Bao Dai, the former Emperor of Vietnam, enjoyed visibility and status. But the pliability that recommended him to France and the United States alienated him from the Vietnamese people, and he soon became a lingering symbol of the old regime in an age of new nationalist aspirations. Nevertheless, Ho's endorsement of the principles enshrined in the American and French revolutions was insufficient to retain the backing of the United States, which was alarmed by his communist sympathies and hampered by a commitment to uphold France's ambition of regaining its position in Vietnam. From 1948 Ho turned increasingly to the Soviet bloc for support, thus setting the scene for the deadly confrontations that were to follow.

Matysik's study of the URC noted that humanitarian internationalism did not thrive in an era of heightened nationalism and expanding empires. Lawrence shows that the same conditions pertained after 1945, when nationalism was channeled into the Cold War and a final effort was made to reinvigorate Europe's imperial mission. The seemingly benign universals promoted by the West and the Soviet Union alike were domesticated only after they had been transformed by the fire of war. Rivalry between the two super-powers warped Ho Chi Minh's nationalist movement and destroyed large parts of the region and its people. Ho eventually succeeded in setting Vietnam on the path to independence, and in due course it emerged as an amalgamation of the forces that had made it, including a centralized and authoritarian government with a strong military base. Self-determination has produced weak states, rogue states and a good many more that fail to live up to their founding principles. As Schad and Lawrence show, the rivalry of the great powers in the Middle East and Vietnam contributed to the fragmentation of borders and loyalties, and to the instability that ensued. These problems are products of the imperial age of globalization rather than of its recent postimperial form.[87] The idea that these conditions can be put right by a new style of "benign imperialism," as has been advocated recently, omits the evidence of history, and now, it might be said, the evidence of experience too.[88]

White's contribution, the last of main chapters, provides a broad discussion of the term "nation state" and its accompanists, "nation," "nationality," and "nationalism," which appear in specific forms in many of the preceding chapters. These terms are, of course, both well established and highly controversial, but few historians have considered them in the context of the new literature on globalization. It is probably fair to say that historians use the term "nation state" far more often than they define it. White's analysis shows that an awareness of this literature can contribute to the study of history by reminding historians that "nation state" and its accomplices are shifting, slippery terms that need to be defined if discussion is not to begin and end at cross-purposes. Social scientists, on the other hand, have long struggled to nail down appropriate definitions. If their efforts have met with limited success, they have undoubtedly pointed to possibilities and pitfalls that historians need to consider. These are especially important in studying the nineteenth and twentieth centuries, when states were being taken apart and remade to an unprecedented extent, and when, as we have seen, attempts were being made to create new nation states in Japan, the Middle East and Vietnam. The acts of nationalizing and renationalizing identities have also had a profound influence on the methods and priorities of modern, professional historical studies since the mid-nineteenth century.[89] List criticized Adam Smith's "boundless cosmopolitanism" and its "disorganizing particularism" because it excluded the nation, with its historic ties of language and custom.[90] The historical profession, which has been concerned to remedy the omission ever since, now faces the challenge of shifting its attention to the "boundless cosmopolitanism" created by globalization.

The study of history can contribute further to this issue by showing how different ethnic and civic conceptions of the "nation state" have evolved, often in parallel but with fluctuating degrees of popularity. These differences are inherent in applying the universal principle of self-determination, which requires particularity if it is to be made operational. The devil, as they say, is in the details. White's analysis here supplements McNeill's wide-ranging interpretation of what he terms polyethnicity, which has been unjustly neglected by historians and social scientists alike.[91] White shows that both ethnic and civic conceptions of nation and nationality long predate the nineteenth century and were far more fluid than reconstructions of the past from the standpoint of the present allow.[92] Ethnic claims associated with nation-building in Europe then achieved prominence between 1789 and the end of World War I, when the principle of self-determination reached a peak of popularity – at the moment, it will be recalled, when the Ottoman Empire was being divided into new states.

Even so, the ideal of an ethnically unitary state was rarely achieved. The best example, Japan, is also exceptional; the United States and Britain, to cite just two of many contrary cases, developed civic conceptions of nationality because the ethnic ideal was considered to be impractical or undesirable – or both. Thereafter, the experience of two world wars cooled enthusiasm for supporting ethnic claims to self-determination, and in Europe for nationalism of any kind as well. Nevertheless, the nation state remained the only model of political development available, and it was puffed up and exported during the era of decolonization that followed World War II – with consequences that we have seen in Lawrence's study of Vietnam. The hope was that the civic conception of nationality would harness diversity without destroying it. The reality was that the late twentieth century witnessed an unexpected and sometimes lethal revival of the idea and politics of ethnicity.

Writing in 1986, McNeill suggested that what he termed polyethnicity would resume its historic role as the predominant basis of state formation. Twenty years later, White has reached the same conclusion, even after taking account of the resurgent politics of ethnicity. The reason, in both cases, is that ethnic nationalism is ultimately incompatible with economic forms of globalization, which require increased flows of migrants across state borders. As for the question of whether globalization is strengthening or weakening the nation state, it ought to be clear by now that much depends on whether the term is equated with ethnic homogeneity or regarded as a contractual, civic, imagined state.[93] The merit of White's contribution is to direct our attention to the crucial importance of defining the terms of the debate.

The relationship between universals and particulars is indeed complex. However, the chapters that follow have made it possible to lay out a spectrum of relationships and outcomes. At one end stand examples of universal principles that interact with particular localities to joint, if not always equal, advantage. This does not imply either the existence of an iron law of ever expanding universals or the operation of a benign, civilizing mission to uplift the fallen. In the cases under review, universal principles made headway because mutual interest dictated a compromise that harnessed the energy and enterprise of the locality instead of subverting it. Navajo weavers, Indian musicians, and Japanese politicians have this much in common. The corollary is that universals fail to extend their domain, or else destabilize the locality in the attempt, when they refuse to concede a sufficient degree of validity to the region and peoples concerned. The Middle East and Vietnam stand together as examples of such intransigence, which is enhanced when the power of the state is mobilized to support a universal ideology.[94] But Hegel, too, was intransigent: his universal succeeded, to his own satisfaction at least, not by trampling upon the opposition but by dismissing it. The Universal Races Congress, on the other hand, recognized and respected the problem of diversity, but in doing so failed to produce a universal blueprint that could also deal with difference.

Two general conclusions can be drawn from these studies. The first is that there are few, if any, pristine universals. Wherever universals appear, they bear the marks of the locality that produced them and of the contributions made by other sources, which might be both distant and unacknowledged. For the most part, universals are jointly produced and sometimes recycled, which, put another way, is to say that we have lived in a globalized world for longer than we realize or perhaps wish to recognize. The second conclusion is that, once we understand the longevity and extent of these interactions, it becomes harder to trample on or dismiss the values of others because we can see more clearly that we share the basic predicaments of what Hannah Arendt called the human condition.[95] Universals succeed best, it seems, when they tolerate difference, concede validity to others, and thus contribute to a cosmopolitan outcome.

Application

"Human history becomes more and more a race between education and catastrophe." So wrote H. G. Wells at the close of his *Outline of History*, published in 1920.[96] Wells was writing in the immediate aftermath of the devastation brought about by World War I. He saw around him, as did Norman Angell and other commentators, forms of integration that today would be classified as evidence of globalization.[97] Europe had developed what Wells called economic "fusion." Economic growth allied to technical advance was drawing the world together. The process had thrown up new issues, such as arms control, the spread of disease and the need to manage global airways, which were beyond the jurisdiction of any one state. The state, indeed, was part of the problem: economic integration was pulling different countries together; political considerations were pushing them apart; national rivalries had just wrecked them. Wells saw only one way forward: "Nationalism as a god must follow the tribal gods to limbo. Our true nationality is mankind."[98] Existing states needed to be placed under a federal world government if the disaster of the recent past was to be avoided and the issues arising in the postwar world addressed. Only by this means could basic needs be assessed and a "rough equality of opportunity" given to the children of the world. Education had a crucial part to play in this process by developing what today would be called a "global civic consciousness."

We do not have to agree with Wells's proposed solution to acknowledge that he had a good grasp of the problem. In the immediate aftermath of Nine Eleven and amidst the "war on terror," we survey a world that is even more integrated economically than it was a century ago. Yet it is still subject to much the same national rivalries, to which have now been added a layer of supra-national forces such as terrorist organizations and a presumed clash of whole civilizations. Today, it is not only capital that knows no boundaries. As for the solution, leaving aside the promise or threat of a federal world government, Wells was surely right in allocating a key role to education. Even so, we need to proceed carefully: the difference between education and propaganda is the difference between a friend and an enemy, and the two are not always distinguished easily. Accordingly, it would be unfortunate if a book like this, which tries to unmask a number of claims to universal truth, should fail to be aware of the danger of seeing others in the image of ourselves. Equally, we would be naïve to suppose that the literature on globalization provides a universal template of its own that fits neatly over the study of history.

Nevertheless, in recognizing these difficulties, we have tried to make a case for a new type of history, one that rises above the nation state and itself becomes part of the process of globalization. The modern, professional study of national history began with the formation of nation states in the nineteenth century. Now that we live in a globalized world, it is appropriate, and we would argue necessary too, that we should rethink the way we study the past to take account of the much changed present. The literature on globalization has a part to play in this enterprise in amplifying the contributions already made by studies of world history and international history. The intellectual purpose of the explorations undertaken here should now be self-evident: to enquire as systematically as possible into relations between the study of history and the new literature on globalization. In pursuing this enquiry, we have tried to make aspects of this literature accessible while also adhering to the requirements of professional historical research. We hope to have shown that the exercise produces gains for both parties. Historians can take up, apply and amend hypotheses that have been generated by social scientists whose principal concern is with contemporary globalization; social scientists can enlarge their understanding of the present by incorporating a larger historical dimension into their work.

We also hope that this study will be of practical value in contributing to the way in which history is taught. There is no doubt that the interests of the current generation of students are moving beyond the study of national history, important though it is. The students of today travel across national boundaries far more readily than their parents did. Their e-mails circumnavigate the globe in an instant, sustaining imagined communities on a scale that not even H. G. Wells's science fiction envisaged. Television brings them war, famine, politics, and sport from the four corners of the world. Curiosity and logic, if combined, ought to lead to a rethinking of the content, presentation and status of world history. Progressive departments of history are beginning to explore ways of altering their programs to take account of these developments.[99] However, the message is not as self-evident as it ought to be. There is also opposition, whether to adjusting established priorities in general or to promoting world history in particular.[100] If the study of history is to bear some relationship to the world we live in, world history needs to be seen as more than low-level preparation for high-level specialization that, once achieved, absolves practitioners from communicating with others beyond their own narrow domains. The literature on globalization provides a means of advancing the study of world history. It is not a talisman or a quick fix, but it is an opportunity that should be taken.

In this connection we are especially fortunate that William McNeill, the pioneer and untiring advocate of world history, has contributed an "Afterword" to this book, thus adding an independent voice to a work that otherwise is written entirely by members of the Department of History at the University of Texas at Austin. McNeill recalls us, appropriately, to a longer and larger tradition of thinking about the "great transformation" that is both a preface to and a part of the process we consider here under the heading of globalization. His example, which shows how the universal of American culture helped to destroy the "age-old local way of life" in the Greek villages he studied, provides a further instance of the diverse outcomes of globalization. In this case, it seems, globalization is producing uniformity by creating urban man. Bsumek's study, which McNeill refers to, shows how local communities can maintain their way of life by harnessing the process of globalization for their own purposes. McNeill's final appeal reminds us of the importance in the new century of studying the "interconnected whole" of human history. Our book tries to promote that study and also advance the means of teaching it.

We have tried to practice what we here advertise by showing that colleagues in one department can rise above their separate specializations and develop a sense of collective purpose that joins together widely different and seemingly disparate pieces of research without sacrificing their individuality. In this way, we have become a microcosm of the world we have studied. Our quest for commonality has flowed into distinct localities without, we hope, submerging them. The result, if we have been successful, has been to reconstruct elements of a world whose interacting parts need to be understood both for the sake of their own past and for their relevance to the present.

Notes

1   It is possible that his opponent, John Kerry, was damaged by his knowledge of the world, especially his connections with France, because understanding implied sympathy and sympathy suggested a possible division or at least dilution of loyalties.

2   Richard H. Pells, *Not Like Us: How Europeans Have Loved, Hated and Transformed American Culture since World War II* (New York, 1997); and Karl Miller's contribution to this volume (Ch. 6).

3   Two good introductions are: James L. Larsen, *Interpreting Nature: The Science of Living Form from Linnaeus to Kant* (Baltimore, MD, 1994); and Lisbet Koerner,

Linnaeus: Nature and Nation (Cambridge, MA, 1999). The analogy could be expanded in ways that fit the analysis of this book – not least by inserting subsequent modifications of Linnaean theory showing, for example, that there were multiple centers of diffusion rather than one. See James Larson, "Not without a Plan: Geography and Natural History in the Late Eighteenth Century," *Journal of the History of Biology*, 19 (1986), pp. 447–88. Linnaean universalism, like present-day globalization, also had a strong moral (and in his case spiritual) imperative. See Lisbet Rausing, "Underwriting the Oeconomy: Linneaus on Nature and Mind," *History of Political Economy*, 35 (2003), pp. 173–203.

4   A thorough and balanced account is Ernst Breisach, *On the Future of History: The Postmodernist Challenge and its Aftermath* (Chicago, 2003).

5   The social science literature is as extensive as the historical literature is sparse. Helpful introductions for historians include: David Held, Anthony McGrew, David Goldblatt and Jonathan Perraton, *Global Transformations: Politics, Economics and Culture* (Cambridge and Stanford, CA, 1999); David Held and Anthony McGrew (eds), *The Global Transformations Reader* (Cambridge and New York, 2000); David Held and Anthony McGrew, *Globalization/Anti-Globalization* (Cambridge and Malden, MA, 2002); and Manfred B. Steger, *Globalization: A Very Short Introduction* (Oxford, 2003).

6   Convenient and necessary expansions of the definition can be found in Held et al., *Global Transformations*; and A. G. Hopkins (ed.), *Globalization in World History* (New York, 2002), pp. 18–25.

7   At the time of writing, there are few general studies that treat the subject from a historical perspective. See, for example, Hopkins, *Globalization in World History*; Jürgen Osterhammel and Niels Petersson, *Globalization: A Short History* (Princeton, NJ, 2005); Bruce Mazlish and Akira Iriye (eds), *The Global History Reader* (New York, 2005). See also the important, though more specialized work of Kevin H. O'Rourke and Jeffrey G. Williamson, *Globalization and History: The Evolution of a Nineteenth-Century Atlantic Economy* (Cambridge, MA, 1999).

8   Bruce Mazlish, "Comparing Global History to World History," *Journal of Interdisciplinary History*, 28 (1998), pp. 385–95. An excellent guide to the current state of teaching world history is Patrick Manning, *Navigating World History: Historians Create a Global Past* (New York, 2003).

9   The pioneering work is that of William H. McNeill, *The Rise of the West: A History of the Human Community* (Chicago, 1963; new ed. 1991). See also his reflective essay, "*The Rise of the West* after Twenty-five Years," *Journal of World History*, 1 (1990), pp. 1–21.

10 Indeed, globalization has challenged the social sciences, as well as history, to think beyond the framework of the nation state.

11 Hopkins, *Globalization in World History*; Bruce Mazlish and Ralph Buultjens (eds), *Conceptualizing Global History* (Boulder, CO, 1993).

12 Hopkins, *Globalization in World History*.

13 An introduction to these issues is Ian Clark, *Globalization and Fragmentation: International Relations in the Twentieth Century* (Oxford, 1997).

14 It might be added that theorists of globalization have not provided suitable definitions either, so the present discussion may be of value to them as well as to the historians to whom it is primarily addressed.

15 The growth of universalism as a religious doctrine (that all men can be saved) in Britain and the North American colonies in the seventeenth and eighteenth centuries is outlined by Geoffrey Powell, "The Origins of Universalist Societies in Britain, 1750–1850," *Journal of Ecclesiastical History*, 22 (1971), pp. 35–56. A striking account of the universal Christian empire is James Muldoon, *Empire and Order: The Concept of Empire, 800–1800* (London, 1999).

16 Richard Falk, *Human Rights' Horizons: The Pursuit of Justice in a Globalizing World* (New York, 2000); Micheline Ishay, *The History of Human Rights: From Ancient Times to the Globalization Era* (Los Angeles, 2004).

17 A notable discussion of international distributive justice can be found in Onora O'Neill, *Bounds of Justice* (Cambridge, 2000). For a study relating to non-governmental organizations see the discussion of *Médicins sans frontières* and *Médicins du monde* in Bertrand Taithe, "Reinventing French Universalism: Religion, Humanitarianism and the 'French Doctors,'" *Modern and Contemporary France*, 12 (2004), pp. 147–58.

18 It has also been used in a derogatory sense that is not implied here. References to cosmopolitanism in Eastern Europe in the nineteenth century commonly referred to intellectuals and Jews as individuals whose loyalty to the nation state were thought to be suspect.

19 Such as Friedrich List, as noted by Mark Metzler in Ch. 8. H. G. Wells was among those who popularized the idea early in the twentieth century. See his *The Outline of History*, Vol. 4 (London, 4th ed. 1922), Ch. 41.

20 Relationships between universals, nation states and cosmopolitanism in the present-day, multi-cultural world are considered in Pheng Chean and Bruce Robbins (eds), *Cosmopolitics: Thinking and Feeling Beyond the Nation* (Minneapolis, MN, 1998).

21 A helpful review of the literature, though one dealing more with migration than with diasporas, is M. Kearney, "The Local and the Global: The Anthropology of Globalization and Transnationalism," *Annual Review of Anthropology*, 24 (1995), pp. 547–65.

22 A fuller statement than is possible here would examine the ways in which empires projected universals that also acquired a cosmopolitan character as a result of interacting with diverse localities.

23 A lucid introduction is Peter J. Taylor, *Modernities: A Geohistorical Interpretation* (Cambridge, 1999). See also Gilbert Rist, *The History of Development: From Western Origins to Global Faith* (London, 1997).

24 Tracie Matysik notes in this study (Ch. 5) how Felix Adler, one of the prime movers behind the Universal Races Congress of 1911, was influenced by

Kant's universalism, while others in the movement leaned more towards Benthamite utilitarianism.

25 Ronald Meek, *Social Science and the Ignoble Savage* (Cambridge, 1976); Terence W. Hutchison, *Before Adam Smith: The Emergence of Political Economy, 1662–1776* (Oxford, 1988); Walt Whitman Rostow, *The Stages of Economic Growth: A Non-Communist Manifesto* (Cambridge, 1960).

26 Jo-Ann Pemberton, *Global Metaphors: Modernity and the Quest for One World* (London, 2001).

27 Francis Fukuyama, *The End of History and the Last Man* (New York, 1992).

28 Muldoon, *Empire and Order*, pp. 140–1.

29 My position here is in accord with that outlined by Bruce Mazlish, "Global History in a Postmodern Era?," in Mazlish and Buultjens, *Conceptualizing Global History*, pp. 113–27. For nineteenth-century elements of postmodern thought see Pemberton, *Global Metaphors*, Ch. 2.

30 Ch.3.

31 Kerwin Lee Klein, "In Search of Narrative Mastery: Postmodernism and the People without History," *History and Theory*, 34 (1995), pp. 275–98.

32 An important recent exploration of these themes is Claudia Moscovici, *Double Dialectics: Between Universalism and Relativism in Enlightenment and Postmodern Thought* (Lanham, MD, 2002). Patrice Higonnet, *Sister Republics: The Origins of French and American Republicanism* (New York, 1988) explores the tensions between universalism and individualism in these movements.

33 Moscovici, *Double Dialectics*, Ch. 3.

34 See the valuable study by Karen O'Brien, *Narratives of Enlightenment: Cosmopolitan History from Voltaire to Gibbon* (Cambridge, 1997). To make matters even more complicated, the connection could run in the opposite direction too, as in (Abbé) Guillaume Thomas Raynal's *Histoire philosophique des deux Indes* (1770), which started from a cosmopolitan standpoint and ended with a vision of a universal society united by trade. Ibid., p. 236.

35 Moscovici, *Double Dialectics*, Ch. 4.

36 Maryanne Horowitz, "Montaigne's 'Des Cannibales' and Natural Sources of Virtue," *History of European Ideas*, 11 (1989), pp. 427–34. Montaigne, writing in the late sixteenth century, was also largely responsible for introducing the idea of the noble savage into European thought.

37 One chapter (9), by Philip White, is predominantly historiographical, but it seems apposite that a book concerned with the changing nature of historical studies should include at least one study of this kind – and in this case the theme of the chapter, the nation state, is central to both modern history and to the literature on globalization.

38 On this subject see Ernest Gellner, "Civil Society in Historical Context," *International Social Science Journal*, 43 (1991), pp. 495–510.

39 Hiram Caton, "The Preindustrial Economics of Adam Smith," *Journal of Economic History*, 45 (1985), pp. 833–53. Smith used the term "nation" to refer generally to forms of political organization as varied as "the savage nations of

hunters and fishers," and the "civilized and thriving nations" of Europe. *The Wealth of Nations* (New York, 1937 ed.), pp. lviii–lix.

40   A. G. Hopkins, "The 'New International Order' in the Nineteenth Century: Britain's First Development Plan for Africa," in Robin Law (ed.), *From Slave Trade to Legitimate Commerce* (Cambridge, 1995), pp. 240–64; P. J. Cain and A. G. Hopkins, *British Imperialism, 1688–2000* (London, 2001), especially Chs 8–13.

41   Jeffrey G. Williamson, "Globalization, Convergence and History," *Journal of Economic History*, 56 (1996), pp. 277–306; Harold James, *The End of Globalization: Lessons from the 1930s* (Cambridge, MA, 2001).

42   Thomas M. Campbell, "Nationalism in America's UN Policy, 1944–1945," *International Organization*, 27 (1973), pp. 25–44.

43   John Boli and George M. Thomas (eds), *Constructing World Culture: International Nongovernmental Organizations since 1875* (Stanford, CA, 1999); Akira Iriye, *Global Community: The Role of International Organizations in the Making of the Contemporary World* (Berkeley, CA, 2002).

44   Michael E. Latham, *Modernization as Ideology* (Durham, NC, 2000); Jefferson P. Marquis, "Social Science and Nation-Building in Vietnam," *Diplomatic History*, 24 (2000), pp. 79–105; Mark T. Berger, "Decolonisation, Modernization and Nation-Building: Political Development Theory and the Appeal of Communism in South-East Asia, 1945–75," *Journal of South-East Asian Studies*, 34 (2003), pp. 421–48.

45   A lively collection of relevant essays is in Lloyd C. Gardner and Marilyn B.Young (eds), *The New American Empire* (New York, 2005).

46   The primary source is Samuel P. Huntington, *The Clash of Civilizations and the Remaking of World Order* (New York, 1996), which developed from a debate in *Foreign Affairs* in 1993.

47   Sevket Pamuk, "The Ottoman Empire in the Eighteenth Century," *Itinerario*, 24 (2000), pp. 104–16.

48   Joseph Klaits and Michael H. Haltzel (eds), *The Global Ramifications of the French Revolution* (Cambridge, 1994), Chs 7–8. The best short guide to the reforms is Donald Quataert, *The Ottoman Empire, 1700–1922* (Cambridge, 2000).

49   Ussama Makdisi, "Ottoman Orientalism," *American Historical Review*, 107 (2002), pp. 768–96.

50   Nader Sohrabi, "Global Waves, Local Actors: What the Young Turks Knew about Other Revolutions and Why it Mattered," *Comparative Studies in Society and History*, 44 (2002), pp. 45–79. The complexities of the movement are explored by M. Sukru Haioglu, *Preparation for a Revolution: The Young Turks, 1902–1908* (Oxford, 2001).

51   Charles Desnoyers, "Towards 'The Enlightened and Progressive Civilization:' Discourses of Expansion and Nineteenth-Century Chinese Missions Abroad," *Journal of World History*, 8 (1997), pp. 135–56.

52   Ch. 4.

53 The best concise guide is Quataert, *The Ottoman Empire*. On the consequences of economic penetration see Cain and Hopkins, *British Imperialism*, Ch. 12; Jacques Thobie, *Intérêts et impérialisme français dans l'Empire Ottoman, 1895–1914* (Paris, 1977).

54 A short guide to the last days of the Ottoman Empire is A. L. Macfie, *The End of the Ottoman Empire, 1908–23* (Harlow, 1998).

55 A valuable guide to the historiography is Zachary Lockman, *Contending Visions of the Middle East* (Cambridge, 2004).

56 As argued in Hopkins, *Globalization in World History*.

57 James L. Hevia, *Cherishing Men from Afar: Qing Guest Ritual and the Macartney Mission of 1793* (Durham, NC, 1995), p. 25.

58 Unsurprisingly, sinologists are divided on this issue. Some claim that Chinese philosophy is too deeply embedded in its particular context to be exportable to other cultures; others disagree. Roetz, for example, has argued recently that the Confucian concept of *ren* (humanness) is a good candidate for being an enlightened universal. Heiner Roetz, *Confucian Ethics of the Axial Age* (Albany, NY, 1993).

59 Gang Deng, *The Premodern Chinese Economy* (London, 1999), pp. 87–99.

60 Helen Dunstan, *Conflicting Counsels to Confuse the Age: A Documentary Study of Political Economy in Qing China, 1644–1840* (Ann Arbor, MI, 1996), p. 332.

61 J. J. Clarke, *Oriental Enlightenment: The Encounter between Asian and Western Thought* (London, 1997), pp. 49–50.

62 Ibid., p. 50. See also Christian Gerlach, "Wu-wei in Europe: A Study of Eurasian Economic Thought," *Global Economic History Network Working Papers*, 12 (2005).

63 Tessa Morris-Suzuki, *A History of Japanese Economic Thought* (London, 1989), pp. 8–14.

64 The economic history of the period is covered by L. M. Cullen, *A History of Japan, 1582–1941: Internal and External Worlds* (Cambridge, 2003), Chs 3–4.

65 Morris-Suzuki, *A History of Japanese Economic Thought*, pp. 14–43.

66 See for example, James O. Gump, *The Dust Rose Like Smoke: The Subjugation of the Zulu and the Sioux* (Lincoln, NA, 1994), idem, "A Spirit of Resistance: Sioux, Xhosa, and Maori Responses to Western Dominance, 1840–1920," *Pacific Historical Review*, 66 (1997), pp. 21–52. For ritualized resistance see Dominic J Capeci and Jack C. Knight, "Reactions to Colonialism: The North American Ghost Dance and East African Maji-Maji Rebellions," *Historian*, 52 (1990), pp. 584–601. See also the articles on globalization in the special issue of *Ethnohistory*, 52, Winter (2005).

67 For an overview see John Joyce, "The Globalization of Music: Expanding Spheres of Influence," in Mazlish and Buultjens, *Conceptualizing Global History*, Ch. 9.

68 The role of the firm in the emerging global economy is explored by Geoffrey Jones, "Business Enterprise and Global Worlds," *Business History*, 3 (2002), pp. 581–605; and Alfred D. Chandler and Bruce Mazlish (eds), *Leviathans: Multinational Corporations and the New Global History* (Cambridge, 2005).

69 Lakshmi Subramanian, "The Reincarnation of a Tradition: Nationalism, Carnatic Music and the Madras Music Academy, 1900–1947," *Indian Economic and Social History Review*, 36 (1999), pp. 131–63.

70 Jocelyne Guilbaut, "On Redefining the 'Local' Through World Music," *The World of Music*, 35 (1993), pp. 33–47. The whole of this issue (No. 2) is relevant to the discussion of globalization and world music.

71 And Chinese musicians and consumers too, if we include the complementary study by Andrew F. Jones, *Yellow Music: Media Culture and Colonial Modernity in the Chinese Jazz Age* (Durham, NC, 2001).

72 The standard biography is W. O. Henderson, *Friedrich List: Economist and Visionary, 1789–1846* (London, 1983).

73 In addition to the German states and the United States, List was also familiar with Belgium, France, Austria, and Hungary.

74 Henderson, *Friedrich List*.

75 Friedrich List, *The National System of Political Economy* (London, 1885 ed.), p. 419.

76 Ibid.

77 Ibid. pp. 420–1.

78 David E. Mungello, *Leibnitz and Confucianism: The Search for Accord* (Honolulu, HI, 1977); Walter W. Davis, "China, the Confucian Ideal, and the European Age of Enlightenment," *Journal of the History of Ideas*, 44 (1983), pp. 523–48.

79 Michael A. Schneider, "The Intellectual Origins of Colonial Trusteeship in East Asia: Nitobe Inazo, Paul Reinsch and the End of Empire," *American Asian Review*, 17 (1999), pp. 1–48.

80 Mauricio Tenorio Trillo, "Stereophonic Scientific Modernisms: Social Science Between Mexico and the United States, 1880s–1940s," *Journal of American History*, 86 (1999), pp. 1156–87.

81 Dorothy Ross, *The Origins of American Social Science* (Cambridge, 1991); and for the application of these principles to the study of history, idem, "Grand Narrative in American Historical Writing: From Romance to Uncertainty," *American Historical Review*, 100 (1995), pp. 651–77; and Peter Novick, *That Noble Dream* (Cambridge, 1988).

82 Margaret Olwen MacMillan, *Paris 1919: Six Months that Changed the World* (New York, 2002).

83 The history of this well known phrase is covered by Alan Cunningham, "The Sick Man and the British Physician," *Middle Eastern Studies*, 17 (1981), pp. 147–73.

84 MacMillan, *Paris 1919*.

85 Ross, *Origins of American Social Science*.

86 Mark W. McLeod, "Indigenous Peoples and the Vietnamese Revolution, 1930–1975," *Journal of World History*, 10 (1999), pp. 353–89.

87 There is a discussion of these issues in Clark, *Globalization and Fragmentation*, pp. 188–91.

88 Among many examples, which already read like echoes from another age, see Sebastian Mallaby, "The Reluctant Imperialist," *Foreign Affairs*, 81 (2002), pp. 2–7, and Kenneth M. Pollack, "Next Stop Baghdad?," ibid., pp. 32–47.

89 The variety of this historiography, as it has affected the history of Germany, Britain, France and Italy, is fully explored in Stefan Berger, Mark Donovan and Kevin Passmore (eds), *Writing National Histories: Western Europe since 1800* (London, 1999).

90 List, *The National System*, p. 174.

91 William H. McNeill, *Polyethnicity and National Unity in World History* (Toronto, 1986).

92 Anthony D. Smith, *The Ethnic Origins of Nations* (Oxford, 1986); also idem, *Chosen Peoples* (Oxford, 2003). The key study of the diversity and fluidity of ideas and practice is by the medievalist, Patrick J. Geary, *The Myth of Nations: The Medieval Origins of Europe* (Princeton, NJ, 2002). David R. Roediger traces the changing meanings of race and ethnicity in the United States in the twentieth century in *Working Towards Whiteness: How America's Immigrants Became White* (New York, 2005), Ch. 1.

93 A clear, accessible guide to these issues is Robert J. Holton, *Globalization and the Nation-State* (New York, 1998). Contrasting points of view can be found in Susan Strange, *The Retreat of the State: The Diffusion of Power in the World Economy* (Cambridge, 1996), and David A. Smith, Dorothy J. Salinger and Steven C. Topik (eds), *States and Sovereignty in the Global Economy* (London, 1999).

94 McNeill's "Afterword" (Ch. 10) provides a further example of a universal (US influence) that overwhelmed the local (Greek villages) after World War II.

95 Hannah Arendt, *The Human Condition* (Chicago, 1958).

96 The quotation is from Vol. 4 of the 4th ed. (London, 1922), p. 1305.

97 Angell made the mistake, repeated by others, of assuming that increasing integration would make war impossible. See his *The Great Illusion* (London, 1910). Also J. D. B. Miller, *Norman Angell and the Futility of War: Peace and the Public Mind* (New York, 1986).

98 Wells, *Outline of History*, p. 1290.

99 Examples are now becoming too frequent to list. Sample illustrations include: a two-day program of seminars and discussions held at the University of Rochester in April 2003 to explore "educational programs that various colleges and universities around the country have organized under the 'global studies' rubric," a three-day conference organized by graduate and postdoctoral students in Cambridge (UK) in March 2005, and a program sponsored by the Center for Historical Analysis at Rutgers University during the academic year 2005–06 on "Approaching World History in an Era of Globalization."

100 William H. McNeill, *The Pursuit of Truth: A Historian's Memoir* (Lexington, KY, 2005), pp. 131–2, records how world history was closed down after his retirement from the University of Chicago in 1987. Patrick Manning, who

founded the World History Center at Northeastern University in 1994, also had to oversee its closure in 2004 for lack of support. See Manning, *Navigating World History*, pp. viii, xi–xiii. The Chicago story may have a happier ending because Michael Geyer, McNeill's successor, has moved increasingly into world history and is now teaching as well as writing about the subject.

2

Value Added in the Production and Trade of Navajo Textiles: Local Culture and Global Demand

Erika Marie Bsumek

The Navajo Indians are the largest Indian nation in North America. Over 290,000 members of the Navajo Nation live on a reservation that spans more than 25,000 square miles in the four-corners region of the Southwest – an area that includes parts of Utah, Arizona, New Mexico and Colorado (Map 1, p. 45). Given the size of the reservation and its population, it should come as no surprise to learn that the Navajo Indians have been touched by the forces of globalization and have recently made an appearance in the globalization literature.[1] Commentators from a variety of perspectives have uncritically, or selectively, accepted scholarship that casts Navajo textile art as a derivative product resulting from trade with external communities. Hence the appearance of the argument that the development of the Navajo textile industry proves that local cultures have benefited, and continue to benefit, from the processes of globalization and free trade. For instance, economists have utilized a narrow understanding of Navajo weaving to emphasize the validity of the gains-from-trade model, which argues that "individuals who engage in cross-cultural exchange expect those transactions to make them better off, to enrich their cultural lives, and increase their menu of choice."[2] This model limits the agency of local communities because it ignores the ways they integrate goods, ideas, and skills into their culture on their own terms and downplays the control that specific communities have had over their own world-views. It also ignores the techniques that local communities have used to control their engagement with external forces. This essay shifts our attention from the global to the local by revealing the ways that Navajo weavers maintained their own culture while still engaging with universalizing forces.

The question asked here is not whether trade makes communities culturally richer but rather, how local cultures have understood trade encounters and influenced their subsequent development. This chapter addresses this question by linking the Navajo to the debate on globalization in three ways. First, it points out that Navajo interactions with cultures far beyond their borders long pre-date the globalizing forces of today, underscoring the antiquity of practices that many modern globalization specialists claim are new. Navajo culture was at the center of many cross-cultural adaptations and Navajos have long dealt with issues that theorists have only recently identified as being central to the ways that the "local" can shape, if not always trump, the "global." Second and far less well known, these historical connections were not discrete bilateral exchanges. The case of Navajo weaving complicates any simple distinction between universal and local. From an external perspective it is easy to think of Navajos as occupying a locality that was acted on by successive colonial powers, yet such an interpretation obscures the active role Navajos played in such encounters.

This ambiguity raises a third and final set of issues, referred to here as recycling,[3] which have current geopolitical implications. I define recycling as a process whereby goods, patterns, and materials from distant global communities are partly absorbed, partly reprocessed by local communities and then re-exported to their centers of origin, where they are greeted as novelties. In this scenario, global communities recycled, as did local ones. As this occurred, Navajo culture came to be viewed as a unique variant of American national culture. Still, this process did little to change the cultural meanings that Navajos associated with the process of weaving. The control maintained by Navajos during the recycling of global influences into their culture represents one important way in which they have shaped and solidified their own cultural and economic identities, even as political boundaries and economic conditions changed around them.

I begin with a brief overview of the history of Navajo weaving and note some of the ways that Navajo history has been misused in discussions of globalization. I then demonstrate the evolving cultural importance of Navajo arts and crafts to the Navajo themselves, explaining how the Navajo have shaped their culture in relation to universal and local forces. I end with an extended discussion of the current controversy surrounding geopolitics and the sale of "Navajo-style" blankets made by Zapotec Indians in Mexico to show how the intervention of the nation state in regulating commerce has placed the Navajo Indians in an ironic and difficult position. Navajo rugs have become highly desired commodities as part of the recycling process, but consumer demand has also spawned an extensive market that pits Navajo Indians, as Americans, against Zapotec Indians, as Mexicans. Political boundaries have given additional value to some goods, and undercut others, as expressions of different national entities. Despite this, imposed political boundaries alone have not controlled the way local cultures evolve.

Stereotyped interpretations: the history of Navajo arts and crafts

Economist Tyler Cowen asserts in his book, *Creative Destruction: How Globalization is Changing the World*, that globalization supports artistic development and diversity in local communities. Invoking the gains–from–trade model, Cowen claims that "trade [across cultures] gives artists a greater opportunity to express their creative inspiration." He employs historical examples, positing that Navajo weaving "owes its existence to technology, growing wealth, and cross cultural exchange."[4] Cowen emphasizes this point to prove his core argument that technology and exchange have had a positive effect on the people they have touched. Cowen's focus on Navajo weaving as a cross-cultural phenomenon is a familiar one and is based on literature that traces the Navajos' supposed "borrowing" of skills and wares from the original inhabitants of Mexico, the Puebloan peoples of the Southwest, the Spanish colonizers they encountered, and the Anglo traders with whom they transacted business in order to develop the textiles for which they have become so well known.

The standard non-Navajo interpretation of the development of Navajo weaving may be summarized as follows: the Navajos entered what is now the American Southwest sometime between 1200 and 1400 AD.[5] They migrated from, perhaps, the Pacific Northwest, and are linked linguistically to the Apache as well as other Athapaskan peoples of Alaska and Canada. Once they arrived in the region, they came into contact with the array of Southwestern Pueblo Indian groups who were mostly sedentary farmers but who had already established long-range trade networks. It was at this time that anthropologists note that the Apache and Navajo, or the Southern Athapaskan speakers, split into separate groups. While the Apache maintained a hunting and gathering lifestyle, Navajos "began to incorporate many of the subsistence features and cultural features of their new neighbors."[6] These new techniques included weaving with reeds, cotton, and then, finally, wool as they acquired sheep from the Spanish and Puebloan peoples. Through intermarriage, slave raiding, and trade with local and distant Puebloan people, and then later, following the arrival of the Spanish, a distinctive Navajo craft culture developed around livestock production and trade.[7]

Non-Navajo historians frequently contend that, as the Navajo integrated sheep-herding into their daily activities, wool became the primary material for Navajo textiles, which were additionally "transformed from a purely utilitarian practice into an art" when they were traded with their neighbors to the south for Mexican serapes, blankets and floor coverings. This is an example of the trans-cultural flows which advocates of globalization, like Cowen, regard as encouraging creativity:

> The serape pattern, with serrated zigzag lines, was derived from the ponchos and clothing of the Spanish shepherds in Mexico, which in turn drew upon Moorish influences in Spain. Navajo design drew heavily upon these sources, although the Navajo altered them to suit their own visual language, introducing deliberate distortions and eliminating the notion of border.[8]

Additional alterations in the craft occurred as factory-made cloth, such as European-made bayeta red cloth, became available to Navajo weavers though long-distance trade. The weavers used the cloth in distinctive ways by unraveling it and incorporating the reddish thread into their textiles.

Scholars of Navajo textiles agree that the classic period of Navajo textile production was between 1650 and 1868. Global processes, especially trade between divergent local communities, such as European cloth manufacturers, Mexican traders, and Navajo weavers, occurred during this period and were woven together through the textile trade, often in ironic ways. For instance, Navajo weavers found the brighter-colored material from Spain appealing as a contrasting hue to the muted shades they made using vegetable-based dyes. The irony was that bayeta was made in Europe from cochineal, a beetle parasite extract that was imported into Europe from Mexico; bayeta cloth was then transported back to Mexico and used in what is now the American Southwest by local groups such as the Navajo.[9] Textiles from this period, like the bayeta weavings, are often used to illustrate interactions between the Spanish, the indigenous people of Mexico, and the Navajos.

Supporters of the gains-from-trade model often focus on the next period in the development of Navajo textiles to prove their point. The classic period in textile development was followed by what has been called the "transitional period," which lasted from 1868 to 1890. During those years, as textile scholars have noted, the market for Navajo blankets was changing from native to tourist consumption.[10] Like other populations within the United States, Navajos were affected by national trends like industrialization and the growth of a consumption-oriented society. Navajo weavers obtained the brighter, chemically dyed yarns, like those from the textile hub of Germantown, Pennsylvania, and started to weave rugs instead of saddle blankets or articles of clothing. They also began experimenting with new patterns like the eyedazzler (Illustration 1), a textile made of contrasting colors and geometric interlocking designs.

The influential agents of change in the transitional period were the reservation-based traders who instructed weavers about color usage, the incorporation of an outside border, and preferred dimensions so that the rugs they produced would better meet non-Indian consumer demand.[11] In the 1870s and 1880s, machine-made dyes and yarns reached the Southwest by way of the traders. Traders claimed that these new yarns enabled Navajo weavers to improve their skills because these materials were of finer quality than the hand-carded and dyed yarn used previously. Such refined products afforded Navajos the opportunity to experiment with new patterns, designs, and styles and led to the invention of the bold eyedazzlers.[12]

Interpreters of Navajo weaving commonly pay a large amount of attention to the traders who directed the sale of Navajo textiles to white consumers and altered the craft in the process. It is true that towards the end

Source: Durango collection, Ft Lewis Museum

Illustration 1   Navajo eyedazzler

of the nineteenth century Navajo traders encouraged local weavers to use certain kinds of yarn, to integrate design elements found in Persian and Turkish textiles, and to alter the patterns of the rugs to otherwise fit the marketplace.[13] Evidence that the traders were kept abreast of market trends is easy to find. For instance, in 1916 Alfred Hardy, a dealer in Indian goods from Long Beach, California, informed Navajo trader Don Lorenzo Hubbell that, although consumers wanted textiles made by the so-called "primitive" Navajo Indians, the most marketable were those rugs that both reminded consumers of how different Indians were from "civilized" Americans and met middle-class standards. Hardy wanted "Navajo rugs: *un*-dyed – no matter what the *weavers* think. I have been asked time and time again for these as they can be easily cleaned. *They* could be sent to a good laundry."[14] As Hardy suggested, demand for the rugs hinged on the ability of traders to meet consumer tastes. So, as consumer demand changed, traders hesitated to buy brightly colored, commercially dyed rugs from weavers. Not surprisingly, the production of the eyedazzlers tapered off and vegetable-dyed rugs became popular once again. By paying a disproportionate amount of attention to the traders economists have bolstered the claim that Navajo design is more derivative than unique and indigenous.[15] Although traders did affect the development of Navajo weaving, their influence represents a fraction of a larger story.

These historical interpretations lay out a basic history of the evolution of Navajo textile production, yet they are simplistic, diverting attention from the complex interplay between tradition, influence, and creativity among Navajo weavers themselves. Cowen fails to grasp the cultural importance of weaving, trade, and artistic achievement among the Navajo, offering instead a truncated and misleading portrayal of Navajo artisans responding uncritically to outside forces. His definition of value is also too narrow. To understand the value attached to Navajo textiles it is necessary to give weight both to the dynamism and creativity of the indigenous society and to the role of extra-economic considerations. In addition, basic accounts of Navajo weaving often fail to take into account Navajo understandings of history and the meanings that Navajo have associated, and continue to associate, with the production of textiles. As contemporary weavers have emphasized, Navajos have had agency in these matters, and it is important to note that although weaving may be a material representation of contact with different groups, interaction does not automatically render Navajo weaving a derivative process.[16]

Simplistic explanations not only lack Navajo understanding of the culture of textiles, but also ignore the United States' conquest of the region in the 1840s. The integration of the Southwest into the nation, which occurred during the same years that mark the "classic period" and continued into the "transitional period," separated Mexico and the United States and divided

The Zapotec live in Oaxaca

Map 1   The Navajo Reservation

the indigenous peoples of Mexico and the United States into different national populations: Americans and Mexicans. In this way geo-political forces created specific local regional economies that were governed by federal regulatory entities and national laws controlling trade between Navajos and white Americans and between Americans and Mexicans in general. Yet, before we can move to an analysis of the Navajo recycling and geo-politics, a more expansive history of Navajo cultural interaction and craft development is needed.

The importance of culture to value

An examination of the cultural importance of weaving to the Navajo reveals how local crafts have responded to and controlled changes within the global marketplace. In the case of Navajo weaving, textile production was linked both to the subsistence of weavers and their families and to the prosperity of traders. It was also tied to a newly emerging sense of where Navajos fit into a larger American national project.[17] Yet, assessments of the Navajo craft industry have been repeatedly filtered through an essentialized understanding of so-called "primitive" or pre-industrial people. Navajo artisans were (and are) depicted as either making products strictly for exchange, with creativity emerging as a by-product, or as manufacturers of goods that served the cultural needs of non-Navajo consumers, as in the case of so many coffee table books on Navajo textiles. In short, "authentically" cultural and "modern" economic motivations have been mistakenly seen as mutually exclusive categories. In reality, as we shall see, Navajo trade and craft culture were entwined from the beginning.

Advocates of globalization often make this mistake, even when they get the basic facts of the evolution of textile production and trade correct. They fail to mention the ways in which the skill of weaving was originally tied to Navajo understandings of their universe and they neglect the fact that Navajo textiles were important to the Navajo themselves, even as they became valued trade items to the Puebloan peoples, the Spanish, or later, to the American consumers who desired Navajo rugs as popular additions to their homes in the early 1900s. Yet weaving and its importance can be found in the most fundamental expressions of Navajo culture: accounts of the creation of the Navajo themselves. Thus, an understanding of value that goes beyond a narrow formal definition of price-times-quantity helps to explain the resilience and dynamism of local production.

Although there are many interpretations of the Navajo creation story, there are some commonalities that occur in almost all versions.[18] It is generally understood that there were three or four subterranean worlds characterized by different forms of disorder that continually propelled Navajo ancestors to travel from one world into the next. The journey ended when the ancestors emerged onto the earth's surface. This left the Earth Surface People (or the Nihookáá Dine'é) dependent upon the Holy Ones to teach them to survive. Changing Woman, the most important of the Navajo Holy People, told the Nihookáá Dine'é where to live – the area marked by four sacred mountain ranges – while others among the Holy People established rules of conduct and taught the Earth Surface People skills to survive.

Spider Woman, another of the Holy People, taught Navajo women how to weave. According to oral tradition, two Navajo women sought Spider Woman's assistance to survive in their new world and Spider Woman responded by casting her web to lift the weary women up to the summit of her home. She then built the women a loom and taught them how to shear sheep and to turn the wool into yarn that could be dyed with colors from plants and other organic materials. Finally, as anthropologist Kelli Carmean demonstrated, Spider Woman taught the women that, to weave blankets, weavers should always hold beautiful thoughts in their minds and put "their whole souls into their work."[19] At the time, the women were not sure why Spider Woman wanted to teach them how to weave but they respected her and became skilled at the craft. Still, they "wondered how this new knowledge could possibly help their people." In an act of individual assertion, which stemmed in part from a misunderstanding of Spider Woman's true intentions, the women included an intentional flaw in their designs by leaving an opening in the textile so that, if necessary, "their souls could escape" and return to their loved ones.[20]

Spider Woman is credited with helping Navajos to stay warm in the winter and giving them an item of value to trade. Creation accounts contend that, when Spider Woman saw the flaw, she first responded with anger, which was quickly tempered by compassion, and she sent the women home. Upon leaving, they felt that they had failed at their primary task: to help their people survive. Yet, wanting to give something to their people, they began to teach the other Diné women, just as Spider Woman had taught them. As time passed, the women became the creators of the beautiful textiles that kept them warm in the winter and also provided them with an item to trade with their neighbors for food and other necessities. Hence, the craft of weaving is usually viewed as a culturally gendered economic activity, but men were not prohibited from learning the skills necessary to weave.[21]

The cultural underpinnings of weaving remained strong even as modern commercial trends influenced the growth of certain styles over others. Nor did modern commercial trends determine the meaning attached to weaving among the Navajo. Noted weavers D. Y. Begay, Kalley Keams, and Wesley

Thomas reveal this when talking about the importance of weaving to Navajo culture today, stating that: "Our mothers and fathers ... encourage us to continue to weave ... as our great-great-grandmothers have; they say it is a way of survival. It's the Navajo way. Navajo weaving is part of our religion, oral history, language, and *k'e* (family structure)."[22] For Thomas it is the entire process, from start to finish, that strengthens his sense of cultural identity and economic security. "Through the actual construction of the loom and the process of weaving," he explained, "I learned about Navajo spirituality." Like those who learned the craft from Spider Woman, he reports that a weaver still "must have clear and positive thoughts while weaving, thereby creating a 'sacred space.'" More importantly, Thomas's grandmother repeatedly told him that his weaving tools are his "defenders," his "weapons against hunger or any form of 'hard times.'"[23] Thomas's statement makes it clear that weaving has both cultural and economic purposes that cannot be separated.

The integration of Navajo products and Navajo culture can be seen at all stages of production. Holding beautiful thoughts in mind during the production of textiles was, and is, tied to one of the key cultural elements of Navajo life – *hózhó* or beauty. *Hózhó* expresses a "unity of experience" that connects spiritual, economic, intellectual, and aesthetic endeavors. As Gary Witherspoon has shown, "Navajo life and culture are based on ... the creation, maintenance, and restoration of hózhó."[24] Importantly, beauty is expressed through creation, and not "through perception and preservation" as it tends to be among Euro-Americans. In this way, beauty is not necessarily "so much a perceptual experience as it is a conceptual one." Witherspoon attributes the sale of beautiful Navajo-made goods to outsiders as complementary parts of this concept.[25]

The sale of Navajo-made rugs and jewelry to non-Indians, who locate "beauty in things" rather than in the production of them, reveals how the Navajo, who were seen as outsiders in a more centralized domestic market, maintained their supposedly peripheral cultural traditions in the face of the dominant society's potential hegemonic power. In other words, Navajos would produce beautiful goods even if whites did not buy them, but they also produce them specifically to trade. Culture and economic rationale were always intertwined. Thus, even as weavers incorporated new materials and technologies into the design and production of their textiles, their own cultural markers were reinforced. By selling the goods they made, weavers and their families have maintained and strengthened the core cultural beliefs that were trade-oriented from their inception.[26] Navajo weavers have not simply responded to outside influences. Nor have they relinquished their own culture; instead they struggle to maintain their cultural traditions and the value of the products they make.[27] The sale of goods to non-Navajos has provided an additional and important economic rationale for culturally based production. In this case, the universal has supported the local.

An examination of Navajo ethnogenesis reveals that the Navajo were active participants in trade from the seventeenth century onwards, incorporating changes to meet market demands, often on their own terms. An enhanced understanding of Navajo culture demonstrates that economic development and artistic evolution can be conjoined categories. The cultural values of local communities were, and are, ingrained in the production of the goods they manufactured. Yet, weavers have struggled, and still struggle, to have those values acknowledged by outsiders. When Navajo values are misunderstood or ignored, it can have – and has had – tangible consequences for the producers. For instance, when theorists of globalization neglect the cultural importance of Navajo weaving, they obscure the crucial economic role the art has played within the Navajo community.[28] Further, interpretations that cast the Navajo as borrowers who gain only aesthetically from their interactions with others, as in the gains-from-trade model, undervalue the labor involved in the manufacture of textiles: creativity and not financial remuneration takes precedence in such accounts. Those who have historically underpaid weavers and undervalued textiles, and the scholars who fail to recognize the importance of culture in the production of weaving, devalue the skills possessed by Navajo weavers and Navajo culture itself.

This brings larger questions in the globalization literature into the discussion. As demonstrated earlier, Navajo weaving has been used to consider whether the net effect of globalization leads to a flourishing of creativity or a homogenization of culture. But simplistic accounts of Navajo history should not be used to argue that cross-cultural exchanges prove, or disprove, one argument or the other. Globalizing influences are felt, and managed, on a number of complex levels by both local and global communities.[29] What is clear is that a fuller understanding of Navajo culture helps to explain the resilience of the local when confronted with outside forces. In order to explore this theme further, we need to turn our attention to the way in which interactions between global influences and Navajo communities engaged in a process of recycling.

Recycling and geo-politics: the representation of Navajo culture as national culture

Just as materials and patterns from distant global communities were partly absorbed by Navajos, so they were also re-exported to global markets, where they were consumed as commodities that carried symbolic meanings. Those meanings grew out of the ways Navajos were incorporated into the developing American nation. As Navajo lands became part of the Southwestern United States, American Indians were integrated into the expanding nation in the mid to late nineteenth century in ways that were both representative and real, and the reality of incorporation for American Indians was often characterized by forced assimilation, brutality, and oppression. The Navajo were no exception.

Declared enemies of the Federal Government in 1864, more than eight thousand Navajos were interned at Fort Sumner in Southeastern New Mexico, where they suffered from disease, starvation and death. Upon their release in 1868, the year that also marks the end of the "classic period," Navajos returned to their homeland, which had become a reservation encompassing only a small section of what had previously been their domain. Many Navajos ended up living "off reservation" as a result. Throughout the 1870s, 1880s, and 1890s, as both the white and the Navajo populations grew, the government addressed land disputes by expanding the reservation in a checkerboard pattern that placed Navajo lands next to lands owned by cattle ranchers and railroad companies. Not only did this strain relations between business interests and the Diné, it also created a situation where the "boundaries of the reservation were widening, but the actual land area available for Navajo use was shrinking."[30] Land loss was just one of the ways the relationship with the federal government affected the Navajos, but it also exemplifies how the Navajos were both a "sovereign nation" that could petition to expand its land base, and a population whose "domestic dependent" status meant they had to rely on whatever solutions the federal government devised.[31]

Given that Navajos were first viewed as "enemies" who needed to be imprisoned and then seen as "primitives" who needed the guidance of the federal government, it seems ironic that their material culture, along with a stereotyped American Indian culture in general, became one of the markers of American national identity in the late nineteenth century.[32] This irony provides us with another way of understanding the instability of the categories of center and periphery and the power of the recycling process. The idea of an American "frontier" is central to our understanding of how supposedly "primitive" Navajo culture became a national culture. One of the most powerful ideas in American culture during the late nineteenth century was that the frontier had provided a "safety valve" that enabled subsequent waves of immigrants and Americans to spread across the country onto "free" land.[33] This safety valve supposedly enabled democracy to flourish in the United States. By 1890, however, many observers feared that the "frontier" was on the verge of "closing." Due to impressive advertising campaigns launched by the Atchison, Topeka, and Santa Fe Railway and the Fred Harvey Company, by the early twentieth century Pueblo and Navajo Indians of the Southwest were represented not only as America's own "ancient" population but also as "portals" to the rapidly vanishing "frontier." These businesses encouraged white Americans to travel to the region and sought to demonstrate that, in the words of anthropologist Rosemary J. Coombe, the "frontier that defined the national imagery of democracy" still existed and was also about vacations and consumption.[34]

By 1900 native-born white middle-class and wealthy Americans were encouraged to declare their "American-ness" by traveling to historic sites and by interacting with "primitive" peoples, like the Navajo and Puebloan peoples of the Southwest.[35] At Fred Harvey Hotels, like the Alvarado Hotel in Albuquerque, New Mexico, tourists could see Navajo Indians on display, they could sign up to take an "Indian detour" to an Indian reservation, and they could buy a Navajo rug or a piece of jewelry to take home in one of the many gift or curio shops in the region. As the widely circulated tourist literature for Fred Harvey's Indian building put it, tourists could connect with the ancient past in a modern setting:

> In the Indian building are displayed some of the most interesting collections in this country. Indian villages, remote cliff dwellings and isolated hogans throughout the Southwest have been searched by experts for the rarest exponents of Indian life … Patient Navajo squaws may be seen weaving blankets while their men are making crude articles of jewelry.[36]

By literally displaying contemporary indigenous peoples next to material excavated from ancient cliff dwellings, the Harvey Company created a visual and narrative picture where Navajo Indians were both connected to the long history of the nation and bound to its future – as living representations of its past – through the goods they made.

Navajos were cast as a unique American population. They were depicted as creative, industrious, and as more than one observer noted, adept "cultural borrowers." Like other "outsider" populations, this made their ultimate demise seem unavoidable. They would either be assimilated, with the guidance of whites, or would slowly die out. As one editor claimed in 1887, Navajos would either develop into civilized beings or would remain "demons or brutes" doomed to extinction if left without the improving influence of education.[37] President Grover Cleveland concurred with such sentiments, and urged the Bureau of Indian Affairs to support assimilationist agendas in Indian boarding schools.[38] By the early 1900s, others, like Stewart Culin, ethnologist and curator at the Brooklyn Museum, went as far

Source: Curtis Photo, *The Vanishing Race*, 1904

Illustration 2   "The Vanishing Race"

as to predict that the ultimate assimilation of the Navajo was a natural part of their evolution.[39]

Images like Edward Curtis's "The Vanishing Race" (Illustration 2) reinforced the idea. In this popular photo, Curtis depicted a line of Navajos slowly plodding toward the sun-drenched buttes. Their backs to the camera, the Navajos were moving away from civilization, not towards it. This type of highly-staged imagery of disappearance became part of the standard marketing ploy that imparted a sense of urgency among American consumers.

Consumers were told that they should lose no time if they wanted to take home part of the mythologized West that Navajos represented; consequently by the 1910s they had purchased millions of dollars worth of Navajo-made textiles and jewelry from traders, dealers, and curio store owners.[40]

White consumers viewed the popular and stylized Navajo rugs as novelties because they evoked the "frontier" and reaffirmed the racial status of the tourists in the process.[41] As occurred with other "exotic" populations in other tourist destinations, material representations of Navajo culture became popular souvenirs.[42] Navajos, and the goods they made, came to represent a place – the Southwest; a time – the past; and an ideology of racialized national pride – the triumph of white "civilized" American democracy. Yet, even as Navajo weavers made textiles with the American marketplace in mind, replete with attention to consumer tastes and desires, weaving retained its importance to the weavers who made the rugs, the kinship networks that depended on the sale of such rugs, and the larger community for whom they served as cultural expressions.

In the process of producing rugs for American consumers, Navajo weavers differentiated themselves from each other and from other Americans. Navajos continued to weave, recycling new yarns, color schemes, and designs into the textiles they made, never losing sight of Spider Woman and *hóhzó* in the process. Along with the traders who supported their development, weavers took pride in the creation of specific styles. These unique styles, such as the subtle Wide Ruins rugs, the dramatic Ganado Reds, the symbolic Storm Patterns, and the religiously inspired Yei Bi Chi designs, soon came to represent both a general product, a Navajo rug, and specific regional populations of the Navajo reservation. Thus, the highly stylized and differentiated Navajo-made rugs assumed a general trademark status while maintaining cultural and regional specificity. As Rosemary Coombes has revealed, trademarks can be "logos, brand names, characteristic advertising images, or other (usually visual) forms that condense and convey meaning in commerce."[43] She also contends that the "ubiquity of trademarks in *national social arenas* and their currency both as culture and as private property create generative conditions for struggles over significance."[44] As Navajo rugs evoked specific images that had been made by non-Navajos like Curtis and Harvey Company managers, and differentiated by the Navajos themselves, struggles over the control of those images bubbled to the surface.

By the 1930s, conditions in post-Fordist America were ripe for a struggle over the meaning of Navajo "Indian-made" goods. Court cases in the 1930s illustrate exactly how the state intervened not only in regulating Indian affairs, long an arena of government activism, but also in codifying markers of Navajo identity, further entrenching a cultural trademark associated with Navajo "Indian-made" goods. In the mid-1930s, the Federal Trade Commission (FTC) took up the issue of protecting American consumers from false, "Indian-made" goods that had been mass-produced either in factories to resemble Navajo Indian rugs and jewelry, or by Southwestern Indians in machine-shops.

In the most contentious of the trade cases, the *FTC v. Maisel Trading Post* in 1932, the 10th Circuit Court of Appeals ruled that mechanized production methods were harmful to the integrity of the trade and deceptive to consumers and therefore should be banned. According to the court, Navajo

"Indian-made" goods – in this case Navajo jewelry – needed to be hand-crafted by Indians and made according to the "primitive" Indian traditions in order to be labeled "Indian-made." The larger effort, out of which this and other FTC cases arose, sought to protect consumers from purchasing mass-produced Navajo-style goods when they really desired Navajo handicrafts. The ruling also reveals the power of the recycling process. The interaction between the local (Navajo) and the global (American consumerism) was such that imported influences, like the demands of consumers, were absorbed by Navajo weavers.[45] They were also reprocessed by the Navajo in ways that made them uniquely their own, imbued with the *hózhó* and economic value. Rugs were unique Navajo creations but were also exported to American and foreign consumers. The originator in this case was consumer demand, but as it became filtered through the lens of Navajo culture it assumed a unique symbolic form. The market value of Navajo hand-made rugs and jewelry was, in large part, derived from that form.[46] Coming on the heels of the FTC's regulatory efforts, Congress established the Indian Arts and Crafts Board in 1935 to police the sale of "Indian-made" products, including those made by the Navajo. The intent of this act was two-fold: to preserve indigenous craft cultures and the economies that surrounded them, and to protect consumers from deceptive marketing practices.

Recycling and geo-politics: contemporary controversies

As Kathy M'Closkey has claimed, "The appropriation of popular Navajo patterns is not just a pilfering of pretty designs. It is theft of a way of life." Moreover, "It threatens the destruction of activities vital to Navajo culture. And it is one of the more recent threats that perpetuate processes begun more than a century ago."[47] Current debates surrounding Navajo-made goods no longer focus on the mass production of goods. Rather, observers of Navajo craft industries now report that the brisk expansion of foreign textiles that reproduce Navajo designs puts pressure on what has been a relatively strong market for Navajo rugs and blankets (and other Indian arts and crafts) since the early twentieth century. M'Closkey and other critics of this trend believe that the importation of "fake" textiles fundamentally harms the Navajo weavers and the larger Navajo community.[48] Consumer advocates worry that the sale of Navajo reproductions misleads consumers who aspire to buy authentic Navajo-made rugs as ethnic artifacts or as items that continue to represent the diversity of American nationality.

The Navajos recognize the complexity of this situation. On April 8, 1998, *USA Today* featured a front-page article on the economic crisis caused by the production of faux "Indian-made" goods that were flooding the

American market. The headline warned: "Indian Art: Buyer Beware, Artisans Pay Price of Counterfeiting." The newspaper informed its readers that each year hundreds of thousands of tourists traveled to the Southwest and spent more than a billion dollars on American Indian arts and crafts. "Increasingly," reported John Shiffman, "much of what's for sale isn't hand-made or crafted by [American] Indians." As a result, American Indian crafts-men and women lost up to 90 percent of the trade to foreign production. Lee Yazzie, a Navajo silversmith from Gallup, New Mexico explained: "When you rob people of their design and take it overseas (for production) and get another people there to do it for peanuts, then two groups of people are being taken advantage of." Yazzie added that, when consumers unwit-tingly purchased faux "Indian-made" goods, they were the victims of deception and fraud.[49]

The most commonly noted "threat" to the Navajo textile market comes from the Zapotec Indians. M'Closkey reports that "sophisticated copies" of Navajo rugs "are created by thousands of Zapotec weavers active in cottage industries" and that the entrepreneurs "who appropriated Navajo patterns to this region [and] import the finished products into the United States" mark up the price of the rugs between 200 and 1,000 percent.[50] Anthropologist W. W. Wood reveals that the once distinctive "Zapotec textiles are no longer sold as Zapotec textiles but as Southwestern U.S. textiles" or rather "as inexpensive, vaguely ethnic or Native American textiles" that have specific "Navajo-like" patterns.[51] Whereas Wood sees this competition as part of an expansion of local production and trade networks wherein the Zapotec have become local producers of a product connoting the distinc-tive regional, Southwestern style, M'Closkey approaches the topic from a different vantage point. She believes that these rugs are produced by a people who place little cultural meaning on their manufacture. Since Zapotec rugs are sold for significantly lower prices than rugs made by Navajo weavers, even with the high retail markup, M'Closkey and others fear that their escalating sales in hotel gift shops, curio stores, ethnic art galleries and through websites will further undermine the economic well-being of weavers on the Navajo Reservation and destroy a "way of life" in the process.[52]

Lee Yazzie's quotation about the exploitation of two groups of people directs our attention to the complexity of the situation and the ubiquity of recycling. Navajo culture, as that of a uniquely American population, became an expression of national culture. As the market for Navajo-made goods grew, representations of Navajo-made goods were exported to distant local communities. In some ways, this led to the replication of an earlier cycle among the Zapotec. Like the Navajo, the Zapotec have been weaving since before the arrival of the Spanish. Like Navajos during the early period, Zapotecs initially manufactured textiles to trade with surrounding communities but trade networks among the Zapotec were not as extensive as were those of the Navajo. If we consider other similarities, we can see that intermediaries, like the early Navajo traders, connect stores in the US with weavers in Teotitlán. In the last 30 years, the Zapotec have experienced their own "transitional period" of sorts. Since 1970 many changes in the production of goods made by Zapotecs have occurred, including the expansion of Zapotec local craft industries, the growth of a local merchant class, and the mass exportation of rugs.

This process was made possible in part by of the development of national consciousness. Just as Navajo-made products connoted American national pride, Mexican nationalists promoted Zapotec textiles during a key period in Mexican history. It was during the postrevolutionary period in Mexico, after the 1910s, that many intellectuals and politicians "worked to create a sense of Mexican national identity in which indigenous culture was a prominent feature" and helped to develop ethnic pride and tourism.[53] Government-sponsored programs featured Zapotec textiles to highlight indigenous crafts as a matter of Mexican national pride. Based on their own tradition of textile production, Zapotec weavers wove rugs with their own geometric designs. These unique designs became popular expressions of Mexico's indigenous and Aztecan past. Yet by the 1970s and 1980s, the textiles were made not only for tourists within Mexico but were also for export to the American Southwest, where they were, and are still, sold.[54]

Exporting Zapotec rugs required a highly coordinated effort on the part of the US retailers, Mexican middle-men, and Zapotec weavers who wanted to take advantage of the fad for Southwestern designs that flourished in the 1980s. By 1980, wholesale buyers of Zapotec rugs brought books and museum catalogues with photos of Navajo rugs to Oaxaca. Retailers and middle-men told the weavers what to make in an attempt to control products destined for specific markets in Santa Fe and Taos.[55]

The organization of the Zapotec weaving industry has again changed in the last 15 years. American consumer demand has led to a situation where Zapotec textiles are no longer produced exclusively in Teotitlán by Zapotec weavers for Zapotec intermediaries. Rather Zapotec rugs are now part of a larger global process. The Zapotec weavers reproduce Navajo designs, while American businesses coordinate production and trade. In a globalized world, the production of a Zapotec textile now starts with an order from a business in the United States.[56] The Zapotec have kept their traditions alive by integrating international market demands into the production of their goods. They have been able to keep families together and employed by working to meet the demands of the ever-growing market for Southwestern-style goods.

Here again, Lee Yazzie's observation about two sets of people being taken advantage of directs our attention to the complexity of the situation produced by the recycling process. Navajos are affected by the importation of so-called fake rugs, yet so too are the Zapotec artisans who manufacture the Navajo-style rugs. As Wood suggests, when Zapotec textiles enter the marketplace "the various 'traditions' for woolen 'serape style' textiles on both sides of today's US/Mexico border are so completely intertwined that they are neither products of Mexico nor the United States exclusively."[57] Instead, Wood views the hybridity of indigenous designs as "the product of a set of distinct but interconnected weaving traditions that ... span an international border."[58]

Wood's assessment forces us to wonder whether local Navajo and Zapotec weaving communities and cultures have been changed as a result of the global marketplace. Have the global influences intervened in ways that make what is happening to the Zapotec an extension of an earlier recycling pattern that affected the Navajo? According to the gains-from-trade model and its simplistic retelling of history, around 1900 Navajo textiles were valued by white middle-class consumers as cheaper versions of Persian rugs. The intermediaries (traders and dealers) encouraged the use of new patterns and designs (Persian rugs), facilitated, and then discouraged, the use of new dyes and materials (Germantown yarns), and marketed Navajo textiles to middle-class American consumers as representations of the frontier-era "vanishing race" of American Indians. The skill of weavers – who worked only with their hands – was represented as the key characteristic of the authenticity of the product. Just as Navajo weavers reproduced design elements from Persian rugs to meet consumer tastes, Zapotec rugs have become popular down-market tourist items because they mimic Navajo styles. An interesting difference between the two is that Zapotec Indian identity is downplayed in this process of exchange whereas in the case of the Navajo markers of Indian identity were highlighted to stimulate demand for Navajo-made products in the early part of the twentieth century.

The ethnicity and national identity of Zapotec Indians have been conflated to assert the inauthenticity of their rugs and the illegitimacy of their makers as "Native Americans" in a transnational world. In 1992, a Zapotec weaver named Antonio attempted to sell rugs directly in Santa Fe during the popular and lucrative Indian Market week. As Antonio carried the rugs around Santa Fe's plaza, trying to catch the attention of potential buyers, an elderly customer approached him and asked: "What tribe are you from?" He answered that he was a Zapotec Indian. "'Oh ... Zapotec," the man responded, "And where is that reservation located?" When the seller replied that his village was in Mexico, the prospective buyer retorted, "Mexico, no ... I'm not interested in a Mexican blanket," and walked away.[59] As this episode reveals, the Zapotec have been drawn into a globalized market for a locally manufactured and nationally symbolic product in which their own ethnicity has little or no value. The Navajo-made rug has value in part because it is a cultural "brand." It is a product built on both the recycling of external sources into its production *and* on the value local producers attach to it.

As federally recognized Native Americans, Navajos are citizens of their own nation – the Navajo Nation – and of the United States. This dual nationality points to how Navajo culture has been maintained in the face of shifting political borders while also demonstrating exactly how arbitrary such distinctions can be. Cultural traditions separate groups, but so too do national borders. Borders matter, especially when the regulation of trade affects the marketing of products that are seen as conveying meaning about nationalism and identity. Since Zapotec rugs are sold in American shops, owners of those shops need to find a way to make these goods appealing to American consumers who are largely interested in goods made by American Indians, not "Mexicans." Shop owners do this by cleverly emphasizing the generic "Indian-ness" of the weavers or the "primitive nature" of the hand-woven textile in question. The omission of the fact that such goods are made in Mexico by the Zapotec is creatively managed. As the elderly gentleman quoted above revealed, Zapotec textiles are still viewed as "not worthy of purchase in their own right as Native American crafts but as cheaper substitutes for the 'real thing': a Navajo textile."[60] In essence, shops downplay Zapotec ethnicity and Mexican nationality.

This strategy on the part of dealers has paid off. As Antonio's story reveals, it has placed Zapotec weavers in a weak position when they attempt to intervene in the larger process where they have very little agency in direct market interactions. Intermediaries and consumers play an important role in constructing variations of Navajo and Zapotec identity in the global market. Within this image-making schema, the history of local craft industries, the transformation of local economies, and the cultural importance of skills like weaving to the community are almost wholly obscured.

Navajo representatives have tried to publicize these issues by proposing to register for official trademarks for their cultural products. Contemporary Navajo weavers, like Wesley Thomas, want to preserve market opportunities while maintaining the cultural importance of the goods they make. At the same time, they want to protect non-Navajo weavers and consumers from being "taken advantage of." As a result, they acknowledge the necessity of passing on the craft to subsequent generations, the need for effective state regulation – even though they are suspicious of the federal government – and the value of improving marketing strategies. At a 1998 meeting of the Navajo Arts and Crafts Forum, Ferdinand Notah, Executive Director of the Navajo Division of Economic Development, noted the importance of marketing Navajo arts and crafts as expressions of the Navajo Nation in order to emphasize their role in the world.[61] Navajo silversmith Ray Tracey even advocated marketing Navajo culture, much like Air Jordan basketball shoes, Perrier bottled water, and Levi Jeans. "Name recognition is vital in business," he said.[62] When Andy Abieta, an activist who works "to protect and promote authentic Indian arts and crafts", spoke, he stressed "the importance of artwork for education and the preservation of culture." Abieta reminded the other artisans in attendance that their primary "communication" with the world at large "is through arts."[63] Edward P. Howard, a lawyer from the Center for Law and Public Interest, told forum members that he was committed to "solving once and for all the problem of fraudulent competition" of Indian Arts and Crafts. He charged audience members to bring him a case he could prosecute, so that a precedent could be set in law.

As Wesley Thomas's comments and the discussion made at the Arts and Crafts Forum illustrate, Navajos are aware of the economic and cultural importance of their arts and crafts as markers of their identity. Although the 1990 Arts and Crafts Act was passed by Congress to provide a mechanism to stem the importation of "fakes" or goods manufactured by people outside the United States and sold under false pretenses, it has yet to be utilized due to lax enforcement and cultural attitudes towards the law. Audience members told Howard, for instance, that "suing someone in a court of law is against the ways of traditional Navajo society" even though it sounded like an effective way of stemming the flow of Navajo knock-offs into the marketplace.[64] Again, Navajo culture maintains its key role in Navajo society.

The 1990 Act was the culmination of several earlier attempts to regulate the trade in "Indian-made" goods. In the case of the Navajo/Zapotec dispute, the act determines which indigenous group or groups can sell products using the "Indian-made" label and simultaneously enables shop owners to sell markers of identity as constructed by earlier state efforts. Consumers look for indications of authenticity when purchasing such products – and an official label is therefore appealing.[65] Unfortunately for the Zapotec, a product has to be hand-made by a member of a federally recognized tribe if it is to bear the "Indian-made" label. This means that goods made by indigenous peoples outside the United States cannot be sold as "Indian-made." It also makes it difficult for Indians like Antonio, who are proud of their heritage, to sell goods openly and honestly. Ethnic art dealers skirt these regulations in a variety of creative ways. Some dealers do not tag Zapotec rugs at all, but simply place them in close proximity to "certified" Navajo weavings. Others include tags that name a specific weaver – and those names are often invented by dealers – without mention of a tribal or national identity. Others still, simply claim that a rug is made of one hundred percent wool and dyed with natural vegetable dyes. These are features that consumers have associated with Navajo textiles since the turn of the twentieth century. An additional strategy is to emphasize the "primitiveness" of the Zapotec Indians while minimizing the fact that the weavers live, work, and weave in Mexico. All of these strategies are designed to reinforce images of "Indianness" which have developed within "the particular social and cultural space of the Southwest, images that have been successfully manipulated in the marketing of arts and crafts of the past."[66]

Conclusion

An observer looking at Navajo weaving today might conclude that it has been shaped by recent global influences. However, the cultural production that surrounds this craft rests on both its antiquity and the subsequent commingling of "local" meanings and outside interventions. The category of the local includes: the cosmological or spiritual, and the use of the craft of weaving to transmit culture, history, religion and economic security from one generation to the next. The exchanges that accompanied Navajo rugs from the "classic period" and beyond were not simply static, bilateral trades but were the outcome of continuous interactions between the original center (Navajo local culture) and its periphery (the Pueblo, Mexican, Spanish, and whites with whom they came into contact), so much so that those terms lose their accuracy. Prior to 1848, Navajos and the indigenous people of Mexico could trade with each other, although there is no evidence to suggest that Navajos and Zapotecs exchanged products directly. North American Indians and the indigenous people of Mexico have exchanged styles, ideas, and cultures through a series of interactions with a variety of people, acting sometimes through guidelines defined by an intervening state. From the beginning of the twentieth century, consumer demand has fuelled the engine that drives such exchanges. Yet, when Zapotec reproductions of Navajo rugs are purchased in the United States, it is the Navajo weavers who feel the pinch. Within this context, a fascinating theme emerges in the relationship between economics and politics: prior to the establishment of the modern United States/Mexico border, economic flows were unhindered by official intervention. Yet, contemporary political intervention (in part on behalf of Navajos and their marketing strategies) has sought to claim cultural ownership and certify the authenticity of a product, even though it carries different meanings for different groups. In essence, Navajos argue they have made a trade-name for themselves that needs to be preserved, whether or not it is a codified "brand." In this case, we might consider, perhaps, that globalization has strengthened tribal identity by helping to codify craft products and secure them for Navajo society.

Such codification points to the reciprocal influence of "peripheries" and "centers." As ideas, skills, technologies and materials entered Navajo culture, they were altered to fit the needs and world-views of the community.[67] Similarly, Navajo-made products such as textiles were "exported," yet local ideas and cultural views about what such exchanges encompassed were not exclusive to either profit-centered economic development or aesthetic enhancement. When considering the processing and "recycling" of goods, ideas, and practices that occurred during these exchanges, any attempt to distinguish between origins and additions distorts the cultural process it seeks to explain. In this scenario, two final questions remain unanswered. If notions of Navajo ethnicity are strengthened by global competition, what has happened and what will happen to local Zapotec textile industries producers now that the forces of globalization have expanded the market for their goods they make but do not take full account of the value of their identity? Finally, what are we to make of an economy that values a culturally specific understanding of Navajo identity but not the full worth of Navajo labor?

Notes

1   A number of individuals provided invaluable feedback on this article. I would like to thank the other authors in this volume as well as Julie Hardwick, James Sidbury, Vincent Cheng, Phoebe Kropp, Martin Summers, Colleen O'Neill, Michael Topp and Peter K. Bsumek. Tyler Cowen, *Creative Destruction: How Globalization is Changing the World's Culture* (Princeton, NJ, 2002). Benjamin Barber offers a critique of Cowen, see "Globalization and Culture," *Cato Policy Report* (May/June 2003), p. 10. In these interpretations, Navajos are consistently cast as skilled "borrowers" of ideas, materials and technologies and their borrowing is credited with leading to success in their textile market and enhancing their religious traditions.

2   Cowen, *Creative Destruction*, p. 13.

3   I use the term "recycling" rather than "borrowing." For many decades, scholarly and popular interpretations have cast the Navajo as "borrowers" in order to illustrate their lack of innovation. By using the term "recycling" I am not

suggesting that the Navajos lacked in cultural innovation, in fact, just the opposite is the case. Navajos innovated many craft traditions that became both culturally and economically important to them. As I have argued elsewhere, "borrowing" is a loaded concept when applied to the Navajo because it has been used to justify assimilationist agendas: Erika M. Bsumek, "The Navajos as Borrowers: Stewart Culin and the Genesis of an Ethnographic Theory," *New Mexico Historical Review,* 79 (2004), pp. 319–51. Peter Iverson offers another alternative. He asserts that the "expansion of the Diné cultural repertoire therefore came about through infusion of new people rather than by borrowing or duplication." Peter Iverson, *Diné: A History of the Navajos* (Albuquerque, NM, 2002), p. 19.

4   Cowen, *Creative Destruction*, p. 43.
5   The date is currently contested by anthropologists, archaeologists and Navajo oral tradition. Iverson, *Diné*, pp. 12–19.
6   Kelli Carmean, *Spider Woman Walks this Land: Traditional Cultural Properties and the Navajo Nation* (Walnut Creek, CA, 2002), p. 6.
7   For the best scholarship on early Navajo history see Ronald H. Towner and Jeffery S. Dean, "Questions and Problems in Pre-Fort Sumner Navajo Archaeology," in Towner (ed.), *The Archaeology of Navajo Origins* (Salt Lake City, UT, 1996), p. 8; James F. Brooks, *Captives and Cousins: Slavery, Kinship, and Community in the Southwest Borderlands* (Chapel Hill, NC, 2002), p. 95.
8   Cowen, *Creative Destruction*, p. 44.
9   Ibid., p. 45.
10   Nancy J. Bloomberg, *Navajo Textiles: The William Randolph Hearst Collection* (Tucson, AZ, 1988), p. 5.
11   Ibid., p. 6. Erika Marie Bsumek, "Making 'Indian-made': The Production, Consumption and Construction of Navajo Ethnic Identity, 1880–1935," (PhD dissertation, Rutgers University, 2000); Kathy M'Closkey, *Swept Under the Rug: A Hidden History of Navajo Weaving* (Albuquerque, NM, 2002).
12   Cowen, *Creative Destruction*, p. 45. Jane Schneider, "The Anthropology of Cloth," *Annual Review of Anthropology,* 16 (1987), pp. 429–30. I use the term "Navajo traders" to describe non-Navajos who traded with the Navajo on the Navajo Reservation.
13   On the influence of "oriental" designs, see Bloomberg, *Navajo Textiles*, p. 6; M'Closkey, *Swept Under the Rug*, p. 146. There is some debate about whether Navajo weavers were given pictures of Navajo rugs to copy or whether traders encouraged them to add elements like borders to their rugs. Since this question is unresolved, I have not made it a focal point in this essay. It should be noted that Karl Miller's contribution to this book (Ch. 6) shows that agents also influenced the development of the music industry.
14   Alfred Hardy to Lorenzo Hubbell, June 15, 1916, JLHC, Box 36, University of Arizona, Special Collections; emphasis in original.
15   Cowen, *Creative Destruction*, p. 46.
16   D. Y. Begay, Kalley Keams, and Wesley Thomas in Eulalie H. Bonar (ed.), *Woven by the Grandmothers: Nineteenth Century Textiles from the National Museum*

of the American Indian (Washington, DC, 1996), p. vii. Jennifer Nez Denetdale also asserts that "scholars' categorization of weaving within Western paradigms not only has veiled the links between political economy and arts and crafts, but also has served to reaffirm the characterization of Navajos as primarily cultural borrowers who arrived late in the Southwest" and undermines Navajo claims "that contradict Navajo understanding of their own past and origin." Denetdale, "Review Essay for *Under the Rug: A Hidden History of Navajo Weaving* by Kathy M'Closkey and *Navajo Saddle Blankets: Textiles to Ride in the American West* edited by Lane Coulter," *New Mexico Historical Review*, 79 (2004), p. 475.

17 Navajos and other Americans were trying to figure out where the Diné fit into the Nation, in what ways would they become Americans, and in what ways they would remain a distinct group. Americanization programs, often hostile, were launched by the Bureau of Indian Affairs; Iverson, *Diné*, pp. 66–97. See also Alan Trachtenberg, *Shades of Hiawatha: Staging Indians, Making Americans, 1880–1930* (New York, 2004); Shari M. Huhndorf, *Going Native: Indians in the American Cultural Imagination* (Ithaca, NY, 2001).

18 I do not mean to imply that all creation stories are the same. There is a great amount of detail and nuance that cannot be included here.

19 Carmean, *Spiderwoman Walks this Land*, p. xix.

20 Ibid.

21 On gender roles and weaving see Erika M. Bsumek, *Indian-made: The Production and Consumption of Navajo-ness, 1868–1940* (forthcoming, University Press of Kansas).

22 Begay et al. in Bonar, *Woven by the Grandmothers*, p. vii.

23 Wesley Thomas, "Shil Yóólt'ool: Personification of Navajo Weaving," in Bonar, *Woven by the Grandmothers*, p. 36.

24 Gary Witherspoon, *Language and Art in the Navajo Universe* (Ann Arbor, MI, 1977), p. 154. According to Witherspoon, "Hózhó expresses the intellectual concept of order, the emotional state of happiness, the moral notion of good, the biological condition of health and well-being, and the aesthetic dimension of balance, harmony, and beauty. In Navajo art we find all these concepts, states, and conditions expressed."

25 Ibid., pp. 151–2.

26 Just because culture is maintained does not meant that weavers have been fairly compensated. See Denetdale, "Review Essay," p. 478.

27 Ibid., pp. 471–9; M'Closkey, *Swept Under the Rug*, pp. 234–55.

28 For many years observers of Navajo textile production have asserted that Navajo women wove for "pin money." More recent analysis reveals that during World War II more than 60 percent of the Navajo economy was based on weaving. Other evidence suggests that over the last two centuries over 100,000 Navajo women have woven more than 1 million blankets and rugs. Still, in spite of their popularity and importance detailed economic analysis reveals that weavers typically made between 0.05 and 0.17¢ per hour for their labor, far

below economic standards for a "living wage" of the time the figures were calculated. M'Closkey, *Swept Under the Rug,* pp. 78–84; Colleen O'Neill, *Working the Navajo Way: Labor and Culture in the Twentieth Century* (Lawrence, KS, 2005), pp. 69–70.

29   A. G. Hopkins, "The History of Globalization – And the Globalization of History," in idem (ed.), *Globalization in World History* (New York, 2002), p. 26.

30   Richard White, *The Roots of Dependency: Subsistence, Environment, and Social Change among the Choctaws, Pawnees, and Navajos* (Lincoln, NE, 1983), p. 219.

31   On the complicated legal status of American Indians see Gail K. Sheffield, *The Arbitrary Indian: The Indian Arts and Crafts Act of 1990* (Norman, OK, 1997), pp. 32–5.

32   Philip J. Deloria, *Playing Indian* (New Haven, CT, 1998), pp. 1–9; Bsumek, "Making 'Indian-made.'"

33   Frederick Jackson Turner, "The Significance of the Frontier in American History," in idem, *The Frontier in American History* (New York, 1920); Gregory H. Nobel, *American Frontiers: Cultural Encounters and Continental Conquest* (New York, 1997); David Wrobel, *The End of American Exceptionalism: Frontier Anxiety from the Old West to the New Deal* (Lawrence, KS, 1993). I use Turner to demonstrate that people felt anxious about a "closing" frontier, not to argue that the frontier either existed or was closing.

34   Rosemary Coombe, "Embodied Trademarks: Memesis and Alterity on American Commercial Frontiers," *Cultural Anthropology,* 11 (1996), p. 213.

35   Marguerite S. Shaffer, *See America First: Tourism and National Identity, 1880–1940* (Washington, DC, 2001), p. 4. Shaffer claims, "In teaching tourists what to see and how to see it, promoters invented and mapped an idealized American history and tradition across the American landscape, defining an organic nationalism that linked national identity to a shared territory and history."

36   "The Great Southwest – Along the Santa Fe Trail" (Kansas City, KS, 1914); Center for Southwest Research (CSWR), Albuquerque, NM, MSS 115.BC, Box 1, Folder 5.

37   "Ramona Days," Number 1, March 1, 1887, Indian Department of the University of New Mexico, p. 6.

38   Ibid; letter from Grover Cleveland, unnumbered page, CSWR, call number E97.6 R3 V1 #1.

39   Bsumek, "The Navajos as Borrowers," pp. 319–47.

40   By 1931, more than $1 million dollars' worth of Navajo rugs had been sold to American consumers. See Bsumek, "Making 'Indian-made,'" p. 27.

41   This is similar to what George Lipsitz calls a "possessive investment in white-ness," in Lipsitz, *Possessive Investment in Whiteness: How White People Profit from Identity Politics* (Berkeley, CA, 1998).

42   A. G. Hopkins, "Globalization With and Without Empires: From Bali to Labrador," in Hopkins, *Globalization in World History,* p. 230; Michael F. Brown, *Who Owns Native Culture?* (Cambridge, MA, 2003), Hal Rothman,

Devil's Bargains: Tourism in the Twentieth Century American West,(Lawrence, KS, 1998); Sarah H. Hill, "Marketing Traditions: Cherokee Basketry and Tourist Economies," in Carter Jones Meyer and Diana Royer (eds), *Selling the Indian: Commericializing and Appropriating American Indian Cultures* (Tucson, AZ, 2001).

43   Coombe, "Embodied Trademarks," p. 203.
44   Ibid.; emphasis mine.
45   Karl Miller also notes (this volume, Ch. 6) how consumer demand influenced the music industry.
46   Bsumek, "Making 'Indian-made,'" pp. 186–230.
47   M'Closkey, *Swept Under the Rug,* p. 15.
48   Ibid; W. W. Woods, "Rapport is Overrated: Southwestern Ethnic Art Dealers and Ethnographers in the 'Field,'" *Qualitative Inquiry,* 7 (2001), pp. 484–503, idem, "Flexible Production, Households, and Fieldwork: Multisited Zapotec Weavers in the Era of Late Capitalism," *Ethnology,* 39 (2000), pp. 133–48.
49   John Shiffman, "Indian Art: Buyer Beware, Artisans Pay Price of Counterfeiting," *USA Today,* April 8 (1998), 1A–2A.
50   M'Closkey, *Swept Under the Rug,* p. 196.
51   Wood, "Flexible Production," p. 137.
52   "Even the Experts Are Being Duped," *USA Today,* April 8 (1998), 2A, column 1. This fear is based on the fact that a high percentage of the Navajo Nation's 200,000 (or more) members "are involved in the trade" of selling rugs and other "Indian-made" goods.
53   W. W. Wood, "Stories from the Field, Handicraft Production, and the Mexican National Patrimony: A Lesson in Translocality from B. Tavern," *Ethnology,* 39 (2000), p. 184; Lynn Stephens, *Zapotec Women* (Austin, TX, 1991), pp. 91–3, 133.
54   W. W. Wood, "Oaxacan Textiles, 'Fake' Indian Art, And the Mexican 'Invasion' of the Land of Enchantment," unpublished paper in possession of the author, pp. 4–5.
55   Ibid., p. 5.
56   Wood, "Flexible Production," p. 135.
57   Wood. "Oaxacan Textiles," p. 12.
58   Ibid.
59   Wood, "Rapport is Overrated," pp. 491–2.
60   Ibid., p. 493.
61   "Tourism Office Hosts Unique Forum to Examine Arts and Crafts Issues," *Navajo Times,* May 14 (1998).
62   Ibid.
63   Ibid.
64   Ibid.
65   Sheffield, *The Arbitrary Indian,* pp. 102–20.
66   Wood, "Rapport is Overrated," p. 494.

3

Universals of Yesteryear: Hegel's Modernity in an Age of Globalization

Roger Hart

In Hegel, Contradiction then passes over into its Ground, into what I would call the situation itself, the aerial view or the map of the totality in which things happen and History takes place ... These are lessons we can still put to use today, not least in our attempts to grasp the still ill-defined and ever-emerging effects of that phenomenon we have begun to call "globalization."[1]
– Fredric Jameson

"Globalization," for all its alleged unprecedentedness, has been theorized through a series of questions that are, in contrast, not particularly original. First, what are its defining features (features, that is, that mark a sufficiently radical break with the past to necessitate this neologism)? Second is periodization – when did globalization first begin, and which historical events best indicate the shift? And third, what are the consequences of globalization, and what interventions are possible?

As we will see below, while contentious debates over these issues have yielded little consensus on the characteristics, periodization, or consequences of what has been termed the "age of globalization," most studies concur that globalization is an intensification or acceleration of various processes over a period of decades or even centuries. In contrast, characterizations of "our age" as a period of globalization can be dated with some precision: while the term "globalization" has been in use since at least

1961,[2] it has become a keyword in the titles of academic conferences, articles, books, and anthologies only in the last 15 years. This suggests we might be suspicious of the assumption that proclamations of an age of globalization innocently reflect some underlying reality, and instead inquire into the disproportionate proliferation of the use of the terms "global," "globalism," and "globalization." That is, if globalization is not a sudden break which occurred only 15 years ago, how do we account for the sudden shift in discourse? And if a central defining feature of the "age of globalization" is just the *act* of defining "our times" as such, what can we learn from the history of similar performative acts in the past, for example, attempts to fashion "our times" as "modern"?

This chapter presents one possible role for critical history in debates over globalization and the attendant questions of the local and universal. Of course, we cannot write a history of the ideologies of globalization just as they are beginning to emerge; nor can we simplistically claim that they are doomed to repeat the history of past ideologies, such as those of modernity. However, I will argue, the shift we are now experiencing from a discourse of modernity to globalization provides an important opportunity for reflection: to the extent that the discourse of globalization has already displaced that of modernity, proclamations about modernity have lost much of the unquestioned self-evidence that lent them credibility; and to the extent that the discourse on globalization appropriates or "recycles" modernity, to use Erika Bsumek's helpful term, a historical analysis of the ideologies of modernity can provide a critical perspective on globalization. The first section of this chapter presents a preliminary inquiry into the relationship between the discourses of modernity and globalization. The second section explains the focus in this chapter on one particular vision of modernity, that presented by Hegel in his *Philosophy of History*: on the one hand, Hegel's conceptualization of modernity is arguably the most important and philosophically profound; on the other hand, his assignment of modernity to the "Germanic nations" alone – precisely because it now seems so startling – provides a particularly striking example of the ideological fashioning of collective identities. The following three sections analyze how Hegel manipulates the local and universal to imagine the "Germanic nations" alone as modern: Hegel first makes spirit – the subject of world history – universal; he then localizes spirit in a single nation; having localized world spirit in a single nation, Hegel excludes the remainder of the world from world history. The conclusion of this chapter then develops some of the implications of this historical analysis of Hegel's modernity for the emerging discourse fashioning our age as the age of globalization.

From modernity to globalization

Several important questions about possible connections between conceptualizations of modernity and globalization are raised, if only to be dismissed,
by Arjun Appadurai, one of the most prominent theorists of globalization,
in the opening paragraphs of his seminal *Modernity at Large*. At first,
Appadurai seems prepared to reflect on the checkered history of social
science theory's disjunctures with historical fact:

> One of the most problematic legacies of grand Western social science
> (Auguste Comte, Karl Marx, Ferdinand Tönnies, Max Weber, Émile
> Durkheim) is that it has steadily reinforced the sense of some single moment
> – call it the modern moment – that by its appearance creates a dramatic and
> unprecedented break between past and present. This view has been shown
> repeatedly to distort the meanings of change and the politics of pastness.[3]

However, in the very same paragraph, Appadurai ventures that what went
awry with all of these past theories is not the positing of some "dramatic and
unprecedented break," but rather that it was incorrectly identified: "the
world in which we now live ... surely does involve a general break with all
sorts of pasts. What sort of break is this, if it is not the one identified by
modernization theory?" Appadurai's answer appears in the next paragraph,
which begins, "implicit in this book is a theory of rupture." His thesis is that
the "rupture" is globalization, which he calls "modernity at large."[4]

Appadurai's assertions immediately suggest several questions about
conceptualizations of modernity and globalization. How can "modernity,"
if it is as theoretically suspect as Appadurai suggests, serve as the basis of his
new theory, just by announcing that it is now "at large"? How does the
extension of "modernity" to the world "at large" constitute the rupture that
the advent of modernity did not? More fundamentally, is it possible that the
theory Appadurai presents might itself be destined to take a place along with
those of Comte, Marx, Tönnies, Weber and Durkheim – together with
dozens of lesser attempts Appadurai leaves unmentioned – in the pantheon
of "problematic legacies of grand Western social science"? Will it someday
stand accused, to substitute here "globalization" for "modernity" in
Appadurai's critique, of conjuring up "a dramatic and unprecedented break
between past and present," one that will be "shown repeatedly to distort the
meanings of change and the politics of pastness"?

Apparently to allay such suspicions, Appadurai reassures readers that his is
"more than an update of older social theories of rupture and modernization": "First, mine is not a teleological theory"; "Second, the pivot of my
theory is not any large scale project of social engineering"; "Third ... I am

more deeply ambivalent about the prognosis"; "Fourth, and most important, my approach ... is explicitly transnational even postnational" and
moves away from the "fundamentally realist" view of the nation state.[5] If
these are the best arguments Appadurai has to offer to distinguish his work
from these "older" theories of modernity, none seems particularly true. To
take only the most influential social science theorist Appadurai mentions as
an example, Max Weber was famously "deeply ambivalent about the prognosis"; his was not a "large scale project of social engineering," nor fundamentally teleological, nor was the nation state one of his central concerns.

This suggests we reflect on possible similarities between announcements
of an age of globalization and their predecessors. While modernity has often
been conceptualized as a break, there has been little consensus on either the
nature of that break, or when it occurred – Comte, Marx, Tönnies, Weber,
and Durkheim serve as adequate reminders of a few of these very different
formulations. The same is true for recent theories of globalization. For
David Harvey, the key is "time-space compression," which reached a turning point in 1846 and 1847, was "peculiarly strong" at the beginning of the
20th century, and has been "intense" since 1973.[6] Anthony Giddens's
"globalizing of modernity" plots "the increasing intensification of world-
wide social relations" along four dimensions – the nation state system,
world military order, international division of labor, and world capitalist
economy – beginning in the nineteenth century, and intensifying in the
twentieth.[7] Manuel Castells' "network society" proclaims a "brave new
world of informational, global capitalism" that is "profoundly different"
from earlier forms of capitalism, in which labor is increasingly localized and
capital increasingly globalized in network flows.[8] For Michael Denning, the
shift occurs in 1989 from the age of three worlds – capitalist, communist,
and third world – to a global culture where "everyone thinks there is now
one world."[9] And Jean Baudrillard, whose work is often cited in globalization theory, proposes "orders of simulacra," a semiotic reformulation of
Marxist modes of production.[10]

More problematic still is the relationship that theories of globalization
postulate between globalization and modernity. On the one hand, the
break globalization is held to represent is often conceptualized as an intensification of modernity in, for example, Marc Augé's "supermodernity" and
"hypermodernity," or as a spatial extension of modernity in, for example,
Appadurai's "modernity at large" and Giddens's "globalizing of modernity"
– breaks, that is, which might not seem like much of a break at all.[11] On
the other hand, globalization is often represented as a radical break with
modernity, particularly in formulations that in their previous incarnations
signaled this break with the once ubiquitous prefix "post-": examples

include post-modernists, such as Jameson and Harvey; post-colonialists, such as Appadurai; post-marxists, such as Jameson and Denning; and post-structuralists such as Baudrillard. In such theories, any assertion of a break with modernity is again complicated by a well-founded skepticism toward "modernity" itself. Indeed, the fissures between the cognates "modernity," "modernism," and "modernization" were only the most obvious warning signs for those who, ignoring Wittgenstein's analysis of language, earnestly sought the essence or common thread in all the varied uses of the term "modern."[12]

Hegel's modernity

One way to gain a critical perspective on recent theories of globalization is to revisit the universals of yesteryear – universals, that is, of the not-so-distant past, constructed in a context distinct from the present, and yet constantly appropriated into it. On casual inspection, they can, like the duck–rabbit illusion attributed to psychologist Joseph Jastrow,[13] be viewed in two seemingly incompatible ways: as inextricably local, every bit as bygone as the past that produced them; or as universals, just as valid for our unfolding present as they were for the past. Closer examination, however, reveals the intellectual labor behind the illusion.

In an age now proclaimed to be that of globalization, modernity seems to have become just one such universal, both an ideological product of the past and yet underlying many theories of globalization. I will focus on Hegel's notion of modernity, following the exhortation of Jürgen Habermas, perhaps the most articulate proponent of the "modern West," who argues that to understand modernity and the "internal relation" between it and "Western rationalism" we must return to Hegel. It is through Hegel that Habermas develops his theories of modernity, the public sphere, and civil society, based on "communicative reason," hints of which he finds in Hegel's early writings, but a path, he laments, Hegel "did not take."[14] Indeed, there is arguably no thinker whose views on issues at the intersection of philosophy, history, the world, and modernity are as interesting, profound, or important as Hegel's. His influence is so considerable and so diffuse that it is impossible to trace, whether through Marx, Nietzsche, or Heidegger (to list only the most prominent names), and it is impossible to ignore.[15] While every generation is subject to renewed calls to "return" to Hegel, there are as many "Hegels" as there are returns to Hegel and reasons proffered for the return.[16]

Before we begin, however, we must examine two antithetical misreadings of Hegel's central thesis on modernity. We should first be clear about

Hegel's thesis itself, for in stark contrast to most of Hegel's thought, his conclusion could hardly be clearer or more explicit: modernity belongs to the Germanic nations, and to the Germanic nations alone. In the *Philosophy of History*, as we will see, Hegel first methodically excludes, region by region, the non-European world in its entirety – the Americas, Australia, Africa, China, India, and the Near East. He then excludes, explicitly, by name, most of the remainder of Europe – the Catholics, Austria, Bavaria, Italy, Spain, Portugal, France, and England.

The first misreading, commonly found in encyclopedias and thumbnail sketches of the history of philosophy, simply caricatures Hegel as the state philosopher of Prussia. In these accounts, in which context is substituted for text, politics for philosophy, and sycophantic ambition for intention, Hegel's thesis that the Germanic nations alone are modern is reduced to Prussianism. Such attacks on Hegel date back to at least the publication of his *Philosophy of Right*;[17] more recent versions cite famous critics of Hegel, such as Bertrand Russell and Sir Karl Popper, who are, unfortunately, also famous for not reading Hegel carefully.[18] In sum, this first misreading seeks to localize Hegel not just in space but time, relegating him by association to the fate of "Prussia," which vanished so ignominiously in the past.

While such a misreading might usually best be ignored, without the first misreading, the second might seem incomprehensible. The second is perpetrated by many of the most learned translators, interpreters, and exponents of Hegel, whose studies minimize, ignore, or even purposefully distort Hegel's central thesis about modernity, whether by asserting that the term *germanisch* means "Western," silently substituting "Christian" for "Protestant" and "the West" for "Germanic," offering lengthy alibis, or failing to mention Hegel's central thesis at all. Several examples will suffice: from J. N. Findlay, "the Romantic Modern German Kingdom (in which all Western Europe is included)";[19] from an introduction to the *Philosophy of History*, "Germanic peoples, i.e., Western civilization," which is further explained in the accompanying footnote, "These [Germanic peoples], *nota bene*, include the French, the English, and the rest of Western culture, as well as the Germans, and Sibree [the original translator] is very wrong in translating Germanic (*germanisch*) as German (*Deutsch*)";[20] and from Charles Taylor, "The German nations Hegel means are the barbarians who swarmed over the Roman empire at its end and founded the new nations of Western Europe. There is no particular chauvinism in this use of the word German."[21] These are only a few among numerous examples of the misreading of "Germanic";[22] and this is only the most egregious example of the reinterpretation of several key Hegelian philosophical terms of art, including "reason," "freedom," and "spirit." This second misreading, then, seeks to universalize Hegel, forging interpretations more acceptable to a modern audience. To again take Habermas as an example, while he calls Hegel "the first philosopher to develop a clear concept of modernity," and insists that "we have to get clear on the Hegelian concept of modernity," he cannot quite bring himself to state Hegel's central thesis, never mentions "Germanic nations," and in fact the closest he comes in two chapters of discussion is the circumlocution "the German Christian world that had issued from Roman and Greek antiquity."[23]

Instead of reading Hegel's philosophy as if it actually *is* universal or local, or reading it in a manner predetermined to render it so, I will analyze *how* Hegel marshals ideology, rhetoric, and narrative to imagine the local as universal in his world history. And as an alternative to the false choice between either ignoring Hegel's statements about the "Germanic nations" or ignoring Hegel because of them, Hegel's thesis about modernity will serve a strategic purpose: I wish to use the discomfort and unease generated by his disturbing statements about the Germanic nations to bring into clearer relief the fictiveness of such acts of self-fashioning in general. I will also examine Hegel's views on non-European history, and Chinese history in particular. While Hegel's conceptualization of the modern has been profoundly influential, his writings on the non-European world have largely been ignored outside comparative literature and area studies.[24] Yet Hegel's writings on the non-European world are central to his claims about the modern: without them, his panegyric for the local lacks even the pretense of world history. The focus here on China reflects Hegel's acknowledgement of Chinese history and his familiarity with several of the most important Chinese historical and philosophical texts, which were available to him in translation.

Remarks on a critical approach to Hegel's *Philosophy of History*

The following three sections present a close reading of Hegel's *Philosophy of History*,[25] perhaps his most well known and most accessible work. It is here that Hegel presents his fullest and clearest articulation of modernity,[26] and this is the only work which develops his method for world history.[27] This text is also important for philosophical reasons, for example, as Frederick Beiser notes, Hegel's historicization of metaphysics and God.[28]

The approach taken here to Hegel's *Philosophy of History* represents a departure from previous studies and deserves a brief explanation to better understand the place of this essay within the context of existing scholarship. Excluding polemics from both extremes – contemptuous dismissals and apologetic defenses[29] – the majority of studies of Hegel's *Philosophy of*

History might best be characterized as charitable exegeses,[30] which is true of secondary scholarship on Hegel in general. Indeed, many of the most valuable studies of Hegel's writings have been sympathetic ones, sometimes consisting primarily of extended paraphrase.[31] Unfortunately, these studies often go far beyond the "principle of charity," abdicating the critical role of the philosopher or historian,[32] or worse, refashioning Hegel's philosophy into doctrines imagined to be more acceptable to modern readers.[33] The following sections present an analysis that neither dismisses Hegel nor imagines for him arguments more palatable and modern, neither forging coherence where little exists nor reveling in the alleged inexorability of the deconstructionists' contrived aporias.[34]

There are many excellent studies of the broader historical and philosophical context of Hegel's writings,[35] along with many important studies of European views of the non-European world,[36] and in particular of China,[37] which, because of their scope, do not analyze Hegel's *Philosophy of History* in detail.[38] Most secondary studies that specifically focus on the *Philosophy of History* have sought to interpret it within the context of Hegel's collected writings, conceptualized as a "system," an approach encouraged by Hegel's own description of his philosophy. However, Hegel insists throughout the *Philosophy of History* that his claims are independent conclusions which derive from the study of history. While Hegel's concept of spirit is notoriously difficult and controversial,[39] he develops it here independently of the phenomenological and philosophical explications that are the central purpose of two of his other works, *Phenomenology of Spirit* and *Philosophy of Mind*.[40] Hegel makes no references to these texts in the *Philosophy of History*, and in fact explicitly states that his other works are not necessary to understand the *Philosophy of History*.[41] He repeatedly insists that in the *Philosophy of History*, he will proceed empirically and historically. Indeed, Hegel's "science" countenances multiple, independent, alternative proofs.[42] I will focus on the arguments in the *Philosophy of History* as one such proof.

This approach also recasts other aspects of conventional interpretations of Hegel. Instead of asking the question "What is Hegel's concept of spirit?", to be answered by seeking a coherent definition valid for all passages throughout Hegel's writings, the question posed here is how he constructs, in a particular passage, through narrative, rhetoric, and ideology, an imagined plausibility for a particular statement about spirit. This approach suggests not only a similar reading of other individual Hegelian texts, but also a critical approach to the entire corpus of his work: instead of viewing Hegel's writings as a system and endlessly adducing passages from increasingly obscure manuscripts to defend, for example, one particular interpretation of spirit, we should analyze the problematic relationship between

Hegel's historical demonstration of spirit presented in the *Philosophy of History* and his phenomenological and philosophical explications presented elsewhere.

It should be noted that the *Philosophy of History* is a composite of Hegel's own manuscripts and his students' notes from his lectures on the philosophy of history, which he gave once every two years at the University of Berlin (in the winter semesters of 1822–23, 1824–25, 1826–27, 1828–29, and 1830–31). It is generally accepted that the students' notes are reliable; there are no important philosophical differences between them and Hegel's own manuscripts.[43] This study does not examine in detail the complex issue of the composition of this text, which is addressed by the editors of various editions;[44] it does not trace the development of Hegel's thought through the course of his lectures; nor does it trace the later reformulations and developments of Hegelian thought;[45] instead of presenting a study of Hegel in his times – an approach to intellectual history exemplified by the seminal work of J. G. A. Pocock and Quentin Skinner – this study examines "our times" as imagined by Hegel.

Universalizing spirit

Spirit, Hegel stipulates, is the subject of his "philosophical history of the world" (*philosophische Weltgeschichte*, his most precise term for what he elsewhere sometimes calls "philosophical history" [*philosophische Geschichte*], "world history" [*Weltgeschichte*], or "universal history of the world" [*allgemeine Weltgeschichte*]). Despite his statements to the contrary, Hegel's conception of history is not conventional: history is a means through which spirit attains knowledge of itself. Hegel divides historical writing into three major forms, corresponding to stages in spirit's self-consciousness: "original history" (*ursprüngliche Geschichte*) is "a work of representational thinking for the representational faculty" (*ein Werk der Vorstellung für der Vorstellung*, *WH*, p. 13) through which spirit becomes conscious of itself; "reflective history" (*reflektierte Geschichte*) of a past age allows spirit to reflect upon a different spirit; the final stage is "philosophical history," which is "the record of the spirit's efforts to attain knowledge of what it is in itself" (*WH*, p. 54). Thus Hegel asserts that "world history belongs to the realm of spirit ... the spirit and the course of its development are the true substance of history" (*WH*, p. 44).

At the outset Hegel uses the term "spirit" primarily in the conventional sense of the "spirit of the times," but later in the section "Realization of Spirit in History," he provides a more detailed explanation. "Spirit," I will argue, is made universal just by Hegel's design. He presents a series of examples – including individuals, matter, communities, nations, God, and the world – so incongruous that he seems unable to offer any transition or explanation connecting them, attributing "spirit" to each simply by assignment, that is, by adducing them as examples of spirit:

(1) *Self-consciousness:* Hegel first characterizes spirit as "entirely individual, active, and absolutely alive: it is consciousness, but it is also the object of consciousness"; "the essence of spirit ... is self-consciousness" (*WH*, p. 47, 51).

(2) *The opposite of "matter":* Offering no transition from the previous series of anthropomorphisms, Hegel next asserts that the "nature of spirit can best be understood if we contrast it with its direct opposite, which is matter" (*WH*, p. 47). Hegel's idiosyncratic description of matter seems to be contrived solely for the purpose of defining spirit:

> [Matter] is made up of separate elements and aspires to a condition of unity; it thus endeavours to overcome itself and seeks its own opposite. If it were to succeed, it would no longer be matter, but would have ceased to exist as such; it strives towards ideality, for unity is its ideal existence. (*WH*, p. 48)

Through this opposition Hegel ascribes to spirit "freedom," by which he means not freedom in its current sense, but "self-sufficient being":

> [Spirit's] unity is not something external; it always finds it within itself, and exists in itself and with itself. Matter has its substance outside itself; spirit, on the other hand, is self-sufficient being, which is the same thing as freedom. (*WH*, p. 48)

(3) *Man:* Again with no transition explaining the connection to his preceding example, Hegel describes spirit "when it assumes the shape of a human individual." Here Hegel turns to further anthropomorphisms to ascribe to spirit a process of self-reflection that is fundamental to his characterization of spirit: through self-consciousness, transcending its existence, spirit encounters contradiction which it overcomes in a new unity. He begins with a psychologistic journey so personal that third- and first-person narration merges: man, Hegel relates, is "capable of feeling," but discovering himself to be "determined in some particular way," his feelings are "split up into an external and an internal world," and through the resulting "feeling of deficiency or negativity, I encounter a contradiction within myself which threatens to destroy me. But I nevertheless exist"; through this

knowledge, "I survive and seek to overcome (*aufzuheben*) the deficiency" by seeking "the restoration of my unity" (*WH*, pp. 48–9). Hegel then represents this tale as universal, as defining man's fundamental nature: "the fundamental characteristic of human nature is that he can think of himself as an ego. As a spirit, man does not have an immediate existence but is essentially turned upon himself. This function of mediation is an essential moment of spirit. Its activity consists in transcending and negating its immediate existence so as to turn in again upon itself; it has therefore made itself what it is by means of its own activity" (*WH*, p. 50). Ultimately, Hegel concludes, man "is a spiritual being; in short, he must throw off all that is natural to him. Spirit, therefore, is the product of itself" (*WH*, p. 51).

(4) *God:* Describing God as the "most sublime example" of spirit, Hegel again rehearses this psychologistic journey of man, this time adding to spirit attributes from a theosophic portrayal of the Trinity.[46] At first, the very universality of God impedes – or precedes – self-reflection: God "is the Father, a power which is universal but as yet enclosed within itself." The Son allows God to reflect on himself: God "is his own object, another version of himself, dividing himself into two so as to produce the Son. But this other version is just as immediate an expression of him as he is himself; he knows himself and contemplates himself in it." Finally, spirit represents the reunification in self-knowledge: "it is this self-knowledge and self-contemplation which constitutes the third element, the Spirit as such. In other words, the Spirit is the whole, and not just one or other of the elements in isolation." "It is this doctrine of the Trinity," Hegel asserts, "which raises Christianity above the other religions" (*WH*, p. 51).

(5) *Nation:* Again with little to connect this to his previous characterizations, Hegel describes the spirit of the nation, endowing it with "every aspect of the nation's consciousness and will and indeed of its entire reality; it is the common denominator of its religion, its political constitution, its ethical life, its system of justice, its customs, its learning, art, and technical skill, and the whole direction of its industry" (*WH*, p. 138).

Having assigned to "spirit" its key traits by accretion through anthropomorphisms, contrasts, and analogies, any apparent continuity is the artifact of little more than the recurrence of the same term – "spirit" – in these partially overlapping uses.[47]

Hegel then conflates these different uses of "spirit" through a series of identifications, totalizations, and proclamations of the "all-embracing" nature of spirit (which accounts for the pantheism or panlogism often attributed to him). For example, he states that while it is particular, "the spirit of the nation ... is identical with the absolute universal spirit"; "world spirit corresponds to the divine spirit, which is the absolute spirit"; "spirit of the nation is therefore the universal spirit in a particular form" (*WH*, pp. 52–3). Spirit, Hegel insists, is all-encompassing: "principles of the national spirits in their necessary progression are themselves only moments of the one universal spirit, which ascends through them in the course of history to its consummation in an all-embracing totality" (*WH*, p. 65); "the spiritual sphere is all-embracing; it encompasses everything that has concerned mankind down to the present day" (*WH*, p. 44); "the relationship of men to it [world spirit] is that of single parts to the whole which is their substance ... Since God is omnipresent, he is present in everyone and appears in everyone's consciousness; and this is the world spirit" (*WH*, pp. 52–3).

Localizing spirit in the nation

"In world history ... the individuals we are concerned with are nations, totalities, states" (*WH*, p. 36) – this fiat stands at the very center of Hegel's project of representing the local as universal. That is, from among all the possible choices at Hegel's disposal from the numerous forms of spirit he has delineated – the individual, community, age, nation, God, world, and absolute – Hegel chooses the nation: "the spirits of those nations which [have] become conscious of their inherent principle, and have become aware of what they are and of what their actions signify" are the "object" of the philosophical history of the world (*WH*, p. 12); "The spirit is essentially individual, but in the field of world history ... the spirit in history ... is the spirit of the nation" (*WH*, p. 51).

Hegel reaches this conclusion through two opposing contrivances. First, he subsumes individuals into the nation: the philosophical history of the world "concentrates its attention on the concrete spiritual principle in the life of nations, and deals not with individual situations but with a universal thought which runs throughout the whole" (*WH*, p. 30); "no individual can transcend it ... he can make no such distinction between himself and the spirit of the nation" (*WH*, p. 52). This assimilation of individual to nation has particularly awkward consequences for Hegel's theory: the individual served as Hegel's most concrete exemplar through which he ascribed to spirit its self-conscious, self-reflecting, and self-realizing journey, which he then universalized in mankind as human nature, and projected onto God through the Trinity; but only through jarring anthropomorphisms can the nation assume the attributes of self-consciousness, self-reflection, and self-realization.

Second, Hegel localizes world-spirit within one single nation. That is, Hegel stipulates that from among all nations, one and only one nation represents world spirit at any time, and that world spirit passes from one nation to another. This second device seems even more transparently contrived, apparently having no rationale apart from representing the local as universal. Even the anthropomorphisms and analogies to nature that Hegel adduces here do not fit, and require modification: "The death of a national spirit is a transition to new life, but not as in nature, where the death of one individual gives life to another individual of the same kind. On the contrary, the world spirit progresses from lower determinations to higher principles and concepts of its own nature, to more fully developed expressions of its Idea" (*WH*, p. 63). Hegel stipulates that the spirit of the nation dies, while stipulating that world spirit does not: "The particular spirit of a particular nation may perish; but it is a link in the chain of the world spirit's development, and this universal spirit cannot perish. The spirit of the nation is therefore the universal spirit in a particular form; the world spirit transcends this particular form, but it must assume it in so far as it exists" (*WH*, p. 53).

The destiny which Hegel assigns to the central protagonist of his world history is "freedom." Modern studies have often assimilated Hegel's notion of freedom to the current use of the term.[48] While he sometimes uses "freedom" in a strictly political sense, freedom is for Hegel not found in the state of nature, which he terms "lawlessness and savagery" (*WH*, p. 164); nor is it to be understood as democracy, which he argues against; indeed, his view of freedom is arguably a pact for securing obedience to the state. Since spirit, for Hegel, is the subject of world history, which records the development of self-conscious spirit toward self-realization, "freedom" must be understood primarily in the sense that he assigns to spirit: when "I am self-sufficient, I am also free" (*WH*, p. 48). It is in this specific sense of freedom – the self-sufficient, self-conscious, self-reflection of spirit – that Hegel claims that "world history is the progress of the consciousness of freedom" (*WH*, p. 54). Hegel then further insulates this evolution of spirit toward freedom through the famous device, the "*cunning of reason*" (*WH*, p. 89, emphasis in original).[49] Strictly speaking this is not a theory – Hegel presents no evidence for it – but rather an alibi put to the service of further isolating Hegel's philosophical history of the world from the events of history.

The fate of the world in Hegel's history

In contrast to the complexity with which Hegel portrays his central protagonist, spirit, and its destiny, freedom, the subsequent emplotment of his world history is simplistic. World spirit is transferred, Hegel famously posits, from one world-historical nation to the next, from East to West, from the Orient to Greece, the Romans, and in his conclusion, the Germanic nations: "The Orientals ... only know that one is free ... this one is therefore merely a despot ... The consciousness of freedom first awoke among the Greeks ... like the Romans, they only knew that some, and not all men as such, are free ... The Germanic nations, with the rise of Christianity, were the first to realise that man is by nature free, and that freedom of the spirit is his very essence" (*WH*, p. 54). This anticlimactic denouement can be understood by examining the stock roles Hegel assigns to other nations. Hegel's approach to the history of the world, I will argue, might best be termed eliminative. That is, in Hegel's hands, world history is not an attempt to present history from all regions across the globe; instead, with spirit localized in a single nation, the remainder of the world is cast outside world history.

An analysis of Hegel's views of the wider non-Western world is not as tangential as it might first appear: if Hegel is to claim to write anything more than a local history, he necessarily must address the history of the rest of the world. The point of my analysis here is not to show that Hegel's statements are just in some way historically inaccurate, or Eurocentric, or orientalist – undeniably they are all three, as has been widely noted. Indeed, Hegel's pronouncements on the world are so embarrassing to modern Hegel scholars that they hesitate to even include these sections in modern editions and translations.[50] Although apologists occasionally offer defenses,[51] Hegel's writings are not Eurocentric only if by that we mean to specify more precisely that his central point is to celebrate not all of Europe but the Germanic nations. And it certainly is not difficult to find explicit orientalism in Hegel's writings: "it is the necessary fate of Asiatic empires to be subjected to Europeans; and China will, some day or other, be obliged to submit to this fate" (*PH*, pp. 142–3).[52] Hegel's chapter "The Oriental World" has earned notoriety, Haun Saussy notes, "as the model of a Eurocentric world history, a narrative that selfishly seizes every opportunity to crowd its protagonists out of the story, a book, in short, unsuited to being either a *world* history or a world *history*."[53]

Hegel does not posit a homogeneous "peoples without history," but instead addresses each region separately, providing specific pretexts for excluding each from world history, sometimes eliminating entire continents, and sometimes specific nations. For example, "the torrid and frigid regions ... are not the theatre on which world history is enacted ... such extremes are incompatible with spiritual freedom," and therefore it is the "temperate zone which must furnish the theatre of world history" (*WH*, p. 155). He then excludes from world history the indigenous peoples of the Americas and Australia.

On India, Hegel asserts that "it is obvious to anyone with even a rudi-
mentary knowledge of the treasures of Indian literature that this country, so
rich in spiritual achievements of a truly profound quality, nevertheless has
no history" (*WH*, p. 136). Historical writing is for Hegel, as we have seen,
the record through which the self-conscious spirit of a nation comes to
reflect on itself, and it is on this pretext that Hegel excludes India from
world history in the opening passages: "Nations whose consciousness is
obscure, or the obscure history of such nations, are at any rate not the object
of the philosophical history of the world"; "the real objective history of a
nation cannot be said to have begun until it possesses a written historical
record. A culture which does not yet have a history has made no real
cultural progress [and this applies to the pretended history] of India over
three and a half thousand years" (*WH*, pp. 12–13, interpolation is Nisbet's).

Hegel does acknowledge Chinese historical writings: in contrast with
India, Hegel describes China as "an empire which possesses a highly distinguished and detailed historical record going back to the earliest times" (*WH*,
p. 136); "no people has so strictly continuous series of [historical] writers as
the Chinese" (*PH*, p. 116); to Europeans "a matter of special astonishment
is the accuracy with which their historical works are executed" (*PH*, p. 118).
These writings might seem to be a promising source for Hegel, since his
world history was supposed to begin with original history recording the
spirit of the times, and then developing to reflective and philosophical
history.

However, Hegel never bothers with the methodology he purports to
formulate for the philosophy of history: he never demonstrates nor even
explains, using Chinese historical writings, why he thinks spirit never
attained in China the "second principle" – "substantial mind endowed with
knowledge ... and also self-awareness."[54] Indeed, he seems to care so little
for his methodology that he never even uses Chinese sources to demonstrate
that world spirit originated in the East. These sources were available to
Hegel in translation, and he uses them for various purposes, just never those
he outlines in the *Philosophy of History*.

One important source available to Hegel was the *Document Classic* (*Shu
jing* or *Shang Shu*),[55] which records the speeches of Chinese rulers and
ministers, together with a preface for each conventionally attributed to
Confucius (traditional dates 551–479 BCE). In fact, Hegel apparently used
the translation of the *Document Classic* extensively to prepare his lectures on
the philosophy of religion.[56] Despite his familiarity with this work, Hegel
offers little analysis of the speeches, and no specific criticisms of the *Document
Classic*, either as original or as reflective history. Instead, Hegel simply
dismisses it: "Thus the *Document Classic* is not an actual historical work

(*eigentliches Geschichtswerk*), but a collection of individual portrayals (*Darstellungen*),[57] romances without coherence and without definite consequence" (*VPW*, v. 2, p. 281).

Another important general history available to Hegel in translation was the *Guideline and Commentary to the Comprehensive Mirror for Aid in Government* (*Zi zhi tong jian gang mu*),[58] compiled by Zhu Xi (1130–1200), the most influential philosopher of middle- and late-imperial China. This work is based primarily on a history by the statesman Sima Guang (1019–1086), *Comprehensive Mirror for Aid in Government* (*Zi zhi tong jian*), which covers the period from 403 BCE up to the beginning of the Song Dynasty in 959 CE, organized in a chronological style, and to this Zhu Xi added judgments based on his moral and political philosophy. Hegel mentions it only once, without any quotations, citations, analysis, or criticisms, and provides no explanation why this work is not a general history.

In contrast with his lengthy discussion and criticism of European histories, Hegel offers few specific criticisms of Chinese historical writings, except to claim, quite falsely, that "*history* among the Chinese comprehends the bare and definite facts, without any opinion or reasoning upon them" (*PH*, p. 135) – in fact, the Chinese historical texts available to him are filled with opinion and moral evaluations. Hegel dismisses Chinese history without further explanation: "we cannot go further into the minutiae of their annals ... as they themselves exhibit no development" (*PH*, p. 118). Hegel's statements about China correspond so tenuously to translations of original Chinese historical and philosophical writings – despite the number and volume available to him – that it is difficult to determine any place in his lectures on China, beyond six brief citations, where he used them. Instead, Hegel relies primarily on anecdotes, caricatures, and misrepresentations apparently from newspaper accounts and the European universal histories he derides.

His negative pronouncements on China are not in any way dictated by his sources, either primary or secondary. In fact, Hegel's views were stated in opposition to what has been called the Oriental renaissance, to the positive assessments of numerous sinophiles including Leibniz, Voltaire, and Wolff.[59] It seems reasonable to speculate that Hegel's polemics may have been a reaction against the pretensions to competing "universals" found in the writings of the European sinophiles and in the translations of Chinese works themselves.

Hegel's placement of China outside world history is then simply the tautological result of his conceptualization of spirit: localized, world spirit belongs to a single nation; nations without world spirit are then excluded from world history. That is, because self-sufficient, self-conscious, self-reflective spirit developed only in Christianity, "everything which belongs to spirit – unconstrained morality, in practice and theory, heart, inward religion, science and art properly so-called – is alien" to China (*PH*, p. 138). He misrepresents China as a theocracy, but because of its alleged lack of spirit, he concludes that China lacks religion: "Chinese religion, therefore, cannot be what we call religion. For to us religion means the retirement of the spirit within itself, in contemplating its essential nature, its inmost being" (*PH*, p. 131). Similarly, although he acknowledges that Confucian morality "has received the highest praise and the most flattering tributes" from some Europeans, because of the absence of spirit, Hegel dismisses it without further examination: China is "lacking – indeed completely lacking – in the essential self-consciousness of the concept of freedom" (*WH*, pp. 144–5). These dismissals cover a wide range of subjects in which Hegel has little if any expertise, including mathematics, science, medicine, technology: because there is no "contrast between objective existence and subjective freedom" to allow spirit to self-consciously self-reflect, "every change is excluded," there is only a "fixedness of a character which occurs perpetually" (*PH*, p. 116).

Hegel's historical treatment of those nations which he pronounces absent of spirit is perhaps best summarized in a passage where he implies that without spirit, "their deeds are lost without trace ... and no enduring achievement remains. Or the only traces they leave are ruin and destruction" (*WH*, p. 145). Spirit encompasses "every aspect" of the nation, and Hegel ascribes Oriental despotism to every aspect of Chinese society – administration, government, and religion. Hegel marshals anecdotes and misrepresentations to portray China as an absolute despotic unity: "Chinese regard themselves as belonging to their family, and at the same time as children of the State"; the "duties of the family are absolutely binding," and "the universal will immediately commands what the individual is to do, and the latter complies and obeys with proportionate renunciation of reflection and personal independence" (*WH*, pp. 120–1). Hegel ignores central tenets of Confucianism, including remonstrance, the principled disobedience of the emperor. In Hegel's China, "the Orientals do not know that the spirit or man as such are free in themselves ... They only know that one is free; but for this very reason, such freedom is mere arbitrariness, savagery, and brutal passion ... This one is therefore merely a despot, not a free man and a human being" (*WH*, p. 54).

Ultimately, in the section "The New Times" (*Die neue Zeit*), Hegel eliminates most of the remainder of Europe, leaving only the "Germanic nations" as the embodiment of world spirit. Hegel excludes much of Europe on the grounds that the Reformation, which "originated in Germany, and struck firm root only in the purely Germanic nations," was "limited to certain nations": "in Austria, in Bavaria, in Bohemia, the Reformation ... was indisputably stifled"; "the Sclavonians ... could not share the benefits of the dawning of freedom"; "the Romanic nations" ("Italy, Spain, Portugal, and in part France") "hindered the attainment of spiritual freedom" by maintaining "the principle of disharmony" (*PH*, pp. 419–21). And although the Reformation also "established itself in Scandinavia and England" (*PH*, p. 419), it is only Frederick II's "immortal work," the Prussian municipal code, in the secular sphere that ushers in the *"last stage in history, our world, our time"* (*PH*, p. 442, emphasis in original).[60] Hegel eliminates England, for example, by charging that it "maintained itself on its old foundations," its Constitution was "a complex of mere particular rights," and the "institutions characterized by real freedom are ... nowhere fewer than in England" (*PH*, pp. 453–4). Hegel, throughout his writings, repeatedly characterizes this "new times" as "Germanic," stating, for example, "This phase can be described as the *Germanic world*, and those nations on which the world spirit has conferred its true principle may be called the Germanic nations" (*WH*, p. 206, emphasis in original).

Conclusions

We are now in a position to summarize the key formulas in Hegel's philosophical history of the world: spirit is the subject of world history; universalized, spirit encompasses the world; localized, world spirit is particular to one single nation alone; and, in the final step, the local is universalized – modern world spirit is assigned to the Germanic nations alone while the remainder of the globe is eliminated from world history.

Hegel first transforms history into a record of spirit's development. Original history is a means through which spirit represents itself, gaining consciousness of its principle; reflective history is a means through which, using the difference with the spirit of a past age, spirit comes to reflect upon itself. Philosophical history of the world is a record of self-conscious, self-reflective spirit's attainment of self-knowledge. Spirit is the subject of Hegel's philosophical history of the world.

Spirit is, by Hegel's design, universal, and this is accomplished in two ways. First, Hegel proceeds by fiat, directly pronouncing spirit – in some of its forms at least – to be universal, all-embracing, and all-encompassing. Second, Hegel proceeds by conflation, presenting various terms and phrases in which the term "spirit" appears as if there was a single spirit and these examples were just instantiations of its differing forms, thus establishing by assumption a unity from the diverse forms of spirit which he attributes to entities as disparate as individuals, communities, nations, God, and the world. It is through this resulting conflation that Hegel selectively ascribes traits to spirit by accretion, through equally incongruous anthropomorphisms, contrasts, and analogies. He first attributes to "spirit" life and consciousness; as the opposite of matter, spirit "exists in and with itself" and is thus "free"; as a "human individual," spirit is self-conscious, self-reflective, and self-producing; as God, spirit is omnipresent, omniscient, and omnipotent; as the Trinity, spirit is universal, self-contemplating, and self-knowing; and as a nation, spirit is "all-embracing," including "every aspect" of the nation. But this apparent unity is achieved at the cost of coherence: because his examples are so tenuously related, Hegel must in addition present a series of identifications to forge unity among these disparate forms of spirit. The analysis of the narrative construction of spirit presented here, though limited to the *Philosophy of History*, suggests reasons why, as Robert Williams puts it, "a successful, comprehensive interpretation of *Geist* [spirit], and with it, Hegelianism, has thus far eluded interpreters."[61]

Next Hegel localizes universal spirit in the "spirit of the nation." That is, against his pronouncements of the universality of spirit, and contrary to the unity of spirit he so painstakingly forges, Hegel designates, from among the numerous forms of spirit he adduces, the spirit of the nation as the subject of world history. The spirit of the individual, in this scheme, is subsumed within the spirit of the nation; the spirit of the nation is a totality encompassing all of the nation's culture, art, science, and philosophy. Then, in one of Hegel's most clumsily conceived contrivances, he stipulates that one nation, and only one nation, is the spirit of the world in any age; spirit passes, in this arrangement, from one nation to another.

This localization of universal spirit serves to transform the local into the universal. A personal if imagined journey of self-reflection, contradiction, and overcoming, resulting in a self-produced unity of spirit, is projected by Hegel onto mankind as human nature, and further projected onto the Trinity, culminating in self-contemplating, self-knowing universal spirit. This fiction alone, however, is in itself hardly adequate to transform world history into a panegyric for the Germanic nations. Hegel must further assign to world history the ultimate destiny of self-sufficient, self-conscious, self-reflective universal spirit achieving self-knowledge; he must further designate the sole protagonist of this pilgrimage to be the spirits of nations, not individuals, and of one and only one nation in any age.

With the local represented as universal, all that remains is for Hegel to dispense with the remainder of the globe. The world and its history, which Hegel must by necessity address, are irrelevant to Hegel's panegyric, and are introduced only to be explained away. And it is Hegel's localization of universal spirit – with the nation as the subject of world history, all individuals and all culture subsumed in the totality of the nation, and one and only one nation as universal spirit – which serves as Hegel's theoretical alibi for his dismissal of all other nations along with all of their historical particulars. Then what are the larger implications of this study, beyond, that is, rescuing Hegel from Habermas's reinvention of him as a failed Habermasian – the "first philosopher to develop a clear concept of modernity" who stumbled in his early years onto the path of the critique of subject-centered reason through communicative action, only to fail to follow it through?[62] We might summarize the preliminary considerations we began with as follows. As with modernity, there is no consensus on a definition for globalization, but only that it defines "us"; there is no consensus on a date, but only that globalization marks an unprecedented break. Globalization is sometimes defined as a break which intensifies modernity, or as opposed to a modernity that is held never to have existed, or sometimes both within the same theory. Theories of an age of globalization, themselves hybrids of post-modernism, post-structuralism, post-colonialism, and post-marxism, have come into prominence with surprising suddenness in the past 15 years; perhaps all we can be certain of is that we now know what lies beyond modernity, "past the last post-,"[63] and the name of the language-game is "globalization."

What if, at this liminal moment in the history of self-fashioned representations, instead of looking forward to a future termed the "age of globalization" from a past called "modernity," we instead imagine ourselves looking back at modernity from a globalist future? Modernity, I have suggested, is a universal of yesteryear, something that, at this point, we can still envision in two incompatible ways. On the one hand, the idiom of modernity, its claims, and its conclusions, are certainly still familiar to us. On the other hand, from the perspective of the global twenty-first century, the discourse of modernity seems to be a relic of a bygone past. Consider, for example, the twentieth-century historiography that offered explanations for China's asserted "failure" to achieve "modernity." This discourse was sustained not so much by the validity of its claims, but rather by what Deleuze and Guattari call the "redundancy" of statements with "little plausibility or truthfulness"[64] that circulated as central themes through many fields of Chinese studies. Why did China fail to develop capitalism? Why was there no scientific revolution in China? Why was there no industrial revolution in China? Why did China never develop modern political institutions? Prominent among these were the debates culminating in a symposium in 1993, inspired at least in part by Habermas's misreading of Hegel's thesis on modernity, addressing China's alleged failure to develop a public sphere and civil society.[65] Was an alternative modernity for China even possible?

In these "comparative" studies with the West, virtually every feature of Chinese culture was adduced as the explanans for this "failed" modernity. While, with the exception of the "public sphere"/"civil society" debates, few of these claims derive directly from Hegel, there are notable similarities to Hegel's writings on China. At what is just the beginning of the global twenty-first century, this historiography is already rapidly becoming outdated: convening a major academic conference now to inquire into China's failed modernity is scarcely conceivable. Furthermore, in this historiography we consistently find China continuing to play a role homologous to that which Hegel had imposed – that of a civilization without change. Historians whose work has made important and in some cases considerable contributions to our knowledge of China have adopted as their central thesis concepts that are not historical explanations at all but instead little more than updated language roughly synonymous with Hegel's view: examples include "cybernetic" or "homeostatic" (Joseph Needham), "high level equilibrium trap" (Mark Elvin), "involutionary" (a term Philip Huang borrows from Clifford Geertz), and "quasi-involutionary" (Jack Goldstone), to cite only a few from a vast literature. Even in recent works explicitly critical of Eurocentric narratives of "modernity," China continues to assume this role. For example, a central thesis of Kenneth Pomeranz's recent and influential book, *The Great Divergence: China, Europe, and the Making of the Modern World Economy*, is that China hit a "cul-de-sac."[66] The real cul-de-sac, the analysis of Hegel presented here suggests, is the conceptual one behind studies of China's "failure."[67] Will theories of globalization merely provide a new discourse for retelling this narrative, one in which the local effects of globalization are anointed as the new universals, and China stands accused of failing to be "global"?[68]

Theories of globalization, while not the first to manipulate the local and universal to imagine the global, are not a simple "update" of theories of the modern. The point of this critique of the historically specific manner in which Hegel imagined the modern cannot be to draw a direct line from Hegel to theories of globalization, however influential Hegel might be. Hegel himself inveighs against crude applications of the "lessons" of history into the present which, he argues, is always particular (*WH*, p. 21). While no historical study can predict the future, whether it is indeed the destiny of theories of globalization to share the fate that Appadurai assigns to those of modernity, can these theories in the end avoid the fate of Hegel, and the dozens of grand social theories of the modern? Will they look any less parochial, will they be any less embarrassing than Hegel's formulations? Nevertheless, might we at times pause to marvel at their ingenuity, and at least in the case of Hegel, their sheer philosophical beauty? Perhaps in this sense we might liken these ideological products to the Navajo rugs that Bsumek so vividly describes in this volume: we might admire these tapestries for their creativity or inquire into their construction and the history of their components, often so incongruous, without placing too much credence in their claimed authenticity.

The criticisms presented here can scarcely diminish the importance of these grand performative acts of self-fashioning:[69] the power of collective self-representations cannot be overstated, whether in the form of the imagined communities of nation states criticized in recent scholarship, the ethnicities examined by Philip White, or as "modern," "Christian," "Muslim," "Marxist," or "National Socialist." We cannot know for what political purposes the ideologies of globalization will be appropriated, and because of the power of these ideologies, critical theorists must not abdicate their responsibilities as critics and become traffickers themselves. Ultimately, history suggests that we must keep foremost in our minds the consequences of past ideologies, as we take as our task the analysis of how these ideologies are fabricated.

Notes

1 Fredric Jameson, concluding paragraph of "Notes on Globalization as a Philosophical Issue," in Jameson and Masao Miyoshi (eds), *The Cultures of Globalization* (Durham, NC, 1999), p. 77.

2 The earliest use of the term "globalization" given in the OED is 1961 (*OED*, "global," s.v.); the earliest important academic use of the term "globalism" seems to be George Modelski's *Principles of World Politics* (New York, 1972). I would like to thank Antony Hopkins for the latter point; for an analysis of the history and use of these terms, see his introduction to this volume.

3 Arjun Appadurai, *Modernity at Large: Cultural Dimensions of Globalization* (Minneapolis, MN, 1996), p. 3.

4 Appadurai, *Modernity at Large*, p. 3. For a discussion of the relationship between historical research and social science theory, see A. G. Hopkins, "The History of Globalization and the Globalization of History?" in Hopkins (ed.), *Globalization in World History* (New York, 2002), pp. 11–46.

5 Appadurai, *Modernity at Large*, p. 9.

6 David Harvey, *The Condition of Postmodernity: An Enquiry into the Origins of Cultural Change* (Cambridge, MA, 1990).

7 Anthony Giddens, *The Consequences of Modernity* (Stanford, CA, 1990).

8 Manuel Castells, *The Information Age, Vol. 1, The Rise of the Network Society* (Cambridge, MA, 1996).

9 Michael Denning, *Culture in the Age of Three Worlds* (New York, 2004), p. 42.

10 Jean Baudrillard, *Symbolic Exchange and Death*, trans. Iain Hamilton Grant (Thousand Oaks, CA, 1993); originally published as *L'échange symbolique et la mort* (Paris, 1976).

11   Marc Augé, *Non-Places: Introduction to an Anthropology of Supermodernity* (New York, 1995); originally published as *Non-lieux: Introduction à une anthropologie de la surmodernité* (Paris, 1992).

12   See Jürgen Habermas, "Modernity's Consciousness of Time and Its Need for Self-Reassurance," Ch. 1 of *The Philosophical Discourse of Modernity: Twelve Lectures* (Cambridge, MA, 1987); originally published as *Der philosophische Diskurs der Moderne: Zwölf Vorlesungen* (Frankfurt am Main, 1985); Marjorie Perloff, "Modernist Studies," in Stephen Greenblatt and Giles B. Gunn (eds), *Redrawing the Boundaries: The Transformation of English and American Literary Studies* (New York, 1992); and Susan Stanford Friedman, "Definitional Excursions, the Meanings of *Modern/Modernity/Modernism*," *Modernism/Modernity*, 8 (2001), pp. 493–513.

13   This optical illusion is a drawing that can be seen as representing either a rabbit or a duck. It is reproduced as a line drawing in Ludwig Wittgenstein, *Philosophical Investigations*, trans. G. E. M. Anscombe (New York, 1958), p. 194e, first published posthumously in 1953 as *Philosophische Untersuchungen*. Thomas Kuhn also uses this illusion to explain "paradigm changes" in "Revolutions as Changes of World View," Ch. 10 of *Structure of Scientific Revolutions*, 2nd ed. (Chicago, 1970), p. 114.

14   Habermas, *Philosophical Discourse of Modernity*, p. 30.

15   "One is well warned by Heidegger, Bataille, Derrida, and, of course, Hyppolite that Hegelianism extends its power even when ignored, turned away from, and the Hegelianism emerging as a result is often of the worst type. Hegel makes it impossible for one to treat him lightly, even when one refuses to treat him, and he makes it difficult to break from him." Arkady Plotnitsky, "Foreword: Reading and Rereading Hyppolite and Hegel," in Jean Hyppolite, *Introduction to Hegel's Philosophy of History* (Gainesville, FL, 1996), p. ix. Certainly Michel Foucault, along with many others, could also be added to this list.

16   In "The Return to Hegel: The Latest Word in Academic Revisionism," Louis Althusser, revising Glockner's 1931 comment that what was at stake in the return to Hegel was Kant, asserts that the latest "Great Return to Hegel is simply a desperate attempt to combat Marx, cast in the specific form that revisionism takes in imperialism's final crisis: *a revisionism of a fascist type*." Althusser, *Spectre of Hegel: Early Writings*, trans. G. M. Goshgarian (New York, 1997), p. 183; emphasis in original. "Return to Hegel" was first published in *La Nouvelle Critique*, 20 (1950).

17   According to Terry P. Pinkard, in *Hegel's Phenomenology: The Sociality of Reason* (Cambridge, 1994), the view of Hegel as the state philosopher for Prussia dates back to Hegel's contemporaries: "Almost all the contemporary reviews virtually ignored the content of the book [*Philosophy of Right*] (or badly misunderstood it) and focused instead on the Preface; the consensus among the reviewers came down to the notion that Hegel had turned into an apologist for Prussian royalist autocracy and had come to embrace a kind of unattractive absolutistic view about his own philosophy" (p. 460). Ironically, Hegel's lectures were

apparently intended to dispel rather than reinforce that view: "stung by criticisms that he was a pawn of the ruling powers in Prussia, Hegel used his lectures to clear up several misunderstandings that had been left over from the publication of the *Philosophy of Right*." Pinkard gives the following example: "He thus made it clear to his audiences that despite his argument for the 'absolute right' of the bearers of the meaning of world history at any given time to do what they had to do, he was not defending any type of view that authorized people to do what they wished to do with those whom they regarded as 'lesser' people"; "moralistic criticism of [world] historical figures was, from the standpoint of understanding world history and its progress, simply beside the point; condemning Caesar as a 'bad man' did not help one any better understand freedom or Caesar's role in the history of the development of the 'Idea' of freedom" (p. 493).

18   Stephen Houlgate, in *Freedom, Truth and History: An Introduction to Hegel's Philosophy* (London, 1991), notes that "there is a strong tradition of Hegel criticism, running from Hegel's contemporary, Schopenhauer, through Rudolf Haym and Nietzsche, to Bertrand Russell and Karl Popper, which sees in Hegel little more than an apologist for the conservative (Prussian) status quo ... For some critics, indeed, Hegel's political philosophy is a direct precursor of corporate fascism and National Socialism ... In the minds of many people, then, Hegel is associated with the veneration of the Prussian state, with proto-Hitlerian German nationalism." Houlgate notes that "the severest critics of Hegel have frequently reacted to what they have perceived to be the deleterious effects of *Hegelianism* and have not actually read much of Hegel himself" (p. 78).

19   John Niemeyer Findlay, *Hegel, a Re-Examination* (New York, 1958; reprint, 1962), p. 336.

20   C. J. Friedrich, Eaton Professor of the Science of Government at Harvard from 1955 to 1971, "Introduction to the Dover Edition" (unpaginated), in *Philosophy of History*, trans. J. Sibree (New York, 1956).

21   Charles Taylor, *Hegel* (New York, 1975), p. 398.

22   While Walter Kaufmann uses the term "Germanic nations" in the text, his footnote states that "The term *die germanischen Nationen* obviously refers to the Protestant nations of northern Europe and cannot by any stretch of the imagination be taken to mean merely 'the Germans'; yet this is a point where Hegel has been mistranslated and misrepresented again and again." Kaufmann, *Hegel: Reinterpretation, Texts, and Commentary* (New York, 1965), p. 255, n. 2. Houlgate mentions only in passing that Hegel assigns modernity to "certain Protestant countries such as Germany and England." Houlgate, *Freedom, Truth, and History*, p. 231. Joseph McCarney, in *Hegel on History* (New York, 2000), does note, in the middle of a chapter, that Hegel is talking about the Germanic nations, but later suggests that in the broad outline Hegel is correct in his views on history. One clear exception is Knox's *Hegel's Philosophy of Right* (Oxford, 1977 [1952]), which accurately and straightforwardly uses the term "Germanic nations."

23 Habermas, *Philosophical Discourse of Modernity*, pp. 4–5.

24 The most important critiques of Hegel's writings on the non-West include Haun Saussy, "Hegel's Chinese Imagination," in *The Problem of a Chinese Aesthetic* (Stanford, CA, 1993); idem, "No Time Like the Present: The Category of Contemporaneity in Chinese Studies," in *Great Walls of Discourse and Other Adventures in Cultural China* (Cambridge, MA, 2001); Gayatri Chakravorty Spivak, *A Critique of Postcolonial Reason: Toward a History of the Vanishing Present* (Cambridge, MA, 1999), pp. 37–66; Ranajit Guha, *History at the Limit of World-History* (New York, 2002); Partha Chatterjee, "Communities and the Nation," Ch. 11 of *The Nation and Its Fragments: Colonial and Postcolonial Histories* (Princeton, NJ, 1993), pp. 220–39; and Susan Buck-Morss, "Hegel and Haiti," *Critical Inquiry*, 26 (2000), pp. 821–65. Two important dissertations are Stuart Jay Harten, "Raising the Veil of History: Orientalism, Classicism and the Birth of Western Civilization in Hegel's Berlin Lecture Courses of the 1820's" (Ithaca, NY, 1994); and Gregory Mahlon Reihman, "Constructing Confucius: Western Philosophical Interpretations of Confucianism from Malebranche to Hegel" (Austin, TX, 2001). Other studies include Heinz Kimmerle, "Hegel und Afrika: Das Glas zerspringt," *Hegel-Studien*, 28 (1993); Yoshinori Takeuchi, "Hegel and Buddhism," *Il Pensiero*, 7 (1962), pp. 5–46; K. A. Wittfogel, "Hegel über China," *Unter dem Banner des Marxismus*, 5 (1931), pp. 346–62; A. Chi-Lu Chung, "A Critique of Hegel's Philosophy of History," *Chinese Culture* [Yang-ming-shan, Taiwan], 5 (1963/64), pp. 60–77; Michel Hulin, *Hegel et l'Orient: suivi de la traduction annotée d'un essai de Hegel sur la Bhagavad-gita* (Paris, 1979). See also Donald M. Lowe, *The Function of "China" in Marx, Lenin, and Mao* (Berkeley, CA, 1966). I would like to thank Tracie Matysik for bringing to my attention Buck-Morss's article and Harten's dissertation.

25 For Hegel's "Introduction," I have used the *Lectures on the Philosophy of World History: Introduction*, trans. H. B. Nisbet (Cambridge, 1975), hereafter abbreviated *WH*. This translation is based on Johannes Hoffmeister and Georg Lasson (eds), *Vorlesungen über die Philosophie der Weltgeschichte* (Hamburg, 1955), hereafter *VPW*. Other important editions include Hermann Glockner (ed.), *Sämtliche Werke: Jubiläumsausgabe in 20 Bänden* (Stuttgart, 1927–30); Karl Heinz Ilting, Karl Brehmer and Hoo Nam Seelmann (eds), *Vorlesungen über die Philosophie der Weltgeschichte: Berlin 1822/23* (Hamburg, 1996), hereafter *VPWB*; and "Philosophie der Weltgeschichte: Einleitung 1822–1828" and "Einleitung 1830/31," in *Vorlesungsmanuskripte II (1816–1831)*, Vol. 18 of Rheinisch-Westfälischen Akademie der Wissenschaften (eds), *Gesammelte Werke* (Hamburg, 1995). For the remaining sections which are not translated in *WH*, I have used *Philosophy of History*, trans. J. Sibree (New York, 1956, reprint of the edition published by Colonial Press in 1899), hereafter *PH*, originally published as Eduard Gans (1797–1839) and Karl Hegel (1813–1901) (eds), *Georg Wilhelm Friedrich Hegels Vorlesungen über die Philosophie der Geschichte* (Berlin: Duncker & Humblot, 1840). For the sake of uniformity of style and readability, I have on occasion silently altered translations from this latter text.

Other translations (of the introduction only) include *Introduction to the Philosophy of History*, trans. Leo Rauch (Indianapolis, IN, 1988); and *Reason in History: A General Introduction to the Philosophy of History*, trans. R. S. Hartman (New York, 1953). For a comprehensive bibliography of secondary literature on the *Philosophy of History* up to 1975, see "Suggestions for Further Reading" (*WH*, 234–42); a more recent bibliography can be found in Elisabeth Weisser-Lohmann and Dietmar Köhler (eds), *Hegels Vorlesungen über die Philosophie der Weltgeschichte*, *Hegel-Studien*, *Beiheft*, Vol. 38 (Bonn, 1998). For a comprehensive bibliography of secondary works on Hegel, see Kurt Steinhauer (ed.), *Hegel Bibliography: Background Material on the International Reception of Hegel within the Context of the History of Philosophy*, Parts I (up to 1975) and II (1976–1991) (Munich, 1980 and 1998). Many important secondary studies on Hegel have been collected in Robert Stern (ed.), *G. W. F. Hegel: Critical Assessments*, 4 vols. (New York, 1993); see in particular the sections by Benedetto Croce, Alexandre Kojève, Georges Bataille, Jean Hyppolite, Georg Lukács, Theodor Adorno, and Jürgen Habermas.

26 Hegel also presents two short outlines of world history in his other works: "World History," §§341–60, *Hegel's Philosophy of Right*, trans. T. M. Knox (Oxford, 1977 [1952]), first published as *Grundlinien der Philosophie des Rechts* (1821); and "World History" (*Weltgeschichte*, translated as "Universal History"), §§548–52 of *Hegel's Philosophy of Mind: Being Part Three of the Encyclopaedia of Philosophical Sciences*, trans. William Wallace (Oxford, 1971), originally published as *Philosophie des Geistes* (1830). Sections of Hegel's *Phenomenology of Spirit* are also relevant.

27 Frederick Beiser, "Hegel's Historicism," in Beiser (ed.), *The Cambridge Companion to Hegel* (New York, 1993), p. 282.

28 Beiser notes that "history is central to Hegel's conception of philosophy": Hegel "*historicizes* philosophy," famously proclaiming in *Philosophy of Right* that "philosophy is its own age comprehended in thought," ushering in a "revolution" subverting Cartesian philosophy and "historicizing the traditional objects of classical metaphysics, God, providence, and immortality." Beiser very nicely summarizes Hegel's historicization of "metaphysics, God, providence, and immortality" as follows: for Hegel, "metaphysics is possible only if its central concepts are explicable in historical terms"; "God is not an entity beyond the world, but the idea realized in history. Providence is not an 'external end,' a supernatural plan imposed by God upon nature, but an 'internal end,' the ultimate purpose of history itself. And immortality is not life in heaven, but the memory of someone's role in history ... in Hegel, the philosophy of history usurps the traditional function of theodicy: it explains the existence of evil by showing it to be necessary for the realization of the end of history." Beiser, "Hegel's Historicism," p. 271.

29 Duncan Forbes' "Introduction" cites many of the better known polemics against Hegel's *Philosophy of History*, but presents an apologetic defense little better than the works he decries (*WH*, pp. vii–xxxv).

30   For summaries of Hegel's main arguments, see Charles Taylor, "Reason and
     History," Ch. 15 of *Hegel*; Walter Kaufmann, "Hegel on History," Ch. 6 of
     Hegel: Reinterpretation, Texts, and Commentary, pp. 254–96; J. N. Findley, *Hegel:
     A Re-Examination*, pp. 332–7; and most recently, McCarney, *Hegel on History*.
     The most important book-length studies are Jean Hyppolite, *Introduction to
     Hegel's Philosophy of History* (Gainesville, FL, 1996), originally published as
     Introduction à la philosophie de l'histoire de Hegel (Paris, 1948); Jacques d'Hondt,
     Hegel, philosophe de l'histoire vivante, 2nd ed. (Paris, 1988 [1966]); and Dennis
     O'Brien, *Hegel on Reason and History: A Contemporary Interpretation* (Chicago,
     1975). Important criticisms can be found in Theodore Adorno, *Negative
     Dialectics*, trans. E. B. Ashton (New York, 1973), originally published as *Negative
     Dialektik* (Frankfurt am Main, 1966); and Herbert Marcuse, *Hegel's Ontology and
     the Theory of Historicity*, trans. Seyla Benhabib (Cambridge, MA, 1987), origi-
     nally published as *Hegels Ontologie und die Theorie der Geschichtlichkeit* (Frankfurt
     am Main, 1932). Important articles include Beiser, "Hegel's Historicism";
     Clark Butler, "Empirical versus Rational Order in the History of Philosophy,"
     Owl of Minerva, 26 (1994), pp. 29–34; W. H. Walsh, "Hegel on the Philosophy
     of History," *History and Theory*, 5 (1965), pp. 67–82; idem, "Principle and
     Prejudice in Hegel's Philosophy of History," and J. Plamenatz, "History as the
     Realisation of Freedom," in Z. A. Pelczynski (ed.), *Hegel's Political Philosophy –
     Problems and Perspectives: A Collection of New Essays* (Cambridge, 1971);
     Houlgate, "History and Truth"; Benedetto Croce, "The Historicism of Hegel
     and the New Historicism," Philip J. Kain, "Hegel's Political Theory and
     Philosophy of History," Stanley Rosen, "Hegel and Historicism," and Stephen
     Houlgate, "World History as the Progress of Consciousness: An Interpretation
     of Hegel's Philosophy of History," all reprinted in Stern, *G. W. F. Hegel:
     Critical Assessments*, originally published in, respectively, *Filosofia, poesia, storia*
     (Milan, 1951), *Clio*, 17 (1988), pp. 345–68, *Clio*, 7 (1977), pp. 33–51, and *Owl
     of Minerva*, 22 (1990), pp. 69–80. For a collection of essays, see Robert L.
     Perkins (ed.), *History and System: Hegel's Philosophy of History* (Albany, NY,
     1984). Other studies include Burleigh Taylor Wilkins, *Hegel's Philosophy of
     History* (Ithaca, NY, 1974); and Rudolf J. Siebert, *Hegel's Philosophy of History*
     (Washington, DC, 1979).

31   At one extreme is John Niemeyer Findlay's "Analysis of the Text" in *Hegel's
     Phenomenology of Spirit*, which consists almost entirely of paraphrase with very
     few critical interventions to distinguish it from Hegel's thought.

32   While explication of Hegel's texts is difficult and important, one unfortunate
     result has been the abdication of critical perspective. To take one of the best
     studies as an example, in Charles Taylor's *Hegel*, entire pages consist of para-
     phrase of Hegel's claims with few critical interventions from Taylor. Taylor's
     paraphrase is often so lacking in critical interventions that it could be mistak-
     enly interpreted to be an implicit endorsement of Hegel's claims as fact. For
     example, Taylor states, "Hegel makes clear why in his view ancient democracy
     is inappropriate as a model for the modern world," followed by paraphrase of

Hegel. The next paragraph begins "But there is a third reason why ancient democracy is not an appropriate model for our time," followed by more paraphrase. On the following page a paragraph begins, "But these Germans were ideally suited to take history at the next stage," followed by more paraphrase. Taylor, *Hegel*, pp. 396–98.

33 One of the most notable examples is Habermas, *Philosophical Discourse of Modernity*.

34 The "close reading" presented in this essay differs from that of deconstructionists. For examples of Jacques Derrida's analyses of Hegel, see "The Pit and the Pyramid: Introduction to Hegel's Semiology," first published in the seminar proceedings *Hegel et la pensée moderne* (1971), and *Glas*, trans. John P. Leavey (Lincoln, NE, 1986), originally published as *Glas* (Paris, 1974).

35 John Toews, *Hegelianism: The Path toward Dialectical Humanism, 1805–1841* (Cambridge, 1980); Laurence Dickey, *Hegel: Religion, Economics, and the Politics of Spirit, 1770–1807* (Cambridge, 1987); Frederick Beiser, *The Fate of Reason* (Cambridge, MA, 1987).

36 The most important work is Donald F. Lach, *Asia in the Making of Europe*, 3 vols in 9 (Chicago, 1965–).

37 Gregory Blue, "China and Western Social Thought in the Modern Period," in Timothy Brook and Gregory Blue (eds), *China and Historical Capitalism Genealogies of Sinological Knowledge* (Cambridge, 1999); David Martin Jones, *The Image of China in Western Social and Political Thought* (New York, 2001); Julia Ching and Willard G. Oxtoby (eds), *Moral Enlightenment: Leibniz and Wolff on China* (Nettetal, 1992); idem, *Discovering China: European Interpretations in the Enlightenment* (Rochester, NY, 1992); Jonathan D. Spence, *The Chan's Great Continent: China in Western Minds* (New York, 1998); David E. Mungello, *Curious Land: Jesuit Accommodation and the Origins of Sinology* (Honolulu, HI, 1985); Edwin J. Van Kley, "Europe's 'Discovery' of China and the Writing of World History," *American Historical Review*, 76 (1971), pp. 358–85; Raymond S. Dawson, *The Chinese Chameleon: An Analysis of European Conceptions of Chinese Civilization* (London, 1967); Colin Mackerras, *Western Images of China* (Oxford, 1989); René Étiemble, *L'Europe chinoise, Vol. 1, De l'Empire romain à Leibniz*, and *Vol. 2, De la sinophilie à la sinophobie* (Paris, 1988–89); Thomas H. Lee (ed.), *China and Europe: Images and Influences in Sixteenth to Eighteenth Centuries* (Hong Kong, 1991); Virgile Pinot, *La Chine et la formation de l'esprit philosophique en France 1640–1740* (Paris, 1932).

38 The most important is Immanuel Kant, "Idea for a Universal History from a Cosmopolitan Point of View," reprinted in John F. Rundell and Stephen Mennell (eds), *Classical Readings in Culture and Civilization* (New York, 1998), pp. 39–47, first published in 1784; other important works include "universal" or world histories by Voltaire, Johann Gottfried Herder, and Johannes von Müller.

39 For an important study of Hegel's use of the term "spirit," see Robert C. Solomon, "Geist," in Alasdair C. MacIntyre (ed.), *Hegel: A Collection of Critical*

Essays (Garden City, NY, 1972), pp. 123–49; and Robert R. Williams, "Hegel's Concept of *Geist,*" reprinted in Stern (ed.), *G. W. F. Hegel: Critical Assessments,* originally published in Peter G. Stillman (ed.), *Hegel's Philosophy of Spirit* (Albany, NY 1987). See also John McDowell, *Mind and World* (Cambridge, MA, 1994); and Robert B. Pippin, *Hegel's Idealism: The Satisfactions of Self-Consciousness* (Cambridge, 1989). Many studies, such as O'Brien's "contemporary interpretation," for the most part downplay the importance of spirit.

40 Arnold V. Miller and J. N. Findlay (eds), *Phenomenology of Spirit* (Oxford, 1977), originally published as *Phänomenologie des Geistes* (1807). For a critical analysis, see Robert C. Solomon, *In the Spirit of Hegel: A Study of G. W. F. Hegel's Phenomenology of Spirit* (New York, 1983); Michael N. Forster, *Hegel's Idea of a Phenomenology of Spirit* (Chicago, 1998); and Pinkard, *Hegel: A Biography.*

41 The only other work which Hegel refers to is the section on world history from the *Philosophy of Right*: "I have no text book [compendium] on which to base my lectures; but in my *Elements of the Philosophy of Right* [*Grundlinien der Philosophie des Rechts*], §§ 341–360 (i.e. the conclusion), I have already defined the concept of world history proper, as well as the principles or periods into which its study can be divided" (*WH,* p. 11).

42 See, for example, Findlay, "Foreword," in *Hegel's Phenomenology of Spirit,* pp. v–vi.

43 Joseph McCarney offers several quotations, from various editors, as evidence of the reliability of the students' notes. McCarney notes that "there is, one should add, nothing in the student transcripts that jars with, or stands significantly apart from, the manuscript content," and concurs with Dennis O'Brien's conclusion, "I have not been able to discern any *philosophical* difference between what is said in the notes and in the manuscript." McCarney, *Hegel on History,* pp. 7–10.

44 For detailed notes on the problems in the reconstruction of Hegel's *Vorlesungen über die Philosophie der Weltgeschichte* (for the edition edited by Hoffmeister and Lasson), see Georg Lasson's "Notes on the Composition of the Text" (*WH,* pp. 221–6).

45 Secondary studies of the development of Hegelian thought include Toews, *Hegelianism;* William J. Brazill, *The Young Hegelians* (New Haven, CT, 1970); Karl Löwith, *From Hegel to Nietzsche: The Revolution in Nineteenth-Century Thought* (New York, 1964), originally published as *Von Hegel zu Nietzsche* (1941); Michael Kelly, *Hegel in France* (Birmingham, 1992); Michael Roth, *Knowing and History: Appropriations of Hegel in Twentieth Century France* (Ithaca, NY, 1988); David Boucher et al., "British Idealism and the Political Philosophy of T. H. Green, Bernard Bosanquet, R. G. Collingwood and Michael Oakeshott," *British Journal of Politics and International Relations,* 7 (2005), pp. 97–125.

46 See David Walsh, "The Historical Dialectic of Spirit: Jacob Boehme's Influence on Hegel" and comment by Eric von der Luft, in Perkins, *History and System,* pp. 15–46: similar formulations possibly influencing Hegel can be found in the

writings of Jacob Böhme, Walsh argues, or earlier classical sources including Proclus and Plotinus, von der Luft argues.

47 Following here insights into language presented in Wittgenstein, *Philosophical Investigations*, p. 32e.

48 Richard L. Schacht, "Hegel on Freedom," in MacIntyre, *Hegel: A Collection of Critical Essays*, pp. 289–328.

49 On the "cunning of reason," see S. Avineri, "Consciousness and history: *List der Vernunft* in Hegel and Marx," in W.E. Steinkraus (ed.), *New Studies in Hegel's Philosophy* (New York, 1971).

50 For example, Lasson, the editor of the most authoritative German edition, states: "Even this editor had to ask himself here whether the whole corpus of ethnographical information contained in the lecture notes really ought to be included in a contemporary edition, for much of it must appear antiquated today"; Lasson includes it because "information which may have lost its value as practical knowledge may still be of considerable value for an understanding of the way in which Hegel worked and thought" (*WH*, p. 225). These sections are not included in most English translations, including Nisbet, Hartman, and Rauch.

51 Duncan Forbes, in his "Introduction," states "It is also fashionable to display one's broadmindedness by criticizing Hegel for being arrogantly Europocentric or Western orientated ... But isn't Hegel's perspective broadly the right one? Or at least should one not wait until world history has shown its hand a bit more clearly?" (*WH*, p. xxii, n. 1).

52 Elsewhere, Hegel argues that "the civilized nation is conscious that the rights of barbarians are unequal to its own and treats their autonomy as only a formality" (*Philosophy of Right*, p. 219, §351).

53 Saussy, *Problem of a Chinese Aesthetic*, p. 156.

54 Hegel, *Philosophy of Right*, pp. 219–20, §353.

55 Translated and edited by Antoine Gaubil (1689–1759), Joseph de Guignes (1721–1800), Joseph Henri Prémare (1666–1736), and published in 1770 as *Le Chou-king, un des livres sacrés des Chinois, qui renferme les fondements de leur ancienne histoire, les principes de leur gouvernement & de leur morale, ouvrage recueilli par Confucius*. For an overview of the Chinese original, see Edward Shaughnessy, "*Shang Shu*," in Michael Loewe (ed.), *Early Chinese Texts: A Bibliographical Guide* (Berkeley, CA, 1993).

56 "Editorial Introduction," in *Lectures on the Philosophy of Religion, Vol. 2*, trans. P. C. Hodgson, R. F. Brown and J. M. Stewart, (Berkeley, CA, 1988), p. 5.

57 Here the term "portrayals" (*Darstellungen*) stands in contrast with Hegel's use of the term "representation" (*Vorstellung*), discussed above, which he uses for true historical writing.

58 Translated by Joseph-Anne-Marie de Moyriac de Mailla (1669–1748), a French Jesuit missionary to Beijing, and published by Jean-Baptiste Grosier (1743–1823) as *Histoire générale de la Chine, ou Annales de cet empire, traduites du Tong-kien-kang-mou*, a thirteen-volume collection, between 1777 and 1785;

romanized as *Tungkienkangmu* (*VPW*, Vol. 2, p. 283). It should be noted, however, that contrary to the title, the *Histoire générale de la Chine* is only loosely based on the *Guideline and Commentary for the Comprehensive Mirror*, and in fact covers a considerably longer period, from 2953 BCE to 1780 CE. For an analysis of the additional sources used for the period from 959 to 1780 CE, see Richard Gregg Irwin, "Notes on the Sources of de Mailla, *Histoire générale de la Chine*," *Journal of the Hong Kong Branch of the Royal Asiatic Society*, 14 (1974), pp. 93–100.

59 See Raymond Schwab, *Oriental Renaissance: Europe's Rediscovery of India and the East, 1680–1880*, trans. Gene Patterson-Black and Victor Reinking (New York, 1984); originally published as *La renaissance orientale* (Paris, 1950).

60 It should be noted that, contrary to this and similar pronouncements on the "end of history," Hegel's views on this point are ambiguous and contradictory. Elsewhere Hegel states, "America is therefore the land of the future," but "as a land of the future, it is of no interest for us here, for, as regards *history*, our concern must be with that which has been and that which is (*PH*, pp. 86–7; emphasis in original).

61 Williams continues, "Our situation is not unlike that portrayed in the Hindu fable of the blind man and the elephant. About the only safe comment is that in our case the 'elephant' is very big and surpasses our ability to take it all in. The more cynical may harbour the suspicion that not even Hegel knew what he really meant." Williams then states he will present "an important but hitherto ignored or suppressed interpretation of *Geist*." Williams, "Hegel's Concept of *Geist*," p. 538. The argument I have presented in this chapter suggests an alternative: rather than assuming there is something called *Geist*, for which the intentions of the author himself may not be adequate to provide coherence, we might instead analyze the construction and use of *Geist* in specific passages.

62 According to Habermas, Hegel's philosophy "might have given impetus to a communication-theoretic retrieval and transformation of the reflective concept of reason developed in the philosophy of the subject. Hegel did not take this path"; "Hegel did not pursue any further the traces of communicative reason that are so clearly to be found in his early writings" (*Philosophical Discourse of Modernity*, pp. 30–1).

63 From the title of the collection Ian Adam and Helen Tiffin (eds), *Past the Last Post: Theorizing Post-Colonialism and Post-Modernism* (New York, 1991).

64 Gilles Deleuze and Félix Guattari, *A Thousand Plateaus: Capitalism and Schizophrenia* (Minneapolis, MN, 1987); originally published as *Mille plateaux*, Vol. 2 of *Capitalisme et schizophrénie* (Paris, 1980), p. 76.

65 See especially the special issue, "Symposium: 'Public Sphere'/'Civil Society' in China? Paradigmatic Issues in Chinese Studies, Part 3," *Modern China*, 19 (1993): Mary Backus Rankin, "Some Observations on a Chinese Public Sphere," Frederic Wakeman Jr, "The Civil Society and Public Sphere Debate: Western Reflections on Chinese Political Culture," William T. Rowe, "The Problem of 'Civil Society' in Late Imperial China," Richard Madsenand, "The

Public Sphere, Civil Society and Moral Community: A Research Agenda for Contemporary China Studies," Heath B. Chamberlain, "On the Search for Civil Society in China," and Philip C. Huang, " 'Public Sphere'/'Civil Society' in China? The Third Realm Between State and Society."

66 Kenneth Pomeranz, *The Great Divergence: China, Europe, and the Making of the Modern World Economy* (Princeton, NJ, 2000), p. 294.

67 See Roger Hart, "The Great Explanandum," essay review of *The Measure of Reality: Quantification and Western Society, 1250–1600*, by Alfred W. Crosby, *American Historical Review*, 105 (2000), pp. 486–93.

68 One early and important example representative of a growing literature is Hans van de Ven's "The Onrush of Modern Globalization in China," in Hopkins (ed.), *Globalization in World History*. Van de Ven argues that "The question of why China failed to develop a modern capitalist economy … continues to generate some of the best current scholarship on China, as the recent monograph by Kenneth Pomeranz demonstrates. The idea of globalization can add new dimensions to our understanding of such events" (pp. 168–9); he focuses on "modern globalization" from the Late Qing to the present, concluding that "communist globalization failed" (p. 193) and the future is ominous.

69 While recent studies have sometimes used "performative" as a synonym for "fictive," Austin's central concern is statements which have the power to perform an action. See J. L. Austin, *How to Do Things with Words*, 2nd ed. (Cambridge, MA, 1975 [1962]).

4

The Cosmopolitanism of National Economics: Friedrich List in a Japanese Mirror

Mark Metzler

More than twenty-three years have passed since I first had doubts as to the truth of the prevailing theory of political economy ... I perceived that the theory saw only all of humanity, or single individuals, but not nations ... In a word, I came upon the distinction between cosmopolitical and political economy. – Friedrich List, preface to *The National System of Political Economy*, 1841

Three hundred or 350 years ago, bullionism was the most advanced economic technique of the times, [and] the possession of an abundance of gold and silver was the wellspring of national wealth and power [fukoku kyōhei] ... Then about 150 years ago appeared the great economist Adam Smith, who proclaimed that national wealth was more important than gold and silver, [explaining] that the gold and silver that Spain and Portugal had gotten from Mexico and South America had all gone out to England and other countries to pay for goods ... Then just fifty years after that appeared the economist who must be called Germany's Adam Smith, Friedrich List. He proclaimed that more than national wealth, a people's productive power was essential ... But I don't think the views of these two great economists, List and Smith, were necessarily in contradiction: List supplemented points lacking in Smith. One asserted the doctrine of free trade and one the doctrine of protectionism, but we may think that this was only a matter of each asserting the theory most suitable to the contradictory national circumstances of England and Germany at their times. – Takahashi Korekiyo in 1925, shortly after his retirement as Japan's first Minister of Commerce and Industry[1]

The political mission of Friedrich List (1789–1846) was to build an independent, industrialized national economy in Germany, and he is considered one of the architects of German economic unity. His intellectual mission was to create an alternative, "national system" to counter the universalist "cosmopolitical" economics of the Smithian school. Takahashi Korekiyo (1854–1936) was a statesman rather than a theorist, and is most famous for guiding Japan's early recovery from the Great Depression after 1932. Takahashi's mission was likewise to build an independent, industrialized national economy, and he was a principal framer of what would later be called the "Japanese model" of development. List, despite his six years in America and his US citizenship, was until recently almost forgotten in the English-speaking world. Takahashi, who also learned his English in America, remains largely unknown outside his home country. But one might use these two economic nationalists to give an "ex-centric" account of modern economic globalization that reverses currently dominant definitions of universal norm and local exceptionalism.

Since the demise of Marxism-Leninism, no social science tradition has been so given to notions of the "legislative" and universal nature of its theoretical constructions as the classical/neoclassical tradition in economics. The metaphysical ground in this tradition is the idea of governmental "not doing" – laissez faire – to allow the naturally balancing economic activity of individuals to function. Applied to relations between nations, this means that governments should not attempt to direct trade or monetary flows or otherwise stand in the way of the spontaneously arising global division of labor. Put crudely, markets are an expression of universal principle and an arena where competing individual interests harmonize productively. States and indeed nations are local and artificial constructions; within this political arena, competing interests frequently produce destructive effects. This understanding of economic nature (and political artifice) is also a universalizing *program*, in the form of the movement for open economies and global free trade. It was this latter claim that List was most concerned to counter with his "national system of political economy." On the face of things, we thus see a globalizing universalism – liberalism in the classical sense – facing a protective and reactive localism – economic nationalism – that appears as resistant and "anti-globalizing."[2]

Takahashi's invocation of List suggests a less binary picture, and the present chapter explores its sources to reveal a bundle of complex interactions. We will see first that competing foreign "universals" were reconstructed locally, using existing local materials – recycled, in the usage introduced by Erika Bsumek and extended by Karl Miller, both in this volume. Some of the resulting policy constructions have since been re-exported as the "Japanese model" of development. Second, liberal and national–protectionist policies have cycled over time. Each set of policies has historically addressed a distinctively different set of developmental problems, with liberalism focused on "deconstructive" (or deregulatory) tasks, and protectionism directed at "capitalist construction." These rival policy sets have reshaped and succeeded one another – developmentally, in line with the phasing of national industrialization, and cyclically, in line with the oscillations of prosperity and depression.

The question of liberal versus national economics also touches on some current and long-running polemics. List was a representative figure among the first generation of writers to criticize Smith's already popular doctrines. After being nearly written out of the English-language narrative of economics, List's name began to crop up again in the 1980s and especially the 1990s, in connection with the rise of "Listian" developmentalist states in Japan and East Asia. The recycling of a Germanic cliché to identify the essence of the Japanese economy has also been criticized, and the point made that List's "essentially German" economics was in many ways American. As Bruce Cumings has put it, one might equally well explain modern Japan by invoking the name of the now forgotten American protectionist Henry C. Carey.[3] While Cumings's point suggests the complex international circulation of ideas that I explore here, there is in fact much to gain by thinking about Japan and Friedrich List together. List has also been honored in connection with East Asian developmentalism more as a symbol, removed from historical context, than as a subject of historical analysis. The real connections turn out to be dense, and Takahashi's own career is a good place to start.

At the founding of the Ministry of Commerce and Industry

Japanese industrial policy, as it crystallized around the middle of the twentieth century, may well be the most comprehensive, systematic, and successful program of industrial nurturing so far developed. No one would say that it has been without costs, and many would say that the whole subject now belongs to history.[4] The Ministry of International Trade and Industry (MITI) has been the institutional fountainhead of Japanese industrial policy, and the often emotional debate over MITI and the nature of Japan's high-speed growth forms the larger stream of analysis and polemic within which the question of Friedrich List's economics has recently been revived. MITI was organized under that name in 1949, but the Ministry dated its own life story to 1925, when "MITI's past body (*zenshin*), the Ministry of Commerce and Industry [MCI], was born," out of the splitting of the old

Ministry of Agriculture and Commerce.[5] The role of midwife was played by Takahashi Korekiyo, who was briefly the first MCI minister. Takahashi also seems to have considered the Ministry of Commerce and Industry to be a final legacy in his career of government service: three days after the new Ministry was inaugurated in April 1925, he announced his retirement and resigned from the cabinet and from the presidency of the Seiyūkai party.[6] At this moment of self-reflection, Takahashi evidently was thinking of two past economic nationalists, Maeda Masana (1850–1921) and Friedrich List.

"Ah, revered Maeda Masana! Revered Maeda Masana! Your friend Takahashi Korekiyo stands solemnly before your memorial, tears pouring down," Takahashi called to Maeda's departed spirit at the dedication of a stone memorial that he and other admirers of Maeda erected at a temple in Kyoto on April 15, 1925. "With no thought of profit or fame, even when facing death," Takahashi told those gathered together, Maeda's "one concern was for the nation." Maeda's great achievement, Takahashi further reminded them, was a 40-year old book, *On the Promotion of Industry* (*Kōgyō iken*), which was dedicated to his life's mission of "building the nation on the basis of industry" (*sangyō rikkoku*).[7] In fact, the slogan, "build the nation on industry" was being taken up at the time by Takahashi's own Seiyūkai party. And in 1884, Takahashi himself had helped draft Maeda's *Promotion of Industry*, which has since been regarded as the world's first comprehensive national development plan. It was also a plan that reflected Maeda's drive, conceived when he went to Paris as a young man in 1869, to make Japan equal to the Western countries.

Takahashi's own experience of the West went back even earlier than Maeda's, to his thirteenth year, 1867, when the government of his feudal domain, Sendai, sent him to study English in California. He also learned how East Asian workers were integrated into the global division of labor when he was "sold as a slave," as he later told it, to work on a farm in the town of Oakland.[8] After hearing of the revolution in Japan a few months later, his Sendai fellows helped buy him out of his indenture and the group returned home at the end of the year. After various jobs as an English teacher and translator, Takahashi in 1881 joined the newly established Ministry of Agriculture and Commerce, where he became the first head of the patent office and created Japan's first system for the protection of "intellectual property."[9] Takahashi worked on Maeda's staff in 1884. After Maeda's *Promotion of Industry* project was cancelled, Takahashi left the government and tried and failed in the enterprises of managing a coal mine, a dairy farm (then a modern, Western-style undertaking), and a silver-mining venture in Peru. He then entered the banking world, and as the Japanese government's first overseas financial commissioner negotiated the giant foreign loans that financed Japan's war with Russia in 1904–05. Takahashi thereby rose to the summit of national financial policymaking, becoming governor of the Bank of Japan in 1911–13 and minister of finance in 1913–14 and 1918–22. Takahashi was also president of Japan's conservative political party, the Seiyūkai, from 1921 to 1925, prime minister in 1921–22, and minister of agriculture and commerce in 1924–25. His effort to retire in 1925 was unavailing, and he was recalled as finance minister in 1927. He was/recalled again in 1931, at the depths of the global economic crisis, when he implemented the world's most successful anti-depression policy. Although known for advocating a pro-growth "positive policy" (*sekkyoku seisaku*), Takahashi also opposed runaway military budgets, and so it was that at the age of 81 he was murdered by mutinous soldiers on February 26, 1936.

In June 1925, a month after his invocation of Maeda Masana, the newly retired Takahashi discussed his own philosophy of economics in a speech to the Industrial Promotion Society in Osaka.[10] Takahashi's starting point, typically for him, was the question of the then-current (post-World War I) recession. Indirectly criticizing the budgetary retrenchment policy of the current cabinet (led by the rival Kenseikai party), Takahashi said that industrialists were following the government's lead and thinking that they too must retrench. But if everyone did so, Takahashi said, it would worsen the recession. The present task was less to restrain imports than to expand exports. Unless industry invested in the new mass-production technologies, Japan would be left behind other countries. It was in this context of post-World War I retrenchment and heightened international economic competition that Takahashi – uncharacteristically – turned for justification to a foreign economist and expounded upon Friedrich List's idea of national productive power.

One might wonder also at turning to "Germany's Adam Smith" in 1925, when defeated, bankrupt Germany had just been placed into Anglo-American financial receivership under the Dawes Plan, and the "German model" hardly seemed an object of emulation. Takahashi's invocation of List, falling into a national discourse in which domestic policy differences were expressed in terms of foreign developmental models, was motivated partially by a perceived incongruence with the British model. Six weeks before Takahashi's speech, Britain's Chancellor of the Exchequer, Winston Churchill, had announced that Britain would restore the gold standard at the old prewar parity. Japan's Kenseikai party cabinet began preparations to do the same. The restoration of free gold flows would require further budgetary austerity and would intensify the price deflation and depression that had followed the war. When the Kenseikai's successor party finally followed

Britain's lead four years later, Takahashi openly broke with the liberal monetary orthodoxy.[11] Although Takahashi seems not to have realized it, Friedrich List had in fact articulated his own critique of British liberal orthodoxy in the face of an analogous deflationary conjuncture following the Napoleonic wars.

A point of deeper structural congruence between List's Germany and Takahashi's Japan was their shared developmental position. Relative to Britain, Germany was a "late-developing country," as Takahashi had explained on an earlier occasion, anticipating Alexander Gerschenkron's famous analysis.[12] As opposed to British free trade, Germany had therefore adopted a policy of protectionism; as opposed to British individualism, it adopted a "principle of national unity." Japan faced the same circumstances, Takahashi thought, and "if we attempted to adopt British-style liberalism, we would only get the negative effects of it." List's analysis of the situation of a backward, less productive economy confronted with a more advanced and productive one was thus especially apt.

Friedrich List and the temporality of nations

Adam Smith stood on the eve of the industrial revolution but did not really perceive it,[13] and Friedrich List was one of the first economic thinkers to grasp the world-historical significance of industrialization. Whereas Smith's problem was the dissolution of mercantilist restrictions on trade, List's was the "belated" development of the disunited German states. His advocacy of protective tariffs was part of a larger concern with the practical problems of development: administrative reform, the promotion of trade and industry (later called industrial policy), and the creation of a national transportation infrastructure and unification of a national market.[14] Like Hegel, List began his exposition from history, not from first principles. He thus traced a supersession of national economic ascendancies, beginning with the Renaissance ascendancy of the North Italian city-states (and the parallel Northern ascendancy of the Hanseatic League). This gave way to the commercial ascendancy of the Netherlands, and finally to that of England, which was now "among the countries and empires of the earth, that which a great city is in relation to the plains around it" and "a standard and model for all nations."[15] This historical picture has since elaborated into much more sophisticated theories of a historically shifting capitalist core and of successive national hegemonies within an expanding capitalist system.[16] As List explained it, the critical causes of national rise or decline were the presence or absence of personal freedom and enterprise, appropriate state policy, and national unity. Each successive national ascendancy represented an increase in national scale. By thus historicizing Britain's current primacy in industry (and by extension in political-economic theory), List also relativized it, foreseeing that "the same causes that have raised Great Britain to her present high position will – probably already in the course of the next century – raise the United States of America to a degree of industry, wealth, and power which will surpass the level at which England stands so far as England now surpasses little Holland."[17]

In fact, it was in the United States that List systematized his economic ideas in the late 1820s, and he considered the young republic to be the great model of state-enabled national economic development – much as Japan would appear to members of newly industrializing Asian countries 150 years later. The analogy with Japan also deserves some thought in connection with List's national activism. List began his turbulent and peripatetic career in 1805 as a government official in a small German state, Württemberg, which was comparable in size to one of the larger feudal domains in Tokugawa Japan. He became known as a liberal and advocate of constitutionalism, and was in 1818, for a few months, the first professor of public administration (Staatswissenschaft) at the University of Tübingen.[18] Notably, List did not study the established cameralist doctrines taught there and was relatively little influenced by German academic and administrative ideas of economic statecraft.[19] He did learn from German businessmen and he championed their cause, in 1819 helping organize a Union of German Commerce and Industry (Deutsche Handels- und Gewerbsverein) in Frankfurt and beginning the campaign for a German customs union (Zollverein). Hitherto List had followed the ideas of the free-trade school, but his exposure to French protectionist ideas helped convert him to protectionism.[20] List's aggressive and disputatious character, combined with his liberal advocacy, antagonized not only the local authorities but also Austria's Prince Metternich. In 1822, when List was an elected representative in the Württemberg assembly, he was convicted of slandering the authorities and violating the press law. After two years as a fugitive, he was confined to a fortress for five months and then exiled, thus becoming in the Japanese language of that time a *rōnin*, or masterless samurai – which is to say, an unemployed government official – like so many of the activists who led Japan's national unification movement in the 1860s. Also like many of these "stateless" national agitators, List came to a violent end, though in this case it was by his own hand.

In 1825, List left with his family for America, "where life itself is the best work that one can read on political economy," and where it seemed to him that the "stagewise development of a national economy," which took many centuries in Europe, "proceeds here before our eyes."[21] List's friendship with General Lafayette, whose entourage he joined soon after arriving in the United States, secured him a high-level reception. He settled in Pennsylvania, where after a brief, failed effort at farming and distilling, he found a more advantageous place in the local division of labor writing for and editing a German-language newspaper and helping found a coal-mining and railroad company, one of the first in the country. America was in the midst of its own struggle over free trade and protection, which arose in the deflationary aftermath of the War of 1812. When List was in America, this dispute became sharply sectionalized, as Northern industrialists called for import-substitution policies while export-oriented Southern planters wanted free trade, and the fight over trade policy combined with that over slavery and states' rights.[22] Pennsylvania was the heartland of the protectionist cause, and List quickly took sides, sounding like an American nationalist in his advocacy for the "American System" of industrial promotion and protection of "infant industries." Influenced by the ideas of Alexander Hamilton (1755–1804) and the protectionist and abolitionist writer Daniel Raymond (1786–1849), List associated with members of the Pennsylvania Society for the Promotion of Manufactures and Mechanic Arts including Charles Ingersoll and Matthew Carey (the father of Henry Carey).[23] List was "naturalized" as a US citizen in 1830, and he immediately returned to Germany, holding office for a time as US consul to the Kingdom of Saxony. He continued to promote the expansion of the German Customs Union and in 1837 helped found Germany's first long-distance railway, from Leipzig to Dresden, part of his vision of a pan-German and pan-European railway network.

For an ardent nationalist, List was thus remarkably cosmopolitan. This is equally clear in the successive presentation of his ideas, which were first published in English as a series of letters to Ingersoll, assembled as *Outlines of American Political Economy* in 1827. Ten years later, in Paris, List presented his ideas more systematically in *Le système naturel d'économie politique* (1837). In 1841, he published *Das nationale System der politischen Ökonomie* in Stuttgart. In this sense, List became a "German" economist only five years before his unhappy death.[24]

List is often misperceived as an anti-Enlightenment thinker (or as an "anti-economist" in one recent misconstruction), who argued in concert with contemporary romanticism that economic truth was relative and culture-specific.[25] In fact, List's argument was more universalist in that he saw national economic development as proceeding through distinct, universal stages. Thus, appropriate policies were stage-specific. The stagewise transformation which concerned List was that facing Germany: the transition from developed agriculture to industry. He connected this idea to a concept of import-substitution industrialization, as a country proceeded from the export of agricultural goods, to the production of simple finished goods, to the development of domestic machine-building and the export of manufactured goods. List was optimistic about the possibilities of technology transfer, which he thought must be coupled with protection for infant industries.[26]

However, this stagewise developmental process was not automatic but existed only as a developmental potential. Nations were typically stuck in a particular stage and held there by the existing international division of labor, if not further peripheralized. Given existing disparities in industrial development, universal free trade would mean only that "all England would be developed into one immense manufacturing city." Germany would have little more to offer this English world than "children's toys, wooden clocks, and philological writings," and perhaps an occasional auxiliary corps for use overseas.[27] It was only by great, national efforts – by subordinating individual interests to those of future generations through heavy investment and the deferring of present consumption – that a nation could progress to the next level.[28]

Thus, as Takahashi Korekiyo would, List saw the development of a nation's *productive powers* as the foundation of all else.[29] The concept of productive powers encompassed not only the physical capital of a country but, more importantly, its "human capital" (to use a more recent term) and its institutions. The social whole exceeded the sum of its individual personal components and had its own distinctive dynamics that were not derivable from a simple extension of individual or household dynamics. Takahashi too emphasized this point, which underlay his own "Keynesian" understanding of the use of macroeconomic policies to stimulate consumer demand.[30] List also had a holistic concern for merging and linking different sectors of the economy in what he called the "confederation of the productive forces," and as Hamilton had, he insisted that agriculture and industry developed in harmony, not in opposition. This idea resembled the balanced-development ideas of Maeda Masana, who developed a fuller understanding than List of what would later be called "leading sectors" and "linkages," also greatly influencing Takahashi.[31] If many of List's ideas were originally American, this holism – expressed above all in regard to the nation – falls more squarely into the German intellectual tradition, and contrasts with the more mechanistic conceptions of British political economy. List's thinking was also characterized by an obsessive concern with national power as a prerequisite of development and at times verged into the kind of metaphysical statism most famously expounded by his contemporary and fellow Württemberger, G. W. F. Hegel (1770–1831), whose own national universalism is explored in Roger Hart's chapter in this volume.

This holistic ideal contrasts with List's own fragmented life. Hoping now to promote an Anglo-German alliance in the face of the rising continental powers of the United States and Russia, List traveled to London in 1846, just at the point when free trade was being fully implemented there. Confronted by the ascendant globalizing power of British industry, he left despairing of Germany's industrial prospects. This national *angst*, together with List's personal failure to find a suitable permanent post, seems to have ruined his mental and physical health. Hoping to recuperate in the warmer climate of the South Tyrol, List attempted to travel alone across the Alps in late November. He met miserable weather, and outside Kufstein, he shot himself. As List had feared, the free-trade movement developed vigorously in Germany itself, culminating in commercial treaties between Prussia and France in 1862 and Prussia and Britain in 1865.[32] Nonetheless, stimulated by the new German common market List had helped to foster, German industry developed apace.

At the same time, free trade was "battering down Chinese walls" in East Asia. In 1839–42, as List finished writing his *National System*, Britain fought its first war to open up trade with the Chinese empire. In 1844–46, the French attempted to force open the kingdom of Ryūkyū, which was controlled by the Japanese domain of Satsuma. The Western threat spurred Satsuma's own "technonationalist" response.[33] In March 1854, six months before Takahashi Korekiyo was born in Edo, a US naval flotilla induced the Tokugawa government to open formal relations with the United States. In 1858, against the backdrop of a second British and French war to open Chinese commerce, the Tokugawa government acceded to treaties that provided for open ports, free trade, and strict limits to Japanese tariffs. Open trade abruptly transformed the economic situation in Japan and provoked a constitutional crisis that ended in the overthrow of the Tokugawa shogunate in 1868 by imperial loyalist forces from the Satsuma and Chōshū domains. Thus, Japan's market-opening shock was conjoined with its internal unification in its modern, national form. List's ideas came to Japan shortly after, in the context of Japan's own national debate over protectionism and free trade.

Liberal solutions and national constructions in Japan

In many ways, "mercantilist" national economics was invented independently in Japan, and Western ideas were combined with existing conceptions. The Tokugawa state's "maritime restrictions" (*kaikin*) were originally motivated by national security rather than economics, and the volume of licensed foreign trade (handled after 1633 by foreign carriers) increased substantially over the seventeenth century. By 1715, however, when new restrictions were placed on the export of gold and silver, national seclusion policies had been reconceptualized in bullionist terms. In line with this view, the shogunal government later experimented with limited import-substitution and export-promotion measures.[34]

More radically mercantilist developments took shape in the local lordly domains. The Tokugawa "world" (referred to by the self-magnifying Chinese term *tenka*, "all under heaven") can in fact be thought of as a small interstate system in that individual domains, while under strict shogunal authority in certain respects, enjoyed more or less exclusive taxation, legislative, administrative, judicial, police, and military powers within their own territories. Many domainal governments also issued their own paper money and operated domainal monopolies over various locally produced goods that they "exported" to the national (Tokugawa-administered) markets in Osaka and Edo, in competition with other domains that pursued similar import-substitution and export-promotion strategies. As the political economist Kaiho Seiryō (1755–1817) explained in 1813, "This is an age when ... one must be on guard not from his neighbor's violent attack, but rather from loss through trade ... If a domain does not innovate to increase its lands' produce relative to its neighbors, the neighbor will grow rich and the domain will grow poor. And ... gold and silver will flow to the prosperous land." Thus, a national market and a national division of labor developed integrally with an "intra-national" mercantilism, conceptualized under the name of *kokueki*.[35] A modern translation of *kokueki* is *national interest* (or literally, *national profit*), but here the "country" (*kuni* or *koku*) was the individual feudal domain. *Kokueki* ideas were developed and disseminated by traveling administrative and economic policy advisers, who loosely approximated the cameralist "consultant administrators" of eighteenth-century Germany. In this comparative view, *kokueki* could be translated as the eighteenth-century Latin-German term *"policey"* (Germanized as *"polizei"*), which is what the cameralist advisors called their own statecraft practice.[36]

The most important domain in terms of its heritage for the national economic policies of the Meiji era (1868–1912) was that of Satsuma in the far south of Kyushu island. Satsuma was also one of the most economically backward and late developing domains and maintained some of the most draconian and feudalistic social and economic controls. Uniquely, it had its own overseas "colony," Ryūkyū, through which it maintained a limited international trade.[37] Satsuma was also one of the first modern "countries" to launch a comprehensive economic development plan, drawn up in 1830 by the consultant administrator Satō Nobuhiro. By 1856, well in advance of the central government's own "technonationalist" response, Satsuma had built its own reverberatory steel furnace and began casting modern cannon. Three of Meiji Japan's most important economic statesmen also began their careers as officials managing the Satsuma economy. The first of these was Ōkubo Toshimichi (1830–1878), who until his assassination was the most powerful man in the new government and who directed a program of state-led industrial development (*shokusan kōgyō*) that included the establishment of state-owned model factories. The second was Ōkubo's junior, Matsukata Masayoshi (1835–1924), minister of finance from 1881 to 1900, who directed the privatization of the new state-owned enterprises in the early 1880s while simultaneously establishing a central bank, stabilizing the Japanese currency, and setting up other core institutions of the Japanese fiscal and banking systems. The third was the still younger Maeda Masana, who after writing Japan's first national "ten-year plan" was forced from the government by Matsukata.

Historically, tariff protection has not been the most important of the elaborate array of Japanese industrial-policy measures. (Most important, arguably, has been the strategic, state-directed provision of capital to private firms.) In the 1870s, tariff protection was also a theoretical and not yet a practical question because protective tariffs were disallowed by the unequal treaties imposed by the Western powers. It may therefore have been easier to discuss than were issues of current state policy; in any case, protection became the subject of one of Japan's first big public-policy debates at a time when such debates were still novel. It was in this controversy that the Western discourse of what would later be called industrial policy joined a Japanese discourse on the subject.

My focus here is on the "national" side of the liberal–national binary in economic policy. The developmental role of liberalism was also crucial, however, and perhaps never more so than in the years just after the Meiji Restoration of 1868. Inside and outside the new government, reformers embraced liberal ideas as they moved to dissolve feudalistic restrictions that they understood to be holding back Japan's national progress as well as their own careers.[38] The linked ideas of a natural hierarchy of merit and a "natural law of exchange" had the same powerful attraction in Japan as in many other countries. Disseminated by translations and newspapers (also a novelty of the era), liberal economic ideas (not yet associated with Adam Smith's name) enjoyed a sudden vogue during the so-called "Meiji enlightenment" of the 1870s.[39] Japanese commerce under the Tokugawa regime, like German commerce before the creation of the Zollverein, was hampered by myriad local barriers to free trade and enterprise. As Maeda Masana recognized, the first great task in building a national economy was therefore deregulation.[40] Liberal ideas thus inspired and gave direction to a flurry of nationalizing and liberalizing reforms that abolished local barriers to trade and ended feudal restrictions on residence and choice of livelihood, while giving full legal sanction to individual private property and creating a free market in land. Commerce itself, previously scorned by the samurai class, was ideologically legitimated as a form of service to the nation by Westernizers like Fukuzawa Yukichi, who argued for "a nation founded on commerce" (*bōeki rikkoku*) to replace the previous notion of a nation founded on agriculture.[41] Westernizing reformers also introduced Western protectionist ideas soon after, and many of Friedrich List's ideas likewise resonated in Japan before they were associated with his name.

Takahashi Korekiyo took sides early on. "Protectionism is nowadays popular in America and criticized in England," Takahashi declared in 1875 – but conditions in Japan were what mattered, and in order "to plan our national interest" (*kokueki*) and "to promote the happiness of our 30 million countrymen," Japan needed protective tariffs. Takahashi was a 21-year-old teacher of English when he gave this speech. He repeated it 50 years later, shortly after he retired for the first time, when he reread it to an audience of university students and explained to them that since that time, "protection and industrial promotion" had caused all branches of industry to flourish in Japan.[42] Without question, Takahashi acknowledged in 1875, foreign trade was useful in supplying national needs. However, it was also a kind of war in which one could not be off one's guard. Echoing Kaiho Seiryō, Takahashi asserted that, while war itself was becoming rare, now "the enemy uses manufacturing machinery instead of cannon." The "so-called civilized countries," above all Britain, employed this "civilized and enlightened form of war" to widen their territories, gain resources, and build permanent overseas bases.[43] "Our Japan was brought into this war in the Ka'ei era [1848–54] and subsequently forced to sign a [free] trade treaty … and we were at war with them without preparation." In the war between the enemy's well equipped manufacturers and Japan's ill equipped peasants, "it was as if their shells fell in our midst but our arrows could not reach them. Our defeat was inevitable."[44] The measure of Japan's defeat was that every year, ¥8 million in gold flowed out to other countries.

Given protection, Takahashi continued, Japan's manufacturers would compete with one another in the home market to drive down costs. If Japanese textile manufacturers, for example, used machinery as the British did, Japan's lower living costs would ultimately enable Japanese cloth to compete abroad with British cloth. This turned out to be prescient: by the 1930s, a few years after Takahashi reread his speech, it was British textile manufacturers, formerly the great champions of free trade, who clamored for government assistance against Japanese exports. Takahashi thus contradicted those who said that protectionism "violated the natural law of free exchange," or that it hurt the country that practiced it. What was this so-called natural law?, he asked. In reality, property rights were originally established by force and later given sanction by national laws – that is, property was created by human action, not by "natural liberty."[45] If this were the case with property itself, then so too with trade, which was the exchange of property and which was likewise regulated by law.

For models of protection at work, Takahashi turned to the United States and France and explained in detail how tariffs had enabled them to develop, respectively, steel and sugar industries that now competed with the British. Those who argued for free trade overlooked these actual cases and merely argued from an imagined logic. On the other hand, "you all know the condition Portugal, Turkey, and India are in today." These countries had formerly been in the world's first rank in trade, but since the advent of the "civilized-style war" they had been deindustrialized and were now practically reduced to agricultural countries. This transformation underlay the new cultural derogation of these countries that was so conspicuous in the work of early nineteenth-century European writers like Hegel and List – who feared that the same could happen to his own country. India, Takahashi continued, could no longer manufacture even its own former mainstay product, cloth, but sent the raw materials to England and then bought English cloth. Japan could easily suffer the same fate, "and our children and grandchildren will all end up as water drinking [landless] peasants."[46]

Thus, in the same way that Takahashi is credited with implementing a Keynesian policy in advance of Keynes' own presentation of his theory, he also presented a remarkably "Listian" analysis in 1875, some 14 years before List's work was translated into Japanese.

By Takahashi's account, his political-economic views were most powerfully influenced by Maeda Masana, who "taught me the oneness of myself and the state." The new Ministry of Agriculture and Commerce was established in April 1881, at the same time that Finance Minister Matsukata Masayoshi began to cut the budget and privatize government enterprises. Takahashi joined the Ministry in the same year. He met Maeda at the end of 1883, when Maeda was initiating his industrial promotion project. He later recalled their first, intense meeting:[47]

What I first noticed was Mr. Maeda's conception of the national state (*kokka*).[48] Up to then my attitude toward the state ... was a bit like the worship of a believer in Kannon [Guanyin, the boddhisattva of compassion] – I thought it was the highest thing to depend on ... but I felt that myself and the state were distant from one another ... After two days of talking to Mr. Maeda, I realized the shallowness of my former conception of the state. The state is not something distant and separate from me ... Myself and the national state are one thing. I was like a believer realizing the true teaching of the oneness of self and Kannon.

Maeda himself was one of the youngest officials to have experienced working in one of the old domainal administrations. He was also among the first cohort to study abroad, in 1869, aged 20, when the new national government sent him to France for what turned into a seven-year stay. Awestruck by Western civilization, Maeda was initially demoralized by the encounter. He later recalled that some Japanese were even worse affected "and became mentally ill or even committed *hara-kiri*." The fall of Paris to the Prussian army, a year after his arrival, was a turning point for Maeda, who then realized the limits of Western civilization and became "confident [Japan] could catch up."[49] Maeda was especially influenced by the ideas of Eugène Tisserand (1830–1925) of the French Ministry of Agriculture, who emphasized the importance of balancing agrarian and industrial development and of starting from facts derived from detailed local surveys. Their shared view was thus congruent with List's idea of "the confederation of the productive forces."[50]

Back in Tokyo in 1884, Maeda met Takahashi and put him to work in drafting his *Promotion of Industry*, which included detailed surveys of economic conditions in every prefecture of Japan. Its first concern was the adverse national trade balance. Maeda was determined especially that the gold and silver shipped out of Japan over the previous 25 years of open trade be replenished – a concern that might seem quaint to modern economists until it is remembered that in 1881–84 Finance Minister Matsukata was contracting the national paper-money issue to bring it into line with Japan's diminished specie reserves, thereby forcing a general price deflation of some 25 percent and causing a severe agrarian depression. Maeda's proposed solution was to concentrate scarce capital resources where they would achieve the surest and fastest results; this meant strengthening existing rurally based export industries, starting with silk and tea, and promoting import substitution in industries like sugar production and cotton spinning. Accordingly, the *Promotion of Industry* aimed to increase the national income by raising the level of poor peasants' income (reckoned at ¥20 per year) to that of middle-class peasants (reckoned to be ¥60 per year) over the next ten years. National savings were to come out of increased income, not out of restraint, an idea that foreshadowed Takahashi's later "positive policy" ideas. The core of Maeda's original plan was to be a "Development Bank" (*kōgyō ginkō*), which would direct scarce capital to producers and distributors in the priority export sectors; the plan went into detail even to the extent of identifying qualified borrowers in each prefecture.[51]

The *Promotion of Industry* was also a plan that was not implemented. Despite the fact that Matsukata, during his own stay in Paris for the 1878 World's Fair, depended on Maeda to interpret his surroundings and appears to have taken many ideas from him, there were important policy difference between the two.[52] Maeda emphasized rural development and the micro-level organizational and technological strengthening of agriculture and small-scale native industry.[53] Matsukata's centrally oriented program instead concentrated resources on naval buildup, heavy industrialization, and big infrastructure projects, leaving agriculture to develop by itself. The *Promotion of Industry*'s detailed revelations of poverty and rural crisis were also read as criticism of Matsukata's deflation policy. Most crucially, Maeda's comprehensive plan intruded on too many other officials' bureaucratic turf, the proposal for a new bank (which should properly have come from the Ministry of Finance) being only one example.[54] Immediately after the first version of the *Promotion of Industry* was distributed within the government administration, Matsukata forced it to be recalled and gutted of its development bank proposal; the reissued version was the one publicly known.[55] In a major bureaucratic reorganization in 1885, when Japan's modern cabinet system was put into place, Matsukata arranged for Maeda to be dismissed and the project ended. Maeda continued to promote his ideas by setting up private business associations, but without state backing he largely failed in this effort at what Takahashi later called a "private Ministry of Agriculture and Commerce." For the rest of his life Maeda continued to tour the country on foot, in Japanese dress, and to lecture on industrial promotion, but things went badly for him in his later years, as Takahashi recounted. Like List, Maeda was a devotee of the transcendental nation state who was tragically separated from the object of his devotion. Thinking back on it in 1925, Takahashi continued to regret that Japan had not followed the path lined out by Maeda, saying that the correctness of his vision only became clearer with each passing year.[56] The choice of Matsukata's costly militarized heavy-industrial development line − a "strong army" and impoverished country − over Maeda's more civilian, export-oriented, and balanced approach appears even more fateful in post-World War II retrospect.[57]

Maeda's industrial promotion ideas return us to the question of List's own "naturalization" into Japanese social thought. In fact, many of the ideas now more famously associated with List were introduced to Japan through the work of Henry Carey, which was translated in 1884–85 as *Kei-shi no keizaigaku* (Mr Carey's economics) and went through several editions.[58] Here another intellectual circuit is completed, for Carey's translator was Inukai Tsuyoshi (1855–1932). In December 1931, as president of the Seiyūkai party, Inukai led the cabinet in which Takahashi, as finance minister, launched his famous anti-depression policy. Five months after that, Prime Minister Inukai's murder by fascist naval officers ended the brief era of party cabinets. Before he entered national politics in 1890, Inukai became known as a campaigner for industrial protectionism. In 1880, he founded the business journal *Tōkai keizai shinpō* (Tōkai Economic News) to argue the case against the leading liberal economist, Taguchi Ukichi, criticizing Taguchi's "universal economics," in an echo of List, as "empty cosmopolitanism."[59]

In fact, as represented most prominently by Carey, national-economic ideas enjoyed more success in the United States during the middle decades of the nineteenth century than they did in Germany. Carey himself had inherited his father's printing business and built it into a great success, but initially he rejected his father's protectionism and in the earliest of his voluminous and prolix writings advocated a liberal free-trade line. The losses he suffered in the 1837 depression, one of the most severe in the US record, converted him to protectionism. List's *National System* was itself published in an American edition in 1856.[60] With the secession and then defeat of the Southern slaveocracy, US protective tariffs were raised to very high levels, at Henry Carey's strong urging.[61] Meanwhile in Germany, especially after 1847, free trade dominated both theory and practice to the extent that by the early 1870s the idea of protectionism seemed an extinct mercantilist relic. That changed with the great crash of 1873 and the subsequent years of deflation and depression, when List's ideas experienced a first revival in his homeland among a "younger historical school" of political economists, who began to regard List with a few other economists of his generation as having formed an "older historical school."[62] List's book was republished in Germany in 1877.[63] In 1879, Bismarck abandoned his alliance with the free-trade National Liberal party for a protectionist "iron and rye" alliance of industrialists and Junker landlords – who not long before had been grain exporters and avid free traders themselves but were now threatened by the cheap American grain that was flooding European markets. Thus, the German empire joined the United States as an exemplar of industrial protection.

Simultaneously there was a turn in Japan from British to German political economy, part of a larger political and intellectual move away from liberalism. This was the "modern" (=Western) ideological aspect of the nationalist "neotraditionalism" that now became a foundation of both Japanese social science and state ideology.[64] In 1877, Tokyo University was founded to train the elite bureaucratic cadres of the Japanese state. With Takahashi Korekiyo, these officers of the state could say, with more literal truth than could the most absolute monarch, that they as a corporate body and the state were one. In the 1880s, German political economy displaced British political economy at Tokyo University. Liberal economics continued to have a refuge in the private colleges such as Fukuzawa Yukichi's Keiō and Ōkuma Shigenobu's Waseda but had few adherents in government. At its best, as exemplified by thinkers such as Taguchi Ukichi, liberal economics became a critical countercurrent; more typically (with much of academic economics), it became a sterile and abstruse repetition of foreign ideas, little noticed outside a small academic circle.[65]

Japanese interest in German economics was part of an international movement in the 1880s. This movement was especially strong in the United States, as it was in Russia, where List's ideas inspired the "rush" industrialization plans of Finance Minister Sergei Witte in the 1890s. Even in England, there was interest in German ideas, and in 1885, in the context of the rise of the British "fair trade" movement, List's *National System* was retranslated into English and published for the first time in Britain. In 1889, this English translation was translated into Japanese, commissioned by Bank of Japan governor Tomita Tetsunosuke (1835–1916), who was Japan's first real central banker.[66] Tomita entrusted the translation of List's book to his friend Ōshima Sadamasu, a well known translator and a strong advocate of protectionism. Tomita, who had met Henry Carey in America, also commissioned a revised edition of Inukai Tsuyoshi's translation of Carey and wrote the preface to it.

This connection brings us to another main stream in Japanese industrial policy, that of strategic bank-directed financing. This idea did not find a place in List's program, but it arose in Belgium and France at the same time List was active. There, both private and parastatal banks designed to provide long-term industrial capital were first organized in the 1820s and 1830s. This practice is a main subject of Alexander Gerschenkron's idea that industrialization in later developing countries is marked by progressively more conscious and concerted efforts, coordinated by large banks and by the state itself. The model for the Bank of Japan itself was the Banque Nationale de Belgique, founded in 1851 to ensure both financial stability and the stable provision of capital to national industries, and regarded as the state of the art in modern central banking practice.[67] Tomita himself was one of Matsukata's "brains" at the Ministry of Finance and had received his own early education in political economy in the United States. As it happened, Tomita was the leader of the group of young samurai from the Sendai domain who went to America in 1867; as a junior member of the group, Takahashi Korekiyo had stayed in California while Tomita went on to New York, and it was Tomita who helped him escape his debt servitude.[68] Tomita himself returned to New York in 1869, studied economics in the

Newark School of Business, and then served as vice consul in New York before returning to Tokyo to work in the central bureaucracy. Tomita was instrumental in the founding of the Bank of Japan. Matsukata then appointed him the bank's first vice-governor in October 1882 and promoted him to governor in February 1888 but after a conflict forced him to resign in September 1889.[69]

Policy cycling

Historically, liberal ideas have repeatedly been prominent in the work of dismantling restrictive "old regimes." This was Adam Smith's own program: to dissolve state restrictions and liberate the productive forces of enterprise. Thus, as List's translator Ōshima Sadamasu considered it in 1896, "we were fortunate that it was British liberalism that first entered Japan after the opening of the country in the Ka'ei era. Had American protectionism or German eclecticism been first to arrive on the scene, these would not have been enough for us to break through our obstinacy." Ōshima concluded that "without British liberal theory, we would have been insufficiently equipped to see through our confusion of those days"; this "smashing of our obstinacy," he thought, "was very much like Adam Smith rising up to overcome mercantilism."[70]

Friedrich List's task likewise was to break through the entrenched obstinacy of the German states' old-fashioned bureaucracies and tear down the local tariff barriers and other restrictions that were choking intra-German trade – this was *de*regulation, Adam Smith-style. But this is not what List symbolized in other countries. Unlike Smith, List was also dedicated to industrial catching up, concerning which liberalism offered little positive advice. Thus, policy inspiration in the work of "capitalist construction" in the countries that followed England came more from national ideas of economics. Deregulation in early Meiji Japan, notably the dissolution of the Tokugawa-era guild organizations, released new productive forces, but the unregulated entry of new producers led to "excess competition," fraud, and the manufacture of poor-quality products. These damaged the reputation of Japanese exports, which was why Maeda Masana stressed the need for reregulation.[71] After a brief wave of borrowing liberal economic ideas from the "first wave" industrializer, Britain, Japanese policy strategists thus turned to "national" ideas of economics, which they took mainly from "second wave" industrializers. Where a core–periphery model of international relations might lead one to expect a unidirectional flow of policy ideas from the core to the periphery, we see here instead a circulation of policy ideas and practices *around* the core – Britain – as Japanese took ideas of industrial development from the United States, France and Belgium, and Germany. In the 1930s, they also began to take ideas from a fellow "third wave" industrializer, the USSR. The Japanese government (in this respect represented personally by Takahashi Korekiyo) avidly sought British capital for industrial and colonial development after 1898. It frequently sought British technology. But the idea that modern industry would naturally spring up of its own accord was as incredible to Japanese officials as it was to Friedrich List, and the notion that Japan could advance best by conforming to the path of least resistance within the existing international division of labor aroused little interest.[72]

I will not try to summarize here the development of Takahashi's policy ideas as they unfolded in the early 1930s.[73] Suffice it to say that his growth-oriented macroeconomic policy, together with the microeconomic industrial policies developed by junior officials under his auspices, were core components of the "high-speed growth" system that got its full institutional framing in the late 1940s. And this system remained largely in place until the recession and deflation of the 1990s provoked a new round of *liberal* policy solutions. Much more could also be said about Japan's first, 20-year debate over protectionism and industrial policy (although in the way of such debates, participants repeated the same arguments again and again). But it should already be plain that Japanese industrial policy had deep indigenous sources and was shaped by global currents of which Japanese statesmen were acutely conscious. Contrary to two common (and mutually contradictory) images, Japanese national economics was neither an isolated nor a merely derivative discourse, though at this point the international flow of policy ideas was wholly inward, an intellectual "import surplus" corresponding to Japan's import surplus in high-technology goods. Over time, Japan began to export both high-technology goods and ideas, first to nearby Asian countries and then to the rest of the world.

The reader will also have noticed the frequent, even regular turn to industrial protectionism during times of deflation, depression, and "overproduction." This view suggests another type of policy cycling over time, in line with the movement of the economic conjuncture. Here, we can compare the circumstances faced by List's Germany after the Napoleonic Wars with those faced by Takahashi's Japan after World War I. First, trade conditions during the two "Great Wars" themselves (as each was called in its day) served as virtual social experiments in demonstrating the efficacy of import-substituting industrialization at the given stages of German and Japanese development. In this connection, List emphasized the beneficial effects of the British blockade and of Napoleon's Continental System in the Rhine valley, which was simultaneously shielded from British competition and, temporarily, given a larger political–economic unity in the form of the Federation of the Rhine. Thus, "German manufactures of all and every kind" – especially mechanized cotton spinning – "for the first time began to make an important advance." The United States, List noticed, enjoyed a similar surge of import-substituting industrialization during the War of the Revolution, from which Alexander Hamilton drew his own lessons about industrial protection, and again during the blockade and War of 1812.[74] In Japan, World War I likewise forced the rapid progress of import substitution and simultaneously opened vast new markets formerly supplied by the European powers, confirming Takahashi's own ideas of Japan's true potential for industrial growth. Reflecting a characteristically industrial as opposed to a financial standpoint, both List and Takahashi were also sanguine about wartime inflation, seeing high prices as a sign of prosperity.

Following these experiences of rapid industrial development, German industry after 1815, like Japanese industry after 1920, faced the shock of renewed foreign competition during the extended period of postwar deflation. Then, as List saw it, English manufacturers, whose large accumulated capital enabled them to offer better goods, cheaper prices, and much longer terms of credit, "entered into a fearful competition with the German manufacturers," among whom "general ruin" followed.[75] Officials of Japan's Ministry of Commerce and Industry explained their own institutional origins in 1925 by reference to the post-World War I circumstances of "overproduction panic" and intensified international competition.[76] It was in these constrained circumstances that a new policy conception crystalized. Thus, far from constituting a timeless debate from first principles, these successive rounds of argument over economic policy can be understood only in their specific conjunctural contexts. Thus, there is a developmental (or stage-theoretic) aspect of protectionist-style industrial policy practices, and there is a conjunctural one. The same could be said of economic liberalism, instrumentalized as a tool of national policy.

Conclusion: the nationality of economic universalism

This chapter has highlighted the cosmopolitanism of avowedly national economics. One can also delineate the national specificity of avowedly universal free-trade liberalism, a doctrine that today is beginning to find voice among Japanese trade ministers and industrialists.

This question is in part a straightforward matter of ideology, as List suggested: liberal universalism, with its historically British, French, and later North American heritage, has reflected – or served to cloak – the national self-interest of the leading industrialized countries (and of specialized export zones connected to them). Thus, List understood Smith's theory as having a double existence. On one hand, it was the scientific discovery of an economic principle. On the other, it expressed Britain's drive to incorporate the rest of the world into a British-managed division of labor, wherein (to insert more modern language) the British metropole monopolized the higher value-added functions and delegated lower value-added functions to others. British efforts to force free trade onto nations with "infant industries" was thus like someone who, having "attained the summit of greatness," then "kicks away the ladder by which he has climbed up, to deprive others of the means of climbing up after."[77]

But ideology was not the only aspect that List recognized, and liberalism remained for him both telos and ideal, with his own "end of history" being world government and universal free trade. Hence Takahashi (who did not embrace such a globalist ideal) could truly say that Smith and List were not in contradiction and that List supplemented Smith. In this latter view, economic nationalism and liberalism appear more as phases or aspects of a single process. Certainly they were united in the careers of List and Takahashi, both economic nationalists and convinced statists, both broadly international in their outlook, and both advocating national economics for liberal, humanistic ends: "Et la patrie et l'humanité," as List opened his book. Both men also paid for their liberalism: List imprisoned and exiled for his liberal advocacy; Takahashi assassinated for his efforts to restrain militarism. Accused of being a neomercantilist, List was at pains to clarify his debt to liberalism and his selective borrowing from and criticism of mercantilism.[78] In fact, a major part of his originality was to combine liberalism with mercantilism.

The international unfolding of national economics itself, often presented simply as a reaction to or divergence from market-driven globalization, was less a process of market closing than of market *building*, hence at once a "localizing" (nationalizing) and a globalizing movement. States have typically fostered, created, liberalized, regulated, and put boundaries around markets, and they have done this as a means of national empowerment. Self-interested industrialists have often demanded such interventions, typically using patriotic claims as their most powerful ideological weapon. The simple "states versus markets" opposition that forms the stuff of so much contemporary economic mythology cannot capture this complexity.[79] Locally protectionist policies have existed in a complex dialectical relation with universalist free trade, whether as successive stages or as a kind of cycling in line with conditions of prosperity and depression; these "local" policies may in fact be seen as the *intensification* phase of a universal process of successive extensive and intensive market development.

List himself thought that later developing countries making the transition to industrialization would need protective tariffs for only a decade or two. England had "merely gained an advance over others in point of time." By enabling other nations to catch up, "the system of protection appears ... as the most essential means of furthering the final union of nations, and with that, true freedom of trade." National economy, accordingly, was the science of raising every separate nation to that stage of industrial development at which it could freely unite with other equally developed nations. Were all the world to be united as was the United Kingdom of Great Britain and Ireland, "the most vivid imagination will not be able to picture to itself the sum of happiness and well-being that would thereby accrue to the human race." In his imagination of the future, List was thus a universalist and a free trader, and he faulted Colbertian mercantilism for failing to grasp these cosmopolitan moral ends. List thus stands at the beginning of a line of development that leads to the European common market and the European Union.[80]

In such a view, liberalism itself has a stage-theoretic specificity. This idea brings us to the present moment in Japan, where the era of high-speed growth that began in the 1950s was succeeded in the 1990s by a long recessionary hangover and by a widening sense that the jig was up for the old national–protectionist type of industrial policy. The now-old regime of state economic controls that had arisen in the 1930s and 1940s became the target of a barrage of criticism, much of it from insiders. Trade liberalization, in earlier decades a grudging response to American pressure, was taken up as a positive tool of policy in the work of deregulation.[81] This again is the Japanese aspect of a global movement. Neoclassical economics has gained influence in both Japanese universities and government, and contra Takahashi, Smithian liberalism under the banner of "globalization" now seems to be superseding older forms of economic nationalism. By the same token, List's ideas may easily seem a historical dead end of the kind represented by the former Soviet socialist model.

In line with this movement, the Ministry of International Trade and Industry, renamed the Ministry of Economy, Trade and Industry (METI) in 2000, has itself assumed the mission of trade liberalization. METI officials, saying they no longer practice industrial policy, actively foster the development of venture capital firms, research tie-ups between universities and companies, and protections for intellectual property.[82] In the same spirit, the peak Japanese business group Keidanren (the Japan Business Federation), which represents the core big business sectors historically most closely nurtured and guarded by MITI, proposed in 2003 to replace "the old bureaucracy-led model of growth" with a "private-sector-driven society characterized by individual autonomy," wherein globalized Japanese businesses "provided Japan's knowledge and technology to drive economic development around the world, not just on Japanese soil."[83] In the borderless world of the twenty-first century, according to MITI's Vice-Minister for International Affairs, "zero-sum, mercantilist negotiations" would yield to multilateral governance, as the World Trade Organization (WTO) became "something closer to a World Economic Organization (WEO)." Not that competition between nations had disappeared; rather, "those countries which are improving their economic systems through the active promotion of liberalization and harmonization with global standards will be the victors in global competition." Japan has accordingly embraced the World Trade Organization's international legal process as both "sword and shield" in the fight for national economic interests.[84]

Not incidentally, WTO rules conspicuously limit the scope of traditional industrial policies – especially for poorer and less powerful countries that cannot easily ignore or finesse the rules. The question thus arises: is this emerging, professedly liberalizing and globalizing policy package yet another case of a leading industrial country wanting to "kick away the ladder" by which it ascended? Or will it, as its promoters claim, foster development in a form desired not only by leading companies in Japan but also by people in the less industrialized countries where they do business? To raise this question is not to dismiss the latter possibility. Friedrich List also, in one of his more generous moments, freely granted the universal contribution of England's own industrial civilization:[85]

> Who knows how far behind the world might still remain if there had been no England? And if she now ceased to exist, who can estimate how far the human race might be thrown back? Let us then rejoice at the immeasurable progress of that nation, and wish her prosperity for all time.

But of course this was not the end of the thought:

> Should we therefore wish also that she found a universal empire on the ruins of other nationalities? ... The civilization of humankind can only arise from the equalization of many nations in civilization, wealth and power; ... the same path [that England followed] lies open for other nations.

Notes

1 Epigraphs: "Twenty-three years" was mistakenly given as "thirty-three years" in the English translation. This and the following references to List's *National System of Political Economy* are to the 1885 translation by Sampson S. Lloyd (London, 1922 reprint edition), which I have modified by reference to *Das nationale System der politischen Ökonomie*, ed. Artur Sommer (Basel and Tübingen, 1959). Citations are given in the form (e.g., for the opening quotation), *National System*, p. xxxix/pp. 1–2, where the first page reference is to the English and the second to the German edition.

   Takahashi's statement is from "Waga kuni no sangyō ni tsuite," June 18, 1925 (Osaka: Sangyō Shinkō Kenkyūkai), pp. 4–5. Following the Japanese practice, I give the family name first except in English-language bibliographic entries where the names were originally given in the Western order. Unless indicated, Japanese books are published in Tokyo.

2 For the paradoxically combined development of modern nationalism and modern globalization, see A. G. Hopkins, "The History of Globalization – and the Globalization of History?" in Hopkins (ed.), *Globalization in World History* (New York, 2002), pp. 14–16, 29–30, 37; and for related considerations, Tracie Matysik's chapter in this volume. Also relevant here is Benedikt Stuchtey and Eckhardt Fuchs (eds), *Writing World History 1800–2000* (Oxford, 2003), in particular the essays by Sebastian Conrad and Julia Adeney Thomas.

3 The connection has been asserted most prominently by *Atlantic Monthly* editor James Fallows, "How the World Works," *Atlantic Monthly*, December 1993, pp. 61–87, and idem, *Looking at the Sun: The Rise of the New East Asian Economic and Political System* (New York, 1994). For the criticism, Bruce Cumings, *Parallax Visions: Making Sense of American–East Asian Relations at the End of the Century* (Durham, NC, 1999), p. 2; idem, "Japan and Northeast Asia into the Twenty-first Century," in Peter J. Katzenstein and Takashi Shiraishi (eds), *Network Power: Japan and Asia* (Ithaca, NY, 1997), p. 140; or idem, "Webs with No Spiders, Spiders with No Webs: The Genealogy of the Developmental State," in Meredith Woo-Cumings (ed.), *The Developmental State* (Ithaca, NY, 1999), p. 61. A similar point was made by Fallows himself, and more vociferously by Lyndon LaRouche and his adherents (examples at http://members.tripod.com/~american_almanac/ or http://www.larouchepub.com/). See also Keith Tribe, *Strategies of Economic Order: German Economic Discourse, 1750–1950* (Cambridge, 1995), pp. 32–65.

4 See also Woo-Cumings, preface to *The Developmental State*, p. ix.

5 Quoting MITI minister Ikeda Hayato's foreword to the Ministry's 1960 official history, which treats MCI and MITI as the same ministry (Tsūshō Sangyōshō, *Shōkōshō sanjūgonen shōshi*, Tsūshō Sangyōshō, 1960). Chalmers Johnson's *MITI and the Japanese Miracle: The Growth of Industrial Policy, 1925–1975* (Stanford, CA, 1982) launched the ongoing debate and has defined one institutionalist and economically nationalist pole of it. The opposite (universalist/marketist) pole of

the debate has been represented in its most extreme form by theorists espousing "methodological individualism" and "rational choice." Even the debate over the debate now constitutes a body of literature, to which one starting point is David Williams, *Japan and the Enemies of Open Political Science* (London, 1996).

6   Asō Daisaku, *Takahashi Korekiyo den* (Takahashi Korekiyo Den Kankōkai, 1929), p. 273.

7   "Maeda Masana-dan shōtoku kinenhi no mae ni tachite," April 15, 1925, in Takahashi Korekiyo, *Zuisōroku* (Chikura Shobō, 1936), pp. 279–82; Soda Osamu, *Maeda Masana* (Yoshikawa Kōbunkan, 1973), pp. 294–5. See also Richard J. Smethurst, "Takahashi Korekiyo's Economic Policies in the Great Depression and their Meiji Roots," STICERD/Japanese Studies Discussion Paper 381, London School of Economics and Political Science, February 2000; idem, "The Self-Taught Bureaucrat: Takahashi Korekiyo and Economic Policy during the Great Depression," in John Singleton (ed.), *Learning in Likely Places: Varieties of Apprenticeship in Japan* (Cambridge, 1998), pp. 226–38.

8   Takahashi Korekiyo, *Nihon kokumin e no yuigon*, ed. Ōkubo Yasuo (Kobunsha, 1938), pp. 176–81; idem, *Takahashi Korekiyo jiden*, ed. Uetsuka Tsukasa (Chikura Shobō, 1936), pp. 37–70. Takahashi figures prominently in my *Lever of Empire: The International Gold Standard and the Crisis of Liberalism in Prewar Japan* (Berkeley, CA, 2006) and is the subject of a much awaited biography by Richard Smethurst of the University of Pittsburgh.

9   Now associated with free-trade ideas, patent protection was in the mid-nineteenth century considered a form of protectionism and opposed by free-trade advocates. See Fritz Machlup and Edith Penrose, "The Patent Controversy in the Nineteenth Century," *Journal of Economic History*, 10 (1950), pp. 1–29.

10 Takahashi, "Waga kuni no sangyō ni tsuite." Takahashi reworked this statement into several different versions. It was reprinted in September in the Seiyūkai party journal (*Seiyū*, 294, September 15, 1925, pp. 19–30), and later republished in at least two other forms, finally appearing as the introductory section of the posthumously published *Takahashi Korekiyo keizairon* (Chikura Shobō, 1936). In an odd slip that may suggest the channel by which Takahashi first read these "Listian" ideas, he unaccountably referred in one version of the speech to "the American scholar Biriyūsu" instead of to "Germany's Adam Smith, Friedrich List" (Takahashi, "Dō sureba ikkoku no seisanryoku wa yoku nobiru ka?," n.d., in *Zuisōroku*, p. 246). This may be Takahashi's misremembering of the English protectionist J. B. Byles (or *Bairusu* when rendered into the Japanese syllabary), whose book appeared in an American edition in 1872 and was translated into Japanese in 1877.

11 Metzler, *Lever of Empire*, Chs 8–12.

12 Takahashi Korekiyo, "Ōshū taisen no kachū ni arite," November 1915, in *Zuisōroku*, pp. 262–3; Alexander Gerschenkron, *Economic Backwardness in Historical Perspective: A Book of Essays* (Cambridge, MA, 1962).

13 Hiram Caton, "The Preindustrial Economics of Adam Smith," *Journal of Economic History*, 45 (1985), pp. 833–53; also Roman Szporluk, *Communism and*

Nationalism: Karl Marx Versus Friedrich List (Oxford, 1988). In a similar way, List missed one of the biggest stories of his own age: even more than Smith, he entertained a rosy picture of the social and moral effects of factory labor and remained mostly oblivious to the new industrialized forms of poverty and exploitation that were unfolding around him. See W. O. Henderson, "Friedrich List and the Social Question," in idem, *Marx and Engels and the English Workers, And Other Essays* (London, 1989), pp. 105–17.

14 Dieter Senghaas, "Friedrich List and the Basic Problems of Modern Development," *Review* (Fernand Braudel Center), 14 (1991), pp. 451–67, provides an excellent summation.

15 List, *National System*, pp. 3–93/pp. 49–131; quotations from p. 293/p. 311.

16 A stimulating example is Giovanni Arrighi, *The Long Twentieth Century: Money, Power, and the Origins of Our Times* (London, 1994). This national-historical conception was not present in the work of the American economists who seem to have influenced List most, Hamilton and Raymond, who in this regard largely followed the deductive British style of exposition.

17 List, *National System*, p. 339/p. 354.

18 The following biographical details are drawn mainly from the authoritative study of W. O. Henderson, *Friedrich List: Economist and Visionary, 1789–1846* (London, 1983).

19 Tribe, *Strategies*, pp. 33, 44–5. The cameralists, whose great concern was the state and its finances, have been little discussed in English; Albion W. Small, *The Cameralists: The Pioneers of German Social Polity* (Chicago, 1909) remains a standard work on the subject. See also Tribe, *Strategies*, pp. 8–31.

20 W. O. Henderson, "Friedrich List and the French Protectionists," in idem, *Marx and Engels and the English Workers*, pp. 118–32; G. Mompez, *Frédéric List et le nationalisme économique français* (Paris, 1919), pp. 66–9; but see also Tribe, *Strategies*, pp. 46–7.

21 *National System*, p. xlii/p. 7.

22 Again, this fact contradicts simplistic moral equations of liberalism in international trade and liberalism in human rights: British abolitionism became closely associated with free trade, but US abolitionism was frequently associated with protectionism. Southern slave-owners were avid free traders.

23 William Notz, "Frederick List in America," *American Economic Review*, 16 (1926), pp. 249–65; Alexander Hamilton, "Manufactures," in Henry Cabot Lodge (ed.), *The Works of Alexander Hamilton* (New York, 1904), pp. 70–198. Hamilton's report was republished in Philadelphia in 1817 by the Society for the Promotion of American Manufactures and again at least twice in the 1820s. Daniel Raymond's two-volume *Elements of Political Economy* (2nd ed., 1823; reprint, New York, 1964) is often credited as the first authentically American work of political economy.

24 The first is reprinted in Erwin v. Beckerath et al. (eds), *Friedrich List: Schriften/Reden/Briefe*, *Vol. 2* (Berlin, 1931), pp. 97–156, which also contains List's other letters and writings during his years in America; also reprinted in Margaret E. Hirst, *Life of Friedrich List and Selections from His Writings* (London, 1909), pp.

147–272. The second is translated by W. O. Henderson as *The Natural System of Political Economy* (London, 1983). Tribe (*Strategies*, pp. 44–5) says that List should be considered less a "German" economist than an American one.
25 E.g., William Oliver Coleman, *Economics and Its Enemies: Two Centuries of Anti-Economics* (Basingstoke, 2002).
26 See Senghaas ("Friedrich List," pp. 457–8), who described this strategy as "selective integration into the world market and selective decoupling."
27 *National System*, p. 106/p. 142.
28 *National System*, p. 132/p. 166.
29 *National System*, p. 108/pp. 143–4ff; Takahashi, "Waga kuni no sangyō ni tsuite," pp. 5–7; this is also the subject of an entire book by Kobayashi Noboru (*Furidorihhi Risuto no seisanryokuron* [Tōyō Keizai Shinpōsha, 1948]). When translated into Japanese (as *seisanryoku*), the German plural (*Productivkräfte*, or "powers of production") disappears. In Takahashi's usage, the concept also tended to merge with the more modern idea of *productivity* (*seisansei*). For the latter idea, see William M. Tsutsui, *Manufacturing Ideology: Scientific Management in Twentieth-Century Japan* (Princeton, NJ, 1998), esp. pp. 133–51.
30 Takahashi Korekiyo, "Kinshuku seisaku to kin kaikin" (November 1929), in *Zuisōroku*, pp. 247–8; Mark Metzler, "Woman's Place in Japan's Great Depression: Reflections on the Moral Economy of Deflation," *Journal of Japanese Studies*, 30 (2004), pp. 338–40.
31 For one analysis of "leading sectors," W. W. Rostow, *The Stages of Economic Growth: A Non-Communist Manifesto* (Cambridge, 1960); for "backward and forward linkages," Albert O. Hirschman, *The Strategy of Economic Development* (New Haven, CT, 1958), esp. pp. 98–119.
32 John R. Davis, *Britain and the German Zollverein, 1848–66* (Basingstoke, 1997).
33 The phrase is from the *Communist Manifesto*. For Satsuma's policy, see John H. Sagers, *Origins of Japanese Wealth and Power: Reconciling Confucianism and Capitalism, 1830–1885* (New York, 2006), Ch. 3; for "technonationalism," Richard Samuels, *"Rich Country, Strong Army": National Security and the Technological Transformation of Japan* (Ithaca, NY, 1994), who also mentions Satsuma on pp. 81–2 and discusses List on pp. 5–7.
34 Ronald P. Toby, *State and Diplomacy in Early Modern Japan: Asia in the Development of the Tokugawa Bakufu* (Stanford, CA, 1991); Robert Leroy Innes, "The Door Ajar: Japan's Foreign Trade in the Seventeenth Century" (PhD dissertation, University of Michigan, 1980); Tashiro Kazui, "Foreign Relations during the Edo Period: Sakoku Reexamined," *Journal of Japanese Studies*, 8 (1982), pp. 283–306; Kate Wildman Nakai, *Shogunal Politics: Arai Hakuseki and the Premises of Tokugawa Rule* (Cambridge, MA, 1988); Ronald P. Toby and Osamu Ohba, "The Bitter and the Sweet: Import Substitutions in Sugar and Ginseng in Eighteenth-Century Japan" (unpublished manuscript, 1997); Ōishi Shinzaburō, *Tanuma Okitsugu no jidai* (Iwanami Shoten, 1991).
35 Luke S. Roberts, *Mercantilism in a Japanese Domain: The Merchant Origins of Economic Nationalism in 18th-Century Tosa* (Cambridge, 1998); Kaiho Seiryō quoted in Sagers, *Origins*, p. 27; Fujita Teiichirō, *Kokueki shisō no keifu to tenkai, Tokugawa-ki*

kara Meiji-ki e no ayumi (Osaka: Seibundō, 1998), esp. pp. 1–53; Sagers, *Origins*, Chs 1–3; E. Sydney Crawcour, "Economic Change in the Nineteenth Century," in Marius B. Jansen (ed.), *The Cambridge History of Japan, Vol. 5* (Cambridge, 1989).

36   For the "consultant administrators," see J. A. Schumpeter, *History of Economic Analysis*, ed. E. B. Schumpeter (Oxford, 1954), p. 159; and Small, *The Cameralists*. For the recycling of European cameralist ideas back to Meiji Japan, see Katalin Ferber, "'Run the State Like a Business': The Origin of the Deposit Fund in Meiji Japan," *Japanese Studies*, 22 (2002), pp. 131–51.

37   Sagers, *Origins*, from which the information in this paragraph is drawn.

38   Important in this connection is T. C. Smith, "Japan's Aristocratic Revolution," in idem, *Native Sources of Japanese Industrialization, 1750–1920* (Berkeley, CA, 1988), pp. 133–47.

39   Carmen Blacker, *The Japanese Enlightenment: A Study of the Writings of Fukuzawa Yukichi* (Cambridge, 1964); William R. Braisted (trans.), *Meiroku zasshi, Journal of the Japanese Enlightenment* (Cambridge, MA, 1976).

40   Ichiro Inukai, *Japan's First Strategy for Economic Development, with Selected Translation of Kogyo Iken* (Niigata, 2003), p. 29.

41   Byron Marshall, *Capitalism and Nationalism in Prewar Japan: The Ideology of the Business Elite, 1868–1941* (Stanford, CA, 1967); Fujiwara Akio, *Fukuzawa Yukichi no Nihon keizai ron* (Nihon Keizai Hyōronsha, 1998), pp. 150–68.

42   Takahashi Korekiyo, "Hogo bōeki ron – Baba Tatsui no jiyū bōeki ron ni taisuru bakuron," undated speech at Keio University in *Takahashi Korekiyo keizairon*, pp. 96–117. Internal evidence suggests that the speech was given in late 1925 or 1926. The 1875 debate was staged at Takahashi's language school, and he argued in association with Akabane Shirō and the liberal political activist Ono Azusa (1852–86) against the free-trade position taken by the liberal political activist Baba Tatsui (1850–88).

43   Fukuzawa Yukichi and many others were saying similar things at the time. Notably, these perceptions from the global periphery far predate later analyses of Britain's "imperialism of free trade," such as John Gallagher and Ronald Robinson's classic article of that name in the *Economic History Review*, 6 (1953), pp. 1–15.

44   Takahashi, "Hogo bōeki ron," pp. 100–1.

45   "Natural law," *tenri*, literally, "heavenly principle"; "natural liberty," *tenzen no jiyū*; see also Julia Adeney Thomas, *Reconfiguring Modernity: Concepts of Nature in Japanese Political Ideology* (Berkeley, CA, 2001).

46   Takahashi, "Hogo bōeki ron," pp. 110–12.

47   Takahashi, *Jiden*, I, pp. 184–97; Thomas C. Smith, *Political Change and Industrial Development in Japan: Government Enterprise, 1868–1880* (Stanford, CA, 1955); Takahashi, "Shokusan kōgyō no onjin o omou," in *Zuisōroku*, pp. 269–79.

48   The Sino-Japanese words *kokumin* (literally, "national people") and *kokka* (literally, "nation-family," or imperial state) are usually translated as, but do not map directly onto, the European words *nation* and *state*. Among other incongruences, *min*, "people," has historically meant "the *governed* people," as differentiated

from *kan*, "officials" (or the state), which in Tokugawa Japan meant the samurai class. In an illuminating analysis, Ishida Takeshi explores the significant flux in these and other semantically connected terms in *Nihon no shakai kagaku* (Tōkyō Daigaku Shuppankai, 1984), pp. 15–21.

49 Inukai, *Japan's First Strategy*, pp. 11–12; Soda, *Maeda Masana*, pp. 42–6.

50 List was translated into French in 1857 at the instigation of the French Ministry of Commerce and Industry. Although List's ideas were well known in France and Maeda may well have read his book, there no direct evidence of this. See Sidney Crawcour, "*Kōgyō iken*: Maeda Masana and His View of Meiji Economic Development," *Journal of Japanese Studies*, 23 (1997), pp. 103–4. Mompez's brief 1919 dissertation (*Frédéric List et le nationalisme économique français*) makes no mention of Tisserand.

51 Inukai, *Japan's First Strategy*; Crawcour, "Kōgyō iken," pp. 69–104.

52 Inukai (*Japan's First Strategy*, pp. 32–55) emphasizes Matsukata's influence over Maeda and minimizes the conflict between them – but reading between the lines, one forms a completely opposite impression.

53 Recent reconstructions by economic historians suggest that Maeda correctly identified the most powerful dynamic of Japan's actual economic growth during the second half of the nineteenth century, namely the diffusion and adaptation of existing best-practice techniques in "native" industry (*zairai sangyō*), which were enabled and stimulated by the export trade, integration of the national market, and deregulation. ("*Zairai*" industry itself is better described as nativi*zed*, as many techniques had themselves been adapted from Chinese practice.) Surveys are given in Nishikawa Shunsaku and Abe Takeshi (eds), *Sangyōka no jidai, jō* (Nihon Keizaishi 4 [Iwanami Shoten, 1990]), especially in Nishikawa's chapter, "Zairai sangyō to kindai sangyō" (pp. 81–111). For some closely related considerations, see Tessa Morris-Suzuki, *The Technological Transformation of Japan, From the Seventeenth to the Twenty-first Century* (Cambridge, 1994), pp. 71–104. The prehistory of this development is the Tokugawa-era rural "proto-industrialization" analyzed by Thomas C. Smith, *The Agrarian Origins of Modern Japan* (Stanford, CA, 1959); idem, *Native Sources*; Saitō Osamu, *Puroto-kōgyōka no jidai* (Nihon Hyōronsha, 1985); Edward E. Pratt, *Japan's Proto-Industrial Elite: The Economic Foundations of the Gōnō* (Cambridge, MA, 1999); see also David L. Howell, *Capitalism from Within: Economy, Society, and the State in a Japanese Fishery* (Berkeley, CA, 1995).

54 Another, mentioned by Takahashi ("Shokusan kōgyō no onjin," p. 279), was Maeda's proposal to establish a technical school, which angered Education Minister Mori Arinori (who was another of Takahashi's many mentors and patrons).

55 The original, unpublished version of the report was rediscovered and analyzed only in 1969.

56 Takahashi, "Shokusan kōgyō no onjin," pp. 276–7, 281; Richard Smethurst, "Takahashi Korekiyo's Fiscal Policies in the 1930s and their Meiji Roots," *Suntory Centre Papers*, London School of Economics, 1999.

57   This conclusion parallels the important analysis of Meiji economic development
     presented by Yasuba Yasukichi, "Did Japan Ever Suffer from a Shortage of
     Natural Resources Before World War II?", *Journal of Economic History*, 56 (1996),
     pp. 543–60; idem, "Nihon keizaishi ni okeru shigen, 1800–1940," *Shakai keizai
     shigaku*, 62 (1995), pp. 291–312. See also Metzler, *Lever of Empire*, pp. 68, 91.

58   Inukai actually translated the first half of a still lengthy digest of Carey's three-
     volume work by Kate McKean, *Manual of Social Science; Being a Condensation of
     the "Principles of Social Science" of H. C. Carey, LL.D.* (Philadelphia, PA, 1864).
     The second half was translated by Machida Chūji (Tokitō Hideto, *Meiji-ki no
     Inukai Tsuyoshi* [Tokyo, 1996], pp. 54–5). Machida himself was later Minister
     of Agriculture, Minister of Commerce and Industry, and president of the
     Minseitō party in the 1930s. For Carey, see also Andrew Dawson, "Reassessing
     Henry Carey (1793–1879): The Problems of Writing Political Economy in
     Nineteenth-Century America," *Journal of American Studies*, 34 (2000), pp. 465–85;
     Charles H. Levermore, "Henry C. Carey and his Social System," *Political Science
     Quarterly*, 5 (1890), pp. 553–82.

59   宇宙経済ノ空理: an ordinary reading of the first four Chinese characters
     would be *uchū keizai*, literally meaning "universal" (or "space") economics. By
     means of phonetic indicators, Inukai indicated that the four-character
     compound should be read "*kosumupolichisumu*" (Bokudō Sensei Denki
     Kankōkai, *Inukai Bokudō den, jō* (Tōyō Keizai Shinpōsha, 1938), p. 129.

60   *National System of Political Economy*, tr. G.-A. Matile et al. (Philadelphia, PA,
     1856), an edition now rarely referred to.

61   Reinhard H. Luthin, "Abraham Lincoln and the Tariff," *American Historical
     Review*, 59 (1944), pp. 609–29.

62   Note however that the "older historical school" is also often defined as having
     consisted of only four academic economists, a group to which List did not
     belong.

63   Kobayashi Noboru, "*Kokuminteki taikei* ni tsuite," p. 558–9.

64   Andrew E. Barshay, *The Social Sciences in Modern Japan: The Marxian and
     Modernist Traditions* (Berkeley, CA, 2004), especially pp. 37–46; Carol Gluck,
     Japan's Modern Myths: Ideology in the Late Meiji Period (Princeton, NJ, 1985).

65   Regarding the shift to German political economy, Ishida, *Nihon no shakai
     kagaku*, pp. 29–40, and Chūhei Sugiyama and Hiroshi Mizuta (eds),
     Enlightenment and Beyond: Political Economy Comes to Japan (Tokyo, 1988). In the
     1890s, German social policy thought became a new aspect of this connection,
     for which see Kenneth Pyle, "Advantages of Followership: German Economics
     and Japanese Bureaucrats, 1890–1925," *Journal of Japanese Studies*, 1 (1974), pp.
     127–64. For Taguchi, Ōshima Mario, "Taguchi Ukichi no gaikoku bōeki ron
     ni tsuite," *Keizaigaku zasshi*, 100:3 (Ōsaka Shiritsu Daigaku, 1999), pp. 65–81.

66   Friedrich List [Furiidorihhi Risuto], *Ri-shi keizairon*, 2 vols, edited and trans-
     lated by Tomita Tetsunosuke and Ōshima Sadamasu (Nihon Keizaikai, 1889);
     Nihon Ginkō Hyakunenshi Hensan Iinkai (ed.), *Nihon Ginkō hyakunenshi, Vol.
     1* (Nihon Ginkō, 1982), pp. 408–11. The Japanese translation also included the

adulatory short biography of List originally adapted from *Friedrich List, ein Vorläufer und ein Opfer für das Vaterland* (Stuttgart, 1851). Several later editions of List's work were published, including a more recent scholarly translation from the German by Kobayashi Noboru (Furiidorihhi Risuto, *Keizaigaku no kokuminteki taikei* [Iwanami Shoten, 1970]).

67 Although Gerschenkron did not analyze it, Belgium was Europe's second industrialized country after England, and the salience of great investment banks in Belgium's industrialization makes it even more "German" than the German model he did specify. For details, see Michael Schiltz, "The Bank of Japan and the National Bank of Belgium," in W. F. Vande Walle (ed.), *Japan and Belgium: Four Centuries of Exchange* (Brussels, 2005), pp. 121–33; Rondo E. Cameron, "Belgium, 1800–1875," in idem, *Banking in the Early Stages of Industrialization: A Study in Comparative Economic History* (Oxford, 1967), pp. 129–50. The Belgian model was recommended to Matsukata Masayoshi, somewhat ironically, by the liberal French finance minister Léon Say, the grandson of J.-B. Say (who was the number-one target of List's polemic). Matsukata did not speak French, and Maeda Masana presumably translated their conversation.

68 Yoshino Toshihiko, *Wasurareta moto Nichigin sōsai – Tomita Tetsunosuke den* (Tōyō Keizai Shinpōsha, 1974), pp. 405–6; Takahashi, *Jiden*, pp. 63–5.

69 Takahashi himself first joined the Bank of Japan two years after Tomita left it; Tomita's former post of vice-governor was left vacant until Takahashi assumed it in 1899.

70 Quoted in Barshay, *Social Sciences*, p. 42.

71 Inukai, *Japan's First Strategy*, pp. 29–30, 48–9. On the old guilds and their dissolution, see Ulrike Schaede, *Self-Regulation, Trade Associations, and the Antimonopoly Law in Japan* (Oxford, 2000), pp. 224–39.

72 Significantly, the area of economic policy where British ideas had the greatest influence before 1931 was in the theory of monetary stabilization, as practiced by internationalist bankers such as Inoue Junnosuke (1869–1932), who restored Japan's British-style gold standard in 1930 and provoked the crisis that Takahashi Korekiyo was later called upon to fix (and for whom see Metzler, *Lever of Empire*). Another domain in which British policy thought was influential was that of social welfare. In macroeconomic policy, Keynesianism later had considerable influence.

73 This will receive a full treatment in Smethurst's forthcoming study. Summary information can be found in Myung Soo Cha, "Did Takahashi Korekiyo Rescue Japan from the Great Depression?," *Journal of Economic History*, 63 (2003), pp. 127–44; Metzler, *Lever of Empire*, pp. 240–5, 248–52.

74 *National System*, pp. 69, 78–80/pp. 109, 116–18. See also François Crouzet, "Wars, Blockade, and Economic Change in Europe, 1792–1815," *Journal of Economic History*, 24 (1964), pp. 567–88. The destructive result of this "reciprocal blockade," as List called it, was that the "Atlantic" sector of the continental European economies, especially in France, lost access to colonial markets

130 Global History

and sources of supply and never really recovered, causing the deindustrialization
and reagrarianization of whole regions such as those of Bordeaux and Nantes.
75 *National System*, pp. 69–70/p. 109.
76 In the official history cited above (Tsūshō Sangyōshō, *Shōkōshō sanjūgonen
shōshi*), p. 7.
77 *National System*, p. 295/p. 313. Hence the title of a sophisticated neo-Listian
challenge by Ha-Joon Chang, *Kicking Away the Ladder: Development Strategy in
Historical Perspective* (London, 2002).
78 *National System*, p. 272.
79 See also Kiren Aziz Chaudhry, "The Myths of the Market and the Common
History of Late Developers," *Politics and Society*, 21 (1994), pp. 245–74.
80 *National System*, p. 103/p. 139; p. 100/p. 136; p. 272; Emmanuel N. Roussakis,
Friedrich List, the Zollverein and the Uniting of Europe (Brussels, 1968).
81 Or more accurately, reregulation: see Steven K. Vogel, *Freer Markets, More
Rules: Regulatory Reform in Advanced Industrial Countries* (Ithaca, NY, 1996). See
also Hopkins, "History of Globalization," p. 42.
82 Mark Elder, "METI and Industrial Policy in Japan: Change and Continuity,"
in Ulrike Schaede and William Grimes (eds), *Japan's Managed Globalization:
Adapting to the Twenty-first Century* (Armonk, NY, 2003), pp. 159–90.
83 Nippon Keidanren, "Keidanren's Priority Policies," November 24, 2004,
revised February 7, 2005; Nippon Keidanren, *Japan 2025: Envisioning a Vibrant,
Attractive Nation in the Twenty-First Century*, January 2003; at www.keidan-
ren.or.jp/english/policy/
84 Hisamitsu Arai, "Global Competition Policy as a Basis for a Borderless Market
Economy," speech at Columbia University, July 22, 1999; idem, "The Future
of the WTO and the Multilateral Trading System," speech at Asia Pacific
Economic Summit, September 13, 2000; both online at www.meti.go.jp;
Saadia M. Pekkanen, "Sword and Shield: The WTO Dispute Settlement
System and Japan," in Schaede and Grimes, *Japan's Managed Globalization*, pp.
77–100.
85 *National System*, pp. 293–4, 312.

5

Internationalist Activism and Global Civil Society at the High Point of Nationalism: The Challenge of the Universal Races Congress, 1911

Tracie Matysik

When announcements for the first Universal Races Congress (URC) went out, they stated that the express purpose of the Congress was "to discuss, in the light of science and the modern conscience, the general relations subsisting between the peoples of the West and those of the East, between so-called white and so-called coloured peoples, with a view to encouraging between them a fuller understanding, the most friendly feelings, and a heartier co-operation."[1] Prior to the 1911 Congress, organizers had solicited written contributions on the global problems of race and race relations that were then circulated weeks before the July meeting. The resulting volume, made available in both French and English, contained contributions from numerous activist and scholarly luminaries. These included: the German-Jewish-American anthropologist, Franz Boas; the former president of Haiti, General Légitime; the founding figure of German sociology, Ferdinand Tönnies; the Nigerian pan-African activist (then listed as the Director of the Niger Delta Mission), Mojola Agbebi; the Hindu scholar, Brajendranath Seal of Cooch Behar's College in India; the African-American social theorist and activist, W. E. B. DuBois; the German-Jewish-American founder of the Ethical Culture movement, Felix Adler; the Chinese diplomat, Wu Ting-Fang; and the Japanese professors of sociology and pedagogy, Tongo Takebe and Teruaki Kobayashi. In reports following the Congress, observers estimated that roughly 2,100 participants attended.[2] If the event was dominated by representatives from Western Europe and North America, it could boast nevertheless that participants came from all corners of the globe. Taking the diverse participation both in terms of contributors and attendees as a sign of success and of global enthusiasm for the project, the organizers of the URC set up a standing committee to plan a Second Universal Races Congress, to be held in 1915 in Honolulu, Hawaii, which was celebrated for its supposed multi-ethnic harmony.[3]

The twenty-first-century reader will rightly guess that the outbreak of World War I prevented the realization of the Second URC. While there are indications that some hopes were carried forward to a more modest version of the URC to be held in Paris in 1915,[4] neither the Honolulu meeting nor the Paris replacement ever came to pass, and the URC's efforts died – one more casualty of the war. The same reader, equipped with hindsight knowledge that World War I was just around the corner, might also have difficulty in grasping the seeming optimism of the Congress's express intent of promoting international, "inter-racial" cooperation and understanding. Yet the two events – the URC and World War I – may be less at odds than they appear. The organizers of the URC hoped to facilitate cooperation and mutual understanding amongst people from all parts of the globe; the all-consuming war would have a similar reach in terms of the physical destruction and social upheaval it would bring. Both were possible because global interconnectedness had become the order of the day by the beginning of the twentieth century.

In the longest perspective both the URC and World War I were products of what A. G. Hopkins has termed the era of "modern globalization." In a preliminary and schematic outline, Hopkins situates "modern globalization" between "proto-globalization" on the one hand, and "postcolonial globalization" on the other, where "proto-globalization" refers to the period between 1600 and 1800, in which modern forms of state sovereignty, economy, and knowledge emerged; and "postcolonial globalization" covers the era beginning roughly after World War II characterized by European decolonization and the realignment of economic power and exchange away from the imperial geographical patterns of the nineteenth century.[5] According to this schema, modern globalization occurred roughly between 1800 and 1950, when the consolidation of the nation state and industrialization coincided with the extension of European imperialism around the globe, creating an international network dependent on overseas trade and empire.

In terms of the production and circulation of knowledge, the modern period of globalization might also be characterized by the challenge of negotiating the universalism of Enlightenment reason and the particularisms of nation, region, and culture.[6] Like Hopkins, Tony Ballantyne describes this development as the "domestication" of Enlightenment universals, as nation states took on for themselves the language of universalism.[7] This modernist negotiation of universalism and particularism might be distinguished from the ascent of postmodern irony[8] and reflexivity that has characterized "postcolonial globalization," and has to a large extent abandoned appeals to universals in favor of cultural difference and multiplicity.

The major part of the scholarly attention paid to the URC has seen it as an ephemeral if extraordinary event that had significance only from particular national or imperial perspectives. Paul Rich, for instance, has provided an excellent account of the role of the URC and its challenge to notions of racial hierarchy in the specific context of British liberalism.[9] Susan Pennybacker has also enriched our understanding of the event by situating it within the diverse political culture of London at the turn of the century.[10] Likewise, first Elliott Rudwick and more recently Robert Gregg and Madhavi Kale have examined the URC as a pivotal moment in the political development of W. E. B. DuBois and his approach both to race politics in the United States and to the Pan-African movement.[11] In addition, several scholars of late have sought to interpret the Congress as the global event it sought to be. Building on a suggestion from Paul Gilroy,[12] Robert John Holton has portrayed the URC as a more postmodern event that accommodated comfortably the tensions of difference. Analyzing the URC sociologically, Holton has suggested that the event should be seen as a model of the "new cosmopolitanism." By this he means a cosmopolitanism that does not make claims to inherently flawed notions of Enlightenment universalism, but rather one that "is broader than any narrowly conceived segment of humankind, yet somehow narrower than humanity as a whole."[13]

This chapter seeks to build on the more recent literature that emphasizes the global dimensions of the URC, while holding to the historical specificity of the event that Rich and others have explored. I examine the event within the context of early internationalist activism that scholars such as Akira Iriye have credited as being initial formations of a "global civil society." Scholars have used the idea of a global civil society quite loosely, usually to connote in some way the kinds of communities and/or organizations that are not beholden to or bounded by the nation state. Some use it to refer to the idea of a "world community," or the general idea that individuals are beginning to bypass national governments in order to advocate causes on behalf of all of humanity.[14] Others stress the rise of both political and economic advocacy groups whose realm of influence exceeds the bounds of any sovereign state.[15] Mary Kaldor, a leading theorist of global civil society, examines the concept in relation to its national precursors. She notes the paradox that conceptions of national civil society have conventionally made universalist claims, usually in the form of individual liberties (both moral and economic). The universalist dimension of individual liberties may refer to liberties that a nation state is supposed to guarantee; in a more activist sense it may refer to those liberties that are held to be universal and upon which a state is said to be infringing unjustly. Kaldor distinguishes these conventional notions of civil society from what she terms a "postmodern" global civil society not only because the latter no longer relies solely upon sovereign nation states to secure (or fail to secure) individual liberties, but also because the latter ironically renounces the pretenses to universalism that its predecessors maintained. In this guise, postmodern global civil society pertains to an "arena of pluralism" that can accommodate more identity-based groups or causes than could the universalism associated with conventional national civil society.[16]

This notion of global civil society – and the tensions between its universalist and particularist dimensions – may be helpful in articulating the conceptual and institutional framework within which the URC was operating. As I will discuss below, the URC's effort to grapple with the notion of race raised broad questions about the normative or morally desirable relationship between individuals, group identities, and something like universal humanity, as well as about the existing cultural and political institutions in which those relations operate. It is thus the URC's examination of the category of "race" in particular that makes it an especially fruitful moment to examine both the potential and the limits of an emerging global civil society in the early twentieth century. From this angle, the participants' concerns continue to appear to be about the critique of imperialism that Rich has rightly depicted; but they appear also to involve the more abstract complexities and contradictions in the notion of a global human community. The explicit theme of "race" at the URC, and participants' efforts to understand it, emerges not only as a contestation of the ideological foundations of imperialism, but also as a means to think about the notion of a universal humanity and the contingency of the intermediate groups into which that humanity divides itself. I keep in sight, however, the critique of imperialism that Rich correctly identified as being an institutional and intellectual motive behind the URC. From this perspective, I am less inclined than recent sociological arguments are to see in the URC a comfortable negotiation of universalism and cultural difference. Rather, I suggest, it was precisely the modernist, internationalist, and imperialist context in which the URC operated that bound it to an extreme logic of universalism, even at the expense of the toleration of difference that it desired. To illustrate what the tensions were, and to consider their relevance for thinking about the URC in terms of globalization debates, I will first discuss briefly how the URC fits into the history of internationalism and internationalist activism. Then I will turn to the URC itself to see just how it approached the question of "race" within the internationalist framework.

Internationalism and the origins of the URC

One of the most common areas of concern in the recent historiography of nineteenth- and twentieth-century Europe has been the rise of nation-building and nationalism. Here a guiding question has been that of how, why, and when individuals learned to identify themselves first and foremost as members of a particular nation state. In a dominant strain of the literature on nationalism, the nineteenth century has been portrayed as a tug-of-war between socialist internationalism on the one hand, and nationalism on the other – both of which could be seen as challenging the limitations of the universalist claims of the Enlightenment, albeit from vastly different starting points.[17] While this focus has been fully justified, it has also obscured the parallel growth of international organization in the same period.

More recently, scholars of diverse disciplines have begun to look at the rise of other forms of internationalist activity during this period. Here the literature has extended well beyond the Second International to include developments such as international women's organizations, international cooperation in the provisioning of health and medicine, and international peace and pacifist movements, to name just a few.[18] This recent trend has sought to understand the movement towards internationalism not just as a set of anomalies, or even as indications that a degree of sanity survived the nationalist furor leading to the war, but rather as a phenomenon constitutive of the era. From this perspective these intimations of what, today, would be called globalization might substantially alter how historians understand the whole period. It might, for instance, cast the seemingly inevitable "road to war" in a slightly more contingent light.[19] From the road-to-war perspective, 1914 is usually seen as the great break that vastly separates the nineteenth from the twentieth centuries; in contrast, a focus on the development of institutions such as internationalist activism and international non-governmental organizations (INGOs) may offer a means to see more continuities across traditional lines of rupture. In this light, Akira Iriye has suggested that, through the study of INGOs in particular, "we shall gain an understanding of one aspect of the phenomenon of globalization and of the historical process that has created transnational, global, and human forces and movements defining the world today."[20]

Although the vast majority of INGOs came into existence after 1945, their growth was already increasing in the decade before 1914. Numbers vary according to the specific criteria used in calculations, but recent estimates suggest that between 175 and 200 INGOs existed in 1900, compared with more than 26,000 by 2000.[21] Internationalist activism increased at the end of the nineteenth century due to the political evolution of the European state system and its imperial expansion on the one hand, and changes in technology and industry on the other. As European imperialism spread to all parts of the globe towards the end of the nineteenth century, so did the European system of territorial sovereignty. At the same time, changes in transportation and communication fundamentally altered the way individuals perceived the globe. Railways and steamships enabled previously unimaginable transcontinental and transoceanic travel and commerce, while the invention of the radio was to revolutionize the transmission of information.

This combination of economic, political, and technological developments prompted the establishment of commissions to facilitate travel, communication, and the transportation of goods. The earliest of these included commissions for the free navigation of the Rhine (1815) and Danube (1856) rivers, the first of which was concerned solely with Western and Central European diplomacy, the second including the Ottoman Empire as well. But soon organizations such as the International Telegraphic Union (1865), the Universal Postal Union (1878), and the International Bureau of Weights and Measures (1876) extended in principle to all parts of the globe. INGOs, which were usually expressions of international-humanitarian and social-reform efforts, grew at an even faster pace than the international governmental organizations (IGOs), and were enabled by the same political, economic, and technological developments. The World Anti-Slavery Convention (1840) is often credited with being the first such organization, followed shortly by the International Committee of the Red Cross (1864). Slowly such organizations became ever more popular, so that by the 1890s roughly ten new organizations were founded each year.[22] These included such diverse groups as the Young Women's Christian Associations (1894), the International Central Bureau for the Campaign against Tuberculosis (1902), the Universal Esperanto Association (1908), and the International Union of Ethical Societies (1896)[23] which was so central to the formation of the URC.[24]

The URC came together largely through the cooperation and efforts of the International Union of Ethical Societies and the Inter-parliamentary

Union.[25] The public face of the event was to a large extent that of the Inter-parliamentary Union, which was an exceptional type of organization situated between an IGO and an INGO.[26] It had its origins in the international peace movement, which had been growing steadily in the last quarter of the century. While most early peace associations were entirely non-governmental – sometimes affiliated with specific religious denominations, at other times with free-trade associations – the Inter-parliamentary Union was founded when sitting members of French and British parliaments, who were themselves active in the non-governmental peace associations, first began petitioning their fellow representatives on matters pertaining to international arbitration, and then strengthened their efforts through collaboration. From here it was a short step to reach out to other European and ultimately non-European parliaments. The first Inter-parliamentary Conference took place in Paris in 1899, but quickly changed its name to the more permanent sounding Inter-parliamentary Union. Its primary aim was to take advantage of members' proximity to governments in order to urge them to adopt arbitration procedures in cases of international conflict. By the time the URC met in 1911, the Inter-parliamentary Union had a well established foundation, and even received funds from a number of members' governments. It was in the light of the Inter-parliamentary Union's established prominence that Philip James Stanhope – by then Lord Weardale and twice president of Inter-parliamentary conferences – served as the official president of the URC.

If the prominent members of the Inter-parliamentary Union, such as Lord Weardale, provided the public face of the URC and facilitated its connection to the international peace movement, the idea for the event itself, its organization, and its intellectual ambition derived from the International Union of Ethical Societies and its founder, Felix Adler. An international organization of a very different type, the International Union of Ethical Societies was based not so much on the ambition to influence governmental policy, as on the pursuit of intellectual exchange and individual moral education.

The Ethical Culture movement, as it was known, began as a secular Jewish organization in New York City in 1876. Adler, its founder, had been preparing to enter the rabbinate when he concluded that Judaism, along with all organized religions, had lost its ability to provide moral guidelines for individual and social life.[27] Adler understood this to be an inevitable consequence of modernity and the demystification of social life; he understood also, however, that like-minded individuals nevertheless desired some basis or guideline for moral orientation. Ethical Culture thus came about as a forum in which to debate in secular terms the pressing moral problems that its members confronted in the rapidly changing world around them. Its tone oscillated between explicit secularism and religious tolerance. No religious doctrine would be allowed to dominate the agenda of Ethical Culture, but neither would individuals who were devoted to specific religions be excluded from the organization.[28]

The organization spread quite quickly beyond both its New York City beginnings and its secular Jewish starting point. By 1886 Ethical Culture Societies had been founded in Chicago, St Louis, and Philadelphia, with memberships dominated by secular thinkers with Christian backgrounds.[29] Then, largely through personal connections, Ethical Culture founded its two other strongholds: in Britain, and in Germany and Austria.[30] The first meeting of the nascent International Union of Ethical Societies took place in Switzerland in 1896, at which point the Union consisted of branches primarily from Europe and North America.[31] By the time of the URC, however, the Union included branches from Japan, India, and New Zealand as well.[32]

The ideological ambitions of Ethical Culture centered on the question of applied ethics. Adler himself had been most influenced by Kantian universalism, while his British and German counterparts tended to lean more in the direction of a softened Benthamite utilitarianism. The fact that these intellectual starting points might be irreconcilable mattered little to the overall project of Ethical Culture, as that project aimed less to provide a unified intellectual stance than to foster discussion of the moral foundations upon which reform efforts and the critique of tradition might be based.[33] The one unifying presupposition was a general commitment to universal humanitarian welfare, which was to be achieved through a combination of careful consideration of competing moral perspectives and concrete social action. International cooperation among the regional branches of Ethical Culture operated along this divide between moral philosophical questions and social reform. The first international congress adopted a manifesto that listed a number of general principles of the organization, such as the commitment to the "moral training and instruction of the young," and "resistance against injustice and oppression." Delegates also agreed that they would "leave it to the various Societies to apply the above tasks according to the circumstances of their own countries."[34] In short, internationalism was to work as a means of intellectual exchange, but advocacy for social reform remained an explicitly local, nationally specific project. This split between intellectual exchange and applied reform efforts or political advocacy, and the corresponding split between internationalism and localism, would have a substantial impact on the shape and aims of the URC itself.

Motives for the meeting

The URC extended well beyond the hitherto limited internationalist networks of both the Inter-parliamentary Union and the International Union of Ethical Societies. What exactly motivated this outreach? Almost all organizers and participants of the URC were in agreement with the sentiment expressed by Paul Reinsch, a Wisconsin- and Berlin-based scholar of international law (and later US Ambassador to China), who claimed that:

> the cardinal fact of contemporary civilisation is the unification of the world, the emergence of organic relations, world-wide in scope, uniting the branches of the human family in all parts of the earth. This result is due primarily to the really marvelous advances made in all the methods and processes of communication. Distance has been annihilated, and lands on the opposite sides of the earth, formerly mysterious to one another, are now next-door neighbours.[35]

Similarly common, however, was the general sense that problematic conceptions of "race" allowed the even more troublesome phenomenon of what Weardale called "race arrogance."[36] For the organizers and many participants of the URC, it was this combination of world proximity and misguided understandings of "race" that posed the greatest threat to world peace, and thus necessitated a forum such as the URC. How exactly this "unification of the world" and challenges to ideas of racial superiority and/or racial conflict were related and should be most productively evaluated and responded to, however, varied considerably between the different organizers.

Weardale saw these challenges primarily from a strategic perspective. Speaking explicitly about the international peace movement, he noted that it had hitherto consisted almost exclusively of "members of the Caucasian race."[37] With enthusiasm, he claimed that world developments were such that it was now possible to imagine a "brotherhood of man."[38] This expansion of the peace movement's reach was due, he argued, largely to a recent redistribution in global power as a result of what he called a "tremendous though silent revolution" in the East.[39] Though Weardale was referring primarily to the Japanese victory in the recent Japanese–Russian war, he was echoing a growing awareness in Europe of the potential cultural and political powers of China and East Asia more generally. Seeking to distinguish his position from what he called the "yellow peril" paranoia of "yellow journalists" – even if his own language tended to mirror that which he criticized – Weardale aimed explicitly to call into question the distinction between "East" and "West," noting in particular how many of the cultural developments of the West were expressly indebted to technological innovations in

China.[40] The danger, in his view, emanated not from the East, but from the misguided policies of Western European countries that presupposed racial difference and racial superiority and thereby threatened to enlarge the arena of international conflict. It was consequently the task of the international peace movement to become more global than it hitherto had been. And it was the corresponding task of the URC to delegitimate conceptions of race that enabled such claims of racial difference and hierarchy.

Adler, on the other hand, viewed the issue of global race politics in a much more localist fashion. He had first proposed the foundation of the URC at the meeting of the International Union of Ethical Societies in 1906 because he was becoming increasingly aware of the problems of race and human inequality in American politics. While not entirely overcoming racial stereotypes himself (like his contemporaries, he routinely referred to "backward races"), he had developed a considerable admiration for both Booker T. Washington and W. E. B. DuBois. He traveled to their respective institutions to speak and invited both men to speak at his own New York Society for Ethical Culture.[41] Then, in 1898, just when Adler had been developing ever more antipathy towards the conditions of racial segregation at home, the US entered into a war with Spain, the outcome of which made the US an occupying imperial power. Quick to join sympathies with the Anti-Imperialist League, Adler made his stance clear through public lectures and through pamphlets with titles such as "Can We Afford to Rule Subject Peoples?"[42] His primary argument against US imperialism was that it would compromise the premises of equality upon which democracy rested, and would thereby undermine the principles of US domestic politics.

It was thus the explicitly local problems of the US, in terms of both racial segregation domestically and imperial conquests abroad, that prompted Adler to propose the Congress. To be sure, he shared with Weardale concerns and enthusiasms about the growing integration of all parts of the globe, and the potentially disastrous problems that ill-begotten conceptions of race might have for all parties involved. But his focus always returned to the local implications of global intellectual exchange. While he did not maintain that local issues such as those the US was confronting could be resolved through an event such as the meeting of the URC, he did hope that a more global discussion about race would shed light on the specific domestic manifestations of conflict. He made this sentiment very explicit in his official "Report of the First Universal Races Congress" that he presented to the United States Bureau of Education, his official sponsor for the conference. Referring to the motivation that he hoped participants at the URC would take away with them, Adler suggested that each participant will perhaps have been compelled to pause and acknowledge to himself how immense is the problem with the fringe of which, and only a fringe, he is dealing. I do not, of course, for an instant imply that we should therefore be less zealous and less concentrated upon that portion of the field which it is appointed to us to till, or that we should feel less earnestly that in attempting to solve a fraction of the problem we are contributing what we can to the solution of the whole. I only meant that we should see our work *sub specie humanitatis*, and I venture to express the belief that such undertakings as the Universal Races Congress help us to do so.[43]

It was thus with these combined global and local motivations of Weardale and Adler that the URC came about.

The primacy of the individual in a universal humanity

True to the idealist investments of Ethical Culture, the form of the URC was in many ways more significant than its content. Ethical Culture had always been committed to the idea of the transformative potential of rational conversation, and the URC would be no different. The organizers' attention to issues of representation was especially significant in terms of the URC's global ambitions. The organizers did not want to host a conference in which Europeans simply talked to one another about non-Europeans. Accordingly, they explicitly requested that individuals speak about the regions of the globe from which they came. At the same time, the organizers were especially insistent that all individuals speak with full autonomy, subordinating neither themselves nor the Congress to any group affiliation or political cause.[44] As a consequence of these formal emphases on rational discussion, it is unwise to try to sum up the intellectual or political stance of the URC. But it is possible to trace the competing convictions within the discussions that took place.[45]

Around the central issue of race, however, there emerged a general consensus, if not a unanimous voice. This consensus began first and foremost with the discrediting of any biological basis for definitions of race, placing emphasis rather on a fundamental "unity of humanity." The conference organizers had issued in their general announcements of the conference a broad request for papers that would in some way address the issue of race and its relation to international cooperation around the globe. While the general call was very vague, Gustav Spiller – the "Honorary Organiser" of the URC, as well as an active participant in and historian of the Ethical Culture movement – had appended a questionnaire, consisting of questions such as the following:

(a) To what extent is it legitimate to argue from differences in physical characteristics to differences in mental characteristics? (b) Do you consider that the physical and mental characteristics observable in a particular race are (1) permanent (2) modifiable only through ages of environmental pressure, or (3) do you consider that marked changes in popular education, in public sentiment, and in environment generally, may, apart from intermarriage, materially transform physical and especially mental characteristics in a generation or two?

In keeping with the political motivations of the organizers, he also asked: "How would you combat the irreconcilable contentions prevalent among all the more important races of mankind that *their* customs, *their* civilisation, and *their* race are superior to those of other races?"[46] The responses that came in greatly surprised the organizers. In particular, there was near unanimity on the idea of "the monogenetic theory of the origin of the different races," or the idea that all humans developed fundamentally from the same biological species.[47]

For scholars such as Paul Rich, the consolidation of this "monogenetic" conception of the human species was the single most important accomplishment of the event.[48] Rich situates the URC's discussions of race within a nineteenth-century set of debates between "monogenists" and "polygenists," as to whether the human species had emerged from one or many original "stocks." He notes that Darwinism initiated a break from explicit debates about origins, as attention shifted to variations and patterns of evolution. Yet he argues that the issue returned implicitly towards the end of the century when physical anthropologists turned to craniometry and anthropometry as means of documenting different racial "types." Other scholars have suggested that, technically speaking, the monogenetic thesis was already established by the time of Darwin, since most race scientists were willing to concede that humanity must constitute one species in so far as reproduction across racial groups was possible and common.[49] Nevertheless, the search for evidence that races constituted radically different sub-species took the place of the strictly polygenist arguments of the earlier nineteenth century.[50] In a study of the professionalization of anthropology in the United States, Lee Baker observes how one strain of Social Darwinist thought in anthropology took up where the polygenists left off, and came to dominate the field's approach to race.[51] Less interested in the question of origins, this school of thought emphasized the problem of cultural evolution. Led especially by Daniel Brinton in the United States, this school tended to fuse the biological with the cultural, and maintained that some "races" were not equipped to evolve into advanced states of civilisation.[52] It was at these positions – both the explicitly polygenist and the newer cultural evolutionist – that Spiller's questionaire had been aimed; and it was their presupposition of "race" as being distinct and unalterable that the URC challenged.

Admittedly, the anthropologists at the URC debated the issues rather heatedly, and without definite resolution.[53] To the non-specialists, however, the monogenist thesis was not passé, and they were quick to latch onto it in order to reach their political conclusions. Adler, for instance, took it to mean that "at least one of the principal arguments, or rather pretexts, for the proud scorn of one race by another is destroyed."[54] It may be significant in this regard that the executive council changed the name for the proposed second conference from the "Second Universal Races Congress" to "Second World Conference: for Promoting Concord Between all Divisions of Mankind," as the biologically laden notion of "race" no longer held relevance for participants at the URC.[55]

The case of Franz Boas who, in the words of Vernon Williams, initiated "the anti-racist creed in American social science," is an interesting example in this regard.[56] At the time of the URC, Boas was in the midst of his own transition from physical to cultural anthropology and of his battle against the cultural evolutionists. Since the 1890s Boas had opposed the tendency of physical anthropology and cultural evolution to view cultural development as a direct manifestation of physical potential, even while himself relying at times on physical anthropological data.[57] By the time of the URC, however, Boas was beginning to make a more definite break from anthropometrics altogether. It was thus that his written contribution to the Congress explicitly challenged the premises upon which anthropometrics were based. He drew particular attention to the effects of environment on the physical growth of individuals. For instance, he examined physical characteristics of members of a single family who were born alternately in Europe and North America, and drew attention to specific moments in an individual's physical development in which environmental factors such as nutrition were especially important.[58] Arguing that "an absolute stability of human types is not plausible," he effectively shifted the question of "race" or "human types" onto one of *individual* variation amidst an otherwise universal humanity. Gone was the idea that "race" could operate as a natural intermediary group for identity purposes.

If Boas's argument was the most radical, in so far as it explicitly used the methods of physical anthropology to move from the rhetoric of race to that of individuals and universal humanity, it was typical of URC participants' efforts generally to challenge the idea that race denoted anything fixed or permanent. In their ambition to depict race as both dynamic and contingent, most participants drew attention in particular to the cultural pressures that induced group identity formation. The French sociologist Alfred Fouillée,

for instance, offered the Congress what might be called a cultural construc-
tivist understanding of how group identities have formed to produce notions
of race. He stressed how important self-conceptions of racial identity in a
group are, in that they "[impart] to each of its members a kind of racial
personality" that elicits "a tendency to affirm this personality more and more
strongly, to oppose it to other racial types and secure its predominance."[59]
J. Tengo Jabavu, of Kingwilliamstown, South Africa, who was to become
president of the South African Races Congress of 1912, employed a similar
framework in his account of the formation of racial groupings in South
Africa. He detailed how individuals in southern Africa came to describe
themselves as Bantu, and to designate all who did not "answer to this
description" as being somehow different, "either by their colour or by some
striking peculiarity in their physique."[60] If this attention to the contingency
of group identity formation circled most pressingly and frequently around
issues of race, it was not confined to that one phenomenon. Indeed, D. S.
Margoliouth, a professor of Arabic at Oxford, issued an ardent critique of
nationalism using a parallel logic. He emphasized the primacy of language in
group and national formation, while noting the essential instability of
languages and of language-based group identities.[61]

The universalist commitments that underwrote these efforts to denatu-
ralize group identities turned most forcefully to concerns about individuals
in the Congress's advocacy of universal human rights. At the urging of
Emile Arnaud, a French representative, the Congress proclaimed "the
universality of the principles contained in the Rights of Man, made at the
time of the French Revolution, and notably the following: Men are born
and live equal and free under the law."[62] What is especially interesting here
is that the Congress was not content to leave the protection of human rights
to their traditional guarantors: sovereign nation states. Rather, it called
expressly for an "International Tribunal for the Rights of Man and of the
Rights of Nations." To be sure, the idea that human rights could best be
defended at an international level was not unique to the URC. Nor was it
especially realistic, exceeding by a stretch the institutional capacity of existing international cooperation. But it coalesced remarkably well with the
general critique coming out of the URC not only of "race," but also of
naturalized group identities generally, because it bespoke the premise that
individuals might exist most fundamentally as members of humanity. While
in the more anthropological discussions, it was "race" as a category that the
individual seemed to transcend, here in the political discussion of human
rights, it was the nation state that the individual should exceed in order to
participate in universal humanity.

In terms of the formation of global civil society, it is easy here to see the classically universalist and activist dimensions of the URC. At a purely normative level, organizers and participants envisioned all individual human beings as equal members of humanity, as individuals first and foremost, with specific geographical, national, cultural, or linguistic identities only secondly. If they lacked the means to enact this normative vision in global political institutions, they sought to enact the vision in the framework of the URC itself. They successfully brought together individuals from all parts of the globe, and guaranteed that all individuals at the meeting spoke as equals.

Negotiating cultural difference

The emphasis on individuals as members of universal humanity represented only one strain of discussion at the URC. Although many at the Congress understood individuals to transcend intermediary groups such as "nation," "race," or "culture," to which they belonged, very few of them sought to deny the reality and thus the relevance of those intermediary or local groups. For most participants, however, there was no contradiction between the "unity of humanity" thesis and the celebration of cultural difference. Felix Adler, for instance, was very explicit about this. "The thesis of the essential unity of mankind," he took pains to clarify:

> was not taken in the sense of universal sameness, it was not understood to mean that each of the several component groups of humanity is capable of reaching the same degree of excellence along every line. The unity spoken of is an organic unity. It implies that the same essential faculties are present in all, and that it is to be assumed that every group is capable of contributing to the common stock something uniquely its own, something that in the full fruition of civilization can not be spared.[63]

Brajendranath Seal expressed a similar sentiment in his rather optimistic depiction of history as an evolution towards a "Universal Humanity." He did not understand this Universal Humanity to be a homogeneous entity, but rather to be something that would grant universal equality while "respecting each National Personality, and each scheme of National values and ideals."[64] To aid both in mutual understanding between cultures and in self-understanding of a culture, Seal stressed in particular the importance of self-representation. He proposed not only further meetings such as the URC, at which "thinkers from the East [would] be regularly invited to explain their own national or racial cultures and standpoints at meetings organised by the different branches in the West; and *vice versa*," but also the establishment of endowed professorships and even an international journal through which individuals from diverse cultures would educate others about their own cultures.[65]

With less emphasis on the notion of "Universal Humanity," or the "unity of humanity," Jabavu echoed this theme of cultural self-representation in his depiction of the destruction that European settlement had brought to Bantu culture. In particular, he lamented the destruction of the "old tribal system," and with it, "the wholesome restraints of tribal law and custom and morality." As a remedy, he called in particular for self-education and the establishment of a South African College to be run by and for indigenous South Africans.[66] Mojola Agbebi similarly commented upon the destruction of social order in West Africa following the imposition of European institutions, noting that the lack of knowledge about African cultures among colonial rulers had brought considerable social disruption. Consequently, he called for "the cultivation of knowledge of the African," in a fashion that "is calculated to engender respect and consideration for him and his institutions."[67] He concluded that, although the Congress had been established primarily to foster mutual knowledge and respect between Occidental and Oriental peoples," its organizing principles and ambitions would "go a long way towards the solution of the African problem."[68]

At this level of intellectual exchange, the URC seemed to be negotiating rather successfully a commitment to universalism on the one hand, and a valorization of cultural difference on the other. The commitment to universalism occurred first at the level of biology, in the insistence on a singular human species. This claim coincided with a universalist commitment to individual human rights. It was at the level of culture, tradition, and history that the overall tone of the URC celebrated difference. To this point, there was no contradiction. As we have seen, however, a divide often existed in Ethical Culture and at the URC between theory and practice. In this regard, the comfortable negotiation of universalism and cultural difference at the URC was no different, and proved less comfortable when practical political considerations arose. In this light, it is interesting to note that organizers of the URC had sought from the outset to exclude explicitly "political" matters from the Congress. The initial announcement of the conference stated that "all schools of thought which sympathise with the Object of the Congress are hereby invited to take part in the proceedings," and that "*resolutions of a political character will not be submitted.*"[69] It further stated in no uncertain terms that "*the Congress is pledged to no political party and to no particular scheme of reforms.*"[70] Were the URC just an academic conference, such an exclusion might not be all that surprising. And it certainly coincided with the idealist premises of the International Ethical Union because its members wanted to demonstrate how the exploration of ideas would itself transform material and political reality. But the URC was more activist than academic, and its effort to exclude practical political matters was not entirely successful. Amidst a general sentiment at the URC for dismantling imperial rule around the globe, the question of self-government for all peoples arose repeatedly in papers, discussion, and formal resolutions by the Congress Business Meeting. It was consequently here, in considering what political self-government meant and the circumstances under which it could be realized as a global norm, that the URC's supple negotiation of universalism and cultural difference gave way to a harder and less accommodating universalism.

The arguments for self-government tended to coincide with the moral aims of the Congress. A special "suggestion" formally adopted by the Congress Business Meeting is illuminating in this regard. Originally proposed by Sir Charles Bruce of Scotland, it read as follows:

> In the treatment of dependent peoples and communities the modern conscience rejects as a fallacy the claim of Western civilisation to a monopoly of the capacity of self-government based on an indivisible inter-relation between European descent, Christianity, and the so-called white colour. It recognises that, while this inter-relation has evolved a capacity for self-government in an appropriate environment, a similar capacity has been evolved by an inter-relation of other races, creeds, and colours appropriate to other environments. It maintains, therefore, that the conflict between West and East must be adjusted on the same principle that has adjusted the conflicts of race and creed in the West, the principle of freedom interpreted as liberty of person and conscience and equality of opportunity for all, without distinction of race, creed, or colour under a settled government.[71]

In this passage, the themes of fundamental human equality together with that of cultural difference appeared complementary once again, providing the justification for dismantling colonial rule and replacing it with self-government for all defined social groups. In short, the premises of human equality and cultural difference were to be the basis for extending the Westphalian system of state sovereignty to all societies around the globe.

But when the discussion turned to *how* this moral ideal of a world made up solely of self-governing societies might be realized, the notion of cultural difference lost ground. Here the basic premise was that colonized groups needed to be "prepared" for self-government. To this effect, the Congress Business Meeting passed a "special resolution" to support the institution of "public international law guaranteeing equality to nations of divers races, facilitating the entrance of civilised peoples into the community of nations, and stipulating the duty of now existing nations of preparing the emancipation and autonomy of said peoples."[72] This officially adopted sentiment was prevalent among attendees at the URC. Already in 1900 Adler had been very clear on this issue in his opposition to the US occupation of the

Philippines. Adler undoubtedly favored self-government for all people. On this note, he maintained: "It is far better for a people to learn to manage its own affairs, even if it is at the sacrifice of certain of the benefits of good government; better to have less good government, and more of the power, gradually acquired, of securing in the end good government."[73] It was in this regard that he denounced in particular British rule in India for failing to facilitate Indian independence. Nevertheless, Adler held that self-government should not occur prematurely. But with reference to the Philippines, Adler had not argued for immediate withdrawal. Rather, he argued for independence, "not necessarily immediate independence, but independence, finally."[74] Once the occupation had begun, he maintained, the US had a duty to *prepare* the Philippines for self-government. Likewise, John Robertson, a Member of Parliament from London, explicitly maintained at the URC that the monogenist thesis regarding the human species "precluded the idea of the inherent superiority of any race whatever," and that consequently no group could legitimately rule over another. Even so, he could only endorse "the *ultimate* possible freedom by all races alike [my emphasis]," much as Adler had done a decade earlier in regard to the Philippines.[75]

It was here, in the discussions of what was to constitute preparedness for self-government that interest in cultural difference tended to fall by the wayside. The official stance of the Congress Business Meeting was to endorse the sovereign nation state as the single desirable telos of all societies. While this emphasis on nation states as the most desirable model for global organization might not have implied cultural uniformity, delegates could only conceive of "preparedness" for sovereign nation state status in one uniform fashion. The Congress Business Meeting resolved accordingly to encourage "in all lands a universal and efficient system of education – physical, intellectual, and moral." Moreover, it moved "to collect records of experiments showing the successful uplifting of relatively backward peoples by the application of humane methods, and to urge the application of such methods universally."[76] So much for respect for cultural difference; universal education to a very particular model of self-government became the order of the day. The pleas by Jabavu and Agbebi, both of whom had stressed the importance of culturally specific moral norms, education, and structure of social order were irrelevant to the discussion of political aims. To be sure, some saw a paradox in the URC's stance, in so far as it tended to repudiate the sentiment of respect for cultural difference. Robertson had noted of the paradox of political autonomy as he and many like-minded progressive thinkers conceived of it: "It really amounts to confessing that all peoples who have not hitherto governed themselves are relatively undeveloped; that, in short, self-government is the pre-requisite of any high level of social organisation and general capacity."[77] In other words, a society needs to have been self-governed in order to have built up the customs and institutions such that it would be prepared for self-government on the model of the European nation state. This contradiction, he noted, "is not always avowed." And yet, the resolutions by the Congress Business Meeting regarding universal education and universal moral advancement held firm.

Towards a conclusion: global civil society, then and now

Because of the outbreak of World War I, the URC did not meet in 1915 as planned, and in fact never convened again. As a result, the outcome of the event was very diffuse. As already noted, many participants celebrated the event as a consolidation of a humanist, anti-imperialist ethic and of the monogenist thesis in race science. Historians have been more inclined to point to the intellectual energy and confidence the URC inspired in its participants for future, less universal ventures. Both Elliott Rudwick and Robert Grave and Madhavi Kale, for instance, cite the URC as significant for DuBois (who saw the meeting as the most significant event of the young twentieth century), first, in providing him with a community of peers sharing a world vision; and second, in indicating the relevance of the international stage for problems pertaining to race.[78] Likewise, Akinola Akiwowo notes the significant place of the URC in the biography of Mojolo Agbebi. While Akiwowo does not credit the URC as the impetus to Agbebi's involvement in the pan-African movement, he does identify the URC with being a significant step in giving Agbebi international prominence, and in Agbebi's understanding of the international dimension of race politics.[79] Probably the most concrete outcome of the event in terms of its race politics was Muhamed Ali Duse's founding of the *African Times and Orient Review*, a short-lived periodical (running from 1912 to 1918) intended to foster communication between races and nations around the globe. While Duse did not identify the periodical as an official organ of the URC, he did insist that it was directly inspired by the conference.[80]

In the realm of world politics, the aftermath of the URC is equally diffuse. To an extent, the founding of the League of Nations realized some of the aims of the Inter-parliamentary Union, which had co-sponsored the event and had always made the cause of arbitration between antagonistic states its foremost aim. Not all participants from the URC, however, were so enthusiastic about the League – including Felix Adler. Already at the URC, Adler had expressed his reservations about a "parliament of man" or a "federation of the world,"[81] something he feared would provide only the facade of human equality around the world, while neglecting the real ends of Ethical Culture, namely the moral recognition of human equality. He expanded this argument in his response to the League of Nations after the war. He had contested the Allies' presentation of the war as the preservation of democracy, viewing it rather as a battle for imperial power. The League of Nations, he subsequently held, served as a progressive cover for the victors' pursuits of territorial acquisition.[82] For Adler, then, neither the League of Nations nor any comparable institution would be in a position to realize the goals that Ethical Culture had envisioned with the URC so long as the globe was dominated by imperial powers. Given these diverse responses by participants at the URC to the League of Nations, it seems fair to say that some of the common ground that participants had found on largely cultural matters depended precisely on the fact that a political institution such as the League of Nations had only been a hypothetical possibility – and hence could be bracketed out of discussion – in 1911.

I want to conclude, then, not on this diffuse outcome of the event, but rather on the phenomenon that the URC illustrated so well, namely the phenomenon of conflicting universalisms and the specific form it took at the turn of the century, as nationalism was at its height and internationalism was finding its own uncertain feet.[83] On the one hand, we have the idealist-universalist conception of humanity that had promoted respect for cultural difference. The URC called into question the naturalness of group identities, claims to which tended to support notions of racial or national hierarchies. In doing so, it asserted fundamental human equality and the absolute priority of individuals over groups. On the other hand, the URC advocated a universalism that emphasized political autonomy in a community of sovereign nations that would erode that same cultural difference by cultural assimilation. In this sense, the URC sought to promote universal human rights and equality, even as its preconceptions regarding state sovereignty and coincident cultural norms exerted normative pressures on non-European cultures to conform. One might conclude that this dimension of the URC's project reverted from the notion of cultural difference to a logic akin to the eighteenth- and nineteenth-century anthropological argument about "civilization" that presupposed a universal humanity in which different societies exhibited specific phases along a universally shared path of progress.[84] In this case, the achievement of sovereign nation state status came to signify in the official pronouncements of the URC the most advanced states of human societal development.

Given this situation of conflicting universalisms at the URC, we must ask what this assessment prompts us to say about the early formation of global civil society at the turn of the century. First, it is safe to conclude that the

URC had a vision of a world community on two levels: that of individuals as part of universal humanity; and that of interaction between social groups (races, nations, cultures, language groups). To recall Kaldor's terminology, we can say that the URC was operating between universalist and postmodern conceptions of civil society. We can also say that this divide for the URC occurred between its normative moral ambitions and its contention with existing communities and political-institutional rules regulating their co-existence. In terms of its normative moral ambitions to negotiate universalist notions of the individual with valorization of existing cultural differences, the URC might thus be seen as leaning towards, or yearning for, something that would be referred to anachronistically as "postmodern global civil society," with its ironic negotiation of universalism and difference. But when the realities of imperial domination and related concerns for political autonomy asserted themselves, another variant of universalism returned that precluded cultural difference and rendered that postmodern irony moot. Seen in this light, the dilemma of the URC centered not around negotiation of cultural difference, but rather around competing versions of universalism.

This is in no way intended as a general criticism of the ambitions of the URC and its organizers. The URC was one of the most progressive initiatives of its era. Rather, it is simply to caution against reading turn-of-the-century internationalist activism too quickly as a seamless precursor to recent globalizing developments. One way to put this is to suggest that the implied multiculturalism of both the "new cosmopolitanism" and "postmodern global civil society" may be easier to assert and maintain in a postcolonial world than in a world in which imperialism and heightened nationalisms were the reality to be challenged. In that world, the progressive position that sought to challenge claims to national, cultural, and racial difference and superiority sometimes required critics to promote an unyielding universalism – even if at the cost of the very cultural difference that they wanted to celebrate.

On another level, however, the challenges that the URC faced were not so different from issues confronting more recent efforts to conceive of global civil society. To be sure, the framework of international governmental institutions has increased exponentially in the last century, and with it has grown in the civil sphere a wealth of global activism. And yet nothing like a world government has arisen to succeed the full range of operations performed by the nation state. Certainly political theorists debate how relevant the nation state is, given the range of international conventions that now curtail national sovereignty. Yet few are eager to renounce regional, still less national, institutions altogether, even as they may defend on a moral-normative level notions of universal humanity and universal human rights.

Arguments can be made in the political realm that regional political entities – be they nation states or sub-national entities – are necessary to preserve a sense of participatory politics. In the cultural realm, ethnic and religious affiliations are supposed to preserve a diversity of cultural traditions that is said to enhance human experience. It is in this regard, then, that the URC's strained efforts to negotiate something like universal humanity together with cultural specificity ran up against a set of problems that is also highly relevant to more recent globalization debates. If participants at the URC addressed this complex in ways that reflected the specific currents of their era – namely, through reference to heightened nationalisms, the reign of imperialisms, and claims to racial superiority – it was their eagerness to confront the issues as a global phenomenon that perhaps sets them apart from their context, and that enables their deliberations to transcend their immediate context in order to contribute to debates on similar issues today.

Notes

1   "Circulars Issued by the Executive Council," in Gustav Spiller (ed.), *Papers on Inter-Racial Problems Communicated to the First Universal Races Congress Held at the University of London July 26–29, 1911* (London, 1911; Boston, MA, 1911), p. xiii.

2   Felix Adler, "Report of the First Universal Races Congress, Held at London July 26–29, 1911," in the *Report of the Commissioner of Education for the Year Ended June 30, 1911, Vol. 1* (Washington, DC, 1912), p. 609; *Record of the Proceedings of the First Universal Races Congress Held at the University of London July 26–29, 1911* (London, 1911), p. 5.

3   Ibid., p. 11.

4   Notice in *Crisis* VIII (1914), p. 166, cited in Elliott M. Rudwick, "W. E. B. DuBois and the Universal Races Congress of 1911," *Phylon*, 20 (1959), p. 375; Michael D. Biddiss, "The Universal Races Congress of 1911," *Race*, XIII (1971), p. 45.

5   A. G. Hopkins, "Globalization: An Agenda for Historians," in Hopkins (ed.), *Globalization in World History* (New York, 2002), pp. 6–11.

6   See ibid., p. 7; and Tony Ballantyne, "Empire, Knowledge, and Culture: From Proto-Globalization to Modern Globalization," in Hopkins (ed.), *Globalization in World History*, pp. 116–40. See also Ann Laura Stoler and Frederick Cooper, "Between Metropole and Colony: Rethinking a Research Agenda," in Stoler and Cooper (eds), *Tensions of Empire: Colonial Cultures in a Bourgeois World* (Berkeley, CA, Los Angeles and London, 1997), pp. 1–3; and Robert John Holton, "Cosmopolitanism or Cosmopolitanisms? The Universal Races Congress of 1911," *Global Networks*, 2 (2002), pp. 156–8.

7   If with a slightly different emphasis, many scholars of European Enlightenment and modernity have argued that the contentious relationship

between universalism and particularism is not dependent on national appropriations per se, but rather is an intrinsic product of the Enlightenment tout court.
See for instance, Harold Mah, *Enlightenment Phantasies: Cultural Identity in France
and Germany, 1750–1914* (Ithaca, NY, 2003); Judith Butler, Ernesto Laclau and
Slavoj Žižek, *Contingency, Hegemony, Universality: Contemporary Dialogues on the
Left* (London and New York, 2000). See also the full issue of *Differences*, 7
(1995), which was devoted to the topic of universalism in the light of post-
structuralism.

8   Irony as a category was long an important tool of literary criticism, but came to
have a broader relevance in the era of postmodernism. Conventionally, irony
referred to statements that were meant to imply the opposite of what was literally stated. It relied upon the notion that there was a "true" condition, and that
the ironic statement referred thus in an oblique way to the true condition,
though often in a critical or revelatory fashion. It was supposed to provide a
means to get beyond superficiality to expose what lies beneath the surface. In
the era of postmodernism, however, the notion of truth itself, along with grand
narratives, came under question. In such a situation, "irony" came to refer to
statements that were made despite the knowing awareness that there was no
fundamental "truth" to which they referred. Richard Rorty provides a particularly helpful definition of the "ironist" as one "who fulfills three conditions:
(1) She has radical and continuing doubts about the final vocabulary she
currently uses, because she has been impressed by other vocabularies, vocabularies taken as final by people or books she has encountered; (2) she realizes that
argument phrased in her present vocabulary can neither underwrite nor dissolve
these doubts; (3) insofar as she philosophizes about her situation, she does not
think that her vocabulary is closer to reality than others, that it is in touch with
a power not herself. Ironists who are inclined to philosophize see the choice
between vocabularies as made neither within a neutral and universal metavo-
cabulary nor by an attempt to fight one's way past appearances to the real, but
simply by playing the new off against the old." See Richard Rorty, *Contingency,
Irony, and Solidarity* (Cambridge, 1989), 73. For further discussion of irony, see
also Linda Hutcheon, *Irony's Edge: The Theory and Politics of Irony* (London,
1994); Hutcheon, "Power of Postmodern Irony," in B. Rutland (ed.), *Genre,
Trope, Gender: Essays by Northrop Frye, Linda Hutcheon, and Shirley Neuman*
(Ottawa, 1996), pp. 33–50.

9   Paul Rich, "'The Baptism of a New Order': The 1911 Universal Races
Congress and the Liberal Ideology of Race," *Ethnic and Racial Studies*, 7 (1984),
pp. 534–50. See also Rich, *Race and Empire in British Politics* (Cambridge and
New York, 1990), esp. pp. 44–9.

10   Susan D. Pennybacker, 'The Universal Races Congress, London Political
Culture, and Imperial Dissent, 1900–1939," *Radical History Review*, 92 (2005),
pp. 103–17.

11   Rudwick, "W. E. B. DuBois," pp. 372–8. See also Akinsola Akiwowo's treatment of Mojola Agbebi, which does not take the URC as its primary focus, but

does note its role in the intellectual and political biography of Agbebi and his part in the development of the pan-African movement. Akinsola Akiwowo, "The Place of Mojola Agbebi in the African Nationalist Movements: 1890–1917," *Phylon*, 26 (1965), pp. 122–39. For more of a survey account of the event, see Michael Biddiss, "The Universal Races Congress of 1911," *Race*, XIII (1971), pp. 37–46.

12   Paul Gilroy, *Black Atlantic: Modernity and Double Consciousness* (Cambridge, MA, 1993), p. 144.

13   Robert John Holton, "Cosmopolitanism or Cosmopolitanisms? The Universal Races Congress of 1911," *Global Networks*, 2 (2002), p. 155; paraphrasing an argument from Bruce Robbins, "Actually Existing Cosmopolitanism," in Pheng Cheah and Bruce Robbins (eds), *Cosmopolitics: Thinking and Feeling Beyond the Nation* (Minneapolis, MN, 1998). Treating two URC participants from Iran and the Ottoman Empire, Mansour Bonakdarian has recently added to the "global" interpretations of the event. Bonakdarian examines how the Iranian and Ottoman representatives negotiated the universalism of Western scientific claims and the particularities of local knowledge. Of the existing literature, Bonakdarian's interpretation most closely matches my own. I, however, identify these tensions in the overall logic of the URC. See Mansour Bonakdarian, "Negotiating Universal Values and Cultural and National Parameters at the First Universal Races Congress," *Radical History Review*, 92 (2005), pp. 118–32.

14   The advocacy may also include non-human animals. On "world community," see especially Akira Iriye, *Global Community: The Role of International Organizations in the Making of the Contemporary World* (Berkeley, CA, 2002). The notion was also present in his earlier book, *Cultural Internationalism and World Order* (Baltimore, MD, 1997).

15   Further uses abound. See for example contributions in David Held and Anthony McGrew (eds), *The Global Transformations Reader: An Introduction to the Globalization Debate*, 2nd edition (Cambridge, 2003). See in particular Michael Mann, "Has Globalization Ended the Rise and Rise of the Nation-State?," pp. 135–46; David Held, "Cosmopolitanism: Taming Globalization," pp. 514–29; and Held, "The Changing Structure of International Law: Sovereignty Transformed?," pp. 162–76; Susan Strange, "The Declining Authority of States," pp. 127–34; Jessica Matthews, "Power Shift," pp. 204–12.

16   Mary Kaldor, *Global Civil Society: An Answer to War* (Cambridge, 2003), pp. 6–10. For a very comprehensive analysis of the phenomenon of global civil society, see the yearbooks produced by the London School of Economics: Mary Kaldor, Helmut Anheier and Marlies Glasius (eds), *Global Civil Society, Vols 1–3* (Oxford and New York, 2001–03).

17   Two theorists who have dominated the literature on nationalism are Benedict Anderson and Ernest Gellner. See Anderson, *Imagined Communities: Reflections on the Origin and Spread of Nationalism* (New York, 1991); Ernest Gellner,

Encounters with Nationalism (Oxford and Cambridge, MA, 1994); Gellner, *Nations and Nationalisms* (Oxford and Cambridge, MA, 1983). See also Eric Hobsbawm, *Nations and Nationalism since 1780: Programme, Myth, Reality* (Cambridge and New York, 1990). Examples of the more cultural focus on the production of national belonging can be found in the work of George Mosse, *Nationalism and Sexuality: Middle-Class Morality and Sexual Norms in Modern Europe* (Madison, WI, 1985); *Nationalization of the Masses: Political Symbolism and Mass Movements in Germany from the Napoleonic Wars through the Third Reich* (Ithaca, NY and London, 1975). A very good, recent example of the focus on the more state-oriented political strategies of producing national identity can be found in Geoff Eley, "Making a Place in the Nation: Meanings of 'Citizenship' in Wilhelmine Germany," in Eley, *Wilhelminism and Its Legacies: German Modernities, Imperialism, and the Meanings of reform, 1890–1930* (New York and Oxford, 2003), pp. 16–33. On viewing this rise in nationalism within the history of globalization, see A. G. Hopkins, "The History of Globalization and the Globalization of History?" in Hopkins, *Globalization in World History*, pp. 12–44.

18   Some examples include: John Boli and George M. Thomas (eds), *Constructing World Culture: International Nongovernmental Organizations since 1875* (Stanford, CA, 1999); Akira Iriye, *Cultural Internationalism and World Order*; Iriye, *Global Community*; H. L. S. Lyons, *Internationalism in Europe 1815–1914* (Leiden, 1963); Leila J. Rupp, *Worlds of Women: The Making of an International Women's Movement* (Princeton, NJ, 1997); Paul Weindling (ed.), *International Health Organisations and Movements, 1918–1939* (Cambridge, 1995); Margaret E. Keck and Kathryn Sikkink (eds), *Activists Beyond Borders: Advocacy Networks in International Politics* (Ithaca, NY and London, 1998).

19   Iriye, *Global Community*, pp. 11–12.

20   Ibid., p. 8.

21   John Boli and George M. Thomas, "INGOs and the Organization of World Culture," in Boli and Thomas (eds), *Constructing World Culture: International Nongovernmental Organizations Since 1875* (Stanford, CA, 1999), pp. 14, 23; Robert O. Keohane and Joseph S. Nye Jr, "Globalization: What's New? What's Not? (And So What?)," in Held and McGrew, *The Global Transformations Reader*, p. 182.

22   Iriye, *Global Community*, p. 11; Boli and Thomas, "INGOs and the Organization of World Culture," p. 22.

23   This International Union of Ethical Societies also went by the name of the International Ethical Union.

24   For a comprehensive account of INGOs at the turn of the century, see Lyons, *Internationalism in Europe*.

25   Susan Pennybacker identifies nineteenth-century slavery and the war in Southern Africa as the real incentives behind the meeting. This essay focuses more on the *institutional* origins of the URC. See Pennybacker, "Universal Races Congress," p. 106.

26 Information for this paragraph comes from: Lyons, *Internationalism in Europe*, pp. 327–9; and Christian Lange, "The Interparliamentary Union," *International Conciliation*, 65 (1913), pp. 3–14.

27 Howard B. Radest, *Felix Adler: An Ethical Culture* (New York, 1998), p. 10. The most thorough account of Adler's turn away from Reform Judaism is Benny Kraut, *From Reform Judaism to Ethical Culture: The Religious Evolution of Felix Adler* (Cincinnati, OH, 1979). See also Horace L. Friess, *Felix Adler and Ethical Culture: Memories and Studies*, ed. Fannia Weingartner (New York, 1981); James F. Hornback, *The Philosophic Sources and sanctions of the Founders of Ethical Culture* (New York, 1983).

28 Friess, *Felix Adler and Ethical Culture*, p. 49. Adopted from one of Adler's early speeches, the motto of the organization was: "Diversity in the Creed, unanimity in the deed."

29 Ibid., pp. 81ff.

30 On British variants of Ethical Culture see Gustav Spiller, *The Ethical Movement in Great Britain: A Documentary History* (London, 1934); Ian Duncan MacKillop, *The British Ethical Societies* (Cambridge and New York, 1986). On the German Society for Ethical Culture, see Horst Groschopp, *Dissidenten: Freidenkrei und Kultur in Deutschland* (Berlin,1997); Frank Simon-Ritz, *Organization einer Weltanschauung: die Freigeistige Bewegung im Wilhelminischen Deutschland* (Gütersloh, 1997).

31 See Spiller, *Ethical Movement in Great Britain*, pp. 186–95; Felix Adler, "The International Ethical Congress," in Adler, *Ethical Addresses III* (October 1896), pp. 133–50.

32 Wilhelm Börner, *Die ethische Bewegung* (Gautzsch bei Leipzig, 1912), pp. 11–12.

33 "In our times," Georg von Gizycki, a founder of the German Society for Ethical Culture, noted, "it is often harder to recognize what is good than it is to do that which is already recognized as good." Georg von Gizycki, Letter to Editor in *Vorwärts: Berliner Volksblatt*, 9 (October 25, 1892), p. 3.

34 "Manifesto of the Delegates at the First Congress of the International Ethical Union in Zurich, September, 1896," reprinted in Spiller, *The Ethical Movement in Great Britain*, pp. 186–7.

35 Paul S. Reinsch, "Influence of Geographic, Economic, and Political Conditions," in Spiller, *Papers on Inter-Racial Problems*, pp. 49–50.

36 Lord Weardale, *The First Universal Races Congress*, Vol. 42 of *International Conciliation* (1911, reprinted in Buffalo, NY, 1997), p. 7.

37 Ibid., p. 3.

38 Ibid., p. 4.

39 Ibid., p. 3.

40 Ibid., p. 5. On China and the West, please see the contribution in this volume by Roger Hart.

41 Friess, *Felix Adler and Ethical Culture*, pp. 194–5.

42 Felix Adler, *Can We Afford to Rule Subject Peoples?* (New York, 1890). See also Felix Adler, "The Philippines: Two Ethical Questions," in Adler, *Ethical*

Addresses (Philadelphia, PA, 1902), pp. 171–90. The two ethical questions were: "1. Is it treason to condemn a war waged by our country while the war is still in progress? 2. Are civilized nations justified in adopting uncivilized methods of warfare?" (p. 171).

43 Adler, "Report of the First Universal Races Congress," p. 617.

44 Gustav Spiller, "Preface", in *Papers on Inter-Racial Problems*, pp. v–vi.

45 Susan Pennybacker rightly insists that there was no shared political project at the URC. Pennybacker, "Universal Races Congress," p. 106. There were, however, shared tensions. These shared tensions are the object of the present analysis.

46 Spiller, "Questionnaire," pp. xiv–xv.

47 Adler, "Report of the First Universal Races Congress," p. 611.

48 Rich, " 'The Baptism of a New Era,' " p. 536.

49 See Paul Weindling, *Health, Race and German Politics Between National Unification and Nazism, 1870–1945* (Cambridge, 1989), p. 49; Nancy Stepan, "Biology and Degeneration: Races and Proper Places," in J. Edward Chamberlin and Sander L. Gilman (eds), *Degeneration: The Dark Side of Progress* (New York, 1985), pp. 97–120.

50 Ibid., pp. 536–7. For other accounts of turn-of-the-century anthropological understandings of race, see George Stocking, *Race, Culture, and Evolution: Essays in the History of Anthropology* (New York, 1968); Vernon J. Williams, *Rethinking Race: Franz Boas and His Contemporaries* (Lexington, KY, 1996); Rich, *Race and Empire*; George Mosse, *Toward the Final Solution: A History of European Racism* (New York, 1978).

51 Lee D. Baker, *From Savage to Negro: Anthropology and the Construction of Race, 1896–1954* (Berkeley, CA, 1998).

52 Ibid., esp. pp. 32–8.

53 See especially the "First Session: Fundamental Considerations," in Spiller, *Papers on Inter-Racial Problems*, pp. 1–39; and "Opening Proceedings – Discussion of Anthropological Problems," in *Record of the Proceedings*, pp. 22–8. For an interesting analysis of competing theories of race by DuBois and Felix von Luschan in the context outside of the URC, see John David Smith, "W. E. B. DuBois, Felix von Luschan, and Racial Reform at the *Fin de Siècle*," *Amerikastudien*, 47 (2002), pp. 23–38.

54 Adler, "Report of the First Universal Races Congress," p. 611.

55 *Record of the Proceedings*, p. 7.

56 Williams, *Rethinking Race*, p. 1. For an interesting discussion of Boas's efforts to professionalize anthropology and to universalize its practices, see Mauricio Tenorio, "Stereophonic Scientific Modernisms: Social Science Between Mexico and the United States, 1880s-1930s," *Journal of American History*, 86 (1999), pp. 1156–87.

57 Discussed in Williams, *Rethinking Race*, p. 10. See also Stocking, *Race, Culture, and Evolution*, esp. pp. 195–233.

58 Franz Boas, "Instability of Human Types," in Spiller, *Papers on Inter-Racial Problems*, p. 101.

59 Alfred Fouillée, "Race from the Sociological Standpoint," in Spiller, *Papers on Inter-Racial Problems*, p. 24. For more on Fouillée, see J. E. S. Hayward, "Solidarity and the Reformist Sociology of Alfred Fouillée," *American Journal of Economics and Sociology*, 22 (1963), pp. 205–22.

60 J. Tengo Jabavu, "Native Races of South Africa," in Spiller, *Papers on Inter-Racial Problems*, p. 336.

61 D. S. Margoliouth, "Language as a Consolidating and Separating Influence," in Spiller, *Papers on Inter-Racial Problems*, pp. 57–61.

62 *Record of the Proceedings*, p. 10.

63 Adler, "Report of the First Universal Races Congress," p. 611.

64 In this sense, Seal could be seen to be articulating a different reading of Hegel's world history than that offered in this volume by Roger Hart. According to Seal's logic, all cultures participate uniquely in the evolution of humanity, and are distinct, particular manifestations of the universal. No one culture – including Protestant Prussia – would be seen to be *more* universal than another.

65 Brajendranath Seal, "Meaning of Race, Tribe, Nation," in Spiller, *Papers on Inter-Racial Problems*, pp. 12–13.

66 Jabavu, "Native Races of South Africa," p. 341.

67 Mojola Agbebi, "The West African Problem," in Spiller, *Papers on Inter-Racial Problems*, p. 343.

68 Ibid., p. 348.

69 "Circulars Issued by the Executive Council," in Spiller, *Papers on Inter-Racial Problems*, p. xiii; emphasis in original.

70 Ibid., p. xiv; emphasis in original.

71 Ibid., p. 14.

72 *Record of the Proceedings*, p. 10.

73 Adler, *Can We Afford to Rule Subject Peoples?*, p. 10.

74 Ibid., p. 4.

75 *Record of the Proceedings*, p. 36.

76 Ibid., p. 8.

77 John M. Robertson, "The Rationale of Autonomy," in Spiller, *Papers on Inter-Racial Problems*, pp. 40–1.

78 Rudwick, "W. E. B. DuBois," p. 376.

79 Akiwowo, "The Place of Mojola Agbebi," pp. 122–39.

80 Gabriele Schirbel, *Strukturen des Internationalismus. First Universal Races Congress, London 1911* (Münster and Hamburg,1991), pp. 1065–6.

81 Felix Adler, "The Fundamental Principles of Inter-racial Ethics, and Some Practical Applications of It," in Spiller, *Papers on Inter-Racial Problems*, pp. 261–7.

82 Radest, *Felix Adler*, pp. 13, 122. See also Felix Adler, *The World Crisis and Its Meaning* (New York and London, 1915); and Adler, *The Moral Prerequisites of a League of Nations* (New York, 1919).

83 On this issue I find a schema put forth by Etienne Balibar very helpful. Balibar suggests rather that we consider three different manifestations of universalism:

"real," "fictive," and "ideal." According to this breakdown, "real" universalism speaks to the global unity that has resulted from economic, political, and technological developments of modernity. "Fictive" universalism speaks, on the other hand, to those Enlightenment ideals of human equality and the rights of man. It may also, however, carry with it the threat of normalization and/or exclusion, as individuals are expected to conform to the model of the ideal subject in order to qualify for universal equality and rights. "Ideal" universalism is resistance to normative constraints or exclusion in the name of equality on the part of individuals or groups. These categories are themselves ideal types. In any concrete situation, these various moments of universalism may interact in complex and even vacillating fashion. See Etienne Balibar, "Ambiguous Universality," *Differences*, 7 (1995), p. 48. For an explicit discussion of universalism and race, see also Balibar, "Racism as Universalism," in Balibar, *Masses, Classes, Ideas: Studies on Politics and Philosophy Before and After Marx* (New York, 1994). For a very good discussion that situates Balibar's explanation of universalism within other recent reconsiderations of the concept, see Amanda Anderson, "Cosmopolitanism, Universalism, and the Divided Legacies of Modernity," in Pheng Cheah and Bruce Robbins (eds), *Cosmopolitics: Thinking and Feeling Beyond the Nation* (Minneapolis, MN and London,1998), pp. 265–89.

84 See George W. Stocking, *Race, Culture, and Evolution: Essays in the History of Anthropology* (Chicago and London, 1982), pp. 195–233; George L. Mosse, *Toward the Final Solution: A History of European Racism* (New York, 1978), pp. 3–16. For select examples of more recent accounts of the multiple forms that racism and race-thinking can take, see: Ann Stoler, "Racial Histories and Their Regimes of Truth," *Political and Social Theory*, 11 (1997), pp. 183–206; Anthony Appiah and Amy Guttman, *Color Conscious: The Political Morality of Race* (Princeton, NJ, 1996); Mara Loveman, "Is 'Race' Essential?," *American Sociological Review*, 64 (1999), pp. 861–98; Jonathan Glassman, "Slower than a Massacre: The Multiple Sources of Racial Thought in Colonial Africa," *American Historical Review*, 109 (2004), pp. 720–54.

6

Talking Machine World: Selling the Local in the Global Music Industry, 1900–20

Karl Hagstrom Miller

In the summer of 1920, the *New York Evening Post* interviewed Edmond F. Sause about the state of the international recording industry. Sause was in a good position to answer the query. The middle-aged export manager had begun working in the phonograph trade in 1903 as a basement stock clerk at the Columbia Graphophone Company store in Manhattan. Eventually, Sause became a salesman and store manager. Literally rising through the ranks, he ascended to an office on the twentieth floor of the Woolworth building where he oversaw one of the largest international departments in the business. "Like the sewing machine, typewriter and cash register, the talking machine can be said to be an American product," Sause told the *Post*. "Its possibilities in foreign trade were appreciated practically from the beginning. While the industry was still struggling in home markets, progress was being made in developing foreign trade. Few American industries can show as large a percentage of foreign trade to its total turnover as the talking machine industry during the last twenty years." Sause's comments were brief, yet his message was clear: the phonograph, invented by Thomas Edison in 1877, may have been an American product, but its early history was one of international success and domestic difficulty. What did Sause mean by this? And how does his characterization of the industry force a reconsideration of the history of music, commerce, and globalization in the twentieth century?[1]

First, Sause suggested that globalization and recorded music had been together almost from the start. This runs counter to most of what has been written about both the phonograph and musical globalization. Standard industry histories focus primarily on the United States with nods to Great Britain, Germany and France. They rarely mention the foreign trade that Sause found so significant to the industry as a whole.[2] The large body of literature about musical globalization, on the other hand, is dominated by discussion of the years since the 1970s, an era noted for the rapid movement of media, people and money, and the integration of global markets. For all of its diversity, recent literature largely agrees that musical globalization is a story of the late twentieth century.[3] Yet Edmond Sause's comments came after more than two decades of rapid global expansion by the fledgling phonograph industry. In these years, major patent-controlling firms such as Columbia, Edison's National Phonograph Company, the Victor Talking Machine Company, and its British affiliate Gramophone scrambled to establish markets throughout the world. Companies spread across Western Europe in the 1890s. They systematically expanded into Latin America, Asia and Eastern Europe in the first years of the new century. Business grew quickly.[4] By 1910, companies had established sophisticated global networks of production and distribution for their machines and phonograph records. They had recorded thousands of musicians in dozens of countries, and the quantity of "foreign" or "ethnic" records in their catalogs outnumbered domestic releases by a significant margin. The industry's largest trade journal, founded in 1905, was called *The Talking Machine World*. The title was no mistake. Phonograph dealers and company executives understood themselves as part of a global industry.

Second, Sause implied that there was something wrong with phonograph marketing in the United States. Again, the current literature is of little help here, for it focuses primarily on the internal development of the United States industry. It is only by contrasting the domestic situation to the global scene – something Sause no doubt did regularly – that the United States' problems come into focus. Sometime between 1901 and 1905, a major split occurred within companies in response to perceived market saturation. Domestic dealers began promoting the *universal* values of Western art music. They attempted to convince American consumers with little interest in the concert hall that they – lo, their very nation – would be better off if they acquired an appreciation for "serious" music. International dealers, on the other hand, developed concepts of *local* music, promoting American technology as a means of listening to native songs and styles. The concept of local music proved a more successful model upon which to build the phonograph business. As Sause implied, touting the universal value of Western music caused the domestic industry to falter. Promoting "serious" music did not create a nation of art-house patrons nor did it alleviate domestic dealers' fears about the future of their industry. In fact, at the very time that the *Post* interviewed Sause, companies were beginning to apply the local-music paradigm developed by their international departments to domestic markets within the United States. This would result in the national flowering of local music styles during the 1920s. Styles such as African-American blues and rural white "hillbilly" or "old-time" music marked the concerted efforts of these groups to promote their own music as well as American consumers' recognition of the nation's powerful local music cultures. They also signified global marketing strategies coming home to roost.

This story suggests a number of conclusions about the historical relationship between the universal and the local in the global music industry. First, claims about the universal value of Western art music did not emerge in opposition to ideas about local music styles. Rather, strategies of marketing universal or local music arose simultaneously as separate alternatives to earlier, exhausted strategies of marketing the phonograph. They shared a great deal in common, as each was propelled by similar assumptions about racial hierarchy, culture and the marketplace. Second, musical globalization cannot be equated with export Americanization. Although it was home to many of the major phonograph companies, the United States nevertheless experienced the industry's local marketing strategies relatively late, long after they were in place in many other corners of the globe. American culture thus was deeply affected by globalization processes taking place beyond its borders. Blues and country music – for many, quintessential symbols of American culture – arose at least in part from marketing strategies imported from Asia, Europe, and Latin America. Finally, the concept of "local music" itself emerged as a byproduct of the global expansion of commercial music production and distribution networks. In this case, the global created the local. By the 1920s, the concept of distinctive local music cultures had become commonplace and relatively uncontested – a universal assumption shared by corporate leaders, musicians who hoped to participate in the burgeoning industry, and even communities tactically resisting the increasing commercialization of culture.

Imagining local music: the creation of global markets

When the phonograph business was in its infancy, few involved talked about the meaning of local music. Hardly any talked about music at all. Early advocates thought Thomas Edison's talking machine was remarkable enough to sell itself. *Scientific American* captured some of this excitement when it announced the invention in 1877. "It has been said that Science is never sensational; that it is intellectual, not emotional," the author began. "But certainly nothing that can be conceived would be more likely to create the profoundest of sensations, to arouse the liveliest of human emotions, than once more to hear the familiar voices of the dead."[5] The writer listed possible applications for the new machine: the recording of political speeches, great works of literature, business correspondence, and famous singers of the day. Possibilities were everywhere – in the business office, in the library, and in children's toys. One thing was certain: there was money to be made.

In the years that followed, dealers scurried to get their products in front of consumers, hoping to cash in on the wonder predicted by *Scientific American*. Nineteenth-century sales efforts focused on placing coin-operated phonographs in arcades, saloons, and other places of public amusement. People were willing to pay a nickel for the spectacle of sound emanating from a box. "When a man can hear the 7th Regiment Band of New York play the boulanger March, a Cornet solo by Levy, or the famous song, The Old Oaken Bucket, for five cents he has little desire to pay five cents to ascertain his weight or test the strength of his grip," wrote the Cincinnati *Gazette* in 1890. "That is the reason the musical machine has killed the business of other automatic machines."[6] Technological novelty – "arousing the liveliest of human emotions" – got the talking machine industry off the ground.

Early dealers did their job almost too well. By the first years of the twentieth century, many began fearing an industry based on novelty was destined to falter as consumers got used to the talking machine. Past successes bred current failures. Dealers decried "the popular impression that the talking machine is still only a scientific toy, and that anything to which the generic name of 'phonograph' can be applied is something capable of emitting only weird screeches and scratchings without the slightest pretensions to musical quality of tone."[7] The burning question confronting phonograph producers was how to build a consistent market for the invention as initial wonder wore thin.

It was within this context that phonograph companies began expanding internationally. New markets offered new consumers, novices who could still wonder at the marvel of mechanical reproduction. In fact, for many within the industry, the first inkling that the phonograph was becoming a global phenomenon came through echoes of the invention's earliest days: stories touting the arousal of lively emotions upon hearing the voices of the dead.

In 1902, engineer Henry M. Blackwell accompanied a surveying company building a railroad track through eastern China. Soon after setting camp in a small village along the route, the crew was alarmed to hear "several hundred chattering Chinamen" gathered outside its quarters. The villagers had caught wind that the surveyors possessed a miraculous talking machine, their military escort explained. The crowd was demanding a demonstration. Once produced, the machine "received more reverence than an ancestor's tomb," recalled Blackwell. Events then took a turn for the worse. As Blackwell dropped the needle, there was a pop followed by stone silence. The machine refused to talk. "Muttering arose from the crowd and a spokesman addressed the interpreter, declaring that there had been unfair discrimination and that if their sovereign rights were withheld, they would 'get hung.' When the little file of soldiers attempted to disperse them the uproar became deafening and the engineers rushed out to find an incipient Boxer outbreak." Several tried to storm the house and take the machine by force, but the soldiers held their ground. Eventually, the crowd tired of the scene and dispersed but not before three "ringleaders" had been arrested. Blackwell and his associates worked half the night to repair the machine. They presented a concert of "'coon' songs and comic opera trifles" the following morning to a "grateful, awestruck" audience. Not in attendance were the ringleaders, who had been sentenced to hang by their wrists for 48 hours for their offences. "Every innovation is bound to have its martyrs," Blackwell concluded.[8]

Henry Blackwell's story of technology, wonder and violence was not unique in the early years of the century. Stock narratives of distant peoples' first contact with the phonograph regularly graced the pages of *Talking Machine World*. From rural China to Chilean forests, Alaska to Central Africa, published stories and photographs depicted exotic foreign populations genuflecting before the talking machine. Phonograph dealers fetishized these images of "uncivilized" people marveling at the phonograph. Victor maintained a collection of such photographs that it would lend to various periodicals for publication.[9] These complex texts and images communicated several contradictory messages. The awe-inspiring magic of mechanical reproduction collided with violence and exploitation. Accounts of racial difference and distance – often finding natives worshiping Western technology or men – mingled with portrayals of the phonograph ultimately smoothing uneasy encounters between civilization and primitivism, colonial powers and colonial subjects. Behind all of these images crept the expanding market for music and machines, a force willing to overcome or reinforce cultural difference as the situations dictated but always able to reframe global cultural clashes as opportunities for consumption. The contradictions contained in these images enabled phonograph dealers to interpret them in multiple ways.

First, stories such as Blackwell's fit into larger tropes about the uses of Western technology in the colonial project. The phonograph joined the rifle, dynamite, fireworks and the pocket mirror as a tool to subdue primitive populations. It held a special place in such narratives for it was a technology of culture rather than force, encouraging colonial metaphors of exchange to eclipse those of conquest. The machine provided what anthropologist Michael Taussig calls "spectaculars of civilized primitivism, exchanges of magic and of metamagic satisfying to both primitive and civilized."[10] The talking machine, like the mirror, invested inanimate objects with human form or function. Ghostly voices arose from a box possessed. It thus could bridge the apparent divide between Western science and primitive superstition, and everyone could delight in its charms. Beyond the scratchy sounds, however, the machine's true magic in these narratives was its ability to evoke commonality while inscribing difference. All were in awe of the talking machine, but there was no doubt that Blackwell and his compatriots were in control. Backed by a military escort, they possessed the machine and proved themselves midnight masters of the technology behind its magic.

White explorers and colonists also controlled the voices emanating from the phonograph, resulting in a firm association between its technological brilliance and white racial superiority. "Huh! Him canned white man," the Alaskan Indian reportedly declared upon hearing his first record.[11] The racial ideology encoded in such stories suggested that white people created and owned the machine, which in turn was haunted by white voices that insinuated themselves into the consciousness of the listener. It was a short leap to the suggestion that primitive people became more civilized through exposure to American technology and culture. One 1905 photograph displayed exotically clothed Aleutian Islanders cocking their heads toward a talking machine in the center of the frame, mirroring the stance of the famous dog in the Victor logo responding to "His Master's Voice." The accompanying article enthused, "It is possible they are hearing for the first time modern music of the leading orchestras, as well as the songs and witty sayings which are current in the large cities. What is true of the Aleutian Islanders is true practically of everywhere the talking machine becomes known. It is a great civilizer and its popularity is founded upon the substantial grounds of giving a tremendous value to every user throughout the world."[12] Author Howard Taylor's 1905 poem, "A Phonographic Legend," further delineated the perceived congruity between the spread of the phonograph and the civilizing effects of American culture. The poem begins with a phonograph washing ashore on a remote island ruled by "King Jamboree." When the mysterious machine begins to speak, the gathered crowd "did not understand the words,/But felt that it must be/A command from their Fetish/To pray on bended knee." Thus, just as in Blackwell's story, Taylor's listeners first associate the talking machine with the supernatural. The mood quickly shifts, however, when the king eats one of the records, thinking it to be a pancake. Others follow, and the technological encounter acquires a specific cultural referent:

> No sooner had they eaten it
> And started for a walk,
> Than with stirring eloquence,
> They all began to talk.
>
> Not in the savage guttural,
> But in old U. S. A.
> The kind you hear in Boston,
> And that is swell, they say.[13]

The talking machine spoke with an American accent. To all others, the stories implied, it was a foreign technology representing an American modernity just now arriving on their uncivilized shores. They literally could consume it, but it would remained possessed by its American creators.[14]

Even as such stories celebrated the unifying magic of the talking machine and its power to transmit American culture, they reveled in their own absurdity. Blackwell's saga, like Taylor's poetic legend, was less reportage than a comedic set piece. It evoked what historian Philip J. Deloria calls an "ideological chuckle" born from the recognition of a cultural anomaly. Stark juxtapositions of primitivism and civilization – chattering Chinamen listening to light opera or island monarchs sporting a Boston brogue – reinforced expectations of racial distance and domination by briefly overcoming them, Deloria explains.[15] The juxtaposition was funny exactly to the extent that one believed it could never happen. The laughter placed oneself and one's culture above that of the primitive protagonists. These stories of first contact thus ambiguously professed a hope that cultural imperialism could make the world a more civilized place, yet they constantly expressed doubts that primitives would be able to appreciate American music when they heard it. The value of civilized culture was simply beyond many foreigners' comprehension.

First contact stories became popular among United States dealers at the precise moment that the novelty of the talking machine was waning among US consumers. They helped express the longings many dealers felt for the not so distant past, an era when American consumers still marveled at mechanical reproduction and the machines sold themselves. *Scientific*

American had identified the emotional power the machine possessed in its 1877 introduction of Edison's invention. Domestic dealers recalled that even as expressions of awe and wonder depicted the complacent colonial subject, they also characterized the ideal consumer. As dealers swapped tales of distant phonograph encounters, they found in "primitives" the wonder and excitement about talking machines that they and their domestic customers no longer possessed. Yet they also read these fantasies of unspoiled consumers through their experiences with the US market. Foreign wonder could not last. A new strategy would be required once international audiences got used to sound coming from a box. It was with this realization that the international phonograph campaigns departed fundamentally from the path pursued in the United States. Initial impetus came from those working in local markets around the world.

In 1905, an anonymous phonograph dealer was asked by *Talking Machine World* to assess business prospects in the Philippines. "I should say, from my superficial investigation," the dealer noted, "that the possibilities for a large business here with talking machines is most encouraging. To begin with, the Filipinos take to novelties. They are like children in many respects, and to see them gather around some machine which is sending forth a reproduction of a famous American song, and note the childlike look on their faces, is interesting." The dealer struck the familiar chord of primitive wonder and American culture but then departed from the score. "Of course, all of the records must be in Spanish," the author maintained. "I believe that if the talking machine manufacturers could get some noted Filipino to sing for recording purposes, or some native orator, the records and the machines would have an enormous sale. All people who can, would buy one simply to hear the local singer or speaker."[16] It represented a reinvention of the industry.

Other dealers and investigators were coming to similar conclusions about the importance of recording local music in foreign markets. John Watson Hawd traveled to Calcutta on a fact-finding mission for Gramophone in 1901. He was alarmed at the number of talking machine dealers who were already present in the city. Furniture and bicycle salesmen were adding talking machines to their line of goods. He urgently wrote the Home Office in London suggesting that Gramophone establish an Indian branch office before other transnational and local firms flooded the market with rival machines. Some were using the recording capabilities of Edison's consumer phonographs to capture the singing of their friends and families. Such amateur recordings were selling crisply to Calcutta music lovers. Hawd thus insisted that Gramophone send recording experts to capture the sounds of "native" musicians. Gramophone responded immediately, offering to dispatch Fred Gaisberg, their most successful scout, fresh from recording tours of Europe. Hawd did not wait for Gramophone to act. After sending his request, he quickly befriended Amerendra Dutt, manager of the Classic Theatre in Calcutta. By the time Gaisberg and his recording equipment arrived, Dutt had selected and rehearsed a number of local artists for the scout to record.[17] Similar networks for finding local talent were established in other markets. Quite often these involved tapping into existing arts organizations or infrastructures: music schools in the Philippines, court musicians in India, noted scholars in China.[18]

The scramble for foreign sales was a highly competitive game. Heinrich Bumb, a scout for the German Beka-Record firm, arrived in Hong Kong in 1906 only to discover several others already ensconced there. "The Columbia Graphophone Company had just finished its latest recordings – said to be of 1,000 titles, for which fees of 50,000 dollars had been paid. 'Victor,' 'Grammophon' [sic] as well as 'Zonophon-Records' and 'Odeon' were represented in the colony," he recalled.[19] Successful phonograph companies designed detailed strategic plans for global expansion. In 1907, for example, Victor and its sister company British Gramophone agreed upon a global division of markets so they could spread the use of Berliner disc technology without directly competing with each other. Victor's sphere included North and South America, China, and Japan. Gramophone would sell the Berliner phonograph system in Europe, India, and other Asian countries.[20] Gramophone soon recorded a significant number of musicians in India, Turkey, and Egypt as well as several other smaller national markets. The company cut 14,000 discs in Asia and North Africa during the first decade of the century. Phonograph companies moved throughout Latin American with almost equal speed. Columbia established a presence in Mexico by 1903. Victor and Edison followed within a few years. The Latin American trade grew quickly. In 1913, Argentina imported an estimated 2.7 million phonograph records. Companies that could not afford to set up their own international offices expanded their catalogs by signing licensing agreements with other labels. General Phonograph, the maker of the popular Okeh records, increased its catalog and cache in this way when it became the US distributor for the European Odeon label. By the mid-1910s, when almost all United States recordings were made in a handful of urban centers, the major phonograph companies had made thousands of records in countries around the world.[21]

As the industry expanded, companies developed international networks of production, distribution, and information. Gramophone's production chain provides but one example. Gramophone constructed its machines and cabinets out of wood harvested from around the world: mahogany from

Africa and South America; oak from Great Britain, North America and Russia; and walnut from southern Russia and the United States. Recorded discs themselves were manufactured out of raw materials gleaned from East Asia, India, Spain, France, and the United States. The company maintained even more sophisticated global networks for the production of its recorded music. International recordings were made through the collaboration of company scouts and recording experts with local agents, dealers and talent. Once initial recordings were made, commercial discs were pressed in Hanover, Germany, although by 1912 Gramophone had expanded disc production to plants in Paris, Spain, Berlin, Austria, Russia and India. Discs then were distributed along with machines to exclusive dealerships for sale in the country of origin and migrant communities throughout the world. Gramophone also licensed large portions of its ethnic and classical catalogs to Victor for production and distribution in the United States. This transnational production network was essential to the growth of both Gramophone and Victor. Victor's access to international opera stars through the Gramophone catalog enabled them to dominate the United States opera trade, and the combined geographic reach of the two powerhouses allowed them to claim one of the most comprehensive catalogs of "ethnic" music.[22]

In the beginning, United States recording engineers had a very difficult time comprehending the music they encountered on their international expeditions. "Generally they are strangers in the countries to which they may be despatched [sic], knowing little, if anything, of the language or customs of the people and ignorant of the material from which to choose suitable record-making talent," confessed Edward Burns, manager of Columbia's Export Department.[23] Fred Gaisberg concurred, "On the first day [in Shanghai in 1903], after making ten records we had to stop. The din had so paralyzed my wits that I could not think ... Up to the 27th of March we made 325 records for which we paid $4 each. To me, the differences between the tunes of any two records were too slight for me to detect."[24] American scouts were out of their element. Their skills in assessing and recording musicians from Western art traditions had helped them rise within the ranks of the growing recording industry. Their initial recording successes in the United States and Europe had convinced industry executives that they were the right people to carry out similar ventures throughout the world. Yet they had no framework or aesthetic criteria with which to judge the strange sounds they encountered. "We entered a new world of musical and artistic values," recalled Gaisberg. "One had to erase all memories of the music of European opera houses and concert halls: the very foundations of my musical training were undermined."[25] Many questioned whether the sounds they captured on disc – often based on complex, unfamiliar rhythms and quarter-tone scales "sounding to the Western ear constantly out of tune" – could be considered music at all.[26]

Confronted with such musical and cognitive dissonance, scouts and dealers escaped into the logic of the free market. John Watson Hawd wrote back from India to his Gramophone superiors in 1902, "The native music is to me worse than Turkish but as long as it suits them and sells well what do we care?"[27] S. Porter, a recording engineer working in India, echoed this sentiment in 1905: "To be sure the selections are weird, if not altogether grand, gloomy and peculiar, but they sell like hot cakes." Since "American records are absolutely unknown" and "orchestral records are also little in demand," Porter saw no alternative to supplying the "weird" music to Indian consumers willing to pay the price. In fact, once he focused on "native music", the demand was great enough for him to declare: "India is the best place on earth for talking machines ... I have made records in Russia, Sweden, Norway, in fact all the principal countries of Europe, but India tops them all, and appears to me a great field for American enterprise in this line."[28] Such declarations suggest what American scouts may have been thinking of during their international adventures. Hawd and Porter first pronounced disgust for local musical tastes. Yet failing to arouse interest in American or orchestral music, they threw up their hands, surrendered their own musical tastes, and succumbed to local consumer desires. This new premium placed on local music was born not from an ideology of cultural relativism or equality but from a reassertion of cultural and racial hierarchy.

The primitivist rhetoric perfected in the stories of first contact enabled talking-machine men to focus on local music. A subtle but unmistakable alchemy was occurring as international scouts explained their experiences to domestic readers. From one sentence to the next, stock descriptions of ignorant natives were transformed into detailed analyses of local musical styles and tastes. Primitive stereotypes – particularly the denial that foreign peoples could comprehend Western art traditions – became the justification for taking local music seriously. Reporting on scout Henry Marker's trip through China, one author asserted,

> Talking machine exporters know only too well that the most insignificant nations will buy talking machines if they can hear records made by their own people. A cannibal would flee from a record of Cavalieri but would go almost insane with delight at hearing his own tongue emerge from the horn of a machine.

The author then parsed the Chinese population into a variety of distinct markets, proving his knowledge of Chinese society and geography:

One of the first things that strikes the foreigner when he travels about the Chinese Empire is the lack of homogeneity. This is particularly noticeable in the languages. There is the Pekin dialect and the Canton dialect, and so many others that only a skilled linguist can distinguish them ... so in making talking machine records it is necessary to have actors in all the dialects of the provinces where the goods are to be sold.[29]

Edward Burns, Columbia's export manager, likewise began his summary of the company's Asian expeditions by evoking standard images of foreign superstitions. "In fact, in some countries in the far East," he announced, "the people looked on the talking machine not only with wonder, but positive awe, and approached it with fear and trembling, regarding the mysterious voice from the horn as that of a god." Burns then insisted that Columbia's success throughout East Asia was dependent on a broad and detailed knowledge of local cultures. He offered a running list of his company's work toward this end. In the four years of its campaign, Columbia had studied a variety of local dialects and musical styles; charted the internal and international migration patterns of different ethnic groups; categorized the musical tastes of different economic and social classes; compared the use of music in different religious traditions; chronicled local trade and distribution networks; invented a new recording diaphragm to accommodate the broad dynamics of some local singing styles; learned to promote loud records in areas favoring open air architecture; and even surveyed different locales regarding the colors consumers preferred to see on their record labels.[30] International campaigns were producing serious students of foreign cultures even as they maintained a deep investment in racial and cultural hierarchies.

Some scouts even began to acknowledge the artistic qualities of the music they encountered abroad. T. J. Theobald Noble recorded extensively throughout Europe and Asia in the early 1910s. The prominent engineer chronicled his dawning comprehension of the Hindustani music he captured in Calcutta. "At first I found it unmusical and weird, but eventually began to follow the songs with keen enjoyment and appreciation," he explained. Noble was particularly impressed by an amateur singer accompanied by a harmonium and a set of tabla drums, or "tum-tum". "These instruments are very curious for, although the playing of them appears to be simple, they are in reality extremely difficult," he admitted.

It was many days before I could follow even to a small extent – how the tum-tum was supposed to accompany the singer, and I do confess that to this day I cannot fathom how it is possible to accurately accompany an Indian song on such an instrument. The artist sings up and down the keyboard, and to my mind there are no bars, rhythm or tempo, yet the tum-tumist crescendos, stops, commences and synchronises [sic] perfectly with the singing. It was and still is an enigma to me.[31]

Here was the culmination of the industry's slow recognition of local music and cultural difference. Noble's comments represented a profound, if subtle, change in the conception of foreign sounds. It was a shift from *noise* to *music* – from Fred Gaisberg decrying a paralyzing "din" to the acknowledgement of a conscious, skilled performance. Noble began to hear Hindustani music on its own terms, discovering its difficulty and appreciating its internal logic. In the process, he relinquished some of his power to define cultural value. Even as he acknowledged the music's merits, he admitted that full comprehension and mastery was beyond him. While not admitting its transcendence or even its parity with Western music traditions, Noble allowed that Indians had their own culture and that native musicians understood its artistic characteristics better than American scouts.

At the same time, the local music paradigm placed serious constraints on the music that foreign musicians were allowed to record. It defined local music through its isolation from scouts' own culture and civilization. On the prowl for music that could charm local consumers into purchasing a talking machine, scouts regularly ignored or suppressed evidence that the musicians they encountered in distant lands had already forged their own extra-local connections and cultures. Fred Gaisberg, for example, had no patience for Indian musicians enamored with Western music. Soon after arriving in Calcutta in 1901, he was treated to a female chorus singing "And Her Golden Hair Was Hanging Down Her Back" accompanied by a brass ensemble. Gaisberg cringed. "I had yet to learn that the oriental ear was unappreciative of chords and harmonic treatment and only demanded the rhythmic beat of accompaniment of the drums," he recalled. "At this point we left."[32] Often, such reactions arose out of corporate strategies of market development. Phonograph companies saw little money to be made from recordings of Indians singing British music hall ditties.

Just as often, scouts' reactions in the field were driven by their assumptions about music, race, and primitivism. Henry L. Marker, for example, traveled over 12,500 miles making records for Columbia between 1910 and 1912. In Singapore, Marker arrived for a recording session wearing his standard pith helmet, white suit and matching shoes. He was surprised to discover the scheduled Malay ensemble similarly decked in identical trousers and boots. The scout believed the Western clothes would inhibit the passions of the performers. "Tell that bunch of misguided heathens to take off their boots or there will be no more records made," he declared. The musicians quickly complied.[33] Casting themselves as savvy globetrotters confident in the artistic supremacy of their own Western music traditions, phonograph company scouts imagined they were introducing modern technology to isolated, primitive people around the world. Well shod Malay musicians or Indian brass bands challenged such conceits. They not only demonstrated the worldliness of supposedly isolated, racially inferior people but also suggested that white talking-machine scouts were not as superior or as unique as advertised. Artists or music that challenged scouts' understanding of the dichotomy between primitivism and civilization rarely got recorded.

The global expansion of the phonograph industry thus launched a new conception of local culture. In this new configuration, the local was something separate. It was a distinct, circumscribed space that contained its own musical culture, one demonstrating little apparent relationship to either that of its neighbors or to the music emanating from the United States and Europe. Second, the local was something deeply private. Local culture was known and understood only by insiders and represented something of the essential identity of its practitioners. Finally, local culture was inferior. Scouts did not promote local music because they believed it was equal to the universal values of the Western music tradition. They embraced it because they understood it to be the best that racially inferior foreign populations could achieve. Lacking the capacity to comprehend civilized art, they could be sold music from their own lands. The industry was progressing differently in the United States.

Promoting universal music: cultural uplift in the United States

Domestic salesmen responded to the waning novelty of the talking machine by launching what can be called a campaign of cultural uplift, repositioning their product as an educational tool rather than a parlor trick. In 1905, a vice-president of a major firm declared, "1904 can really, I think, go into history as the year when the talking machine first became generally recognized as more than a toy and as a medium not only of entertainment suitable for the home of the refined and artistic and when it first assumed its place as an educational force."[34] It signaled another reinvention of the industry.

At the heart of the cultural uplift campaign was a dedication to encouraging the use of "serious" art music in the private home. Victor led the pack by promoting its new Red Seal line of classical recordings. The company signed exclusive contracts with Enrico Caruso and other opera singers featured in New York's Metropolitan Opera House. Fine furniture makers designed beautiful cabinets, and interior designers began including the talking machine as an integral part of a modern home's accoutrements. Records by the great opera and concert artists of Europe sold heartily, and dealers often compared the talking machine to a home library of great literature. The industry also promoted the use of art music and opera recordings in state schools.[35]

Perhaps no one epitomized the cultural uplift campaign more than Frances E. Clark, the Supervisor of Music for Milwaukee state schools who in 1911 became the director of Victor's Public School Educational Department. In a 1909 speech before the Wisconsin State Teachers' Association, Clark directly tied American cultural uplift with technological innovation and serious music. "If music is to become the great force of the uplifting of this American people that I firmly believe that it will become, it must be brought about by the next generation knowing more about music and knowing more music itself," Clark declared. The phonograph was an essential tool for this musical education. "It is necessary to reconstruct our old ideas of the wheezy, blaring, blatant, brassy thing we have known in the days agone," she insisted. "The new talking machine with its wood horn, its bamboo needle and the wonderful records obtainable is a joy and delight – an artistic success." With these technological improvements should come more uplifting listening habits:

> The old was almost wholly given over to the lower class of music – the coon song, the ragtime, the cheap popular song heard in saloon and dance hall. The new talking machine is eminently respectable and worthy of a place as an educational factor in every school in the land … By the use of the machine we may enjoy opera, oratorio, orchestra, band, violin, cello, folk songs and ballets over and over again as many times as we like.[36]

Between 1905 and 1917, Clark's opinions about class, race, technology and education became increasingly common within the domestic talking-machine trade. A Columbia sales manager simply echoed standard industry hyperbole in 1917 when he declared: "Music in the home is the greatest addition to the education of man since the printing press was invented."[37]

The cultural uplift campaign seized the imagination of many within the United States industry for it soothed interrelated anxieties concerning American culture, consumerism, and their own identity as cultural brokers. In many ways, cultural uplift was not about transforming American consumer tastes but about changing the very meaning of consumption itself. Though difficult to glean from cultural uplift campaign materials, many citizens outside the industry saw the phonograph's commodification of music as symptomatic of the larger problem of mass-marketed culture. John Philip

Sousa expressed a common feeling when he decried "mechanical music" in 1906. "Sweeping across the country with the speed of a transient fashion in slang or Panama hats, political war cries or popular novels, comes now the mechanical device to sing for us a song or play for us a piano, in substitute for human skill, intelligence, and soul," the composer wailed.[38] Cultural uplift attempted to counter such attacks by imbuing the industry's products with the very "intelligence" and "soul" others reserved for human culture and interaction beyond the cash nexus. It was a bold bait and switch – a Trojan horse in the fragile fortress of uncommodified culture.

The campaign worked as well as it did because it also buttressed the class and racial hierarchies that were marking out United States society and culture. On the one hand, it reinforced the class distinctions that had come to define "highbrow" and "lowbrow" culture during the latter half of the nineteenth century. As historian Lawrence Levine has chronicled, opera itself went through a similar process of uplift as American elites rescued it from popular audiences and recast it as symbol of their own superior social standing, complete with an emphasis on private consumption, a rhetoric of transcendent universal value, and a desire to evangelize the uninitiated about how to approach true art. Levine is quick to point out that the emergent cultural hierarchy was propelled by racial – as well as class – ideology. The terms "highbrow" and "lowbrow" themselves were borrowed from the racist pseudoscience of phrenology that posited racial types and intelligence could be determined through cranial measurements. Opera and orchestral music may have epitomized upper-class refinement, but they also came to signify white cultural supremacy in an era characterized by the racial violence of lynching and Jim Crow segregation, as well as by the growing fear that white children were, in the words of an influential 1913 editorial, "falling prey to the collective soul of the negro through the influence of what is popularly known as 'rag time' music."[39]

Phonograph company spokespeople such as Frances Clark performed this script to perfection, regularly attacking African-American and popular music, predicting national transcendence through the cultivation of high-brow culture, and convincing elite audiences that they could maintain class and racial dominance only by overcoming their misguided objections to cultural commodification and mechanical music. In the process, they projected themselves into the ranks of the nation's cultural elite. This was a dramatic transformation for a group that until very recently had been defined as toy and novelty peddlers, a designation more likely to evoke patent medicine con games than upright professionals rubbing shoulders with renowned conductors and celebrity tenors.[40]

Advocates believed one of the major obstacles to cultural uplift was ordinary citizens' love of inferior local music. They reveled in reports of consumers – particularly those in remote rural locales – learning to appreciate serious music. Thus West Virginia dealer H. C. Farber published a rebuttal to Sousa's critique of "mechanical music," noting that the talking machine had created legions of new Sousa devotees among the nation's rural residents. "The ruralite or hayseed," Farber wrote, "buys himself a 'talker' of some kind, and plays it to beat the band. He hears some of Sousa's pieces and then when the March King comes within one or two hundred miles of his lonely mountain home this very hayseed will put on his store suit and dig down into his jeans for the fare and go to hear the famous bandmaster, whom he would never have heard of if not for the 'talker.' "[41] Once exposed to the great artists of the Western tradition, others agreed, consumers would no longer remain satisfied with the sounds of the amateur or semi-professional musicians from their own communities. "Only a few years ago, when the price of a talking machine was not within the reach of people of ordinary means, I noticed that most especially in the smaller towns and hamlets, a traveling musician, an organ grinder or a 'barn-stormer' show proved a great attraction and was received with the warmest of welcome," explained writer William F. Hunt in 1905. "The people, most in particular those of the rural class, were anxious to hear music, regardless of quality – anything, just so it had some of the characteristics of music about it." Now that the phonograph had arrived in homes across the country, Hunt continued, audiences no longer settled for mediocrity:

> The traveling musician is now rarely if ever seen, and poor class shows are getting scarce. People have been cultivated to the best class of music and entertainments through the marvelous little entertainer – the phonograph – and the above-named class of vendors could now not get a hearing, to say nothing of a recompense for their labor if they put in an appearance.[42]

Hunt was getting ahead of himself. Rural audiences still supported traveling musicians, street performers and local bands. Live music offered a thrill and excitement that could not be banished by the scratchy sounds of the talking machine. It also offered local songs and styles not available on record at the time.

United States dealers were blinded to the value of local music by the dichotomous categorizations behind the cultural uplift campaign. As a 1917 pamphlet entitled "Helping Record Buyers" argued,

> There are two kinds of record customers, one who makes an initial purchase of the latest topical records, and then quickly tires of his Gramophone, and the other type of buyer who when purchasing his instrument selects a variety

of good records, as the base of an ultimate collection. This is the class of customer that is a real asset ... The dealer has a Gramophone enthusiast in embryo, and according to the method of the training so the customer. When it comes to selecting records, the dealer should give his advice, and state his reasons for so advising. Fully 60 per cent of the customers do not know the type of record they require and are probably drawn to the topical and humorous because they have never had the opportunity of hearing good music.

There were two kinds of customers, and there were two kinds of records: topical novelty selections, and uplifting classical recordings. This was the dichotomous vision of American music that drove the domestic phonograph industry. The dealer had a duty to instruct consumers how to make the right decision. It was a matter of economics as well as cultural education. The brochure concluded, "Neglecting an opportunity to familiarize a customer with higher class music than he is accustomed to buying, never did build a business and never will."[43] Local musical tastes, when considered at all, were seen as part of the problem facing the phonograph industry rather than as a potential basis for phonograph sales.

Importing the local: selling foreign music at home

The conceptions of local music that were developed internationally slowly began to influence phonograph marketing in the United States. As global expansion progressed, industry employees crossed borders with ease through travels, transfers and promotions. A stratum of middle-level administrators and technicians thus became well versed in sharing knowledge about selling phonographs and records within a variety of ethnic and national markets. They increasingly brought their international experiences to bear on the domestic market. US native Raphael Cabanas, for example, was the president of the Compañía Fonográfica Mexicana, the exclusive distributor for Columbia in Mexico. In the early 1910s, Cabanas made frequent trips to the home offices in New York and Washington, DC, where he created collaborative marketing campaigns with the Columbia advertising department. In 1913, Cabanas extended the reach of his company by purchasing Columbia dealerships in Texas and Arizona. His Dallas store significantly increased its business following a spate of innovative billboard advertisements, a strategy Cabanas had perfected earlier in Mexico City.[44] Edward N. Burns, Cabanas' chief contact at Columbia, boasted one of the most significant international résumés in the business. Burns was the founding manager of the Columbia Phonograph export department around 1902. He held the position until 1915, when Edmond Sause replaced him so that Burns could be promoted to the vice-presidency of the company. In addition to supervising exports,

Burns served as an adviser to domestic dealers hoping to increase sales among immigrant populations.[45]

It was through fostering sales among US immigrants that international experts had their most direct influence on United States sales strategies. Talking-machine companies began to realize the potential markets that existed in the nation's immigrant neighborhoods during the first decade of the century. Early rhetoric about immigrant sales reflected the emphasis on local singers or speakers developing in the international campaigns. "Remember that in all large cities and in most towns there are sections where people of one nationality or another congregate in 'colonies,' " explained a writer in the *Columbia Record* in 1909. "Most of these people keep up the habits and prefer to speak the language of the old country … To these people RECORDS IN THEIR OWN LANGUAGE have an irresistible attraction, and they will buy them readily."[46]

The arrival of ethnic recordings in the United States was disorienting to some in the industry. Many dealers invoked caricatures of ethnic difference similar to those of the foreign first contact stories when they imagined domestic consumers of foreign records. One dealer related the apocryphal tale of a traveling salesman who sold a machine and twelve records to an Irish immigrant, a Mr O'Toole. The customer was very excited that the traditional Irish songs he ordered arrived in time for his daughter's birthday party. At the appropriate moment, Mr O'Toole hushed the gathered crowd and placed the first record on the machine, stating, "Oi will now give yez Chauncey Olcott's latest song av th' ould country." To the party's surprise a "mysterious tinkle of bells" came forth from the horn, followed by "a series of barbaric shouts." After a second record brought similar results, the crowd demanded the worthless machine be thrown out the window. Just in time, the salesman appeared at the door and breathlessly apologized for mixing up Mr O'Toole's order with that intended for a local Chinese restaurant. The party proceeded as planned.[47] The tone of such stories closely echoed both the violent confusion of Henry Blackwell's Chinese villagers and scout Fred Gaisberg's disorientation while recording the paralyzing "din" of different music traditions.

Yet the role of talking-machine dealers in such tales is notable for two reasons. First, in stark contrast to international scouts, the phonograph company employees in these stories were no longer the ones experiencing anxiety. The shock of encountering the strange music of another ethnic tradition was reserved for other immigrants. The talking-machine man negotiated between multiple ethnic groups, containing and channeling ethnic anxiety by teaching immigrants to be more informed consumers. Second, such stories reveal an important loophole in the industry's cultural uplift campaign. Here are domestic dealers gladly giving customers what they want. It was a double-edged sword. The same racism displayed in the international campaigns excluded many immigrant groups from the possibility of cultural uplift in the eyes of the industry. Yet this very exclusion enabled many American immigrants to demand that phonograph companies grant them recordings of their unique musical traditions.

Companies dramatically accelerated efforts to sell "ethnic" music in the US following the outbreak of war in 1914 in an effort to protect themselves from the possible interruption of global trade networks. As editorialists pleaded for calm and predicted a growing US economy, phonograph companies moved quickly to make up for endangered international profits through increased domestic business. Companies immediately placed their sights on fostering immigrant consumption. "The immense stirring of patriotic fervor due to the European war has given an impetus to the sale of Columbia records of foreign music which is truly phenomenal," a 1914 Columbia publication announced. Victor and Columbia expanded their recording of international material in the United States, setting up recording studios in Chicago to complement their primary New York and New Jersey facilities. Anton Heindl of Columbia's International Record Department was named director of the company's new Chicago studio and promised to place special emphasis on recording the "folk songs, the dances, and the religious hymns" desired by US immigrant populations.[48]

In 1917, Columbia launched a major campaign to pressure their dealers to take advantage of underexploited immigrant markets. "This is harvest time for foreign record business," its advertising copy announced. "Our International Record Department issues records in 37 different languages, and thousands of Columbia dealers in this country are making good, regular money on these records."[49] In the fall, Anton Heindl organized an unprecedented, week-long conference that brought together Columbia executives from both the domestic and international departments to share experiences and develop joint marketing strategies. It was attended by regional sales managers and featured a series of lectures by Edward Burns, the architect of Columbia's global expansion. The conference had the explicit purpose of fostering foreign record sales in the United States. Following the conference, sales managers were to take its message to dealers throughout their territories. Samuel Lenberg, a sales manager out of Chicago, left the conference with orders to "study the conditions in the dealers' territory, collect data and show them how to cultivate successfully trade to which they have not hitherto catered" and "seek to establish new Columbia dealers in localities where there is a large foreign trade and in which the company is not now represented."[50]

It was through this concerted push to increase foreign record sales during the First World War that conceptions of local music and difference – born in companies' international expeditions – came to dominate the United States talking-machine business. First, the campaign changed the way many dealers conceived the history of the industry. Previous dealers had characterized it in terms of its oscillating commitment to cultural uplift, themselves as soldiers in the fight to protect serious, transcendent culture from class or racial degradation. Others now identified the motivating force behind the industry as the search for new markets. "The secret of increasing business lies not alone in redoubling efforts in accepted and familiar fields, but in discovering and operating in new fields where it is possible to create a fresh demand for a product," one author argued. Distinct ethnic markets offered just such possibilities, the author concluded.[51] Second, the foreign record campaign introduced domestic dealers to the marketing magic of local music, the idea that consumers would line up to purchase music that represented their own identity. As one 1917 advertisement explained, "The big foreign-born population of the United States is hungering – yes, *actually hungering* – for its own native music ... These are not just records sung in foreign languages. They are records that have been actually *made in their native land*. That is why they have the indefinable atmosphere which the purchaser immediately recognizes and cherishes."[52]

These were lessons that international scouts had learned many years before, yet they represented a revolution of values to domestic dealers reared on the rhetoric of cultural uplift. Odes to "native music" not only shattered the dichotomous definitions of music behind cultural uplift, they also insisted that consumers – not talking-machine dealers – were in the best position to recognize musical quality. Harry A. Goldsmith, a Milwaukee Victor wholesaler, made this point forcefully:

> Tony Andrianopolis shyly enters your store, hat in hand, and asks if you have some Greek records. Of course you have none, and in the past simply told him so and turned away from him. He slinked out of your store. You soon forgot the incident. Now, had you invited Tony into your office, inquired from him about how many Greeks, for instance, lived in your city, and put it up to him squarely if he thought it would be profitable for you to carry Greek records, you might sit up surprised that you had wasted some wonderful opportunities ... Just hand him a Greek catalog and ask him to mark in this what records he thinks you ought to carry for a starter ... Have faith in Tony. Order every single record he tells you to ... When you get these Greek records in stock let Tony know. Tony will do the rest.[53]

The dealer's role in this transaction was far different from that proposed during the educational and cultural uplift campaigns. The dealer looked to the immigrant customer for musical guidance. By focusing on consumers' current desires rather than trying to foster new ones, phonograph dealers could profit in the foreign record business.

Edmond Sause was interviewed at an important moment in the history of music in the United States. Even as he spoke of foreign success and domestic difficulties in 1920, the local-music model invented in the global marketplace was coming to dominate the phonograph business within the United States. This process, begun by targeting immigrant populations, reached a turning point little more than a month after Sause's words appeared in print. On August 8, 1920, Mamie Smith and Her Jazz Hounds recorded the song "Crazy Blues" for Okeh Records. It was the first significant blues record by an African-American singer and backing band. "Crazy Blues" helped to inaugurate the "race" record industry that sold music made by and for African-Americans. It was a market conception that owed a lot to the local-music paradigm developed internationally. Race records were soon followed by "hillbilly" or "old-time" tunes marketed to rural white audiences. For many Americans, these products traded on their racial, class, and regional authenticity in new ways. Here was music made by artists who lived and performed in the same milieu as their audiences. If previous commercial recordings represented national culture imposed on consumers in every city, race and old-time music often were marketed as local sounds writ large – the triumph of local authenticity over homogenizing bids for universal value.[54] Edmond Sause and others involved in the international industry may have understood these products differently. Race and old-time records in part signified global marketing strategies coming home to roost.

Ralph Peer was a prominent record scout for Okeh, where he supervised Mamie Smith's recording of "Crazy Blues." He later worked for Victor, where he developed a strong catalog of race and old-time records. When asked in 1959 how phonograph companies first got into recording African-American and Southern white music, he quickly credited the immigrant marketing campaigns. "I saw that this was really a business like our foreign record business. We put out German records, Swedish records and what have you. So I decided that, like the German records were all in let's say the 6000 series ... well we need another number series so I started using this 8000. That was the theory behind it," Peer explained.[55] After learning to sell local music to various racial and ethnic groups in the foreign record business, the industry discovered that the United States was as fertile a ground for marketing musical difference as they had slowly discovered the rest of the world to be.

Conclusion: globalization and local music

This story suggests some general conclusions about globalization and the local. First, American music is a product of globalization. Global markets were a major concern of the industry practically from the start, and global experiences were intimately intertwined with the conception and development of music markets in the United States. Some scholars have attempted to locate the emergence of the local-music paradigm within the history of American popular music. A number of scholars have emphasized the 1950s rise of rock and roll, along with its attendant valorization of local "roots," its global appeal, and its apparent anti-commercialism.[56] Others have insisted that the 1920s witnessed the birth of the local-music paradigm as race and old-time records began selling briskly. Unfortunately, such explanations suggest that the local-music paradigm developed in isolation within the US and was then exported. As surely as we must question images of discrete, isolated cultures prior to contact with the phonograph (then or now), we should be skeptical of these portrayals of local US music developing prior to globalization.

Second, within the phonograph industry, concepts of the universal and the local did not arise in opposition to each other. At first glance, proponents of Western classical music or local music appeared to be picking sides in the era's fundamental battle over the meaning of culture. Whether identified in terms of universalism versus the local, high culture versus low, or even Matthew Arnold's "sweetness and light" versus E. B. Tylor's "complex whole," cultural historians have tended to describe these cultural configurations in opposition to each other.[57] The two camps were not as distant as this characterization would suggest. Both were driven by a fundamental faith in racial and cultural hierarchy. Within the phonograph industry, both shared contempt for earlier marketing strategies that pitched the talking machine as a piece of awe-inspiring technology. Both insisted that the future of the machine was as a carrier of culture. The fact of mechanical reproduction mattered less than the ways in which consumers were moved by the music emanating from the horn. Likewise, as historian Michael Denning has suggested, both spoke to an uneasiness about the growing commodification of culture in industrial capitalist societies. Each identified culture as that human activity existing outside the marketplace: the uplift program found it in the fine arts; the international campaigns located it among isolated, supposedly primitive peoples. What is significant about the campaigns for cultural uplift and local music is not that one faltered as the other came to dominate the United States record charts. It is that the industry so quickly was able to commodify two realms of music celebrated for their existence beyond the commercial nexus.[58]

Finally, local music was produced by corporate globalization. Local culture has played a defining role in the recent literature about musical globalization. At its most basic, the local has stood for everything the global is not: rooted in place and tradition, uncommodified, and uninterested in empire-building. Many scholars have challenged the simplicity of this formulation, suggesting that the local emerges through its opposition to globalization or as the specific ground upon which globalization occurs. Yet for all the theorizing, scholars have had a difficult time escaping the basic idea of the local as a thing apart. It remains a way a particular place is defined against the global. The story of the early twentieth-century phonograph industry suggests otherwise.[59]

The local-music paradigm within the phonograph industry arose out of a particular two-pronged historical process. First, the identification of local music was a story of discovery. It involved the slow determination that different locales (defined according to geography, nationalism, race, or class) had developed their own unique musical styles. This discovery of local sounds was partially a byproduct of the capitalist tendency toward differentiation common to the historical quest for new labor and consumer markets. It was also spurred by the Western intellectual revolution in the concept of culture that challenged Arnoldian visions of transcendent "sweetness and light" with anthropological notions of distinct customs and folkways. Second, the identification of local music was accomplished through a process of erasure. Once phonograph companies identified unique musical styles, they limited their depictions of local cultures to these aspects of the scene by ignoring or eliminating musical evidence of outside influences – particularly that of the Western "serious" music they were promoting back home. This aspect of the "local" is rarely discussed in the literature about globalization, yet it is vitally important. Within the commercial recording industry, the local did not develop in opposition to the universal claims of the Western music tradition. On the contrary, it was born out of the belief that some racial or ethnic groups lacked the capacity to comprehend Western civilization. Local music offered a way to increase consumption among inferior populations. The local music paradigm thus reinforced the superiority of the West, the divide between primitivism and civilization, and the Western tendency to hear foreign sounds through the prism of exoticism. Local music was deeply inscribed with the racialism and racial hierarchies of its day. Recent scholars have had such a difficult time defining a local culture that does not perpetuate exoticizing tendencies in part because that was what the concept was designed to do.

Notes

1   "Selling the Talking Machines in the Foreign Markets," *Talking Machine World*,
    July 15 (1920), p. 63; "Edmond F. Sause New Columbia Export Manager,"
    Talking Machine World, February 15 (1915), p. 55.
2   Classic studies include Roland Gelatt, *The Fabulous Phonograph, 1877–1977*,
    2nd rev. ed. (New York, 1977); Walter L. Welch and Leah Brodbeck Stenzel
    Burt, *From Tinfoil to Stereo: The Acoustic Years of the Recording Industry,
    1877–1929* (Gainesville, FL, 1994). A notable exception is the work of Pekka
    Gronow. In addition to the articles cited below, see Pekka Gronow and Ilpo
    Saunio, *An International History of the Recording Industry*, trans. Christopher
    Moseley (London, 1998). See also William Howland Kenney, *Recorded Music in
    American Life: The Phonograph and Popular Memory, 1890–1945* (New York,
    1999), pp. 65–87.
3   For an overview of the debates surrounding music and globalization, see
    Georgina Born and David Hesmondhalgh (eds), *Western Music and Its Others:
    Difference, Representation, and Appropriation in Music* (Berkeley, CA, 2000), pp.
    21–31; Ronald Radano and Philip V. Bohlman (eds), *Music and the Racial
    Imagination* (Chicago, 2000), pp. 28–34. Some important texts on late twenti-
    eth-century musical globalization include: Steven Feld, "Notes on World Beat
    [1988]" and "From Schizophonia to Schismogenesis: On the Discourses and
    Commodification Practices of 'World Music' and World Beat," in Charles Keil
    and Steven Feld (eds), *Music Grooves: Essays and Dialogues* (Chicago, 1994); Veit
    Erlmann, "The Aesthetics of the Global Imagination: Reflections on World
    Music in the 1990s," *Public Culture*, 8 (1996), pp. 467–88; Timothy D. Taylor,
    Global Pop: World Music, World Markets (London, 1997); Robert Burnett, *The
    Global Jukebox: The International Music Industry* (London, 1996); Simon Frith,
    "The Discourse of World Music," in Born and Hesmondhalgh, *Western Music
    and Its Others*, pp. 305–22. A notable discussion of globalization during the late
    nineteenth century is Veit Erlmann, *Music, Modernity, and the Global Imagination:
    South Africa and the West* (New York, 1999).
4   Industry sales statistics are notoriously difficult to determine for the early
    decades of the industry. Educated estimates suggest annual US record sales in
    1900 were approximately three million units. A steady rise occurred through
    1915 when sales were approximately 55 million. The following years saw
    phonograph record sales rise more quickly, reaching about 140 million in the
    early 1920s. International figures are more difficult to determine. Yet available
    figures suggest that sales outside the US in the early 1910s sat at around 50
    million units. See Gronow and Saunio, *An International History of the Recording
    Industry*, p. 12; and Pekka Gronow, "The Record Industry: The Growth of a
    Mass Medium," *Popular Music*, 3 (1981), pp. 59–60.
5   "A Wonderful Invention – Speech Capable of Indefinite Repetition from
    Automatic Records," *Scientific American* (November 17, 1877); quoted in Welch
    and Burt, *From Tinfoil to Stereo*, p. 9.

6   Quoted in Welch and Burt, *From Tinfoil to Stereo*, pp. 32–3.

7   "Will Replace the Cheap Piano," *Talking Machine World*, March 15 (1905), p. 9.

8   "The Talking Machine in China," *Talking Machine World*, June 15 (1905), p. 11.

9   "Columbia Portable Phonograph in Chilean Forests," *Talking Machine World*, October 15 (1927), p. 50; "The Talking Machine in Alaska," *Talking Machine World*, March 15 (1905), p. 3; " 'Talker' Among Savages," *Talking Machine World*, December 15 (1907), p. 4; "Carryola Master Portable in Denver-Africa Trek," *Talking Machine World*, June 15 (1927), p. 34; "Development of the Export Trade," *Talking Machine World*, October 15 (1910), p. 13; "Talking Machine a Civilizer," *Talking Machine World*, July 15 (1905), p. 7; "Jack London's Great Cruise with the Victor," *Talking Machine World*, June 15 (1908), p. 20.

10 Michael Taussig, *Mimesis and Alterity: A Particular History of the Senses* (New York, 1993), p. 193.

11 "The Talking Machine in Alaska," *Talking Machine World*, March 15 (1905), p. 3.

12 "The Talking Machine Excites Interest Among the Aleutian Islanders," *Talking Machine World*, January 15 (1905), p. 6.

13 Howard Taylor, "A Phonographic Legend," *Talking Machine World*, April 15 (1905), p. 22.

14 For a similar point, see Andrew F. Jones, *Yellow Music: Media Culture and Colonial Modernity in The Chinese Jazz Age* (Durham, NC, 2001), pp. 10–12.

15 Philip J. Deloria, *Indians in Unexpected Places* (Lawrence, KS, 2004), pp. 3–14; quote on p. 9.

16 "The Musical Filipinos," *Talking Machine World*, February 15 (1905), p. 3.

17 Michael S. Kinnear, *The Gramophone Company's First Indian Recordings, 1899–1908* (Bombay, 1994), pp. 9–11, 15–17; See also, Regula Burckhardt Qureshi, "His Master's Voice? Exploring Qawwali and 'Gramophone Culture' in South Asia," *Popular Music*, 18 (1999), pp. 63–98; G. N. Joshi, "A Concise History of the Phonograph Industry in India," *Popular Music*, 7 (1988), pp. 147–56; Peter Manuel, "Popular Music in India: 1901–86," *Popular Music*, 7 (1988), pp. 157–76.

18 See "Talking Machines in China," *Talking Machine World*, June 15 (1906), p. 35. Other early calls to record "local color" or "native bands" in foreign markets include: "Great Export Trade," *Talking Machine World*, January 15 (1905), p. 5; "Talking Machine Prospects," *Talking Machine World*, March 15 (1905), p. 22, regarding Puerto Rico; "Chinese Band or Orchestra Making Records in China," *Talking Machine World*, October 15 (1905), p. 28; "Growth of Export Trade," *Talking Machine World*, December 15 (1905), p. 35, which notes the global desire for recordings of local talent; and "Cuban Trade," *Talking Machine World*, April 15 (1909), p. 43, calling for sensitivity to the variety of musical markets in the districts outside of Havana.

19 Heinrich Bumb, "The Great Beka 'Expedition,' 1905–6," *Talking Machine Review*, 41 (1976), pp. 729–33, quoted in Pekka Gronow, "The Record Industry Comes to the Orient," *Ethnomusicology*, 25 (1981), p. 251.

20 Jones, "Gramophone," p. 81; Gronow, "The Record Industry Comes to the Orient," p. 254; John Perkins, Alan Kelly and John Ward, "On Gramophone Company Matrix Numbers 1898 to 1921," *Record Collector*, 23 (1976), p. 57.

21 Gronow, "The Record Industry: Growth of a Mass Medium," pp. 58–60. The phonograph majors' international expansion was part of a larger trend of US companies looking abroad for antidotes to perceived domestic market saturation. The later part of the nineteenth century witnessed a profound increase in US corporate expansion overseas, fostered by government economic policies, fear of domestic overproduction, and anxiety over the perceived closing of the American frontier. See Walter LaFeber, *The New Empire: An Interpretation of American Expansion, 1860–1898* (Ithaca, NY, 1963). Emily Rosenberg, *Spreading the American Dream: American Economic and Cultural Expansion, 1890–1945* (New York, 1982); Fred V. Carstensen, *American Enterprise in Foreign Markets: Studies of Singer and International Harvester in Imperial Russia* (Chapel Hill, NC, 1984).

22 James C. Goff, "An Interesting Letter," *Talking Machine World*, July 15 (1912), p. 63; Gronow, "The Record Industry Comes to the Orient," pp. 252–3; Kinnear, *The Gramophone Company's First Indian Recordings*, pp. 22–3; Jones, "Gramophone," p. 88; Jerrold Northrop Moore, *A Voice in Time: The Gramophone of Fred Gaisberg, 1873–1951* (London, 1976).

23 "Developing Our Export Trade," *Talking Machine World*, February 15 (1908), p. 18.

24 Fred W. Gaisberg, *The Music Goes Round* (New York, 1942), p. 62.

25 Ibid., p. 54.

26 Oscar C. Preuss, "Round the Recording Studios No. 1 – 'Songs of Araby,'" *Gramophone* (March 1928), pp. 411–12; quoted in Gronow, "The Record Industry Comes to the Orient," p. 273.

27 Quoted in Gerry Farrell, "The Early Days of the Gramophone Industry in India: Historical, Social, and Musical Perspectives," in Andrew Leyshon, David Matless and George Revill (eds), *The Place of Music* (New York, 1998), p. 59.

28 "India a Great Market," *Talking Machine World*, April 15 (1905), p. 6.

29 "Around the World with a Talker," *Talking Machine World*, December 15 (1910), p. 49.

30 "Developing our Export Trade," *Talking Machine World*, February 15 (1908), pp. 18–20.

31 Recording Artists of all Castes in India," *Talking Machine World*, April 15 (1913), p. 32.

32 Gaisberg, *The Music Goes Round*, p. 55; Gronow and Saunio, *An International History of the Recording Industry*, pp. 11–12.

33   "Returns from Making Trip Around World," *Talking Machine World*, January
     15 (1913), pp. 43–4.
34   "The Talking Machine is Here to Stay," *Talking Machine World*, January 15
     (1905), p. 3.
35   Mark Katz, *Capturing Sound: How Technology Changed Music* (Berkeley, CA,
     2004), pp. 48–71; Michael Chanan, *Repeated Takes: A Short History of Recording
     and Its Effects on Music* (London, 1995), pp. 30–1; Welch and Burt, *From Tinfoil
     to Stereo*, pp. 113–14; Russell Sanjek and David Sanjek, *Pennies from Heaven: The
     American Popular Music Business in the Twentieth Century* (New York, 1996), p. 24.
36   "A Great Educational Factor," *Talking Machine World*, December 15 (1910), p.
     4. For more information on Clark, see "How to Put Victors in the Public
     Schools," *Talking Machine World*, June 15 (1911), pp. 31–2; "Mrs. Frances E.
     Clark's Address," *Talking Machine World*, July 15 (1912), pp. 29–30. "Victor
     Educational Matter," *Talking Machine World*, September 15 (1914), p. 29,
     reports on Victor promotional material listing 1,783 cities having placed Victor
     machines in their schools.
37   "Music is Approaching its Richest Development," *Talking Machine World*,
     January 15 (1917), p. 47.
38   John Philip Sousa, "The Menace of Mechanical Music," *Appleton's Magazine*, 8
     (1906), pp. 278–84.
39   Lawrence Levine, *Highbrow/Lowbrow: The Emergence of Cultural Hierarchy in America*
     (Cambridge, MA, 1988); quote from Neil Leonard, *Jazz: Myth and Religion* (New
     York, 1987), p. 12. The editorial originally appeared in the London edition of the
     New York Herald. It was reprinted in the United States by *Musical Courier*. On
     industry attitudes toward African-American music, see also Ronald Clifford
     Foreman, Jr, *Jazz and Race Records, 1920–1932: Their Origins and Their Significance
     for the Record Industry and Society* (PhD dissertation, University of Illinois at Urbana,
     1968), p. 46; Neil Leonard, *Jazz and the White Americans: The Acceptance of a New
     Art Form* (Chicago, 1962); Kathy J. Ogren, *The Jazz Revolution: Twenties America
     and the Meaning of Jazz* (New York, 1989), pp. 139–61.
40   In this sense, the cultural uplift campaign in the phonograph industry had paral-
     lels with the contemporaneous uplift campaign in the advertising industry. See
     Roland Marchand, *Advertising the American Dream: Making Way for Modernity,
     1920–1940* (Berkeley, CA, 1985), p. 87–95; Jackson Lears, *Fables of Abundance:
     A Cultural History of Advertising in America* (New York, 1994); Richard
     Ohmann, *Selling Culture: Magazines, Markets, and Class at the Turn of the Century*
     (London, 1996).
41   " 'Talker' Advertises Sousa," *Talking Machine World*, October 15 (1906), p. 5.
42   "Stimulates Musical Taste," *Talking Machine World*, December 15 (1905), p. 6.
     See also, "Talker Succeeds Hurdy Gurdy," *Talking Machine World*, May 15
     (1910), p. 14.
43   "Some Good Retail Sales Tips," *Talking Machine World*, June 15 (1917), p. 126.
     For a very similar argument, see "Importance of Educating Consumers,"
     Talking Machine World, November 15 (1910), p. 3.

44 "Raphael Cabanas Expected," *Talking Machine World*, April 15 (1910), p. 34; "Successful Work in Developing Foreign Trade," *Talking Machine World*, November 15 (1912), p. 6; "The Talking Machine Trade in Mexico," *Talking Machine World*, October 15 (1913), p. 82; "New Columbia Co. Representative in Texas," *Talking Machine World*, December 15 (1913), p. 33; "Building Business in Texas," *Talking Machine World*, May 15 (1914), p. 30; "Conditions in Texas," *Talking Machine World*, June 15 (1914), p. 10; "Becomes Canadian Manager," *Talking Machine World*, October 15 (1915), p. 35.

45 "Edmond F. Sause New Columbia Export Manager," *Talking Machine World*, February 15 (1915), p. 55; "Developing Our Export Trade," *Talking Machine World*, February 15 (1908), pp. 18–20; "Burns Chats of Trip to Cuba," *Talking Machine World*, July 15 (1910), p. 44; "Interesting Views on Mexico," *Talking Machine World*, April 15 (1911), p. 43; "The Old and New World Visited," *Talking Machine World*, December 15 (1911), pp. 37–8; "To Manufacture in Germany," *Talking Machine World*, April 15 (1914), p. 25; "Records in Foreign Languages," *Talking Machine World*, September 15 (1917), p. 96.

46 *Columbia Record*, 7 (1909), quoted in Pekka Gronow, "Ethnic Recordings: An Introduction," in American Folklife Center, *Ethnic Recordings in America: A Neglected Heritage* (Washington, DC, 1982), p. 3.

47 "Chinese Instead of Irish: Tunes from the Talking Machine Aroused O'Toole to Threats of Action," *Talking Machine World*, August 15 (1905), p. 9. For similar stories, see "Chinese Phonograph Records: Delight Chinatown Citizens in New Orleans – Grand Opera in Chinese a Great Attraction," *Talking Machine World*, January 15 (1905), p. 6; "The Good Old Summertime," *Talking Machine World*, October 15 (1906), p. 50. The latter, a veritable encyclopedia of ethnic stereotypes, relates a scene on a crowded New York train featuring "a wonderful mixture of Teutons, Scandinavians, Orientals, Africans, representatives of the Latin races, an Anglo-Saxon or two, and lastly a large talking machine."

48 "New York Trade Discusses European War," *Talking Machine World*, August 15 (1914), p. 24; untitled editorial, *Talking Machine World*, September 15 (1914), pp. 14–15; Howard Taylor Middleton, "Utilizing the War as an Advertising Medium," *Talking Machine World*, September 15 (1914), pp. 28–9; untitled editorial, *Talking Machine World*, October 15 (1914), pp. 14–15; Howard Taylor Middleton, "Fitting the Record to the Customer," *Talking Machine World*, November 15 (1914), pp. 56–7; "Columbia Recording Laboratory Opened in Chicago," *Talking Machine World*, August 15 (1915), pp. 67–8; "Oriental Records," *Talking Machine World*, June 15 (1917), p. 126. See also, Richard K. Spottswood, "Commercial Ethnic Recordings in the United States," in American Folklife Center, *Ethnic Recordings*, pp. 55–6; *Columbia Record*, quoted by Spottswood, p. 55. See also Kenney, *Recorded Music in American Life*, pp. 79–80.

49 Columbia advertisement, *Talking Machine World*, January 15 (1917), p. 54.

50 "Records in Foreign Languages," *Talking Machine World*, September 15 (1917), p. 96; "Promoting Foreign Record Business," *Talking Machine World*, September 15 (1917), p. 83.

51 "An Almost Untouched Record Selling Field with Millions of Prospective Customers," *Talking Machine World*, June 15 (1922), p. 4.

52 Pathé Frères advertisement, *Talking Machine World*, July 15 (1917), pp. 24–5.

53 Harry A. Goldsmith, "Supplying Successfully the Needs of the Buyers of Foreign Records," *Talking Machine World*, June 15 (1918), p. 15.

54 Perry Bradford, *Born with the Blues* (New York, 1965); Jeff Todd Titon, *Early Downhome Blues: A Musical and Cultural Analysis* (Chapel Hill, NC, 1994 [1977]); William Barlow, *Looking Up at Down: The Emergence of Blues Culture* (Philadelphia, PA, 1989); Bill C. Malone, *Country Music USA, Revised* (Austin, TX, 1985 [1968]).

55 Ralph Peer, interview with Lillian Borgeson, January 13, 1958. Tape #FT2772c. Southern Folklife Collection, University of North Carolina at Chapel Hill.

56 Charlie Gillett, *The Sound of the City: The Rise of Rock and Roll* (New York, 1970); Robert Christgau, "Rah, Rah, Sis-Boom-Bah: The Secret Relationship between College Rock and the Communist Party," in Andrew Ross and Tricia Rose (eds), *Microphone Fiends: Youth Music and Youth Culture* (New York, 1994), pp. 221–6; Motti Regev, "Rock Aesthetics and the Musics of the World," *Theory, Culture & Society*, 14 (1997), pp. 125–42; Frith, "Discourse of World Music," pp. 313–14.

57 Raymond Williams, *Culture and Society* (New York, 1958); George W. Stocking, *Race, Culture, and Evolution: Essays in the History of Anthropology* (Chicago, 1982), pp. 72–4; James Clifford, *The Predicament of Culture: Twentieth-Century Ethnography, Literature, and Art* (Cambridge, MA, 1988), pp. 234–5; Michael Denning, *Culture in the Age of Three Worlds* (London, 2004), pp. 76–81.

58 Denning, *Culture in the Age of Three Worlds*, p. 79.

59 Initial accounts of late twentieth-century globalization used the local in this way to articulate a cultural imperialism model, positing discrete, fragile local cultures smothered in a landslide of commodified, mass-mediated Western music. See Bruno Nettl, *The Western Impact on World Music* (New York, 1985); Dave Laing, "The Music Industry and the 'Cultural Imperialism' Thesis," *Media, Culture & Society*, 8 (July 1986), pp. 331–41; Peter Manuel, *Popular Musics of the Non-Western World* (New York, 1988); Andrew Goodwin and Joe Gore, "World Beat and the Cultural Imperialism Debate," *Socialist Review*, 20 (1990), pp. 174–90; Deanna Campbell Robinson et al. (eds), *Music at the Margins: Popular Music and Cultural Diversity* (London, 1991). Later formulations framed the local as a signifier of difference. Influenced by poststructuralism and post-colonialism, writers defined local music not as a distinct entity but as a position that emerged out of a historical power struggle with the West, be it character-ized by its resistance to Western imperialism, its critique of Western music's canonical universalism, or its ultimate exoticism to Western listeners. See Feld, "From Schizophonia to Schmogenesis"; George Lipsitz, *Time Passages: Collective Memory and American Popular Culture* (Minneapolis, MN, 1990); Jocelyne Guilbault, *Zouk: World Music in the West Indies* (Chicago, 1993);

Martin Stokes (ed.), *Ethnicity, Identity and Music: The Musical Construction of Place* (Oxford, 1994); Erlmann, "Aesthetics of the Global Imagination"; Erlmann, *Music, Modernity, and the Global Imagination*; Philip Hayward (ed.), *Widening the Horizon: Exoticism in Post-War Popular Music* (Sydney, 1999). A final conception identified the local as a historically specific articulation of the global, a site in which global flows of media, money, people and power intercut and interacted in unique ways. This school of scholars explored, to paraphrase Stuart Hall, the musical aesthetics of the hybrid, the crossover, the diaspora and creolization. Hybrid musical forms could speak of being a global and local citizen simultaneously, complete with the contradictions such twoness implied. See Arjun Appadurai, *Modernity at Large: Cultural Dimensions of Globalization* (Minneapolis, MN, 1996); Stuart Hall, "The Local and the Global: Globalization and Ethnicity," in Anthony D. King (ed.), *Culture, Globalization and the World-System* (Binghamton, NY, 1991), pp. 38–3; W. E. B. DuBois, *The Souls of Black Folk* (New York, 1989 [1903]), p. 3; Cedric J. Robinson, *Black Marxism: The Making of the Black Radical Tradition* (Chapel Hill, NC, 2000 [1983]); Paul Gilroy, *The Black Atlantic: Modernity and Double Consciousness* (Cambridge, MA, 1993); George Lipsitz, *Dangerous Crossroads: Popular Music, Postmodernism and the Poetics of Place* (London, 1994); Taylor, *Global Pop*.

7

Competing Forms of Globalization in the Middle East: From the Ottoman Empire to the Nation State, 1918–67

Geoffrey D. Schad

The Middle East is an anomaly in discussions of contemporary globalization. Unlike much of the world, the region did not experience a wave of political and economic liberalization in the 1990s. Governments remained authoritarian and economies heavily regulated. Regional integration in the form of intra-regional trade or effective supra-state institutions remained low. Despite growing exposure to satellite television and the Internet, the Arab states were on the poor side of the "digital divide," and the mass media were stifled by censorship. Arab and foreign observers recognized that, at the turn of the twenty-first century, the Middle East was ill equipped to face the challenges of globalization and suffered from a broad lack of freedom, women's empowerment, and effective use of information technologies.[1]

Viewed from North America and Western Europe, the Middle East appeared to be a threatening and violent place. The 1993 Oslo accords between the Palestine Liberation Organization and Israel failed to evolve into a sustainable peace agreement, much less serve as the basis for a "new Middle East"[2] integrating Israel with its Arab neighbors. The ensuing violence reached new depths during the second Palestinian *intifada* that erupted in late 2000. Sporadic terrorism elsewhere, the successive wars over Iraq, civil wars in Algeria and Afghanistan, and vicious bloodlettings nearby in the Balkans, the Caucasus, and Kashmir all indicated that the region was a maelstrom of interminable fighting carried out by violence-prone fanatics. Most spectacular, of course, was the export of violence from the region, with the September 11, 2001 attacks on the United States and their aftermath ushering in a new "global war on terror" and rumination over what was wrong in the Muslim world and what should be done about it.

One explanation that achieved great currency held that the post-9/11 age was witnessing the "clash of civilizations" prophesied by Samuel Huntington in the 1990s,[3] in which "the West" was enmeshed in an inevitable conflict with "Islam." President George W. Bush was at pains to renounce the word "crusade" in describing US actions against the Taliban in Afghanistan and to stress that the wars there and in Iraq were not against "Islam" as such. It was plain, however, that in essence the conflict was perceived as a manichean struggle between "the force of human freedom" on the one hand and "hatred," "tyranny and terror" on the other.[4]

The principal intellectual supporter of this viewpoint is the historian Bernard Lewis. Lewis's view, which recycles arguments he has made for over half a century, is encapsulated in the title of his best-selling book, *What Went Wrong? The Clash Between Islam and Modernity in the Middle East.*[5] Lewis contends that all the problems of the Middle East are fundamentally Middle Easterners' own fault and intrinsic to Islamic civilization. His argument rests on a fusion of two grand dichotomies: the Orientalist distinction between the "civilizations" of "Islam" and the "West" (or, at times, "Christendom"), and that of modernization theory between "modernity" and "tradition." Muslims who point to external actors' roles in shaping the region's political, social, and economic environment are simply playing a "blame game" and indulging in "neurotic fantasies and conspiracy theories."[6] Rather, "what went wrong" is that the Middle East failed to achieve modernity, defined as the allegedly distinctive attributes of Western European society (secularism, social equality, etc.) intrinsic in Judeo-Christian "civilization." If Middle Easterners' principal goal is to achieve "freedom,"[7] they have little choice but to abandon their own culture and to "modernize," or, better, "Westernize," since Lewis equates "modern" with "Western" and because, as he maintains in an earlier essay, of the "authoritarianism, perhaps we may even say totalitarianism,"[8] of an unchanging, monolithic Islamic political tradition.

Despite the popularity of Lewis's diagnosis, and the fact that it mirrors similar dichotomies employed by such Islamists as Usamah bin Ladin, who also believe in a clash of civilizations, it is at base a reductionist, ahistorical vision that discounts or dismisses the major developments in modern Middle Eastern history as well as the literature on globalization. By contrast, this chapter draws on the concept of globalization to interpret the current crisis in the Middle East, attaching explanatory weight to the interaction of the universal and the local during its recent history.

Specifically, the argument is this: the condition of the Middle East today is largely a result of the region's participation in long-term globalizing processes. In the course of the nineteenth century, the Ottoman Empire, which represented the so-called "archaic" style of globalization, had adopted many of the institutions of contemporary Europe in order to remain a participant, albeit a subordinate one, in the "modern" globalizing system produced by industrial capitalism and European imperialism.[9] This posed a paradox, since these institutions were developed for the nation state, whereas the Ottoman state remained a dynastic empire that formally tolerated ethnic and religious difference and local distinctiveness under the aegis of a religio-political order with claims to universal authority. Although the Ottomans thus represented an alternative universal to that proffered by the nation–state system, the process of institutional adaptation meant that the late Ottoman state exhibited hybridity in the interaction of competing universalities and between the imperial center and local provincial peripheries.

This hybridity persisted after the empire's demise in World War I, when the region was reorganized by Britain and France into several territorially delimited successor states conceived of and presented as nation states. As Philip White's contribution to this volume points out, "nation state" is a slippery concept with shifting meanings not always rigorously defined by its proponents. That said, the nation state, as exported from Western Europe, was assumed to be a universal, globally applicable model that would allow all peoples ("nations") to realize the highest stage of political existence. However, for this universal model to be made operational it had to be made specific, by not only recognizing differences but also making them the foundation for political units. On the one hand, the nation state exalted difference, making the locality the basis for smaller polities; on the other, it attempted to suppress both sub-state and supra-state identities and loyalties in the name of building "national" cohesion. Post-Ottoman elites attempted to resolve the resulting tension by constructing ideologies of political identity appropriate to the new situation. Despite nostalgia for the Ottomans and the emergence of modern political Islam in the immediate post-Ottoman years, nationalism was the dominant idiom of political expression during the half-century separating the Great War from the Six-Day War of June 1967. But here, too, paradoxes operated: although nationalism is self-evidently the appropriate organizing ideology for the nation state, for many post-Ottoman Middle Easterners the "Arab nation" was not coterminous with the colonially established state. Consequently, there was a constant tension between Arab nationalism and local (state-based) nationalisms.

If nationalism of whatever variety today appears eclipsed by political Islam, it is not, *pace* Lewis, due to an existential clash between "Islam" and "modernity." Rather, it is a historical consequence of the success of the modernizing project begun by the Ottomans and continued by the rulers of the post-Ottoman successor states. State-building – the maximizing of government power with respect to the component segments of society – was a success; nation-building was less so. State structures enjoyed a high degree of autonomy from society but governments, usually acting in the name of nationalism, alienated the one stratum that, arguably, was essential for the success of the liberal European nation state: the bourgeoisie. After the Arab defeat of 1967, nationalist rhetoric rang hollow. Simultaneously, the economic and social promises of the nationalist regimes went unfulfilled. The resulting social and ideological vacuum was filled by activists offering "Islamic" solutions to society's ills.

Although these broad trends characterize most Arab states, in this chapter the emphasis will be on the Syrian experience. The discussion of the Syrian case here draws on this author's ongoing research on twentieth-century Syria, referred to in notes 41 and 57 below. Syria shows in microcosm these wider trends, although the particularities of the Syrian case put some of them in sharper focus. Here was a congeries of Ottoman provinces that prior to 1918 had no common political identity. Under the French Mandate, Syria was both a truncated local, being much smaller than the imagined Greater Syria, and an expansive one, containing rival foci of identity in the metropolises of Damascus and Aleppo. Syria, later termed the "beating heart of Arabism,"[10] was where the tensions between Arab nationalism and local nationalisms were played out. Mandatory and post-independence Syria was also home to a new class of bourgeois industrialists who saw themselves simultaneously as architects of national economic independence, the vanguard of a reconstituted regional economic order, and equal members of a progressive global bourgeoisie. Finally, Syria is where a political party espousing an expansive Arab-nationalist ideology – the Bacth – emerged and then came to power thanks to *the* institution of the modern state, the military. The bankruptcy of the nationalist project can be seen in contemporary Syria, where the regime mouths republican and Arab-nationalist slogans while ruling through ascriptive ties and upholding dynastic succession.

This chapter will first examine the adaptation of the Ottoman imperial system to the requirements of modern globalization, then discuss the processes by which the nation-state order superseded it in the Middle East. This section discusses the tensions between the universal and the local intrinsic to the state- and nation-building project, referring to how nationalist ideologies attempted to reconcile universality with specificity. The equivocal success of Arab nationalism in the 1950s and the consequences of the Arab states' crisis of legitimacy in the 1960s are presented as accounting in part for the eclipse of nationalism by Islamism from the 1970s onwards. Finally, while no attempt at predicting the future is made, the present situation in the region will be outlined in terms of competition between rival universals and interaction between local and universal to produce hybrid identities.

The Ottoman system and "modern" globalization

The Ottoman Empire was the largest polity of the Middle East from the early 1500s to World War I. The legatee of the great Islamic empires, in its formative centuries it became an exemplar of the type of state characteristic of the so-called "archaic" style of globalization.[11] The Ottomans, like their predecessors, were avowedly Muslim rulers who legitimized their rule in an Islamic idiom. But they were also heirs of an older regional tradition of ecumenical empire in which local linguistic, religious, and other cultural differences were respected so long as sub-imperial groups paid their taxes and did not revolt.

Such an attitude was partially a concession to the limits imposed on coercive power by contemporary technologies, which precluded uniformity, even had it been a policy goal. But it also reflected a manner of rule in which political power was devolved, giving multiple social groups a stake in the maintenance of the system. In the capital, sultans of the Ottoman house ceded effective power to bureaucratic households, garrison commanders, and, on occasion, the Istanbul mob. In the provinces, the sultan's governors relied on advisory councils representing local interest groups in order to govern, and depended on local tax farmers to collect revenue.[12] Throughout the empire occupational groups, tribes, and non-Muslim religious communities enjoyed considerable autonomy.

The genius of the Ottoman approach to local diversity was that it was able to retain its subjects' loyalty even when central authority was weak. During the nadir of Ottoman power in the seventeenth and eighteenth centuries, when the empire lost territory to Austria and Russia, the legitimacy of the Ottoman dynasty and state remained unquestioned, even while provincial governors and tax farmers established de facto dynasties, and revolts in the capital deposed individual sultans. Local rulers and tax farmers depended on Istanbul to recognize their status, and their households were bound to those of central administrators through ties of marriage and mutual interest.[13]

The Ottoman sultan increasingly relied on negotiation rather than command to ensure obedience.[14] He "did not impose uniformity, but rather ordered and regulated the various classes and elements in the empire, in such a way that they should live at peace with each other and contribute their due share to the stability and prosperity of the whole."[15] The Ottomans presided over not so much a coherent territorially delimited state as an archipelago of cities and their agricultural hinterlands, each tied to the sovereign in his capital.[16] In Albert Hourani's words, "[t]he empire then was not so much a single community as a group of communities each of which claimed the immediate loyalty of its members."[17]

This decentralized polity could survive only so long as there was no external enemy strong enough to seriously threaten its existence. By the late eighteenth century such an enemy had appeared with the Russian conquest of Ottoman lands around the Black Sea and Napoleon's seizure of Egypt. These defeats exposed the obsolescence of Ottoman military and fiscal methods, while the after-effects of the French Revolution introduced the idiom of nationalism into what had been controllable provincial rebellions and jacqueries. In consequence, starting in the 1790s under Sultan Selim III and then decisively from the 1820s under Sultan Mahmud II and his successors, the Ottoman leadership embarked on a series of reforms intended to bolster the central state's external power and firmly reassert its internal authority.

These reforms, collectively known as the Tanzimat ("reordering"), entailed modernizing the military, rationalizing and expanding the civil bureaucracy, reforming the provincial administration and regularizing its personnel, and instituting new legal codes and the courts to administer them. Of necessity new schools were required to train officers, bureaucrats, lawyers, and judges. In consequence, a new class of Ottoman officials, familiar with European languages and modes of thought and committed to the empire's preservation and modernization, had evolved by the end of the century. Although Ottoman elites had always been polyglot and cosmopolitan,[18] by the early 1900s they had developed political, social, economic, and cultural attitudes and patterns of personal consumption that exhibited hybridity.[19] Late Ottoman officialdom assimilated the European rhetoric of progress but inverted European racism and prejudice against Islam to present itself as a vanguard of modernity bringing progress to its own retrograde provincials.[20]

Besides producing a new generation of modern bureaucrats, the Tanzimat era generated other new social groupings. The expansion of commercial agriculture geared to export engendered a new landlord class.[21] This class in turn converted its wealth into power by sending its sons into the new government institutions and by exerting direct influence through such innovations as provincial consultative councils and the Ottoman parliament, established by the constitution of 1876. This class of "notables" was the sub-imperial political elite under the Ottomans and then the Europeans, and it was this stratum that provided the initial leadership of the independent Arab states.[22] European economic penetration fostered the rise of a compradorial bourgeoisie in coastal cities while also benefiting merchants in the cities of the interior.[23] However, the evolution of an Ottoman industrialist class was inhibited by the 1838 Treaty of Balta Liman, which eliminated local commercial and industrial monopolies and imposed free trade on the empire. Nevertheless, merchants and artisans adapted to the new environment, which by the end of the century had almost completely destroyed the guild system and substituted capitalist relations for it.[24] Although Ottoman artisans largely adapted by specializing in higher-quality goods for the domestic market, in the case of the rug industry production was geared to the export market, with "traditional" patterns being revamped to meet the tastes of Western European and North American consumers, much as happened with the Navajo textiles examined by Erika Bsumek in this volume.[25]

By the late nineteenth century, key interest groups in the Ottoman Empire were firmly embedded in the European-dominated world economy; they were also subjects of an expanding state that embraced a progressive, modernizing discourse. A hybrid, official "Ottomanism" was propagated to maintain loyalty to this state. The Ottoman state was still a polyethnic, multiconfessional empire presided over by a traditional dynast claiming Islamic legitimacy,[26] but one which had many features of contemporary European nation states and in which old distinctions of status based on religion were being erased.[27] Ottomanism, a quasi-ideology, was not a homogenizing official nationalism, as were contemporaneous Russification policies,[28] but rather an attempt to promote an empire-wide patriotism among all ethnicities and confessions.

"Ottomanism" had limited success. The Balkan peoples, abetted by the Great Powers, rejected their Ottoman affiliation and obtained independence in their own nation states. Tendencies toward greater linguistic and ethnic self-identification as "Arabs" or "Turks" became more marked in the latter part of the 1800s, but with few exceptions most inhabitants of the now truncated empire remained loyal. Ottomanism remained official policy, despite a renewed stress on Islam as the basis of loyalty during the royal dictatorship of Sultan ᶜAbd al-Hamid II (1876–1909), which alienated Christians, and certain policies undertaken during the Second Constitutional Period (1908–18) interpreted by Arabs as promoting Turkish nationalism. Although

198

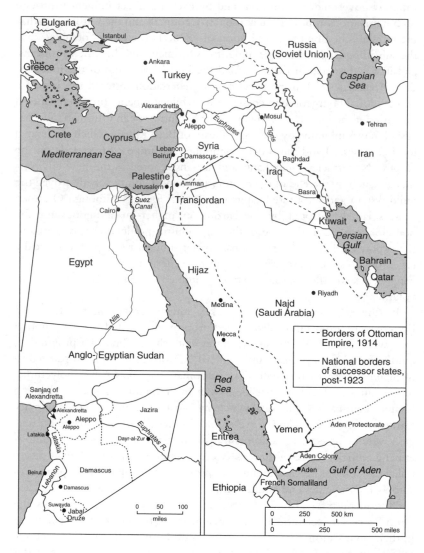

Main map adapted from Richard W. Bulliet et al., *The Earth and Its Peoples: A Global History*, 3rd edition (Boston, MA: Houghton Mifflin, 2005), Map 29.4, p. 796. Inset map adapted from Jere L. Bacharach, *A Middle East Studies Handbook* (Seattle, WA: University of Washington Press, 1984), Map 32, p. 114.

Map 2   The partition of the Ottoman Empire, 1914–23
(*Inset*: The divisions of Syria, 1920–46)

secret societies seeking Arab independence emerged in the last years before World War I, to the extent that Arab nationalism was at all popular it was much more moderate. For example, the delegates to the 1913 Syrian–Arab Congress in Paris asked, in effect, for a partnership between Turks and Arabs in running the empire, rather like that between German-Austrians and Magyars in the Habsburg state after 1867.[29] Even the Great War itself, which saw public hangings of several Arab nationalists and the exiling of others, the outbreak of the Arab Revolt, and a massive famine in Syria[30] did not substantially dent loyalty to the empire. After the Ottoman defeat in 1918, resistance to the European takeover of the Middle East was made as often as not in the name of Ottoman legitimacy, not Turkish or Arab nationalism. In its initial phase the "Turkish nationalist" movement was in fact a struggle for the preservation of Ottoman rights, as was opposition to the French in northern Syria in 1919–22.[31]

The Mandatory order, the independence struggle, and early nationalism

The Entente victors had envisaged dividing the empire among themselves, leaving only a rump Ottoman state in Istanbul and part of Anatolia. However, due to the publication of the secret agreements[32] by the Bolsheviks, the need to reward the Hashimite dynasts who had led the British-sponsored Arab Revolt, and the elevation of national self-determination as a guiding principle by US President Wilson, the victors chose to reconcile imperial interests with nationalist principles in the Mandate system. Rather than directly annexing the Arab provinces, Britain and France obtained League of Nations "Mandates" to prepare the inhabitants of their respective zones (Palestine, Transjordan, and Iraq for Britain, Lebanon and Syria for France) for eventual independence. That the Mandatory scheme corresponded with neither the expressed aspirations of the peoples concerned[33] nor public Anglo-French commitments to support Arab independence[34] did nothing to bar its implementation, legally concluded in 1923 but effectively in force since the San Remo conference of 1920.

Except for Turkey, which established itself by defeating foreign invaders, the Ottoman successor states entered into existence with severely flawed popular legitimacy. Imposed by force of foreign arms, with borders drawn for the convenience of Paris and London, the new states were manifestly European creations. Although local elites, upon whom the exhausted victors had to rely, had grown accustomed to serving distant masters, the new overlords were foreign in a way that the Ottomans had not been. A Damascene or Baghdadi official or army officer, trained in Istanbul and whose career took him all over the empire, could and did regard himself as an "Ottoman"; a Syrian or Iraqi could never aspire to be French or British.[35] In other ways, too, the new states lacked legitimacy. The Mandatory Powers tinkered endlessly with constitutional arrangements to preserve their dominance in what were allegedly to be independent countries. In Syria, France followed the principle of *divide et impera*, repeatedly rearranging administrative divisions. The separate Grand Liban proclaimed in 1920, including majority-Muslim districts previously governed from Damascus, was much larger than the Maronite-Druze homeland of Mount Lebanon that had been an autonomous Ottoman province after 1860.[36] In what remained of Syria, the Druze and Alawite regions were administered for most of the Mandate as entities separate from "Syria."[37] The Alexandretta district, too, had a separate status, and was ultimately ceded to Turkey in violation of the express terms of the Mandate. The Damascus and Aleppo regions were initially constituted as distinct "states," a juridical "Syria" being established only in 1924. The Mandatory Power also manipulated elections, prorogued parliamentary sessions, appointed its clients to high office, and even briefly flirted with crowning an Ottoman in-law as king of Syria.[38]

Apart from the legitimacy problems connected with their creation as alien enterprises, the Ottoman successor states suffered more profound difficulties. In theory these states were nation states, but they were for the most part bereft of the characteristics that had come to define the ideal-type European nation state of the nineteenth century: ethno-linguistic homogeneity and a shared historical experience within the state's boundaries. Although the vast majority of the new states' populations were Arabic-speaking Sunni Muslims, "Arabism" was still a novel concept[39] and the inhabitants were diverse in ethnicity, religion, and mode of life. In addition to Sunni Arabs, Syria contained Kurds, Turks, and Turcomans; Armenian and Syriac Christian refugees from Anatolia; native Christians of all denominations; Jews, both local and immigrant; Shi'i Muslims; and the esoteric Druze and Alawites. Moreover, the population was differentiated into urbanites, peasants, and nomads (who did not respect the new borders). For many Syrians, the principal loyalty was to sect, tribe, clan, or urban quarter, rather than to "Syria." Such diversity had not posed a problem for the Ottoman order, but it was a fundamental threat to the homogeneity of the nation state. This lack of consonance between the community imagined by the architects of the Mandatory system and the communities with which Syrians identified would have but muted political relevance during the Mandate years, when the quest for independence had priority, but would emerge as a significant limitation on state legitimacy following independence.

The states' borders, moreover, did not correspond to what was spatially relevant to their inhabitants, be it previous provincial divisions or imagined unities. For the most part the boundaries were invisible lines drawn on a map at San Remo. Mandatory Syria itself was in effect a rump state, assembled from portions of the old Ottoman provinces of Damascus and Aleppo but excluding others (Palestine, Transjordan, Lebanon) long considered part of an imagined "Greater Syria." The new boundaries isolated both metropolises from their historic commercial hinterlands and forced these rivals into a new, often conflictual relationship. Although this is not the place to enter into the controversies surrounding the notion of Greater Syria, it must be mentioned that historically the *bilad al-sham* had been regarded by its inhabitants as extending from the Sinai to the Taurus, then fading imperceptibly into the vast Syrian steppe/desert. Within this whole Jews, Muslims, and Christians alike regarded Palestine within its biblical bounds between Dan and Beersheba as a special holy land, but while much of Palestine had been administered as a unit from Jerusalem, "Palestine" as such had no administrative existence. Too, there had been set up a "Vilayet of Syria" in the nineteenth century, but it did not correspond to the later Syrian state. Despite the Ottomans' drawing of administrative lines on the map, they had no reality for nomads and little for many others. One should view the settlement and administrative arrangements of Ottoman times as concentric circles radiating from major urban centers rather than as adjacent, cartographically determined entities. It is important to note that the delegates to the Syrian Congress at Damascus in 1920, which named the Hashimite amir Faysal king of Syria, came from Palestine, Transjordan, and Lebanon in addition to the "Syria" he governed, and that the interlocutors of the King-Crane Commission had demanded Syrian unity and independence. Palestinians continued to refer to their area as "South Syria" for several years.[40]

Although the establishment of the Mandatory system marked a definite rupture with the past, there were also continuities. The new states were successors to the Ottomans, and not merely in the juridical sense that they assumed Ottoman international obligations. Ottoman legislation continued in force; justice, taxation, and local administration followed Ottoman forms; and the general development of the states was along the lines pioneered during the Tanzimat. When the Mandatory Powers sought to innovate they heeded Ottoman precedent, with the result that the "traditional" institutions the French and British tried to reform were themselves recent Ottoman innovations based on European, especially French, models.[41] Perhaps most important, late Ottoman patterns of social organization persisted, with landlord-bureaucrat notables maintaining local influence through patron–client networks. Such continuities endured well into the independence period.

For all the artificiality of the states and despite nostalgia for the Ottomans, by the mid-1920s it had become clear to most politically conscious Middle Easterners that the new system was there to stay. It was therefore necessary to foster a sense of identity corresponding to the new reality. As these states were putatively nation states, so nationalisms were evolved as legitimating and mobilizing ideologies. Naturally enough, a range of Arab nationalisms developed.[42] These may be conceived of in generational terms.

The first generation, those who were raised in the late Ottoman period and led the independence struggle against Britain and France, articulated a pragmatic approach. Many of these leaders had been Arabists in the last decades of the empire and retained an ostensible commitment to Arab unity. But since the Mandates precluded the establishment of a unitary Arab state, they focused their immediate attention on the task at hand: achieving the independence of the state as it had been set up. Those who rejected the reality of the new state system and continued to press for Arab integration led the existence of exiled pamphleteers.[43] Those who accepted it sought the available levers of power. There was coordination across borders, and a shared sense of "Arabness," but each "national" struggle took place separately. The relation of the universal and the local had now shifted. Whereas the universal Ottoman state had presided over a host of localisms that lacked operational political content, now a universally applicable local unit, the nation state, had been established. The leaders of these states all claimed loyalty to one universal – Arabism – while also of necessity building local patriotism.

The dynamics of this relationship between universal Arabism and local patriotism varied throughout the region, often in sharply contrasting ways. In Iraq the problem was to find a mode of legitimation in an artificially enlarged locality with an imported ruling class affiliated with a local minority elite.[44] In Syria, the problem was dealing with an unnaturally small unit. Although the major population centers, Aleppo and Damascus, faced in different directions and remained rivals, there was already a sense that they belonged to a Syrian unit, the *bilad al-sham* or "Greater Syria." That conceptual unit was far larger than the "Syria" under French rule. But the Syrian independence leaders – who coalesced in the National Bloc (*al-Kutla al-Wataniyya*) – were practical men. To the extent that they stressed Syrian unity, it was in opposition to French divide-and-rule tactics rather than in seeking to unite all *Syria irredenta* to Damascus. The Bloc sought Syrian independence through "honorable cooperation" with the political institutions established by the French.[45]

As in Iraq, Arabism was stressed in official rhetoric and in the public education system,[46] but was given a local twist. Syria was portrayed as the cradle of Arabism; the anniversary of the May 1916 Ottoman execution of Arab nationalists became a national holiday.[47] History was rewritten, the four centuries of Ottoman rule anachronistically portrayed as four hundred years of Turkish suppression of the Arab nation.[48] But, alongside the stress on Syria's Arabness, there was also the elaboration of a specifically Syrian (and Lebanese) identity fostered by such new institutions as the national museums.[49]

Popular Arab nationalism and its rivals

By the 1930s a new generation, ignorant of the Ottomans, raised in the new states, educated in the public schools and national universities, and linked across borders by such institutions as the American University in Beirut (AUB)[50] and the press, was coming of age. Educated urban middle-class youth, often underemployed, were accustomed to participating in local efforts for independence and bent on eliminating foreign influence. But, for them, a universal larger than the restricted confines of the Mandatory states was needed. It was this generation that came to envisage the Arab nation as a universal that would supplant the old imperial world of their fathers.

Arab nationalism was, of course, not the only new universalizing tendency for this generation. Communism had an appeal for some.[51] But despite the best efforts of local and foreign communists, Marxism never became more than a minority tendency. In the colonized world, socialist internationalism could not trump the quest for national self-determination.

The interwar years also witnessed the emergence of another potent rival to nationalism, although its significance became apparent only decades later: political Islam. The Muslim Brotherhood (*al-Ikhwan al-Muslimin*), to which most modern Islamist movements trace their origins, was founded in Egypt in 1928. The Brotherhood called for a return to a truly Islamic society, arguing that the adoption of Western ways – especially the dilution of the Islamic law (*shari*a) by Western law codes – had harmed Egypt. The goal was an "Islamic order" in which the Qur'an was the fundamental constitution, the government operated according to consultation (*shura*), and the executive was accountable to the laws of Islam and the will of the people.[52] The Brotherhood acknowledged the strength of nationalist sentiment, but claimed that the "only enduring loyalty" possible for a Muslim was to the Muslim nation.[53] But if its ultimate loyalty was to the wider Muslim community, the state the Brotherhood wished to make Islamic was Egypt. For the Brothers, as for most later Islamist groups, the answer to society's problems was the construction of an Islamic order, but the field of action was the existing state. Muslim unity, while desirable, was not the immediate goal.

Although the projected universal and the idiom differed, Islamists faced the same operational dilemma as Arabist politicians and addressed it similarly.

Despite the appeal of communism and political Islam to certain strata, it was Arab nationalism that had the greatest appeal to this generation. An expansive version of the Arabism endorsed by earlier nationalists, this nationalism ultimately rejected the legitimacy of the postwar nation-state order.

This generation defined as Arabs "all who are Arab in their language, culture, and loyalty," the Arab homeland as "the land which has been, or is, inhabited by an Arab majority," and Arab nationalism as "the feeling for the necessity of independence and unity which the inhabitants of the Arab lands share."[54] For them, there was a unitary "Arab nation" deserving independence and unity that was greater than the "Arab state" that had been the Hashimite goal in 1916. Previous Arabists had been concerned with the Ottoman Arab provinces only. This generation's "Arab nation" also included the Arabian Peninsula, Egypt, and North Africa. This extension not only had romantic or theoretical value, but programmatic merit as well. As all the Arabs in the Arab nation faced the same challenge of foreign rule, so they had a common solution: a united Arab struggle for independence.

In stressing the ethno-linguistic character of Arabness, these thinkers downplayed the fact that the vast majority of Arabs were Muslims. While not disparaging Islam, the achievements of the past were presented as national rather than religious in character. Thus the Aleppine Edmond Rabbath wrote of "the astonishing history of the Arabs, wrongly called Islamic."[55] This approach facilitated including Christians (and Jews) among the Arabs, which was crucial to the movement's viability, given the prominence of the Christian community and French efforts to exploit confessionalism. Christians were in a good position to express Arab political aspirations in language comprehensible to Europeans, given their long tradition of Western education. But many Muslims, too, were familiar with the same idiom, through their own studies at European institutions or by passing through high schools in which many teachers had been educated abroad.[56]

This expanded Arab nationalism became the program of new parties whose youthful membership transcended state borders. The leading representative during the Mandatory years was the League of National Action (*ʿUsbat al-ʿamal al-qawmi*), founded in 1933. The League, principally active in Syria, set itself up as the radical alternative to the more conservative older generation of nationalists. Its distinctive approach was underscored by its name: "national" was *qawmi*, that is, of the entire Arab nation (*qawm*), rather than of the local state, or homeland (*watan*). Although *qawmiyya* ([pan-]Arab nationalism) is not necessarily incompatible with *wataniyya* (local patriotism), the two are distinct. Extreme *qawmi* nationalists denigrated local loyalties as being divisive and inimical to the national interest. The Arab nation now took precedence; the local state was merely the field of immediate action. Although the League would be restrained in Syria by the more conservative National Bloc and dissolved in the later 1930s, it left a strong imprint on the shape of Arab nationalism to come. Among its heirs was the standard-bearer of Arab unity efforts, the Ba'th party.

Arab nationalism appealed to more than just a youthful, underemployed intelligentsia. There was another significant stratum for whom Arab unity seemed to be a solution: the business elite. This business class comprised several subgroups. Among them, there was the old, urban mercantile elite, for whom the division of the empire into separate states had also meant its fragmentation into separate, weaker national markets. They were joined by a new industrial bourgeoisie, who by the 1930s had evolved from being patrons of putting-out networks to becoming proprietors of true factories, fostered in part by a French policy of benign neglect and in part by successful lobbying by manufacturers for protective tariffs.[57]

For this business elite economic nationalism was a natural outlook. It derived from late Ottoman efforts to restore the empire's economic sovereignty,[58] but was also inspired by the contemporary discourse linking political and economic anti-colonialism and by the move toward protectionism and autarky by many nations in the early 1930s.[59] Middle Eastern economic nationalism was hardly exceptional, the perhaps unconscious evocation of the ideas of Friedrich List being shared with, among others, Meiji Japan, as Mark Metzler's contribution to this volume underscores. Just as early political nationalists had accepted the post-Ottoman states as the relevant arena of political action, so too economic nationalists initially confined their efforts to the new states. Their goals were protectionism and achieving domestic autarky. These were the impetus behind the 1932 founding of the Syrian Spinning and Weaving Company of Aleppo, the first of many important enterprises known as the "national" (*watani*) companies whose directors were leaders or close associates of the National Bloc.[60] The company's name deliberately linked economic action to political goals, as did that of the Egyptian Bank Misr, which may have served as an example to the Syrians.[61]

But if most industrialists were nationalists, they were not xenophobes. As capitalists they had complex relations with their foreign counterparts. For example Sami Sa'im al-Dahr, a leading Aleppo textile industrialist, was chair of the city's chamber of industry and a vocal partisan of the National Bloc. But he had also been trained in France, was the exclusive agent of a French loom manufacturer, and often directly lobbied the French High Commission rather than the Syrian government.[62]

But autarkic industrial development could only go so far: once the national market was saturated, which did not take long given the low purchasing power of most of the population, there was nowhere to go for continued growth but abroad. With only a limited ability to participate in global markets and unable to penetrate Turkey at all, thanks to Kemalist étatisme,[63] the Arabs had to turn to one another. If there was one Arab nation, logically there should be a common Arab market.

Mercantile support of a broader Arab nationalism was in part a reflection of the bourgeoisie's particular predicament. But also the bourgeoisie sensed, as did the ideologues, that the local character of the new state system was too limiting for full social development. A new universal unit was needed, this time imagined in national terms but covering much the same territory as the bygone Ottoman Empire. Moreover, class interest and outlook could inform the ideology of this new vision. As Hanna Batatu acutely observed:

> From the standpoint of this class, the fragmentation after 1917 of the Arab provinces of the Ottoman empire constituted an abiding hindrance to the old trade channels and the free flow of commerce. Its members resented being confined within narrow borders, and favored large and expanding markets, unencumbered by tariffs and customs duties or by a multiplicity of economic rules and regulations. In brief, to no other element of the population was a pan-Arab horizon more natural.[64]

Independence and the quest for Arab unity

The Arab states achieved effective independence in the late 1940s due to the erosion of British and French power in World War II. With the goal of the first generation of nationalists achieved, new struggles arose within and among the new states. Internally there was a generational and even more a class struggle, as the landlord-notables who had held political leadership during the Ottoman and interwar periods were challenged by lower-middle-class elements representing a wider constituency of peasants and urban workers demanding economic redistribution. The nascent industrial bourgeoisie sought to play a balancing role in this struggle and to present itself as the vanguard of the national future. In the long run, however, the struggle was won by the lower-middle-class forces, who used their predominance in the paramount institution of the modern state, the military, to disenfranchise their opponents.

The internal struggle was complemented by an interstate struggle for regional dominance that took place against the backdrop of Cold War rivalries[65] and the Arab–Israeli conflict. Rulers in Cairo, Damascus, and Baghdad, although motivated by reasons of state, expressed themselves in the discourse of supra-state Arab nationalism. This idiom was no accident, as the young officers who seized power in the 1950s had been indoctrinated by the Arab-nationalist organizations of their youth. These new leaders made this trans-state ideology an article of popular consumption through the new mass media, especially radio. The culmination of this process came in 1958, with the founding of the short-lived United Arab Republic (UAR) of Egypt and Syria.

This paradoxical period, during which governing elites simultaneously advocated supra-state nationalism and jealously guarded the hard-won sovereignty of the new states, is most often associated with Egyptian President Jamal ᶜAbd al-Nasir (1954–70). But the structural changes that Nasir represented were pioneered and carried to their furthest extent in Syria. It was in Syria that the most thorough statement of the Arab-nationalist ethos – Baᶜthism – was elaborated. It was also in Syria that the contest between competing ideologies and classes was most overt. Today, the contemporary Syrian government is perhaps the purest remaining representative of the "Nasirist"-type state.[66]

The rise of the military to power in the Arab states and the outlook of its politicized officers is a complex subject.[67] In broad terms, the military had been neglected during the interwar years. The main defense of Syria was the Armée du Levant, composed of French and colonial troops. The native Troupes Spéciales were a small force, numbering fewer than ten thousand at independence in 1946. Moreover, the military was not a career favored by the notability or the urban bourgeoisie. But after independence, the army was expanded, many veterans of nationalist youth movements becoming officer cadets. The Arab–Israeli war in 1948 found the Syrian army ill prepared. The ensuing defeat made Syrian officers, who blamed civilian politicians, seek to reclaim their honor. The first coup d'état in 1949 came even before armistice negotiations with Israel were completed. The colonels' rule that continued until 1954 made the army a critical actor in internal politics and set an example to be followed after 1963 by the contemporary Syrian regime. Also, crucially, this half-decade was one during which the state managed to firmly establish its autonomy from society and suppress competitive social components, again foreshadowing the policies and politics followed after 1963.

Colonel Adib al-Shishakli, the effective ruler of Syria from late 1949 until early 1954, pursued many policies later associated with Nasir: a neutralist foreign policy, a populist mass rally replacing political parties, the assertion of a strong state role in the economy, and the progressive weakening of the old elites. Although Shishakli achieved some notable successes, including co-opting the nascent industrial bourgeoisie through tax breaks and other concessions,[68] his support was thin and he was deposed in a popular uprising.

The convoluted electoral politics of the post-Shishakli years showed the diversity of competing ideologies. The 1954 elections were contested by the successor factions of the old National Bloc, Islamists, Communists, the Syrian Social Nationalist Party, and others.[69] But the party that dominated the post-Shishakli era, led Syria into the UAR, and won power at bayonet point in 1963, was one espousing a radical, pan-Arab nationalist political and social agenda: the Ba^cth.[70]

The Ba^cth (Renaissance) party was founded in the mid-1940s by two Sorbonne-trained teachers from the Damascene mercantile stratum, Michel ^cAflaq, a Christian, and Salah al-Din Bitar, a Muslim. A party of romantic pan-Arab nationalism,[71] in its early years it was restricted to a small circle of ^cAflaq's and Bitar's devotees. It soon attracted many former members of the League of National Action,[72] and acquired its final form through its fusion in 1952 with the anti-landlord Arab Socialist Party.[73]

As elaborated in its program,[74] the Ba^cth stood for a trinity of interdependent objectives: unity, freedom, and socialism. Unity and freedom formed the first fundamental principle of the Ba^cth, the party constitution proclaiming the Arabs "a single nation, having a natural right to exist within a single state." The Ba^cth went on to declare that "the Arab homeland is an indivisible politico-economic unit. It is impossible for any of the Arab regions to perfect the conditions of its life in isolation from the rest." This Arab nation or homeland, later defined extensively from the borders with Iran and Turkey down through the Arabian Peninsula and across North Africa, is regarded as a cultural unit belonging to the Arabs only.[75] The Arab nation (here, the people rather than the territory) "is distinguished by its special merit" and has "an eternal mission which manifests itself in the form of a complete regeneration through the stages of history, leading to the reformation of human existence, the advancement of human progress, and the enhancement of harmony and cooperation among nations." In expanding on this mission, which links the Arabs to a true universal, that of humanity as a whole, the party proclaims that "the Arabs benefit from world civilization, and they contribute to it in turn." This conceptualization of the Arabs and their place in the scheme of human progress reflects ^cAflaq and Bitar's close reading of German romantic philosophers as well as the Marxism to which they were exposed in their own student days.

The party that was to achieve this regeneration of the Arab nation, the Ba^cth, was identified as nationalist, socialist, populist, and revolutionary, with the specific goals of achieving "absolute freedom for the Arab homeland," uniting all Arabs into a single state, and rebelling "against existing evils affecting all intellectual, economic, social and political aspects of life." The Ba^cth envisioned an Arab state with an executive responsible to a directly elected legislature, an independent judiciary, a unified legal code, and a decentralized administration. The Baᶜth's socialist agenda called for land redistribution, nationalization of public utilities and large industries, a voice for labor in factory administration, and state-led development, but also respected private ownership rights, property, and small industry. The Baᶜth's socialism was a national one, not a Marxist one, and the party rejected class struggle.

On the whole this was a comprehensive if naïve ideology, and one that fitted well with the contemporary ethos of postcolonial nationalism. Indeed, it expressed sentiments that would not be out of place in a European social-democratic party.[76] In Arab terms it contained a few novelties. Arabness was defined in linguistic and affective rather than racial terms, and the ideology was wholly secular. Religion was nowhere mentioned in the party program, although elsewhere ᶜAflaq would write of the foundational role that Islam played in forming the Arab nation.[77] The Arab *qawm* of the earlier pan-Arabs was transformed into a pan-Arab *watan*: the Arab people (*qawm*) inhabits the Arab homeland (*watan*), and in the fullness of time there will be one Arab nation state throughout the homeland.[78] An additional novelty was the linkage of the Arab mission not only to the anti-imperialist struggle but also to the progress of global humanity. The ideology's appeal was demonstrated by the proliferation of party branches in several states in the 1950s.

The Baᶜth was hardly the only force promoting a pan-Arab identity in the 1950s. Once Nasir had established his authority in Egypt, he too came to present himself as an Arab nationalist, as did the post-1958 rulers of Iraq. Moreover, even the Arab states, whose individual sovereignties would have been eradicated by the achievement of the Baᶜthist project, had begun a process of interstate cooperation based on a common Arab identity with the 1945 establishment of the League of Arab States.[79] A voluntary association of sovereign independent states, not a proto-government for the Arab nation, the Arab League's purpose was

> the strengthening of the relations between the member states; the co-ordination of their policies in order to achieve co-operation between them and to safeguard their independence and sovereignty; and a general concern with the affairs and interests of the Arab countries.[80]

Cooperation and coordination are a far cry from unity, and the Arab League has often failed to realize even these minimal goals. The League's member states often ignore agreed-on common Arab policies to pursue their particular interests. Thanks to the continued success of the state-building reforms begun under the Ottomans, the Arab states today are more robust than they were at independence, but the "Arab nation" is no closer to unity than it was 60 years ago.

Of the three occasions when the post–Ottoman state system has been substantially challenged, only the 1958–61 UAR was motivated by pan-Arab ideology.[81] Ba^cthist ideologues in the Syrian government, fearful for their own position, appealed to the newly popular Egyptian leader, who had employed Arab-nationalist rhetoric since the Suez crisis. A reluctant Nasir, his bluff called, acquiesced in the merger, but on his own terms. The new union was one in which Nasirist Bonapartism, not Ba^cthist idealism, would prevail. The price of Arab unity was the Ba^cth dissolving itself, and Syrian interests being subordinated to Egyptian ones.

The 1960s and the bankruptcy of nationalism

As it turned out, the UAR was not the first stage in the building of the Ba^cth's envisaged unitary Arab state. It fell apart in 1961, largely because it was a vehicle for Egyptian domination instead of being an equal partnership. The proximate cause was the extension to Syria of Egyptian decrees nationalizing large industry, alienating the hitherto pro-union Syrian industrialists, who made common cause with the disaffected Syrian army. Although the idea of unity was revived in 1963 by new Ba^cthist leaders in Iraq and Syria,[82] and later unions would be projected among various Arab countries,[83] the UAR experiment was never repeated.

The UAR's collapse was only the first of several debacles that led to a loss of confidence in Arab nationalist leaders and the ideology they professed. The most significant of these were the 1967 Arab defeat by Israel, the failure of the regimes to fulfill their socio-economic promises, their increasing reliance on coercion to maintain their authority, and the progressive narrowing of their support base.

The Palestine issue had long been a principal theme in inter-Arab politics. One of the leading factors in the proliferation of coups d'état in the 1950s had been a desire to compensate for the poor Arab showing in 1948. Both Nasir and the Syrian Ba^cth had made the liberation of Palestine a leading slogan, and Egypt was largely responsible for the creation of the Palestine Liberation Organization in 1964. But with the failure of 1967 Palestinians abandoned reliance on Arab governments and took matters into their own hands: the *fida'iyin* under Yasir ^cArafat seized control of the PLO in 1968. More broadly, the defeat, especially the loss of Jerusalem, made many Arabs and Muslims more receptive to Islamist arguments that it had been caused by the adoption of alien, secular ideologies. Islamist arguments also found a receptive audience because internally the nationalist regimes were seen as failures. At the socio-economic level, the nationalist regimes could not fulfill their promises. The officers had won popular legitimacy by arguing that the existing socio-economic order was unjust. They had promised a more equitable distribution of resources and economic growth under state direction. Land was redistributed, eliminating once and for all the landholding notables who had predominated during the interwar period. The nascent industrial bourgeoisie, which had justified its actions as promoting the national interest, was also dispossessed. Having taken over effective control of the economy, the state now promised a future of growth, opportunity, and full employment.

After a brief period of success with state-led import-substituting industrialization and job creation through infrastructure development, economic growth stalled, and governments could not meet the rising expectations of a youthful, more educated population. Frustration at the lack of economic opportunity on the part of the younger generations of the university-educated meant that the regimes, having deliberately alienated the old commercial and industrial classes, were now losing the support of the "new middle classes" they had come to rely on. This sense of frustration turned to betrayal when, from the late 1960s, economic restructuring reconstituted the bourgeoisie as dependents of the government. The resulting profiteering and crony capitalism made many question what the "revolution" had been for.[84]

After 1967, Arab-nationalist regimes continued to speak of Arab unity while in fact pursuing local state interests and becoming both more narrowly based and more repressive internally. This was especially the case in Syria and Iraq, where the Ba^{c}th, desperate for allies, had made its bed with the army and came to power in Damascus and Baghdad at the point of bayonets. The military Ba^{c}thists eviscerated the civilian leadership of the party and made the organization a hollow shell, a vehicle for careerists mouthing empty slogans to get ahead in one-party states.[85] The Ba^{c}thist states and others continued to trumpet Arabism as their rationale while interfering in one another's affairs for what were transparently reasons of state. Thus the sordid Iraqi–Syrian feuding of the 1970s and 1980s, the meddling of the Arab states in Palestinian affairs and the Lebanese civil war, and the quixotic Iraqi adventures against Iran and Kuwait were all justified in the name of the Arab nation.[86]

Paradoxically, the regimes that were most vocally committed to Arabism were also those in which the regime's support base became narrowest. In Syria, although members of the majority Sunni community were co-opted into the leadership, power was increasingly concentrated in the hands of

Alawite sectarians, especially those tribally linked to the president's family.[87] Similarly, and notoriously, power in Iraq was exercised by Saddam Husayn's kinsmen and other Sunni Arabs from his hometown of Takrit. This reliance upon a small loyal clique recruited by ascriptive criteria, although sensible from the standpoint of regime preservation, only underscored the governments' alienation from large sectors of society and was difficult to reconcile with an official commitment to a much wider framework. It is little wonder that the Syrian government made sure that it had Sunnis in prominent positions,[88] while in Iraq the use of tribal names, which would have highlighted the narrowness of the regime's base, was proscribed.[89]

Unable to generate and maintain popular support, governments came to rely on police power to suppress opposition.[90] In this regard, the independent governments availed themselves of perhaps the most enduring legacy of the colonial state.[91] Arbitrary arrest, compliant courts, and torture accompanied censorship, the channeling of sectoral representation into state-controlled corporatist associations, and a government/party monopoly over education, news and entertainment media, and job opportunities to leave few spaces open for expressing opposition. The regimes that tolerated formal political pluralism (for example, Egypt under Mubarak) made certain that elections would be won by the ruling party. In such conditions, dissatisfaction with the way things were and opposition to the regimes had to be expressed through other means. As it turned out, those means and the idiom they employed would be largely religious.[92] Although in Syria the velvet glove was on the iron fist more often than in Iraq,[93] the regime could and did strike back savagely when challenged. A 1976–82 insurrection by Sunni Islamists of the Muslim Brotherhood, which specifically targeted Alawites, was finally suppressed with the destruction of much of the city of Hamah and the killing of at least five thousand civilians.[94]

This is not to say that Arabism and local patriotism have utterly disappeared as sources of political identity. After all, political Arabism rested on widely shared cultural attributes as well as on intra-Arab migration. This shared sense of Arabness has become available for political mobilization once again at the outset of the twenty-first century, thanks to the new medium of satellite television. Since the founding of the Qatar-based channel al-Jazeera in 1996, this sector has grown to some 150 channels, offering news, commentary, and entertainment independent of government censorship. In the process, it has "created a sense of belonging to, and participation in, a kind of virtual Arab metropolis. It has begun to make real a dream that 50 years of politicians' speeches and gestures have failed to achieve: Arab unity."[95] The building of a trans-state sense of Arab community is also supported by another globalizing technology, the Internet, although government attempts to control Internet access have been more successful and, by most measures, the Arab countries lag far behind most other regions of the world in Internet penetration.[96] The ultimate political effects of this persistent, affective Arabism are difficult to predict. At the local level, patriotic loyalty has also proved enduring. Popular identification with the state as the relevant frame of action remains strong. That it can be mobilized was demonstrated in 2005 by elections in Iraq and Palestine, the popular Lebanese movement after the murder of former Prime Minister Rafiq Hariri, and the *kifaya* ("enough") movement in Egypt against Mubarak's perpetual presidency.[97] That Islamists benefited the most from the 2005–06 Egyptian and Palestinian parliamentary elections does not negate this point. Indeed, the Islamists' willingness to participate in the institutions of the modern state only underscores the widespread acceptance of the post-World War I order.[98] The nation-state order, for all its artificiality, legitimacy problems, and abusive governments, has been remarkably durable and continues to be the arena within which the politics of identity are played out, even when the chosen political idiom is a religious one.

Conclusion

This discussion of the Arab, particularly Syrian, experience of globalization during the nineteenth and twentieth centuries should help put to rest the myth of Islamic/Middle Eastern exceptionalism propagated by Lewis, Huntington, et al. The state of the Middle East and the wider Islamic world is not the result of an unchanging Islamic tradition refusing to come to grips with modernity. Rather, it is the product of the ongoing engagement of the Middle East with globalizing processes and of the particular forms that the resultant hybridities have taken. That is to say that, although globalization offers certain forms of economic, political, and social behavior as modular universals, those on the receiving end of globalization start out with their own notions of what is universal, and adapt the new universals to local conditions. As this chapter has demonstrated, the Middle Eastern experience of globalization was not merely reactive or derivative. Rather, regional elites reinterpreted elements from their own universalistic worldview and from the new universal offered by the West to renegotiate the boundaries between local and universal, producing a hybrid outlook that was neither a blind continuation of "tradition" nor a mimesis of Europe, but something new and different from both. Put another way, there is no singular globalization with a predetermined end result. Rather, there are globalizations with a diversity of outcomes. Seen in this way, the Middle East comes to resemble other parts of the world rather than standing out as the grand exception to globalization.

To recapitulate: during the nineteenth century the Ottoman Empire, representative of the universal empires characteristic of "archaic" globalization, encountered a rival universal in expansionist Europe. By reinterpreting their own legacy and selectively adapting institutions of the contemporary European nation state, Ottoman elites created a new, hybrid social and cultural order. The salient socio-political characteristic of this transformation was that state institutions were strengthened, new state-dependent elites arose, and competing social formations that had acted to check state power, notably the Muslim *'ulama'* (religious leaders), were weakened.

After the partition of the empire into nation states, the state continued to grow in size and autonomy from society. Meanwhile, competing ideologies, drawing on and adapting indigenous sources of inspiration, were advanced to provide a new universal focus of loyalty, with secular Arab nationalism achieving dominance. It is a hallmark of the hybridity of this body of thought that it conceived of the "Arab nation" as not only a territorial entity transcending the colonial borders but also a dynamic force in a reciprocal relationship with world civilization with a mission to promote human progress as a whole. Thus the nation-state order, imposed to serve European imperial interests, was naturalized and reimagined to further a post-Ottoman nationalist agenda that envisaged a new universal in an Arab nation with an historic mission. Paradoxically, the states that espoused this universalist ideology were in practice more concerned with local raisons d'état than with achieving their putative goal of Arab unity.

These regimes faced a crisis of legitimacy from the mid-1960s. Governing elites were able to maintain their power thanks to the autonomy of the state.[99] But the governing ideology was discredited and the estrangement of the state from society meant that criticism and opposition would be expressed in terms of a competing religious universal drawing on indigenous concepts of power and justice.

How does this picture compare to other regions? The Middle East shares certain phenomena with other parts of the non-Western world, particularly those areas which retained formal political sovereignty during the nineteenth century. In common with these countries, the Middle East was subject to strong influence from Europe and a forcible integration into the new world economy. Nevertheless, these countries retained sufficient freedom of action to allow change to come about as the result of a dialogue between the local and the new European universal, rather than as a colonial dictate. Although direct European rule was imposed in the Middle East, the colonial period was too brief and the Mandatories' will too weak to fundamentally alter the long-term trend of hybridization.

In economics, the Middle East's Listian economic nationalism was an attitude shared with many other regions, as explored by Mark Metzler in his chapter in this volume. A case can be made that, absent the chronic political instability, the private sector–state cooperation envisaged by the Syrian bourgeoisie in the early 1950s[100] could have developed into a developmentalist partnership akin to that between the Ministry of International Trade and Industry and the *zaibatsu* (wealthy conglomerates) in Japan. As it was, the shift to state capitalism in the late 1950s and 1960s seemed a viable alternative at the time. That it has been retained, despite its apparent failures, is due to considerations of regime survival rather than to purely economic criteria, at least in Syria.[101]

Politically, the Middle East was hardly the only region where authoritarianism was prevalent in the late twentieth century. The Arab colonels were contemporaries of Latin America's caudillos, the South Korean generals, and Taiwan's one-party state, among others. Some of these regimes have been very long-lived, although longevity of itself does not denote stability or success. But the phenomenon does demonstrate just how strong state institutions have become. In this respect the "Muslim encounter with modernity" can be termed a success, for the governments of the Arab states enjoy a power and autonomy that nineteenth-century Ottomans would have envied.

The religiously expressed cultural reaction to globalizing stresses is also hardly unique to the Middle East. An increase in public religiosity and in efforts to integrate the political and the spiritual have occurred in all regions and within all major faith traditions.[102] Thus Christianity has taken on a heightened political salience in Eastern Europe, post-Soviet Russia, the United States, and Latin America. A militant *Hindutva* (Hinduness) movement reimagines India as an exclusively Hindu patrimony. A messianic religious Zionism exacerbates the secular–religious split in Israel. So the "Islamic revival" in the Middle East, most of which is non-violent and much of which is not political in a conventional sense, is hardly a unique or distinctive phenomenon.

If the Middle East is less exceptional than it appears at first glance, how should one account for the special opprobrium directed at the region? Part of the answer lies in the cultural essentialism epitomized by Lewisian arguments. For complex reasons, the Islamic lands remain the West's "other" in a more profound way than any other region. Beyond that, given the very real tensions in the region and prevalent violence, it is far easier to blame everything on "Islam" or to assert that "terrorists hate freedom" than it is to investigate why and how some Middle Easterners come to embrace extremist Islamism and nihilistic violence.

At a structural level, "what went wrong" was to a great extent a product of externalities, in particular the Cold War and the ongoing Arab–Israeli conflict. The US–Soviet rivalry allowed Middle Eastern rulers to extract strategic rents from the superpowers, while the persistence of the Arab–Israeli conflict similarly allowed relatively poor frontline states (such as Syria) to extract similar rents from rich non-frontline states (such as Saudi Arabia). These strategic rents, supported by the distorting economic effects of the post-1973 oil boom, permitted repressive and inefficient regimes to hold on to power rather than confront their shortcomings. These external influences, however, only reinforced the longer-term development of state autonomy from society, a process having its origins in the Ottoman reforms of the early nineteenth century.

What, then, of the future? The proponents of a homogenizing globalization and of contemporary US policy in the Middle East would argue that the region will inevitably become politically democratic and economically liberal, even if it is necessary to bring about revolution by the application of American military power. The American experience in Iraq since 2003 suggests that this perception may be mistaken. While the opposition – both secular and religious – in the Arab states does desire both political and economic liberalization, it does not wish this result to be imposed from outside or to follow an American model. Rather, just as authoritarian Arab rulers could find inspiration and justification in the hybrid stew created by the region's globalizing interactions, so too can contemporary advocates of both more restrictive and more liberal ways of life.

Notes

1   These are the major conclusions of a series of studies conducted by Arab social scientists under the auspices of the UN Development Programme and the Arab Fund for Economic and Social Development. See Nader Fergany et al., *Arab Human Development Report 2002: Creating Opportunities for Future Generations* (New York, 2002), and *Arab Human Development Report 2003: Building a Knowledge Society* (New York, 2003).

2   The optimistic title of Shimon Peres and Arye Naor, *The New Middle East* (New York, 1993). Peres, then Israeli foreign minister, was one of the accords' principal supporters.

3   See Samuel P. Huntington, "The Clash of Civilizations?," *Foreign Affairs*, 72 (1993), pp. 22–49, and his book *The Clash of Civilizations and the Remaking of World Order* (New York, 1996). The uses that American commentators made

of Huntington's formulation are analyzed in Ervand Abrahamian, "The US Media, Samuel Huntington and September 11," *Middle East Report*, 223 (2002), pp. 62–3.

4 See President Bush's 2005 State of the Union address, text available at www.whitehouse.gov/news/releases/2005/02/20050202-11.html. That politicians' understanding of the struggle is malleable is illustrated by the President's identification of the enemy as "radical Islam" in the 2006 State of the Union address (www.whitehouse.gov/news/releases/2006/01/20060131-10.html).

5 Bernard Lewis, *What Went Wrong? The Clash Between Islam and Modernity in the Middle East* (New York, 2002). Lewis's vision of the Islamic world and his influence on American policymakers are analyzed in Ian Buruma, "Lost in Translation: The Two Minds of Bernard Lewis," *New Yorker*, June 14/21, 2004, pp. 184–91, and Peter Waldman, "Containing Jihad: A Historian's Take on Islam Steers U.S. in Terrorism Fight," *Wall Street Journal*, February 3, 2004, pp. A1, A12. The most extensive critical treatments of Lewis's thought are in Zachary Lockman, *Contending Visions of the Middle East: The History and Politics of Orientalism* (Cambridge, 2004), pp. 130–2, 173–6, 190–2, 216–18, 249–51, and Richard W. Bulliet, *The Case for Islamo-Christian Civilization* (New York, 2004), Ch. 2.

6 Lewis, *What Went Wrong?*, p. 159.

7 Ibid., p. 165.

8 Bernard Lewis, "Communism and Islam," *International Affairs*, 30 (1954), p. 7.

9 This typology of the "archaic" and "modern" forms of globalization follows A. G. Hopkins, "Globalization – An Agenda for Historians," in Hopkins (ed.), *Globalization in World History* (New York, 2002), pp. 1–11.

10 A Ba^cthist slogan, probably attributable to party founder Michel ^cAflaq.

11 Amira K. Bennison, "Muslim Universalism and Western Globalization," in Hopkins, *Globalization in World History*, pp. 73–98. The conceptualization of the medieval *dar al-islam* as a large-scale integrating (globalizing?) system was an element of many early works in world history, even arguably in Fernand Braudel's *Civilisation matérielle, économie et capitalisme: XVe–XVIIIe siècle* (Paris, 1979; English translation *Civilization and Capitalism 15th–18th Century* [New York, 1981–84]). Notable works in this genre include Marshall G. S. Hodgson, *The Venture of Islam: Conscience and History in a World Civilization* (Chicago, 1974), Janet L. Abu-Lughod, *Before European Hegemony: The World System A.D. 1250–1350* (Oxford, 1989), and several of the essays in Michael Adas (ed.), *Islamic and European Expansion: The Forging of a Global Order* (Philadelphia, PA, 1993).

12 How this worked is vividly illustrated in Abraham Marcus, *The Middle East on the Eve of Modernity: Aleppo in the Eighteenth Century* (New York, 1989), Ch. 3.

13 See Donald Quataert, *The Ottoman Empire, 1700–1922* (Cambridge, 2000), Ch. 3, for the relations of elites in the capital and provinces in the eighteenth and nineteenth centuries.

14 Quataert, *The Ottoman Empire*, p. 37.

15 Albert Hourani, *Arabic Thought in the Liberal Age 1798–1939* (Cambridge, 1983), p. 29.

16 See the discussion of "The Dynastic Realm" in Benedict Anderson, *Imagined Communities: Reflections on the Origin and Spread of Nationalism*, rev. ed. (London, 1991), pp. 19–22.

17 Hourani, *Arabic Thought*, p. 29.

18 Ibid., p. 33. A. G. Hopkins's introduction to the present volume indicates the varying connotations of "cosmopolitan."

19 A point underscored by the personal almanacs of an Istanbul official analyzed in Paul Dumont, "Said Bey – The Everyday Life of an Istanbul Townsman," in Hans-Georg Maier (ed.), *Osmanistische Studien zur Wirstschafts- und Sozialgeschichte. In Memoriam Vančo Boškov* (Wiesbaden, 1986), pp. 1–16.

20 As convincingly argued in Ussama Makdisi, "Ottoman Orientalism," *American Historical Review*, 107 (2002), pp. 768–96.

21 Peter Sluglett and Marion Farouk-Sluglett, "The Application of the 1858 Land Code in Greater Syria: Some Preliminary Observations," in Tarif Khalidi (ed.), *Land Tenure and Social Transformation in the Middle East*, (Beirut, 1984), pp. 409–21.

22 The Ottoman state had long depended on local religious, commercial, military, and landholding elites to facilitate its rule in the provinces by mediating between the central authority and the population. But the role of these intermediaries changed along with the institutions of the Ottoman state during the nineteenth century. Those local notables who took part in the new institutions (the secular law courts, the civil bureaucracy, and representative bodies) maintained and increased their influence, while those whose bases of authority were becoming obsolete (largely the *'ulama'*, the religious leaders) saw theirs decline. This same body of notables acted as intermediaries for the French and British Mandatories, and became the ruling classes after independence. The paradigm was first articulated by Albert Hourani in his seminal "Ottoman Reform and the Politics of Notables," in William R. Polk and Richard L. Chambers (eds), *Beginnings of Modernization in the Middle East: The Nineteenth Century* (Chicago, 1968), pp. 41–68. The "politics of notables" paradigm has been applied to nineteenth- and twentieth-century Syrian, especially Damascene, social history in Linda Schatkowski Schilcher, *Families in Politics: Damascene Factions and Estates of the 18th and 19th Centuries* (Stuttgart, 1985); Philip S. Khoury, *Urban Notables and Arab Nationalism: The Politics of Damascus 1860–1920* (Cambridge, 1983); and Philip S. Khoury, *Syria and the French Mandate: The Politics of Arab Nationalism, 1920–1945* (Princeton, NJ, 1987).

23 Laila Tarazi Fawaz, *Merchants and Migrants in Nineteenth-Century Beirut* (Cambridge, MA, 1983).

24 The guild system had already begun to erode with the destruction of the Janissary corps, the obsolete Ottoman military force that had penetrated the

artisanal classes and was the strong arm of the urban mob, in 1826. The conse-
quences for artisans of the changeover to capitalist relations are analyzed in
Sherry Vatter, "Journeymen Textile Weavers in Nineteenth-Century
Damascus: A Collective Biography," in Edmund Burke III (ed.), *Struggle and
Survival in the Modern Middle East* (Berkeley, CA, 1993), pp. 75–90, and Sherry
Vatter, "Militant Journeymen in Nineteenth-Century Damascus: Implications
for the Middle Eastern Labor History Agenda," in Zachary Lockman (ed.),
Workers and Working Classes in the Middle East: Struggles, Histories, Historiographies
(Albany, NY, 1994), pp. 1–19. How Damascene merchants and manufacturers
experienced the change is analyzed in James A. Reilly, "Damascus Merchants
and Trade in the Transition to Capitalism," *Canadian Journal of History/Annales
Canadiennes d'Histoire,* 27 (1992), pp. 1–27, and James A. Reilly, "From
Workshops to Sweatshops: Damascus Textiles and the World-Economy in the
Last Ottoman Century," *Review,* 16 (1993), pp. 199–213.

25 See Donald Quataert, *Ottoman Manufacturing in the Age of the Industrial
Revolution* (Cambridge, 1993).

26 By Articles 3 and 4 of the 1876 Ottoman constitution, the sultan was formally
designated "Supreme Caliph" with the duty of protecting the Muslim religion.

27 Building on earlier decrees, Article 17 of the Ottoman constitution established
the equality of rights and obligations of all Ottoman citizens irrespective of
religion.

28 See Anderson, *Imagined Communities,* Ch. 6.

29 "Resolution of the Arab-Syrian Congress at Paris, 21 June 1913," in J. C.
Hurewitz (ed.), *The Middle East and North Africa in World Politics: A
Documentary Record. Volume 1: European Expansion, 1535–1914* (New Haven,
CT, 1975), pp. 566–7. A thorough discussion of the competing bases of
loyalty in the Ottoman Empire in its last decade is found in Hasan Kayalı,
*Arabs and Young Turks: Ottomanism, Arabism, and Islamism in the Ottoman
Empire, 1908–1918* (Berkeley, CA, 1997). See also Rashid Khalidi,
"Ottomanism and Arabism in Syria Before 1914: A Reassessment," in Rashid
Khalidi, Lisa Anderson, Muhammad Muslih and Reeva S. Simon (eds), *The
Origins of Arab Nationalism* (New York, 1991), pp. 50–69.

30 The *safarbarlik* in Syria of 1915–18 was caused in part by military requisition-
ing of manpower and foodstuffs. See Elizabeth Thompson, *Colonial Citizens:
Republican Rights, Paternal Privilege, and Gender in French Syria and Lebanon*
(New York, 2000), Ch. 1, for a description of the effects of the war years.

31 This resistance was led by Ibrahim Hananu (1869–1935), an Aleppine army
officer of Kurdish origin later regarded as a "Syrian" or "Arab" nationalist.
Keith Watenpaugh, *Bourgeois Modernity, Historical Memory, and Imperialism: The
Emergence of an Urban Middle Class in the Late Ottoman and Inter-war Middle East
– Aleppo, 1908–1939* (PhD dissertation, University of California at Los
Angeles, 1999), pp. 178–90, terms Hananu "the last Ottoman."

32 The most important of which was the Anglo–French Sykes-Picot agreement
of 1916.

33 See the report of the American Section of the International Commission on
    Mandates in Turkey (the King-Crane commission), which visited Greater
    Syria in 1919: US Department of State, *Papers Relating to the Foreign Relations
    of the United States: The Paris Peace Conference 1919, Volume 12* (Washington,
    DC, 1947), pp. 745–863.

34 Notably, the British "Declaration to the Seven" of June 16, 1918 and the
    Anglo–French Declaration of November 7, 1918, texts reprinted in J .C.
    Hurewitz (ed.), *The Middle East and North Africa in World Politics: A
    Documentary Record. Volume 2: British-French Supremacy, 1914–1945* (New
    Haven, CT, 1979), pp. 110–13.

35 See Anderson, *Imagined Communities*, pp. 55–61 and 121ff. on the role of the
    secular or viceregal pilgrimage in fostering national consciousness. See also
    Reeva S. Simon, "The Education of an Iraqi Ottoman Army Officer," in
    Khalidi, Anderson, Muslih and Simon, *The Origins of Arab Nationalism*, pp.
    151–66.

36 In so doing, the French not only rewarded their Maronite Catholic clients
    with, in effect, a state of their own, but also increased the Maronites'
    dependence on France by reducing their proportion of the overall Lebanese
    population.

37 The Druze and the Alawites, as schismatics considered outside the Muslim
    community, had retreated for their own protection to mountainous areas of
    Syria and Lebanon where sectarian identity overlapped with place and tribal
    affiliations to make these groups as much ethnies as confessional units,
    although both were Arabophone. From the start of the Mandate to 1936, and
    then again in 1939–42, these "compact minorities" enjoyed separate adminis-
    trations controlled directly by the French High Commission, not the Syrian
    government in Damascus.

38 The Beirut Circassian aristocrat Ahmad Nami, son-in-law (*damad*) of Sultan
    ᶜAbd al-Hamid II, who served several times as Syrian prime minister.

39 And, at least until the Arabic literary renaissance of the late nineteenth century,
    "Arab" was a term of contempt used by urbanites to identify nomads, just as
    Turkish-speaking Ottomans used "Turk" to refer to bumpkins from the
    Anatolian countryside.

40 For the nineteenth-century origins of a distinctive Syrian consciousness, see
    Fruma Zachs, *The Making of a Syrian Identity: Intellectuals and Merchants in
    Nineteenth Century Beirut* (Leiden, 2005).

41 For example, this was the case with French policy toward labor organizations.
    See Geoffrey D. Schad, "Colonial Corporatism in the French Mandated
    States: Labor, Capital, the Mandatory Power, and the 1935 Syrian Law of
    Associations," *Revue des mondes musulmans et de la Méditerranée*, 105–106
    (2005), pp. 201–19.

42 Turkish nationalism followed its own trajectory, under the guidance of
    Mustafa Kemal, although it faced some of the same problems as its Arab coun-
    terparts. Official Turkish nationalism renounced the Ottoman legacy and

moreover suppressed a strong pan-Turkist ("Turanian") movement intended to unite all speakers of Turkic languages. But the redefinition of Anatolia and Thrace as a Turkish nation state meant that non-Turkish ethnies had either to be expelled (Greeks, Armenians) or have their separate existence denied (Kurds, dubbed "Mountain Turks" by the Kemalists). An official Iranian nationalism was promulgated by Reza Shah Pahlavi (r. 1925–41), although that too ran up against Iran's very substantial ethnic diversity. Zionism, the nationalism of the Jewish immigrants to Palestine, is an altogether special case.

43   As, for example, the faction of Shakib Arslan, a Syrian Arab nationalist from the leading Druze family, who carried on a propaganda campaign against French rule from Geneva.

44   Mandatory Iraq was constructed from the disparate Ottoman provinces of Basra, Baghdad, and Mosul. Its ruling class, the Hashimite dynasty and the Sharifian officers, was imported from the Hijaz, and their local allies, Sunni Arabs, were a minority of the population. The literature on Iraq and its origins grew exponentially following the American-led invasion in 2003. For an overall view, see Toby Dodge, *Inventing Iraq: The Failure of Nation-Building and a History Denied* (New York, 2003). On nationalism in Mandatory and monarchical Iraq, Reeva S. Simon's works are fundamental, for example "The Imposition of Nationalism on a Non-Nation State: The Case of Iraq During the Interwar Period, 1921–1941," in James Jankowski and Israel Gershoni (eds), *Rethinking Nationalism in the Arab Middle East* (New York, 1997), pp. 87–104.

45   The National Bloc's social composition, development, outlook, and style of politics are extensively treated in Khoury, *Syria and the French Mandate*, especially Chs 10–14.

46   See Khoury, *Syria and the French Mandate*, pp. 409–14 on the role played by the school system, especially the Damascus *tajhiz* (high school) in fostering Arab nationalism.

47   And the sites of the hangings in both Beirut and Damascus were renamed "Martyrs' Square."

48   Similarly tendentious nationalist historiographical traditions are common throughout the ex-Ottoman lands, especially in the Balkans. For Turkey itself, although many aspects of the Ottoman past were rejected, the glories of the early Ottoman state were claimed – against the evidence – as the exclusive achievement of the Turks. For a discussion of these issues, see Cemal Kafadar, *Between Two Worlds: The Construction of the Ottoman State* (Berkeley, CA, 1995), Introduction and Ch. 1.

49   Heghnar Zeitlian Watenpaugh, "Museums and the Construction of National History in Syria and Lebanon," in Nadine Méouchy and Peter Sluglett (eds) with Gérard Khoury and Geoffrey Schad, *The British and French Mandates in Comparative Perspectives/Les mandats français et anglais dans une perspective comparative* (Leiden, 2004), pp. 185–202. Public museums and the allied discipline of national archaeology are, of course, principal tools in the building of national identities, as examples from Egypt, Iraq, and Israel attest.

50 Itself an artifact of the Ottoman reform period, founded as the Syrian Protestant College in 1867. AUB was only the most prominent of a network of American, British, and French schools established during the nineteenth century to meet an increased demand for modern education that could not be met by the slow growth of the Ottoman state school system. These foreign missionary schools were complemented by private schools established by Ottoman citizens and those of the Alliance Israélite Universelle.

51 The Communist Party of Syria and Lebanon, first organized in 1923 among Maronite tobacco-workers, was long dominated by Armenians and Lebanese Christians. From 1932 it was under the leadership of Khalid Bakdash, an Arabized Damascene Kurd trained by the Comintern. A classic study of Syrian working-class development from a Marxist perspective is ʿAbdallah Hanna, *Al-haraka al-ʿummaliyya fi suriyya wa lubnan 1900–1945* (Damascus, 1973).

52 Richard P. Mitchell, *The Society of the Muslim Brothers* (New York, 1993), p. 246.

53 Ibid., p. 269.

54 First Arab Students' Congress, "Arab Pledge, Definitions, Manifesto," in Sylvia G. Haim (ed.), *Arab Nationalism: An Anthology*, (Berkeley, CA, 1962, 1976), pp. 100–2.

55 Edmond Rabbath, excerpt from *Unité Syrienne et Devenir Arabe* (Paris, 1937), pp. 43–69, translated in Haim, *Arab Nationalism*, pp. 103–19 (at p. 108). Significantly, this essay approvingly cites Ernest Renan's seminal "Qu'est-ce qu'une nation?." Rabbath (1901–91) was a Christian who had an ambiguous relationship with the Muslim nationalist leadership in Aleppo. See Keith Watenpaugh, "Middle-Class Modernity and the Persistence of the Politics of Notables in Inter-war Syria," *International Journal of Middle East Studies*, 35 (2003), pp. 257–86.

56 Khoury, *Syria and the French Mandate*, p. 411, states that a "majority" of Damascus *tajhiz* faculty were trained in Paris.

57 The discussion in this and subsequent paragraphs is adapted from Geoffrey D. Schad, *Colonialists, Industrialists, and Politicians: The Political Economy of Industrialization in Syria, 1920–1954* (PhD dissertation, University of Pennsylvania, 2001). Unlike many colonial regimes, the French Mandatory power did not deliberately inhibit Syrian industrialization. Since French direct private investment in the Syrian economy was largely limited to transportation and public utilities, the manufacturing sector was left open to Syrian entrepreneurs.

58 Ottoman economic sovereignty had been compromised not only by the 1838 Balta Liman treaty, but also by the centuries-old Capitulations, which granted extraterritoriality to European merchants and their protégés, and by the Ottoman Public Debt Administration, established after the Ottoman default in 1876. Ottoman efforts to break free of these restrictions in turn show the influence of the mid-nineteenth-century European economic nationalism elaborated

by Friedrich List. See Feroz Ahmad, "Vanguard of a Nascent Bourgeoisie: The Social and Economic Policy of the Young Turks 1908–1918," in Osman Okyar and Halil İnalcik (eds), *Türkiye'nin Sosyal ve Ekonomik Tarihi (1071–1920)/Social and Economic History of Turkey (1071–1920)* (Ankara, 1980), pp. 329–50. Showing the way in which economic ideas were cycled and recycled, List's program for the economic unity of Germany, *The National System of Political Economy* (1841) was based not only on the German experience during the Napoleonic wars but also on List's sojourn in the United States (1825–32). List's notion that to be truly independent a nation required a strong industrialized economy, and that late industrialization required protectionist tariffs, became a commonplace of all later economic nationalisms.

59   Thus, a speaker at a 1935 Damascus "Economic Congress" could simultaneously praise Gandhi, Mussolini, and Hitler. See the Mandatory documentation of the meeting in Centre des Archives Diplomatiques de Nantes, Mandat Syrie-Liban, 1e versement, carton 863.

60   The Syrian Spinning and Weaving Company counted among its founders Dr ʿAbd al-Rahman al-Kayyali, scion of a well-established notable family and head of one of the two main factions in the Aleppo National Bloc. Despite its name, the company was often also seen as a deliberately Aleppine enterprise, illustrating the persistence of sub-state identities. See Schad, *Colonialists, Industrialists, and Politicians*, Ch. 7, for details and references.

61   The Bank Misr ("Egypt Bank") was a combine of commercial and manufacturing enterprises, chiefly in textiles, centered on an investment bank founded by Muhammad Talʿat Harb in 1920 and intended to promote Egyptian economic independence. The principal work on it in English is Eric Davis, *Challenging Colonialism: Bank Misr and Egyptian Industrialization, 1920–1941* (Princeton, NJ, 1983). His interpretation of Bank Misr as a nationalist enterprise is disputed by Robert Vitalis in his *When Capitalists Collide: Business Conflict and the End of Empire in Egypt* (Berkeley, CA, 1955), who contends that Egyptian industrialists were chiefly motivated by rent-seeking. These are of course not mutually exclusive motivations, and a similar mixture of motivations can be discerned in the behavior of the Syrian industrial bourgeoisie during the Mandate. The extent of Bank Misr's influence on Syrian industrialists is also in dispute. See Frank Peter, "Dismemberment of Empire and Reconstitution of Regional Space: The Emergence of 'National' Industries in Damascus between 1918 and 1946," in Méouchy and Sluglett, *British and French Mandates*, pp. 415–46.

62   See Schad, *Colonialists, Capitalists, and Politicians*, passim; and Jocelyne Cornand, *L'entrepreneur et l'état en Syrie: le secteur privé du textile à Alep* (Paris, 1994), pp. 56–7, 216.

63   See Roger Owen and Şevket Pamuk, *A History of Middle East Economies in the Twentieth Century* (Cambridge, MA, 1998), pp. 18–20, for an assessment of Kemalist statist policies. The extent to which Turkey served as a model for Arab states is an open question, but there are striking similarities between

Atatürk's authoritarian, protectionist, secular republic and later Arab military-led states.

64 Hanna Batatu, *Syria's Peasantry, the Descendants of Its Lesser Rural Notables, and Their Politics* (Princeton, NJ, 1999), p. 134.

65 Further discussion of the Cold War's effects on Arab politics is omitted here to maintain the clarity of the argument, but there are Middle Eastern parallels to the Vietnamese case discussed by Mark Lawrence in this volume. The difficulties Middle Easterners faced in navigating between the poles of Soviet communism and Western liberalism are examined in Salim Yaqub, *Containing Arab Nationalism: The Eisenhower Doctrine and the Middle East* (Chapel Hill, NC, 2004).

66 There are of course differences. Ba^cthist Syria has always sought to project the image of collective decision-making as against the personalized leadership of Nasir. In Egypt itself Muhammad Husni Mubarak, although the heir of Nasir's mantle, presides over a quite different state than the one Nasir bequeathed Sadat in 1970. A more close approximation of Nasirist authoritarianism may be found in Tunisia since the 1987 coup that deposed the senescent independence leader Habib Bourguiba and installed the current incumbent, General Zayn al-^cAbdin Bin ^cAli.

67 Modernization theorists were at pains to explain the reasons for and meaning of the many coups in decolonizing Latin America, Southeast Asia, and the Middle East. Samuel P. Huntington, *Political Order in Changing Societies* (New Haven, CT, 1968), devotes Chapter 4 to "Praetorianism and Political Decay," with a discussion of Nasirist Egypt on pp. 241ff. See also Michael C. Hudson, *Arab Politics: The Search for Legitimacy* (New Haven, CT, 1977), Ch. 8, esp. pp. 232–3); and Eliezer Be^ceri, *Army Officers in Arab Politics and Society* (London/New York, 1970), among many other sources.

68 Shishakli allowed the business-dominated People's Party to draft the 1950 Syrian constitution, and appointed several business figures to cabinet posts, including Muhammad Sa^cid al-Za^cim, the secretary-general of the Aleppo Chamber of Commerce, who served as minister of finance. See Schad, *Colonialists, Industrialists, and Politicians*, Ch. 10.

69 With a communist (party chief Khalid Bakdash) becoming the first communist elected in an Arab country. See the various party platforms collected in *Al-Ahzab al-siyasiyya fi suriya* (Damascus, 1954).

70 The foregoing is a highly truncated treatment of the very unstable Syrian politics of the 1950s. For more detailed discussions, see Patrick Seale, *The Struggle for Syria: A Study of Post-War Arab Politics 1945–1958* (London, 1965); Steven Heydemann, *Authoritarianism in Syria: Institutions and Social Conflict, 1946–1970* (Ithaca, NY, 1999); and Yahya M. Sadowski, *Political Power and Economic Organization in Syria: The Course of State Intervention, 1946–1958* (PhD dissertation, University of California at Los Angeles, 1984).

71 One of ^cAflaq's early essays opens, "Nationalism is love before everything else." Michel ^cAflaq, *Fi sabil al-ba^cBa^cth* (Beirut, 1959), pp. 29–30, excerpted in Haim, *Arab Nationalism*, pp. 242–3. The essay is dated 1940.

72 Led by an Alawite schoolteacher, Zaki al-Arsuzi, one of many refugees created by the cession by France to Turkey of the Alexandretta province in 1939. For Arsuzi's contribution to the Ba^cth, see Keith Watenpaugh, " 'Creating Phantoms': Zaki al-Arsuzi, the Alexandretta Crisis, and the Formation of Modern Arab Nationalism in Syria," *International Journal of Middle East Studies*, 28 (1996), pp. 363–89.

73 The party was the vehicle for the aspirations of Akram al-Hawrani, a deracinated lower notable from the Hama area who had previously been an SSNP partisan and was the main civilian conspirator in the 1949 coups. The ASP, which mounted land invasions and other direct action, mobilized peasants against Hawrani's personal, family, and political enemies among the Hama landlords. This region was where agrarian income-and-ownership inequality was most stark.

74 "The Constitution of the Arab Resurrection (Ba^cth) Socialist Party of Syria," *Middle East Journal*, 13 (1959), pp. 195–200. All quotations from the Ba^cth program given in this section are from this translation.

75 Separately the party defines an Arab as "anyone whose language is Arabic, who lives in the Arab homeland or aspires to live therein, and who believes in his connection with the Arab people."

76 The canard that Ba^cthism *as such* is a fascist movement, as expressed in such treatments as Kanan Makiya's *Republic of Fear* ("Samir al-Khalil," *Republic of Fear: The Inside Story of Saddam's Iraq* [Berkeley, CA, 1990]), is very largely a back-projection onto the early Ba^cth of the conditions prevailing in Iraq under the dictatorship of Saddam Husayn. Disentangling the Ba^cth's origins from its later exploitation by authoritarian regimes in Syria and Iraq is made all the more difficult by such developments as the 2003 "debaathification" decrees in Iraq that made it analogous to "denazification" in post-1945 Germany.

77 This thus inverts Rabbath's priorities. For Rabbath, Arabism was what made Islam great; for ^cAflaq, Islam was one of the elements of Arab greatness. It is noteworthy that, at the time of his death in 1989 as a favored hostage of the Saddam Husayn regime, ^cAflaq had allegedly converted to Islam.

78 Indeed, in Ba^cthist jargon to this day, there is only one National Command, for the whole Arab nation; the individual states have but Regional Commands, and the gravest ideological error is "regionalism" (*iqlimiyya*).

79 Alexandria Protocol and League Pact in Hurewitz, *Middle East and North Africa in World Politics, Vol. 2*, pp. 732–38. "Arab" is in this context a political rather than an ethno-linguistic term: such Arab League member states as Somalia, Djibouti, and the Comoros are culturally "Arab" only in a very loose sense.

80 Article 2 of the League Pact.

81 The other two examples were the 1990 Iraqi annexation of Kuwait, motivated by greed, irredentism, and a bid for Iraqi regional hegemony, and the 1990 unification of North and South Yemen, a merger with complex origins that had to be enforced during a civil war in 1994.

82 Nasir's contempt for the Ba'th and his scorn for their political ineptness are
    vividly expressed in the transcripts of the abortive unity talks in Cairo in spring
    1963, analyzed in Malcolm H. Kerr, *The Arab Cold War: Gamal 'Abd al-Nasir
    and His Rivals, 1958–1970*, 3rd ed. (New York, 1971).

83 Notably by Libya's Mu'ammar al-Qadhdhafi, who explicitly modeled himself
    on Nasir. A 1971–72 project for a "Federation of Arab Republics" grouping
    Egypt, Syria, Libya, and Sudan was stillborn, although it did lead to a period
    of vexillological unity among the first three.

84 This is a very generalized treatment of a process of economic change that
    moved at differing rates and to differing lengths in Egypt, Iraq, Syria, and
    elsewhere. In the Egyptian and Syrian cases the ability to extract strategic
    rents from outside patrons mitigated somewhat the need to reliberalize the
    economy, while in Iraq access to oil income gave the regime considerable
    autonomy from society. For the general processes of economic restructuring,
    see Roger Owen, *State, Power and Politics in the Making of the Modern Middle
    East* (London, 1992), Ch. 6, and Alan Richards and John Waterbury, *A
    Political Economy of the Middle East: State, Class, and Economic Development*
    (Boulder, CO, 1990), Chs 8 and 9. The role of the Iraqi regime in fostering
    the growth of a dependent bourgeoisie is analyzed in 'Isam al-Khafaji, "State
    Incubation of Iraqi Capitalism," *Middle East Report*, 142 (1986), pp. 4–9, 12.
    "Crony capitalism" in Egyptian agriculture is the topic of Yahya M.
    Sadowski, *Political Vegetables? Businessman and Bureaucrat in the Development of
    Egyptian Agriculture* (Washington, DC, 1991). In Syria, partial economic
    liberalizations under Asad père in the early 1970s and 1991, together with
    the exploitation of Syrian-occupied Lebanon, led to the evolution of a
    "rentier bourgeoisie" of merchants and apparatchiks bound together by
    informal networks. See Raymond Hinnebusch, *Syria: Revolution from Above*
    (London, 2002), Ch. 6, esp. pp. 131–5; and Bassam Haddad, "Syria's New
    Rentier Bourgeoisie: Its Origins and Impact on Socioeconomic
    Transformation in Syria," paper delivered to the Middle East Studies
    Association of North America 39th Annual Meeting, Washington, DC,
    November 2005.

85 There were of course differences in style between the two regimes. Syria's
    Hafiz al-Asad, a former air force officer, rarely appeared in uniform once he
    took office as president, while Iraq's Saddam Husayn, a party apparatchik and
    assassin with no military background, made military fatigues and a beret his
    trademark costume and subordinated the army to party control. With the
    Ba'th in power in both Syria and Iraq, the party was itself split into two rival
    "national" commands, each denouncing the other for alleged deviations from
    orthodoxy. 'Aflaq ended his days an effective prisoner of the Iraqi regime,
    trotted out to give Saddam Husayn's latest atrocities ideological approval,
    while Bitar was assassinated in Paris in 1980, presumably by agents of the
    Syrian regime. In his last interview, published in 1982, Bitar rued many of the
    party's decisions, especially that of attaching its fortunes to the military: "The

major deviation of the Ba^cth is having renounced democracy, liberty" ("Salah ed-Din al Bitar's last interview: 'The major deviation of the Ba^cth is having renounced democracy,'" *MERIP Reports*, 110 (1982), pp. 21–23). In Syria, the reduction of the party to an arm of the state resulted in the acquiescence of the population to a cult of personality in which they did not really believe, analyzed in Lisa Wedeen, *Ambiguities of Domination: Politics, Rhetoric, and Symbols in Contemporary Syria* (Chicago, 1999).

86 Such feuding had marked earlier inter-Arab relations, especially during the Nasirist heyday, when the opposition of "progressive" republican regimes to "reactionary" monarchies degraded into the Egyptian–Saudi proxy war in Yemen, 1962–70.

87 The ascendancy of the Alawites, who had transcended their disadvantages as peasants and minority sectaries by joining the army, began with the regime of Salah al-Jadid, who led the coup of 1963. Since Hafiz al-Asad took power in 1970, the inner circle of power has been the preserve not just of Alawites but specifically of members of the extended Asad family and its tribal confederation, the Kalbiya. See Hanna Batatu, "Some Observations on the Social Roots of Syria's Ruling, Military Group and the Causes for its Dominance," *Middle East Journal*, 35 (1981), pp. 331–44.

88 The regime also sought to defuse Sunni hostility to Alawites, who were viewed as apostates, by obtaining a fatwa from the Lebanese Higher Shi^ci Council that the Alawites were indeed good Shi^ci Muslims. This expedient was necessary since the Syrian constitution required that the head of state be a Muslim. See Patrick Seale, *Asad of Syria: The Struggle for the Middle East* (Berkeley, CA, 1988), p. 173.

89 In Iraq especially, tribalism as a means of dividing and controlling the population actually increased under the Ba^cth even as its existence was denied and denounced.

90 Reaching its nadir in the vast prison that was Saddam Husayn's Iraq, chillingly described in Makiya's *Republic of Fear*.

91 The colonial state during the Mandatory period was very much a police state, with multiple agencies maintaining surveillance over the population. When this author was investigating Syrian economic development in the French Mandatory records at the Centre des Archives Diplomatiques de Nantes, he discovered that a majority of the documents were generated by either the military Service des Renseignements or the civilian Sûreté Générale.

92 This is not to say that secular opposition groups have disappeared. To the contrary, secular nationalist and socialist parties and movements remain important in, for example, Egypt and Syria, but they have been compelled to share considerable political space with Islamist movements.

93 As Raymond Hinnebusch (*Syria: Revolution from Above*, p. 103) observes, "While Syria's Ba^cthist structures resembled Iraq's, the regime eschewed the systematic terror needed to pulverise society in a way comparable to Iraq.

Equally important ... the Ba^cth regime had to seek a modus vivendi with the bourgeoisie which was incompatible with continued totalitarian repression."

94 See Abdul-Karim Rafeq and Geoffrey D. Schad, "Hama," *Encyclopedia of the Modern Middle East and North Africa, Vol. 2*, 2nd ed. (New York, 2004), pp. 980–1; Fred H. Lawson, "Social Bases for the Hamah Revolt," *MERIP Reports*, 110 (1982), pp. 24–8; Middle East Watch, *Syria Unmasked: The Suppression of Human Rights by the Asad Regime* (New Haven, CT, 1991).

95 "Special Report: Arab Satellite Television: The World Through Their Eyes," *The Economist*, February 26, 2005, p. 23. See also the discussion of the sector in Fergany et al., *Arab Human Development Report 2003*, pp. 58–66.

96 Fergany et al., *Arab Human Development Report 2002*, p. 75.

97 The union of the two Yemens in 1990, although followed by a secession attempt by the former South Yemen in 1994, should perhaps be seen in this light rather than as an example of "Arab" unionism. Despite differences connected to the establishment of Ottoman rule in the North and British colonialism in the South, there has long been a sense that Yemen represents a distinctive entity. Interestingly, the former People's Democratic Republic of Yemen (1967–90) was the only Arab state to officially espouse the other great twentieth-century universal, Marxism-Leninism, as its ideology.

98 The Shi^ci victory in the Iraqi parliamentary elections is attributable more to sectarian politics than to the appeal of Islamism as such.

99 It was not just the secular, "progressive" republican states that enjoyed autonomy from society. "Traditional" monarchies such as Saudi Arabia had many of the same advantages, thanks in their case to the ability to extract economic rents due to petroleum receipts. That said, these monarchies also share in some of the same socio-economic stresses and experience similar legitimacy problems, although in the Saudi case the problem is made more acute as both the state and the opposition ostensibly espouse the same religio-political ideology.

100 Which was part of the contemporary World Bank consensus. See International Bank for Reconstruction and Development, *The Economic Development of Syria: Report of a Mission Organized by the International Bank for Reconstruction and Development* (Baltimore, MD, 1955).

101 See Bassam Haddad, "Syria's Curious Dilemma," *Middle East Report*, 236 (2005), pp. 4–12.

102 Religio-political movements were also a notable feature of reactions to the first wave of globalization in the nineteenth century. Thus the United States experienced the rise of such millenarian sects as the Jehovah's Witnesses and the Mormons. In East Asia, religious syncretism helped feed the Taiping Rebellion. Islamic millenarianism marked the Mahdist movement in the Sudan, while the antecedents of modern political Islam are to be found in the career of Jamal al-Din al-Afghani.

8

Universal Claims, Local Uses: Reconceptualizing the Vietnam Conflict, 1945–60

Mark Atwood Lawrence

In his 2002 volume *Rethinking American History in a Global Age*, Thomas Bender proclaims the end of a scholarly era. "One can no longer believe in the nation as hermetically sealed, territorially self-contained, or internally undifferentiated," Bender insists, while challenging his colleagues to write a new kind of history informed by "awareness of subnational, transnational, and global political, economic, social, and cultural processes." The nation state's long and tyrannical reign as the principal unit of historical investigation has, Bender suggests, come to an end.[1] The best evidence that much of the historical profession agrees lies in the fact that even specialists in diplomacy – a category of historians long wedded to the nation as the key subject of study – are increasingly turning their attention to supranational and transnational phenomena. The trend has been especially pronounced among scholars of the Cold War, who have begun to connect familiar narratives of East–West conflict to the other major development that we now understand to have accelerated between 1941 and 1989: globalization.[2] The task of reconceptualizing the Cold War as part of the history of globalization will surely fuel innumerable studies into the indefinite future.

The questions at the heart of this project are huge and complex. Did the East–West confrontation distort, accelerate, or retard the globalizing process, and, if so, how? Conversely, did globalizing trends – the acceleration of the transnational transfer of ideas, information, and money – constrain the options available to nation states embroiled in the Cold War?

Compelling answers to some of these questions have begun to emerge. David Reynolds has argued that the Cold War strongly encouraged one of the principal features of contemporary globalization, the extraordinary power of multinational corporations, by inducing Western governments to pump money into large defense-oriented businesses.[3] Jürgen Osterhammel and Niels P. Petersson have suggested that the Cold War contributed to the development of a global consciousness by confronting people everywhere with the threat of nuclear annihilation.[4] Other commentators have contended that the penetration of Western ideas and practices behind the Iron Curtain contributed powerfully to the delegitimization of the communist empire and thus to the Cold War's end.[5]

Major areas of uncertainty nevertheless remain. Scholars have offered only sketchy ideas, for example, about how to understand the first part of the Cold War – the period before détente and the global economic reconfiguration that began in the early 1970s. Most globalization scholars agree that the early years of the Cold War marked a significant moment. But they disagree about exactly why. Some suggest that the period following the Second World War should be viewed as a key takeoff point for globalizing trends. In his periodization of world history, A. G. Hopkins dates the start of "postcolonial globalization" – the current and most full-blown phase – to roughly the 1950s. By that point, he suggests, the age of European empires was coming to an end. "New types of supranational organization and new forms of regional integration had begun to make their appearance," Hopkins argues.[6] Akira Iriye also contends that the period from 1945 to 1960 was a point of acceleration for global forms of political organization. Across this period, Iriye suggests, the number, scale, and ambition of international organizations grew dramatically, encouraging an unprecedented sense of world community even as US–Soviet rivalry hardened into a bipolar geopolitical order.[7]

For others, the division of the world into rival blocs after 1945 signaled a setback for globalization. In their study of globalization and US foreign policy in the twentieth century, Alfred E. Eckes Jr and Thomas W. Zeiler view the emergence of the Cold War as a point of regression between the surge of integrative forces around the end of the Second World War and the burst of globalizing trends in the 1970s. To be sure, Eckes and Zeiler acknowledge that rapid development of communications and computing technologies during the 1940s and 1950s helped lay the foundation for the technological advances that would drive global integration in later years. But they also argue that the period witnessed significant "deglobalization" as nations gradually abandoned the wartime vision of a new, interknit world order in favor of membership in either the communist or democratic/capitalist camp. "Wartime multilateral dreams of a united, stable global economy supervised by international institutions gradually fell by the wayside, under attack by the competition between two budding superpowers," Eckes and Zeiler assert.[8] The result of this new animosity, contends journalist Thomas L. Friedman, was a world characterized not by integration but by barriers: "The Cold War world was like a broad plain, crisscrossed and divided by fences, walls, ditches, and dead ends. It was impossible to go very far," he adds, "without running into a Berlin Wall or an Iron Curtain or a Warsaw Pact or somebody's protective tariff or capital controls. And behind these fences and walls, countries could preserve their own unique forms of life, politics, economics, and culture."[9]

This essay endeavors to advance the debate over the connection between the Cold War and globalization by arguing that the East–West rivalry of the mid-twentieth century, while fragmenting the world into competing blocs, nevertheless powerfully advanced globalization by enmeshing the entire world in the struggle between two politico-economic systems that claimed universal applicability – between two "opposing versions of European modernist thought," as historian Odd Arne Westad puts it.[10] Unquestionably, the hardening of the US–Soviet confrontation after 1946 put an end to the "liberal moment" that had briefly inspired optimism around the end of the Second World War about the possibility of creating an integrated and harmonious world order based on collective security and trade liberalization. In that period, the coalition of victorious nations led by the United States took strides toward establishing a new order that was, in the words of political scientist Robert Latham, "more comprehensive and international in scope than any previous attempt to bring liberal doctrines to bear in the making of international political life."[11]

The breakdown of the US–Soviet relationship destroyed any chance that the attempt would succeed in ushering in a new era of global integration based on a common acceptance of liberal practices. The new tensions did not, however, mean the end of efforts to forge transnational bonds through the propagation of allegedly universal political and economic principles. On the contrary, the advent of the Cold War only intensified efforts by the most powerful nations to spread particular norms and practices around the globe. It is not, in other words, that globalization ground to a halt after 1947; rather, as Osterhammel and Petersson phrase it, globalization was "split in two."[12] The competition between rival universals proved a catalyst for the global spread of both. Fragmentation was, in the first parts of the Cold War, a powerful motor of globalization.[13]

Much of the hostility and bloodshed that ensued sprang from the conflict between advocates of rival globalizing visions for preeminence, especially in emerging states in Asia, Africa, and Latin America, which lacked strong predispositions one way or the other. These peripheral areas were not mere bystanders, however, as the superpowers – the United States, Soviet Union, and to a lesser extent China, each claiming the universality of its particular set of political and economic principles – vied to control their destinies. To be sure, "Third World" nationalists struggling to establish viable nation states recognized the necessity of siding with one of the great powers in order to obtain badly needed political and material backing. But many nationalists also recognized that the principles espoused by the powers furnished models of development that fitted imperfectly with local needs, grievances, and cultural predilections. Time and again, political forces on the periphery altered, bent, or otherwise manipulated the programs of the great powers in order to achieve not the universal implementation of grand ideas but the solutions to concrete problems closer to home. To appreciate the nature of the conflict between competing "globalizations" during the Cold War, it is necessary to explore the complex interplay between, on the one hand, the architects of policies with universal pretensions and, on the other, the leaders who sought to exploit those grand designs to advance local agendas.

In an effort to suggest patterns that played out in many places around the world, the following pages examine this universal/local dynamic with respect to a single locality, Vietnam, which became a major point of conflict between the democratic–capitalist and communist powers during the years after the Second World War. More specifically, this essay explores the interplay between nationalist elites within Vietnam and the superpower patrons that both sustained them and sought to convert the country into a local articulation of the principles that they espoused. The chapter first examines the relationship between the superpowers and Ho Chi Minh's radical nationalist movement, the dominant Vietnamese political grouping to emerge from the Second World War. It then explores the relationship between the Western powers and the more moderate variant of Vietnamese nationalism that they sought to cultivate beginning in the late 1940s. Both Vietnamese movements tried to gain acceptance and support from abroad while at the same time winning the allegiance of sufficient numbers of ordinary Vietnamese to justify their claims to power.

It was a tricky balancing act that Ho Chi Minh's movement managed far more successfully than the alternative nationalism led first by Bao Dai and then Ngo Dinh Diem. Under Ho's leadership, the Democratic Republic of Vietnam managed to position itself within the communist world without sacrificing its legitimacy within Vietnam. It successfully managed, in short, to manipulate global principles in ways that maintained – and even enhanced – its local effectiveness and credibility. By contrast, the rival moderates aligned with the West failed in this endeavor. Rather than exploiting universal principles for local ends, the moderates were more often manipulated by their superpower patrons and, in the process, lost their legitimacy in the eyes of most Vietnamese. The contrast between the two cases not only helps explain the outcome of the later American war in Vietnam but also suggests that successful political movements in the era of globalization will be those that best manage to bend universal principles and practices to local purposes.[14]

Nationalism, communism, and revolutionary Vietnam

In a speech declaring the independence of Vietnam on September 2, 1945, Ho Chi Minh commiserated with his fellow Vietnamese about the depredations wrought by France over several decades of colonial rule. "They have built more prisons than schools," Ho charged. "In the economic field, they have shamelessly exploited our people, driven them into the worst misery and mercilessly plundered our country." But Ho's main purpose was neither to catalog French abuses nor to stir to action the multitude gathered before him in Hanoi's Ba Dinh Square. Rather he aimed first and foremost to attract international support for his new state, the Democratic Republic of Vietnam (DRV). Again and again, Ho linked the Vietnamese independence struggle to the grand principles allegedly held dear by the world's democracies. "All men are created equal; they are endowed by their Creator with certain unalienable Rights; among these are Life, Liberty, and the pursuit of Happiness," Ho declared in the famous opening lines that echoed the American Declaration of Independence. After similarly invoking the French Revolution's 1791 Declaration of the Rights of Man and Citizen, he appealed to the victorious allied powers to uphold their own ideals, reaffirmed so unequivocally during the Second World War. "We are convinced," Ho Chi Minh asserted, "that the Allies who have recognized the principles of equality of peoples recognized at the Conferences of Teheran and San Francisco cannot but recognize the Independence of Vietnam."[15]

Other Vietnamese leaders dwelt on similar themes. In the first radio broadcast by an official of the broad nationalist front known as the Viet Minh, the Saigon revolutionary Pham Ngoc Thach issued a "pressing appeal" to the allies on August 28, 1945, to abide by their high principles in dealing with Vietnam. After lauding the US plan to grant independence to the Philippines the following year, Pham Ngoc Thach called on American leaders to "defend our cause in the arena of world politics and recognize all the effort, all the courage, we have shown these last 80 years to make heard the voice of a people who want to be free and sovereign." He then praised the people of

Britain and the Soviet Union for showing determination to build "a new world based on social justice and world brotherhood" and called on the French to respect the best historical traditions of their country. "No," he declared, "the people of France, who have already given the world so much of their blood for the principles of justice and liberty, the French people of 1791 and 1917 who have shown the world the rights of the people, will not fail now in their duty."[16] The Viet Minh military chief, Vo Nguyen Giap, professed incredulity about the possibility that the allied powers might disappoint the Vietnamese. "From the Pacific Charter to [the] Teheran, Yalta and San Francisco agreements, the principle of national self-determination has been upheld," Giap averred in a speech on September 2. "The great powers in the democratic front have declared that they were fighting for world peace, so there is no reason why today they would again let French imperialism bring its army here to make war against Independent Vietnam."[17]

Such rhetorical flourishes reflected a simple calculation. If the fledgling Democratic Republic of Vietnam relied entirely on the resources and political legitimacy available to it locally, it stood little chance of resisting the reimposition of French colonial control in the wake of the Second World War. To be sure, the Viet Minh had cobbled together a potent militia during the war against Japan and had convincingly seized the mantle of leadership in the summer of 1945 amid the outpouring of Vietnamese nationalism that came to be known as the August Revolution. But there could be little doubt that France, despite the grievous economic, military, and political damage it had suffered during the war, would soon recover sufficiently to attempt to displace the nationalists and restore colonial rule. For the Vietnamese, the best hope of preserving the revolution lay in tapping into the currents of liberal idealism that dominated geopolitical discourse following the victory over fascism. By tying the local struggle in Vietnam to universalizing appeals for self-determination and individual liberty, the Viet Minh hoped to offset its material weakness through the strength of its ideological appeal.

It was neither the first nor the last time that Vietnamese nationalists sought to exploit grandly stated transnational ideals in order to achieve local objectives. In 1919, a delegation of Vietnamese nationalists led by Ho Chi Minh followed a remarkably similar approach in seeking an audience with leaders of the victorious powers gathered at Versailles to establish a new global order. In that brief heyday of Wilsonian idealism, as in 1945, the Vietnamese called upon Western nations to live up to their own avowed principles by granting self-determination to colonial territories.[18] At other moments, especially after it became clear that the West would do no such thing, Ho's movement tacked in a different direction, seeking solidarity not with liberal internationalism but with another universalizing ideal to emerge with new energy from the First World War, international communism. When Soviet foreign policy swung sharply to the left in 1928, leaders of Vietnam's key nationalist organization, the Revolutionary Youth League, followed suit and, in 1930, replaced the body with a full-fledged Indochinese Communist Party.[19] Lenin, not Wilson, seemed, at least for the time being, to offer the best blueprint for challenging European colonialism.

When Western policymakers first took serious note of Ho Chi Minh's movement, now dubbed the Viet Minh, in 1945, they had great difficulty categorizing it. Ho's obvious communist affiliation seemed to suggest one thing, but his nationalist rhetoric and appeals to liberal anticolonialism seemed to suggest quite another. In fact, as William Duiker argues in his authoritative biography of Ho Chi Minh, Ho's genius as a leader lay in his eclecticism. "Ho Chi Minh was a believer in the art of the possible, of adjusting his ideals to the conditions of the moment," Duiker writes. Commentators make a mistake when they try to determine whether Ho was more communist or nationalist patriot. He was, in fact, "half Lenin and half Gandhi," as Duiker puts it.[20] To phrase the matter differently, Ho Chi Minh – and to a degree the broader Vietnamese nationalist movement that he inspired and often led – was remarkably sensitive to geopolitical vicissitudes and adept at repositioning himself in order to harness the global forces that seemed most likely at a given moment to advance his goals of Vietnamese independence and the establishment of a state conforming to his vision of social and economic justice. None of this is to say that Ho was a mere cynic, grasping at any expedient that would serve his purposes. On the contrary, evidence suggests that Ho, much more a consumer of other people's ideas than an original thinker, was genuinely fascinated by the American as much as the Russian revolution and believed that Vietnam could draw profitably from both examples.[21]

As the Pacific war neared its end in the middle months of 1945, Ho Chi Minh and the rest of the Viet Minh leadership could have little doubt that the United States, with its vision of a world order remade along liberal capitalist lines, stood the best chance of dictating postwar arrangements. Although the Soviet Union held a dominating position in Eastern Europe, it could do little in so remote a place as Indochina. Nor, in China, could Mao Zedong's embattled communists exert influence in Southeast Asia. The United States, by contrast, seemed poised to control the destiny of Asia, if not the world. Washington obviously commanded enormous military and economic power. But even more impressive was the degree to which Washington's vision of a reordered world seemed to be taking hold. Already much of the globe had fallen in line behind American aspirations outlined in the Atlantic Charter signed in 1941 by Franklin Roosevelt and a grudging Winston Churchill. By mid-1945, statesmen from around the world had established the United Nations Organization to ensure global security and the World Bank and International Monetary Fund to regulate a revamped global economy based on open markets and stable exchange rates. Most promising for Vietnamese nationalists, many champions of a liberal world order stressed that the era of European colonization had come to an end. The more open, stable, and prosperous world that Americans imagined rested on a vision of independent nation states participating fully in a vastly expanded international community.

To harness these trends to Vietnamese purposes, the Viet Minh took a number of steps in 1945 and 1946 to demonstrate its desire for full participation in the emerging Pax Americana. The decision by Vietnamese leaders in 1941 to form a broad coalition of nationalist organizations – the Viet Minh – to oppose both France and Japan had marked a first step toward downplaying the role of the Communist Party and positioning Vietnamese aspirations for independence as consistent with the set of principles that underlay the allied war effort. Four years later, with the outcome of the fighting no longer in doubt and decisions about the postwar disposition of colonial territories increasingly imminent, Viet Minh leaders redoubled their efforts to tie their objectives to ascendant Western ideals. Even during the final weeks of the war against Japan, Ho Chi Minh cooperated closely with agents of the American Office of Strategic Services (OSS) who had been sent to Vietnam to recover allied airmen shot down over the area and to help Vietnamese guerrillas mount sabotage operations against Japanese troops. In part, as OSS Major Allison Thomas later speculated, Ho was motivated by a desire to bolster the Viet Minh's standing within the country by demonstrating that Washington considered it a worthy partner.[22] But Ho was also eager to send a message to the United States. "He hoped our being there would help convince the American government to support Vietnamese independence after World War II was over," Henry Prunier, another member of the OSS team in Vietnam, later recalled.[23] In the following months, Ho sought to build on this cooperation by sending at least seven letters to President Harry Truman requesting US support for Vietnamese independence. French efforts to recover colonial control were, Ho complained in one of them, "contrary to all principles of international law and to the pledges made by the Allies during the World War."[24] As if to quash any remaining doubts about where Vietnamese loyalties lay, the Indochinese Communist Party voted in November 1945 to dissolve itself – the only example in history of a communist party abolishing itself after successfully seizing power.[25]

Washington, however, never responded. As the DRV looked to the United States for support in 1945 and 1946, US policymakers stepped back from the enthusiasm that the Roosevelt administration had shown during the war for ending French rule in Indochina. A variety of considerations pushed US policy in this direction. Most important, American leaders concluded that they must avoid any initiative in Vietnam that might alienate France. On the contrary, as tension with the Soviet Union mounted, Washington officials believed that they must help rebuild France into a politically and economically robust nation that could be counted upon to resist Soviet aggression and play its part in a new global order centered on the United States. Looming confrontation with Soviet communism also discouraged American sympathy for Vietnamese nationalism by sharply decreasing Washington's tolerance for instability in the Third World. No matter how much they disliked European rule, a critical mass of US policymakers concluded that it offered the best means to maintain stability through a new period of global uncertainty. Feeding that calculation was mounting alarm about the role of communists within Ho Chi Minh's movement. New studies in 1946 and 1947 emphasized that although the Viet Minh's popularity rested on its nationalist appeal, its leadership consisted largely of dedicated communists who could be expected to cooperate with Soviet designs in Southeast Asia.[26]

To be sure, US leaders did not abandon all interest in ending colonialism in Vietnam. Rather, they struggled between 1945 and 1954 to find a formula for curtailing French control and replacing it with a moderate, anticommunist Vietnamese regime that would simultaneously appeal to local nationalists and cooperate closely with the West. The Truman administration persistently pressed the French government to concede autonomy to Vietnam, especially after Paris drafted the former Vietnamese emperor Bao Dai to lead a quasi-independent Vietnamese regime that, Western officials hoped, would siphon support away from Ho Chi Minh. US officials hoped, in short, that the liberal anticolonialism that Washington had eagerly espoused during the Second World War could be reconciled with the new Cold War imperative to craft an integrated bloc of independent nation states to oppose communist expansion. The trick, of course, would be to establish a Vietnamese government sufficiently independent to win the support of Vietnamese nationalists but sufficiently integrated into the French Union to ensure reliable participation in Western economic and political structures. This quest for a middle-ground solution stumbled along for several years before finally crumbling on the battlefield at Dien Bien Phu.

Long before that point, however, leaders of the Democratic Republic of Vietnam had come to the conclusion that the Western plan to reconcile colonialism and nationalism left little space for their vision of an independent Vietnam. Ho Chi Minh's 1945 attempt to harness Western liberalism to his purposes, in short, had failed. That failure left the Democratic Republic of Vietnam in a difficult position, especially after the start of full-scale war against France at the end of 1946. Although the French military faced great difficulties in Vietnam, Viet Minh forces confronted long odds at the outset of the fighting. Under these circumstances, Ho Chi Minh's government shifted back to the left, hopeful of harnessing the power of international communism. The DRV, it is true, did not immediately abandon all hope of finding sympathy in Americans. Indeed, Viet Minh propaganda continued to express admiration for the United States. Viet Minh-controlled Radio Vietnam flattered the United States in September 1947, for example, as "the first country to fight for independence and democracy, [the] first to free colonies."[27] But it is equally clear that the Democratic Republic of Vietnam, stymied in its appeals to the West, looked increasingly to the communist bloc during 1947.

Initially this approach held little promise. The French Communist Party, eager to display moderation at a time when it entertained reasonable hopes of achieving power through constitutional means, offered little support for the DRV before 1948. Mao Zedong's communist movement in China remained embroiled in a bitter civil war and was unable to lend significant support in Vietnam until 1950.[28] Perhaps most important, Josef Stalin held a distinctly low opinion of the Vietnamese revolution and its leader, Ho Chi Minh. Even as Moscow enhanced its diplomatic presence in Southeast Asia during 1947 – a development that Western policymakers viewed with deep alarm – Vietnamese leaders could have little confidence of receiving meaningful assistance. Indeed, the Soviet Union and the DRV seem to have had no direct contact during the early years of the Franco–Viet Minh war.[29]

Nevertheless, DRV leaders, now operating from their guerrilla base in the mountains north of Hanoi, worked to recast their movement as part of the global communist struggle. There were some reasons for hope. Most important, Stalin's second in command, Andrei Zhdanov, gave a landmark speech in September 1947 proclaiming that the world had been divided into two camps – socialist versus capitalist – and that the communist bloc would lead the armed struggle against imperialism. "Communists must support all the really patriotic elements who do not want their countries to be imposed upon, who want to resist enthrallment of their countries to foreign capital, and to uphold their national sovereignty," Zhdanov declared in comments focused on Europe but with obvious relevance to radical nationalists in the rest of the world.[30] More promising still, communist leaders from around the world established the Communist Information Bureau (Cominform) to coordinate their activities. Hoping to harness these developments to their purposes, Viet Minh officials began emphasizing their communist heritage and their solidarity with the international communist movement. In January 1948, the reconstituted Indochinese Communist Party endorsed the "two camps" concept. A month later, the Viet Minh delegation to a meeting of Asian nationalist organizations in Calcutta strongly emphasized armed revolution. Around the same time, Viet Minh propaganda began highlighting alleged historical connections between the Vietnamese and Russian revolutions, above all the supposed participation of a senior DRV official in the pro-Bolshevik naval mutinies that occurred in the Black Sea following the First World War. All in all, as historian Christoph Giebel contends, "Vietnamese communism from early 1948 on defined and announced itself conspicuously as part of the new communist order."[31]

By the end of the following year, the new approach was paying dividends. Not only had Soviet propaganda turned decisively in the DRV's favor, but also Mao Zedong's victory in China enabled the communist powers to reciprocate the Viet Minh's growing interest in them. In January 1950, China, the Soviet Union, and the rest of the communist bloc granted diplomatic recognition to the DRV, and within weeks Ho Chi Minh traveled to Moscow and China to cement the relationship. By the end of September, China – which, by agreement with Stalin, was to take the lead in promoting communist revolution in Asia – had established a military school to train Vietnamese officers and sent military advisers and equipment to help DRV forces.[32] Tremendous additional quantities of manpower and materiel followed over the next four years.[33] Unsurprisingly, Viet Minh military fortunes improved sharply, beginning in the fall of 1950 with a major triumph over French forces in the mountains along the Chinese frontier and culminating in 1954 with the epic victory at Dien Bien Phu.

Full-fledged partnership with the communist powers marked a major achievement for a Vietnamese movement that had confronted almost total isolation as recently as 1947. Vietnamese revolutionaries had failed in their effort to align themselves with the geopolitical current – Western liberalism – that had seemed all-powerful immediately after the Second World War, but succeeded brilliantly in harnessing the alternative globalizing vision that came to the fore in the late 1940s as communist aspirations, emboldened by Mao's victory, reached beyond the Soviet borderlands. While the Vietnamese revolution generated fear and anxiety among Western leaders, it increasingly meshed with the globalizing program conceived in Moscow and Beijing. As historian Qiang Zhai argues, Ho Chi Minh's revamped program fitted neatly with key objectives of the new Chinese leadership. Most important, Mao believed that supporting the Vietnamese revolution would help consolidate and legitimize revolution in his own country by suggesting that the communist victory was part of a global process in which China had a special role to play. Vietnamese dependence on China also tapped into traditional patterns of Vietnamese political and cultural subordination to China.[34]

Partnership with China did not mean that the DRV leadership ceased its effort to exploit other transnational currents to its advantage after 1950. Above all, Vietnamese revolutionaries sought to draw strength from an emerging "Third World" movement built on the common aspirations of colonized peoples. From 1945 onwards, the Viet Minh had struggled to forge bonds with nationalist movements elsewhere and to cast itself as part of a global current of anticolonial rebellion. By 1948, the DRV had opened diplomatic posts in Thailand, India, Malaya, and Burma and begun participating in regional gatherings, like the youth meeting in Calcutta, aimed at creating unity among colonial and newly independent states. These efforts achieved some notable results. Most important, as historian Shawn McHale argues, the war in Vietnam achieved "iconic status" throughout the Third World as a fight emblematic of the struggles being waged around the globe.[35] Whether that status would bring any tangible results was, however, a different question. To be sure, nationalist leaders and labor unions in India, Burma, and Malaya blocked shipments of French war materiel to Indochina, and DRV diplomats succeeded in obtaining small quantities of weapons from Thailand.[36] But cooperation with fellow South and Southeast Asian nations could not possibly bring even a fraction of the assistance available from the communist powers. The DRV therefore embraced "Third Worldism" only insofar as it was consistent with the partnerships it had created with China and, indirectly, the Soviet Union.

It is important to note that solidarity did not always pay off as Vietnamese leaders hoped. Most significantly, Beijing and Moscow disappointed DRV officials at the 1954 Geneva conference by backing the proposal to settle the Franco–Viet Minh war by splitting Vietnam at the seventeenth parallel. While DRV leaders protested that this solution did not reflect Viet Minh domination on the battlefield, Mao's determination to ease tensions with the West, his fears of outright US intervention, and his desire to gain time to focus on domestic reform dictated moderation in the Vietnamese settlement.[37] Differences between China and the DRV also flared over the land reform program initiated in northern Vietnam during the 1950s. Initially Vietnamese officials embraced the Maoist model that had been carried out across the border in China and welcomed the advice of Chinese experts. When the land reform campaign resulted in mass chaos and violence in 1955 and 1956, however, many DRV leaders turned against the radical Maoist

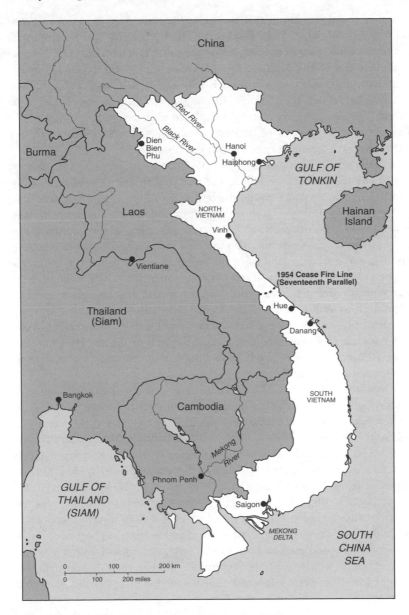

Adapted from Patrick J. Hearden, *The Tragedy of Vietnam*, 2nd edition (New York: Pearson Longman, 2005), p. 11.

Map 3 Vietnam, 1945–63

vision of social revolution that had generally united the two governments until that point. The Maoist model, the critics objected, was not appropriate to the particular circumstances that prevailed in Vietnam. These skeptics had come face to face with the dangers inherent in going too far in importing ideological and economic models without ample consideration of local practicalities. Thereafter, to the disgruntlement of Chinese leaders, the North Vietnamese government downplayed class struggle and mass mobilization as key elements of national ideology, embracing instead a more gradualist Soviet model of communist development.[38]

On the whole, however, Sino–DRV cooperation, supported strongly by the Soviet Union, remained close and was vital to the consolidation of the North Vietnamese state through the remainder of the 1950s. As Qiang Zhai has demonstrated, Beijing and Moscow provided North Vietnam with large quantities of raw materials, technological expertise, and consumer goods through the crucial years in which the new state reconstructed its economy and laid the material foundations for renewed warfare after 1960. Chinese advisers also played influential roles in reorganizing the DRV military, helping with air defense over North Vietnam, and training party cadres.[39] Moreover, as William Duiker has argued, Vietnamese resentment over the Chinese role in the Geneva settlement should not be exaggerated. Many DRV leaders, including most importantly the arch-pragmatist Ho Chi Minh, shared Chinese anxieties about provoking US intervention by pressing for too much too quickly.[40]

Only after 1960 did North Vietnam encounter major difficulties in preserving its smooth relationship with the communist powers. These problems resulted not from Vietnamese doubts about the need for communist solidarity but from rapidly mounting tensions between Moscow and Beijing. As Zhai has suggested, no government in the world had a stronger interest in preserving communist unity than North Vietnam. Indeed, Ho Chi Minh appealed to his country's two patrons to patch up their differences. The possibility of a complete split presented the DRV with a dilemma it had not confronted since the late 1940s: how to reorient itself in order to obtain – or, in this case, keep – the foreign political and military support necessary to overcome its weaknesses and achieve an independent and united Vietnam. The effort, as newly available communist bloc records demonstrate, was fraught with difficulties, not least because it tended to factionalize the North Vietnamese leadership into pro-Soviet and pro-Chinese elements that appear to have dueled for control over DRV policy through the 1960s and marginalized the eclectic pragmatists who had prevailed earlier.[41] The simultaneous escalation of a new war to reunify Vietnam, leading to full-scale US intervention after 1964, only heightened the stakes. North

Vietnam's success in the 1960–73 war resulted from many factors. Hanoi's ability to manage the Sino–Soviet split, just as DRV leaders had earlier managed abrupt changes in the global geopolitical climate, was an important one of them.

The quest for an alternative nationalism

As the Democratic Republic of Vietnam cemented its relationship with the communist powers during the 1940s and 1950s, other political forces attempted to establish an alternative nationalist movement that could tap into the globalizing principles touted by the Western powers – self-determination within a community of nation states, individual liberties, liberalized trade, and domestic market economics. In this effort, Vietnamese moderates, like the radicals who led the August Revolution and then the DRV, self-consciously operated within an international environment that offered challenges but also enormous opportunity. While Ho Chi Minh and his lieutenants positioned their movement within global political currents that would bring them legitimacy and support, the anticommunists were even more successful in linking themselves with foreign powers. This apparent advantage carried with it, however, a major problem. Western governments, though ostensibly championing Vietnamese self-rule, persistently dominated and manipulated the Vietnamese political forces with which they found common interests. The connection between local experience and global principle thus contrasts sharply with the relationship described in the first half of this chapter. In first case, the "local" – the DRV leadership of the late 1940s – manipulated the "global" in order to obtain local purposes. In the case of the two major efforts to establish a moderate nationalist regime in Vietnam – the Bao Dai and Ngo Dinh Diem experiments – the champions of a global geopolitical agenda manipulated the "local" in order to obtain global purposes.

In the final stages of the Pacific war and in the first two postwar years, the French government's principal aim was to isolate Vietnam from any global political current that might challenge colonial rule. Without question, French leaders sought to curry favor with the United States by proclaiming their determination to make thoroughgoing liberal reforms in Indochina. On March 24, 1945, the new French provisional government proclaimed its intention to establish "economic autonomy" and new democratic practices in Indochina. "Freedom of the press, freedom of association, freedom of assembly, freedom of thought and belief, and, in general, democratic freedoms will form the foundation of Indochinese law," the statement declared.[42] French officials took few steps toward putting such grand plans into action, however, and proposed only modest concessions to the Democratic Republic of Vietnam during negotiations aimed at finding a compromise that would avoid war. Meanwhile, French authorities worked hard to prevent direct contact between Vietnamese nationalists and foreign influences, particularly from the United States. Colonial officials harassed activities of the US Information Agency in Vietnam, closely monitored the work of American businesspeople and other travelers, censored foreign reporting, and tightly controlled information about the country. All of these efforts indicate a high level of French anxiety about the possibility that the Viet Minh would succeed in attracting US support by appealing to liberal anticolonial principles. Nothing was more important than to prevent that outcome.[43]

The French government found it impossible, however, to seal Vietnam from the globalizing currents that ran through geopolitics during the 1940s. Paris was unable, in short, to turn back the clock to the day when it could handle Vietnamese affairs as a matter strictly internal to the French empire. The Second World War had put an end to that era by accelerating world-wide information flows and dramatically heightening nationalists' awareness of common interests across South and Southeast Asia. The outbreak of the Franco–Viet Minh war in December 1946 made the implications of this situation abundantly clear. Although French commanders went to war expecting a relatively quick victory, they discovered within a few months that the Viet Minh were a formidable foe that could not easily be defeated. In fact, shortages of military equipment for operations in Vietnam, coupled with the difficulty of meeting growing defense requirements in Europe while France was bogged down in a war in Southeast Asia, led French leaders to much the same conclusion that their DRV enemies had recognized a few years before: France could be successful in Vietnam only if it obtained political and material help from abroad. The question for French leaders, then, was similar to the one that confronted the DRV leadership: how to recast their objectives in a way that would enable them to harness foreign power to their policy objectives. For Paris, the answer lay in succeeding where the Viet Minh failed between 1945 and 1947 – in showing that French policy was consistent with universal Western ideals and thus merited US support.

The principal method for doing so was the Bao Dai experiment, the French government's attempt to manufacture a moderate nationalist movement that could challenge the Viet Minh for leadership of a new Vietnamese state. A number of considerations encouraged the new French policy. Anticommunist nationalism, an important feature of Vietnamese political life across the first decades of the twentieth century, remained significant, especially in the South, even as the Viet Minh took center stage after the Second World War. Indeed, as Neil L. Jamieson has pointed out, the movement to install Bao Dai as head of an anticommunist, independent Vietnam made "spectacular progress" among the Vietnamese public during 1947 as the former emperor returned to political life.[44] There seemed to be reason to believe, then, that Bao Dai could command adequate support. But French leaders also embraced the new policy in the hope of achieving two other goals in Vietnam. They expected that Bao Dai's dependence on French sponsorship would enable France to retain considerable influence over the new state. At the same time, they believed that conceding limited independence would so impress the United States that Washington would line up behind the French effort to destroy the Viet Minh.

As negotiations on the establishment of the new "State of Vietnam" proceeded through 1948 and 1949, French diplomats pressed for American support for the effort. In virtually every encounter with US counterparts, they emphasized the liberal nature of French intentions and urged Washington to view the fight against the Viet Minh not as a war of colonial reconquest but as a conflict that pitted the interests of all the Western democracies against international communism. The interests at stake, they argued, were no longer specifically French: they were now global. In 1949, for example, Paul Devinat, a senior adviser to the French premier on Indochinese matters, told the US ambassador in Paris, Jefferson Caffery, that France had done its part by signing a "liberal agreement" conceding a high degree of independence to Bao Dai's regime. Defending the State of Vietnam, Devinat insisted, was now "an international job" requiring "material and moral support from outside in the next few months."[45] When Washington showed continued caution about aiding the French war effort in early 1950, French officials had little doubt that they must continue to hammer away at the same theme with American interlocutors. "It is only to the extent that we succeed in persuading them that the 'hot war' we are waging in Indochina is part of the cold war that the United States is fighting against Communism that we will be able to depend on their aid in Indochina," the French ambassador in Washington, Henri Bonnet, wrote to his superiors in Paris.[46] Apparently agreeing with that assessment, French premier Georges Bidault pulled out all the rhetorical stops in March 1950, telling US diplomats that the conflict in Vietnam had become "a full-scale war between two ways of life, the results of which would have serious repercussions for all the civilized world."[47]

To a considerable degree, the French succeeded in their effort to recast the fight in Vietnam as part of the global competition between the liberal West and international communism. US leaders did not, of course, need

French officials to point out that the West had a strong interest in seeing Bao Dai succeed or that the new state would require resources beyond what France alone could provide. By 1950, most American policymakers had reached that conclusion on their own and saw no alternative to supporting Bao Dai's regime, which they viewed, despite its weaknesses, as the only possible alternative to a communist takeover. In February, a few days after Beijing and Moscow recognized the DRV, the US and British governments recognized Bao Dai's state. Within a few months, Washington began supplying military aid to support the French war effort. What had begun as a local conflict over Vietnam's post-1945 political status thus became part of the worldwide confrontation between competing geopolitical blocs and the globalizing ideals that distinguished them.

The US and British governments, it is crucial to note, were hardly enthusiastic as they entered the Vietnam conflict on the French side. They clearly recognized that Bao Dai's state meshed imperfectly at best with the broader set of principles that the democratic West allegedly represented – and on which the West's reputation across much of South and Southeast Asia seemed to rest. Most worrying, the new government seemed to command little democratic legitimacy. After a brief flurry of hope in 1950s, Bao Dai generated little enthusiasm among Vietnamese beyond the limited cluster of Catholics, urbanites, and elites that had long furnished the core of the moderate nationalist movement in Vietnam. Despite all the grand rhetoric that surrounded the launch of the new state, there could be no disguising the fact that the French government limited its sovereignty in crucial ways, not least by maintaining control over foreign, defense, and trade policies and preventing Vietnam from having direct diplomatic relations with foreign governments. Nor did the Western powers doubt that nationalists elsewhere in Asia, whose views were perhaps the best barometer of Bao Dai's anticolonial legitimacy, regarded the new Vietnam with deep skepticism. Even as Bao Dai won Western recognition in 1950, the Indian nationalist leader Jawaharlal Nehru dismissed him as "a nice little boy" and "little more than a French puppet."[48] His opinions changed little over the following years, and India refused to recognize the State of Vietnam as part of the community of postcolonial states that it, more than any other country, represented.

Discouraged by the yawning gap between global claims and local practice, Washington and London applied pressure on the French government to concede fuller independence to Vietnam and to set a date by which the new state would have full sovereignty. In doing so, US and British statesmen were no starry-eyed idealists. As Cold War tensions heated up, they increasingly fretted that bold progress toward self-rule would only generate dangerous instability and power vacuums that communists would be well positioned to exploit. But they believed that upholding the principle, or at least seeming to uphold it, in Vietnam was crucial to keeping the area within the Western orbit. Only by somehow reconciling liberal claims and actual policy, US and British officials believed, could Paris enable Bao Dai to win the support of his people and of nationalists elsewhere in Asia – the twin requirements if Vietnam was to be kept from communist domination. The US and British governments quickly ran up against a contradiction, however, as they pushed Paris in this direction. While Washington and London hoped to create an effective multinational combination to fight communism, the French government was struggling in part to perpetuate its colonial prerogatives in Southeast Asia. It could only go so far toward meeting the demands of its Western partners, therefore, without squandering the objectives for which it had gone to war in 1946. After throwing US support behind the French war in 1950, the Truman administration quickly discovered that it had little leverage to force France into granting further independence. Unless the United States was willing to take over the fighting from the French military (which it was assuredly not), it could not demand that France take steps that would undercut the very reason for fighting the war. As a result, American support for the French far exceeded French willingness to cater to US demands. Between 1950 and the end of the war in 1954, the United States contributed a staggering $3 billion in aid – accounting ultimately for more than three-quarters of the cost of the French effort – while the French government did little to enhance Bao Dai's legitimacy as the leader of an independent democratic state.

Four years of intense frustration unsurprisingly left American policymakers eager to break the partnership with France following the Dien Bien Phu catastrophe and the subsequent division of Vietnam into two zones. France, it was clear to the Eisenhower administration, had kept the war going as long as it had through military force, not through any success in transforming Vietnam into a viable, Western-oriented nation state. Now Washington, which emerged from the First Indochina War as the dominant Western influence in Vietnam, discovered a chance to try to accomplish what had eluded Paris over the previous decade. The division of Vietnam into two zones meant that the US effort would have to focus on merely the southern half of the country. But the Eisenhower administration had no doubt that it remained critical to Western security to pull Vietnam – or at least part of it – firmly into the Western camp. The prospect of doing so without the taint of European colonialism generated optimism among many US officials even as the communists consolidated control in North Vietnam in 1954 and 1955.

But it was not just geostrategic necessity or relief over the eclipse of

French colonialism – critical though these were – that left Americans eager to take on the task of establishing a moderate nationalist state in South Vietnam. The challenge of building a nation there, as historian George Herring has written, "tapped the wellsprings of American idealism and took on many of the trappings of a crusade."[49] American rhetoric soared to new heights as Washington worked to succeed where the French had failed – to create a functioning Vietnamese state broadly in line with Western principles. South Vietnam would be the "cornerstone of the Free World in Southeast Asia" and a "proving ground for democracy," as Senator John F. Kennedy put it in 1956.[50] With the French pulling out of Indochina, the United States could return to its "traditional role of supporting the 'independence and legitimate national aspirations' of people," asserted a National Security Council official in the same year.[51]

Helping to sustain this confidence was a powerful set of new ideas, known as modernization theory, which began to emerge during the 1950s. The theory posited that all human societies develop from "traditional" to "modern" along a single, linear pathway and suggested that developed, "modern" states could help guide and accelerate the process in less developed countries through political and economic assistance.[52] Although modernization theory achieved its heyday among US policymakers in the 1960s, its emergence in the preceding years both reflected and gave intellectual legitimacy to various ideas that many Americans held as they contemplated policy toward South Vietnam. It confirmed that what was taking place in Vietnam must be seen as part of a global process by which states achieved adulthood (thus explaining away much of the repression and corruption that characterized the new state). It also made clear that the United States, as the quintessential developed nation, possessed the political and economic expertise to help South Vietnam along the path to development. Finally, the theory suggested that if the United States failed to take the lead, communists would likely step into the void, creating havoc and slowing the advance toward a liberal world order.

Armed with these ideas, US officials struggled during 1954 and 1955 to craft a South Vietnamese state that would serve their short-term geostrategic priorities but also mesh, later if not sooner, with Western ideals. The main challenge, as it had been for the French in 1947, was to bolster a moderate nationalist leadership that could give the new state democratic legitimacy while also playing its part in the desired global order. Although Bao Dai remained formally head of state until he was eased out in a rigged 1955 referendum that established a republic, Americans viewed him as badly tainted by French colonialism and selected a new leader for South Vietnam, Ngo Dinh Diem. Diem possessed a number of appealing attributes. Most important, he mixed fierce anticommunism with unimpeachable nationalist credentials. While many Vietnamese elites had been discredited by collaboration with France, Japan, or the Viet Minh, Diem boasted a record of hostility to all three, precisely the blend that Washington sought. At the same time, Diem, a devout Catholic who had spent many months in the United States, showed a strong affinity for the West – not just its geostrategic aims in the Cold War but also the broader intellectual and moral currents that informed Western hostility to communism. Here, then, was a man who seemed to combine respect for local Vietnamese traditions and interests with a determination to adapt his country to the larger globalizing project led by the United States. "We are not going back to a sterile copy of the mandarin past," Diem declared. "We are going to adapt the best of our heritage to the modern situation."[53]

For a time, Diem's eclectic approach – reminiscent of Ho Chi Minh's ability to swim simultaneously local and international currents – produced promising results. Internationally, Diem found favor in the West by skillfully managing the mass exodus of approximately 900,000 Catholics from North Vietnam to South Vietnam following the division of the country. More important, Diem succeeded in establishing a close partnership with Washington, which not only protected its protégé from various French plots to oust him but also provided so much economic and military assistance that by 1961 South Vietnam ranked fifth globally among recipients of American foreign aid. In all, the United States contributed nearly $1 billion in aid between 1955 and 1961 and, in the late 1950s, had more than 1,500 advisers helping the Saigon government in various ways.[54] Locally, too, Diem achieved considerable successes in the first years of his rule. As he took office, Diem confronted a badly fragmented South Vietnam, with rival religious communities and an organized crime syndicate known as the Binh Xuyen exercising control over significant parts of the country. Through a series of military operations and deft bargaining, Diem defeated or coopted his main rivals and by 1957 had established a South Vietnamese state so coherent and stable that *Life* magazine dubbed him "The Tough Miracle Man of Vietnam."[55]

Diem's early successes, however, masked deep underlying problems that would eventually destroy his effort to satisfy both local and global imperatives. Most damaging was Diem's persistent inability to win support for his regime among the South Vietnamese peasantry, who comprised the vast majority of the population. As scholars have recently made clear, Diem should not be written off as a mere puppet; he did, in fact, have a substantial base of support within South Vietnam.[56] Yet new evidence of Diem's popularity among Catholics and urbanites does little to alter the near-consensus among historians that Diem never achieved legitimacy among the segments of the South Vietnamese population with the strongest grievances against the colonial system and the greatest susceptibility to Ho Chi Minh's brand of Vietnamese nationalism.[57] Diem's disregard for rural conditions and his enthusiasm for repressive police operations to root out adversaries in the countryside demonstrated, as George Herring has written, "a singular lack of concern and near-callous irresponsibility."[58] Even at the peak of his power in the mid-1950s, no reasonable observer doubted that a head-to-head election between Diem and Ho Chi Minh would result in a landslide against the South Vietnamese president.

Diem's inability to deepen his local roots generated serious problems in the international arena as well by the start of the 1960s. His American supporters understood that the South Vietnamese regime could resist communist expansion and contribute to Western political and economic objectives only if it won the backing of its own people – a feat that required considerable attentiveness to the desires of ordinary Vietnamese people. As historian Seth Jacobs has pointed out, Americans doubted that the Vietnamese were prepared for full participation in a democracy. Indeed, that was one reason why Diem's authoritarian streak appealed to Washington in the mid-1950s.[59] But Diem's persistent refusals later in the decade to establish at least the veneer of democracy, to initiate meaningful land reform, or to share power outside a small clique dominated by his family left US officials increasingly frustrated with the man whom they had installed to create a democratic showcase in Vietnam. American anxieties about Diem only increased as attacks on the regime – the opening shots of what would become a new war in Vietnam – escalated around the turn of the decade. The effort to establish a moderate nationalist solution that meshed with the West's agenda would persist for another 15 years before crumbling entirely.

Conclusion

North Vietnam owed its victory to a number of advantages it held over its South Vietnamese enemy, not least superior morale and discipline. Perhaps most important, however, the Democratic Republic of Vietnam managed more effectively than its adversaries – first Bao Dai's state and then Ngo Dinh Diem's – to craft a profitable, dynamic relationship between local needs and the global geopolitical environment in which the Vietnamese conflict took place. At first, the DRV failed in its bid to align itself with Western anticolonial liberalism. But, recognizing the paramount importance of linking revolutionary nationalism in Vietnam with transnational currents that would legitimize it, Ho Chi Minh's government moved in the late

1940s to mesh itself with the other universalizing vision of political and economic development: international communism. Its success in exploiting this transnational phenomenon for local purposes contrasts sharply with the experience of the moderate nationalists who attempted between 1947 and 1975 to find a similar kind of legitimization in the liberal brand of internationalism championed principally by the United States. The key difference is not difficult to identify. While the DRV manipulated global geopolitical currents to suit its local purposes (an independent and unified Vietnamese state) the moderates were manipulated by the Western powers to suit global purposes (a global community of democratic–capitalist states that would participate in a new order centered on the trans-Atlantic West). First France and then the United States failed to overcome the fact that their protégés lacked local legitimacy that could come close to rivaling that of the DRV.

When analyzed in this way, the Vietnamese case suggests the utility of viewing the Cold War as a struggle between rival "globalizations" that, championed by large nations with enormous military and economic power, sought to extend their reach around the world, especially by shaping the destinies of newly independent countries emerging from colonialism and seeking models for political and economic development. The effort was likeliest to succeed in areas where local political elements, with deep understanding of local needs and legitimacy among local populations, could bend the globalizing principles to their purposes. And it was least likely to succeed in areas where globalizing schemes were grafted onto unpromising local conditions. Sheer coercion, it is true, could offset the absence of local leaders interested in "localizing" the broad set of global principles. Indeed, the survival of moderate nationalist schemes in Vietnam for nearly 30 years suggests that military and economic power by themselves could accomplish a great deal in territories where the moderates lacked broad local appeal. The most enduring Cold War partnerships (Cuba's alliance with the Soviet Union, for example, or South Africa's with the United States) often rested, however, on the participation of local elites who could adapt transnational ideals to local goals and thereby maintain a degree of autonomy and the political legitimacy that comes with it.[60]

This struggle between competing globalizations resulted in enormous bloodshed for nearly half a century. Efforts to link local grievances to universal objectives – and vice versa – tended to invest relatively small-scale conflicts with cosmic significance, thus heightening the perceived stakes and the amount of destruction that combatants would be willing to inflict to achieve their goals. The struggle also had other, more ambiguous outcomes. Persistent bids to link local conflicts to universalizing principles made ordinary people around the world much more aware of global phenomena and much more likely than before to see their societies as interlinked. In this way, the Cold War contributed powerfully to the development of a global consciousness that is both cause and effect of globalizing trends that have intensified since the fall of the Berlin Wall. Even as it divided the world into rival blocs, as political scientist Ian Clark has argued, "the Cold War's ultimate effect has been one of integration, not disintegration."[61] Cold War linkages between the local and the universal also helped condition populations around the world to view the victory of one over the other as evidence that the victorious vision of global development held genuine applicability around the globe. Indeed, since the collapse of communism in 1989–91, Western triumphalism has abounded, with one influential current of thought holding that the globe had reached "the end of history" with the virtually worldwide acceptance of liberal internationalism.[62] In fact, as the Cold War showed – in Vietnam, as elsewhere – globalizing ideals cannot be easily introduced into places where they do not mesh with local purposes.

Notes

1   Thomas Bender, "Historians, the Nation, and the Plenitude of Narratives," in Bender (ed.), *Rethinking American History in a Global Age* (Berkeley, CA, 2002), p. 3.

2   For example, Alfred E. Eckes Jr and Thomas Zeiler, *Globalization and the American Century* (New York, 2003); Matthew Connelly, *A Diplomatic Revolution: Algeria's Fight for Independence and the Origins of the Post-Cold War World* (New York, 2002); Jeremi Suri, *Power and Protest: Global Revolution and the Rise of Détente* (Cambridge, MA, 2003).

3   David Reynolds, "American Globalism: Mass, Motion, and the Multiplier Effect," in A. G. Hopkins (ed.), *Globalization in World History* (New York, 2002), p. 255.

4   Jürgen Osterhammel and Niels P. Petersson, *Globalization: A Short History* (Princeton, NJ, 2005), p. 29.

5   For a lively account, see Thomas L. Friedman, *The Lexus and the Olive Tree: Understanding Globalization*, revised ed. (New York, 2000), especially Ch. 4. Notable scholarly studies include Matthew Evangelista, *Unarmed Forces: The Transnational Movement to End the Cold War* (Ithaca, NY, 1999) and Walter L. Hixson, *Parting the Curtain: Propaganda, Culture, and the Cold War* (New York, 1997), especially pp. 229–33.

6   A. G. Hopkins, "Globalization – An Agenda for Historians," in Hopkins, *Globalization in World History*, pp. 9–10.

7   Akira Iriye, *Global Community: The Role of International Organizations in the Making of the Contemporary World* (Berkeley, CA, 2002), pp. 52–62.

8 Eckes and Zeiler, *Globalization and the American Century*, pp. 129–30. In a separate work, Zeiler argues that in the 1930s and 1940s "depression, world war,
   and the Cold War de-globalized – nationalized and regionalized – the international arena." Thomas W. Zeiler, "Just Do It! Globalization for Diplomatic
   Historians," *Diplomatic History*, 25 (2001), p. 550.

9 Friedman, *The Lexus and the Olive Tree*, p. 45.

10 Odd Arne Westad, *The Global Cold War: Third World Interventions and the
   Making of Our Times* (New York, 2005), p. 4

11 Robert Latham, *The Liberal Moment: Modernity, Security, and the Making of the
   Postwar International Order* (New York, 1997), p. 4.

12 Osterhammel and Petersson, *Globalization*, p. 113. See also Ian Clark,
   Globalization and Fragmentation: International Relations in the Twentieth Century
   (Oxford, 1997), p. 122.

13 Mark Metzler's and Tracie Matysik's chapters in this volume make a similar
   point.

14 In exploring the Vietnamese case study, this essay does not so much challenge
   existing interpretations as draw connections that have either been passed over or
   deemphasized by historians largely interested in different questions. Besides the
   works cited below, the essay relies on numerous superb studies of the Vietnam
   wars between 1945 and the early 1960s. See, for example, Philippe Devillers,
   Histoire du Viêt-Nam de 1940 à 1952 (Paris, 1952); Lloyd C. Gardner,
   Approaching Vietnam: From World War II through Dienbienphu (New York, 1988);
   Robert J. McMahon, *Colonialism and Cold War: The United States and the Struggle
   for Indonesian Independence, 1945–1949* (Ithaca, NY, 1981); Andrew J. Rotter,
   The Path to Vietnam: Origins of the American Commitment to Southeast Asia (Ithaca,
   NY, 1987); David G. Marr, *Vietnam, 1945: The Quest for Power* (Berkeley, CA,
   1995); and various essays in Mark Atwood Lawrence and Fredrik Logevall (eds),
   The First Vietnam War: Colonial Conflict and Cold War Crisis (Cambridge, MA,
   2006).

15 Vietnamese Declaration of Independence, September 2, 1945, in Robert J.
   McMahon (ed.), *Major Problems in the History of the Vietnam War*, 2nd ed.
   (Lexington, MA, 1995), pp. 36–8.

16 Broadcast by Dr. Pham Ngoc Thach, August 28, 1945, in Gareth Porter (ed.),
   Vietnam: The Definitive Documentation of Human Decisions (Stanfordville, NY,
   1979), pp. 63–4.

17 Speech by Vo Nguyen Giap, in ibid., pp. 66–71.

18 See William J. Duiker, *Ho Chi Minh: A Life* (New York, 2000), pp. 58–62. For
   the broader context of this initiative, see Paul Gordon Lauren, *Power and
   Prejudice The Politics and Diplomacy of Racial Discrimination* (Boulder, CO, 1988),
   Ch. 3.

19 For the relationship between Moscow and Vietnamese nationalism before the
   Second World War, see William J. Duiker, *The Communist Road to Power in
   Vietnam*, 2nd ed (Boulder, CO, 1996), pp. 29–52.

20 Duiker, *Ho Chi Minh*, pp. 571, 576.

21   On Ho's eclecticism, see especially Mark Bradley, *Imagining Vietnam & America: The Making of Postcolonial Vietnam, 1919–1950* (Chapel Hill, NC, 2000), pp. 30–5.

22   Thomas oral history, in Harry Maurer (ed.), *Strange Ground: Americans in Vietnam, 1945–1975: An Oral History* (New York, 1989), p. 35.

23   Prunier oral history, in Christian G. Appy, *Patriots: The Vietnam War Remembered from All Sides* (New York, 2003), p. 40.

24   Ho Chi Minh to Truman, February 16, 1946, in Porter, *Vietnam*, p. 95.

25   Huynh Kim Khanh, *Vietnamese Communism, 1925–1945* (Ithaca, NY, 1982), p. 329.

26   For shifting US calculations, see Mark Atwood Lawrence, *Assuming the Burden: Europe and the American Commitment to War in Vietnam* (Berkeley, CA, 2005), pp. 45–58, 172–5.

27   Cable, Hanoi consulate to State Department, September 18, 1947, Record Group 59, 851G.01/9-1847, National Archives II, College Park, MD.

28   See Qiang Zhai, *China and The Vietnam Wars, 1950–1975* (Chapel Hill, NC, 2000), pp. 11–13, and Chen Jian, *Mao's China & The Cold War* (Chapel Hill, NC, 2001), pp. 119–20.

29   On Soviet attitudes toward the Vietnamese revolution, see Duiker, *Ho Chi Minh*, pp. 420–3.

30   Zhdanov speech, September 1947, in Jussi Hanhimäki and Odd Arne Westad (eds), *The Cold War: A History in Documents and Eyewitness Accounts* (Oxford, 2003), p. 52.

31   Christoph Giebel, *Imagined Ancestries of Vietnamese Communism: Ton Duc Thang and the Politics of History and Memory* (Seattle, WA, 2004), pp. 47–58.

32   Zhai, *China and The Vietnam Wars*, pp. 18–20.

33   For estimates of Chinese and Soviet supplies during the First Indochina War, see ibid., Chs 1–2, and Chen Jian, *Mao's China*, Ch. 5.

34   Zhai, *China and The Vietnam Wars*, pp. 20–5.

35   Shawn McHale, "Vietnamese, Black Africans, Berbers, and Arabs: The First Indochina War (1945–54) and the Limits of Third Worldism," unpublished paper for the 2005 annual meeting of the Society for Historians of American Foreign Relations.

36   Giebel, *Imagined*, p. 52.

37   For Chinese motives, see Zhai, *China and The Vietnam Wars*, pp. 49–63; Chen Jian, *Mao's China*, pp. 138–44.

38   Duiker, *Ho Chi Minh*, pp. 474–86; Zhai, *China and The Vietnam Wars*, p. 76.

39   Ibid., pp. 73–4, and Nguyen Vu Tung, "Interpreting Beijing and Hanoi: A View of Sino-Vietnamese Relations," in Odd Arne Wested, et al. (eds), "77 Conversations between Chinese and Foreign Leaders on the Wars in Indochina, 1964–1977," Cold War International History Project Working Paper No. 22 (Washington, DC, 1998), pp. 47–64.

40   Duiker, *Communist Road to Power*, p. 172.

41   For insight into divisions within the communist leadership, see Robert K.
     Brigham, *Guerrilla Diplomacy: The NLF's Foreign Relations and the Viet Nam War*
     (Ithaca, NY, 1999); Duiker, *Communist Road to Power*; and Ilya Gaiduk, *The
     Soviet Union and the Vietnam War* (Chicago, 1996).
42   March 24 Declaration, in Philippe Devillers (ed.), *Paris, Saigon, Hanoi: Les archives
     de la guerre, 1944–1947* (Paris, 1988), pp. 53–4.
43   For French efforts to obstruct US influence in Vietnam, see Lawrence,
     Assuming the Burden, pp. 93–5, 131–4.
44   Neil L. Jamieson, *Understanding Vietnam* (Berkeley, CA, 1993), p. 211.
45   Caffery (Paris) to State Department, March 18, 1949, *Foreign Relations of the
     United States, 1949*, Vol. 7 (Washington, DC, 1975), pp. 14–15.
46   Bonnet to Foreign Ministry, April 11, 1950, series Asie/Indochine, file 262,
     Archives of the French Ministry of Foreign Affaires, Paris.
47   Memo by Philip Jessup et al., "Interviews with French Officials," March 13,
     1950, Record Group 59, 751G.00/3-1450, National Archives II, College Park,
     MD.
48   "Nehru to his Chief Minister," February 2, 1950, in *Selected Works of Jawaharlal
     Nehru*, second series, Vol. 14, part I (Oxford, 1993), p. 396; High Commissioner
     in India to Foreign Office, February 5, 1950, series FO371, file 83625, Public
     Record Office, London.
49   George C. Herring, *America's Longest War: The United States and Vietnam,
     1950–1975*, 4th ed. (New York, 2002), p. 54.
50   Quoted Marilyn B. Young, *The Vietnam Wars, 1945–1990* (New York, 1991),
     p. 58.
51   Ibid.
52   Michael E. Latham, *Modernization as Ideology: American Social Science and "Nation
     Building" in the Kennedy Era* (Chapel Hill, NC, 2000), p. 4.
53   Quoted in Seth Jacobs, *America's Miracle Man in Vietnam: Ngo Dinh Diem,
     Religion, Race, and US Intervention in Southeast Asia* (Durham, NC, 2004), p. 37.
54   Herring, *America's Longest War*, p. 69.
55   John Osborne, "The Tough Miracle Man of Vietnam," *Life*, 42 (May 13, 1957),
     p. 156.
56   For example, Philip Catton, *Diem's Final Failure: Prelude to America's War in
     Vietnam* (Lawrence, KS, 2002).
57   For example, Herring, *America's Longest War*, pp. 77–8; Robert D. Schulzinger,
     A Time for War: The United States and Vietnam, 1941–1975 (New York, 1997),
     pp. 94–5; Young, *The Vietnam Wars*, pp. 61–2.
58   Herring, *America's Longest War*, p. 77.
59   Jacobs, *America's Miracle Man*, pp. 36–40.
60   My point here reinforces the idea, explicit or implicit in much recent scholar-
     ship on the Cold War, that "peripheral" actors could, under the right circum-
     stances, exercise a good deal of influence over their ostensible superpower
     masters. See especially Tony Smith, "New Bottles for Old Wine: A Pericentric
     Framework for the Study of the Cold War," *Diplomatic History* 24, Fall (2000),

pp. 551–65; but also John Lewis Gaddis, *We Now Know: Rethinking Cold War History* (Oxford, 1997).

61 Clark, *Globalization and Fragmentation*, p. 122.

62 See Francis Fukuyama, *The End of History and the Last Man* (New York, 1993). For a refined and updated version of the argument, see Thomas L. Friedman, *The World Is Flat: A Brief History of the Twenty-First Century* (New York, 2005). This view spawned a counterargument emphasizing that the triumph of liberal internationalism would result not in uniform acceptance of that model but in a new breakdown of the world into rival visions. See especially, Samuel P. Huntington, *The Clash of Civilizations and the Remaking of World Order* (New York, 1998).

9

Globalization and the Mythology of the "Nation State"[1]

Philip L. White

Innumerable writers have considered the effect of "globalization" on the "nation state." One school argues that the all-encompassing universalism of globalization has made the "nation state" obsolete and will ultimately destroy it.[2] The other insists that the "nation state" with its more local or regional outlook is here to stay, despite the present trend toward globalization.[3] Nearly as universal as globalization is the tendency to use "nation state," with or without a hyphen, for what was formerly called a "nation," as in the League of Nations or the United Nations. Similarly prevalent is the practice of discussing the subject without clearly defining "nation state," "nation," or, for that matter, even "state."

This imprecision conceals an important ambiguity. The "nation state" appears to have two very different meanings. One meaning is a sovereign government. Such a government is expected to serve the interests of all who reside within the government's borders. Some have called such sovereign governments *civic* nations. The other form is what I prefer to call the *ethnic* nation. The ethnic "nation" is a group in which members share kinship (often fictive), language, perhaps a religion, and usually many customs. Each ethnically homogeneous group, advocates of this view insist, is morally entitled to control its own sovereign government and to use control of the government to protect its purported ancestral purity, language, religion, and customs. This view became popular in the nineteenth century, lost much of its popularity after World War II, but has experienced a powerful revival since the end of the Cold War. It has antecedents going back to the Latin word for 'birth' and to Judeo-Christian scriptures.

Assuming that globalization continues unabated, the ethnic version of the "nation state" would appear to have a limited future because migration, spurred by globalization, is eroding whatever ethnic homogeneity may once have existed within major states. The rioting by ethnic minorities in France during 2005 and the widespread discontent among Asian and African Muslims elsewhere in Europe have provided dramatic illustrations of this trend. The reality being created by globalization is that all major "nations" are becoming ethnically heterogeneous rather than homogeneous.

Yet the assumption that "nations" are, or should be, ethnically homogeneous (assumed also by the principle of self-determination) remains popular. In many areas, leaders still wish to see that idea implemented. They insist that the "nation state," defined in ethnic terms, is here to stay because people want it.

If the civic version of the function of sovereign governments prevails, the relationship between "nation states" and globalization becomes more difficult to predict. To the extent that the national government is multi-ethnic or heterogeneous, it would appear to be more compatible with forces, such as international migration, which globalization has propelled. But this is the beginning, not the end, of the problem because sovereign governments of the civic type vary greatly in attractiveness to immigrants, in immigration policy, and in cultural receptivity. Claims made upon them by immigrants can also vary greatly. Consequently, a satisfactory analysis of the impact of globalization upon sovereign governments which are civic in character requires a typology that has yet to be constructed. Clearly those who believe globalization will eliminate the "nation state" have yet to define what it is that will be eliminated or what will replace it.

This chapter will suggest that much of the discussion of the impact of globalization upon "nation states" has been built on shifting sands because the term itself is so rarely defined and its two very different meanings so rarely recognized. No sustainable conclusions about the relationship between "nation states" and globalization can be reached if the terms of debate continue to rest on unspecified assumptions. Both historians and social scientists specializing in the study of globalization, it seems to me, need desperately to clarify precisely what they mean when they use the term "nation state." Even specialists on globalization seem inclined to use the term "nation state" as if its meaning were transparent and non-problematic. It is neither.

Accordingly, it is important to review the history of the term "nation state" to see why, in the context of globalization, its future occasions so much confusion and dispute. This chapter will consider four points relating to the "nation state." First, it will show that, with one possible exception, the leading authorities on the related terms, "nation," "nationality" and "nationalism" have expressed dissatisfaction with even their own understanding of the terms. Second, it will explore the confusion relating to these terms which has persisted from Roman times to the present. Third, it will focus on the development of opposing civic and ethnic conceptions of nation, culminating in the emergence of the concept of the "nation state" in the late nineteenth century. Fourth, it will consider criticisms of the original concept of the "nation state," showing that for most of the developed world, it is a fiction and that globalizing tendencies seem certain to make it remain so. My conclusion will be that, if we are fortunate, globalization will indeed relegate the "nation state," as originally conceived, to the dustbin of history.

Having stressed the confusion arising from failure to define the term "nation state," it is appropriate that I define both globalization and "nation state." Globalization is well, if briefly, defined in the introduction to this volume. For the purposes of the present chapter it is sufficient to note that globalization refers to the accelerating integration of world communities, economically, socially, culturally, and even politically. Defining "nation state" will consume the balance of this essay.

For many observers, perhaps for most in the academic world, "nation state" has become essentially a synonym for a sovereign government. Member states of the United Nations, for example, are now often called "nation states" rather than merely nations. The online version of the *Oxford English Dictionary* (*OED*) now clearly recognizes this equation of "nation state" and nation.[4] To repeat a crucially important point, "nation state" in its original meaning was an ethnic group that controlled its own sovereign government and used that control to serve the interests or the wishes of that ethnic group. This definition, reposing sovereign authority in a homogeneous ethnic group, is the *only* definition of "nation state" to appear in the last published edition of the *OED* in 1989.[5] The earliest use cited there was in 1918, although the current online edition cites a still earlier use in 1895. This ethnic conception of "nation state" is also reflected in the moral commitment that many feel to self-determination.

"Self-determination"[6] is a widely popular doctrine which asserts, as does "nation state" in its original conception, that each of the world's ethnic groups has a moral right to control its own sovereign government and use that control to serve the purposes of the group. If fully implemented, the doctrine of self-determination, or the concept of the "nation state" as defined by the *OED* in 1989, would create two thousand or more "nation states," roughly ten times the current number of UN members. One can imagine, though with considerable difficulty, how such a tenfold increase in the number of UN members would complicate the problems of dealing with globalizing trends already manifest, let alone those to be anticipated in the future.

The ethnic conception of nation, it must be emphasized, contrasts with the civic concept.[7] The civic concept of nation sees sovereign "national" governments as obliged to serve the interests of all the people within their national borders without discriminating either for or against any ethnic group. In practice, purported national governments in the civic sense have often discriminated in favor of the "dominant ethnic group" and against others. Such discrimination and the sometimes distorted recollections of it have been, and continue to be, a major force behind ethnic separatist movements around the world. Those who see globalization as dooming the "nation state" to extinction have a powerful case, providing they refer to the "nation state" as originally conceived, that is as an ethnic group controlling its own sovereign government and using it to serve the interests of that ethnic group. However, if they mean to argue that even civic nations are doomed to extinction under the influence of globalization, the case becomes much harder to make.

Many contemporary commentators who use "nation state" instead of "nation" seem unaware of the original ethnic connotations of the term. For example, all 50 contributors to the otherwise excellent *Globalization Transformation Reader* seem to equate "nation state" with sovereign government.[8] None of the volume's 34 index references to "nation state" even mentions the ethnic definition of "nation." Similarly, few of the contributors who use the term "nation state" seem to be aware that its original meaning assumed that all "nation states" would be ethnically homogeneous. Another recent volume shows a similar reluctance to define "nation state." Karl Cordell and Stefan Wolff's substantial *Ethnopolitical Encyclopedia of Europe*, published in 2004, considers only groups that were "indigenous" to Europe and omits those with roots in Asia or Africa. Despite excluding groups with the greatest cultural differences, the contributors identify some 70 European ethnicities whose history and other distinctive features separate them from those who dominate their national governments. The problems facing those who claim that each ethnic group deserves its own sovereign government to serve the interests of an ethnically homogeneous population are indeed intractable.

With the meaning of "nation state" thus clarified, the disagreement about the future of the nation state, as originally construed, can be restated. The fundamental queries, as I see them, are these. Will our species adapt its political institutions to deal with globalizing tendencies, such as ethnic intermingling, but also the various environmental and other threats common to us all? Alternatively, will we give higher priority to enabling local or regional ethnic groups to preserve their often fictive ancestral purity, their language, religion, or other customs? Will we do so even if it means condoning discrimination against those individuals or groups whose ethnicity is different? Restated in this way, the answers to each question seem obvious. In its more conventional formulation, which often leaves "nation state" undefined, the answer is less clear.

Specialists on globalization who do not define what they mean by "nation state" may have in mind what they see as the obsolescence even of civic nations, as globalization extends its reach. This suggests a further reason for avoiding the term "nation state" or, minimally, for defining it explicitly. As the online edition of the *OED* now makes clear, the term has become ambiguous. Those who use it without defining it inevitably create uncertainty as to which meaning they intend their readers to adopt. Are readers to assume that the writer means a civic nation in which the government seeks to serve the interest of all residents? Or should the reader assume that the intended meaning for "nation state" is that of the 1989 *OED*: an ethnic group that controls its own sovereign government and uses its control to serve the interests of only one ethnic group? In view of the violence engendered by efforts to implement the ethnic definition of "nation state," presumably most writers would wish to leave no doubt as to which meaning they wish their readers to assume. There is a warning here both for historians who are not fully aware of these uncertainties, and for specialists on globalization who predict the demise of the "nation state" without specifying whether they define it in civic or in ethnic terms.

The terminological jungle

Conceptual confusion over the terms "nation," "nationality," and "nationalism" has a long history. The Belgian ethnographer, Arnold van Gennep, expressed it well in 1922. He focused on "nationality" rather than "nation," but early advocates of the "nation state" generally found those terms ("nation" and "nationality") interchangeable. In his *Traité comparatif des nationalités*, Gennep observed: "The social reality currently designated by the word nationality is at the same time so complex in form and content and so variable in time and space that one can never succeed in giving a definition that is not confused and vague."[9]

A few examples will illustrate both the problem and its antiquity. In his famous lecture delivered at the Sorbonne in 1882, Ernest Renan probably helped Gennep arrive at his conclusion 40 years later. Renan answered the question, "What Is a Nation?" by affirming that it was "a soul, a spiritual principle. Two things which are really one constitute this soul, this spiritual principle. One is the possession in common of a legacy of memories; the other is the desire to live together ... ."[10] Whatever else may be said of that definition, it surely qualifies as vague.

James A. H. Murray's *New English Dictionary*, published at Oxford in 1903, set forth another definition that might well have led one to conclude, as Gennep did, that all definitions of terms relating to nationality must be "confused and vague." Murray's 1903 definition of nation reads as follows:

An extensive aggregate of persons, so loosely associated with each other by common descent, language, or [sic] history, as to form a distinct race or people, usually organized as a separate political state and occupying a definite territory. In early examples the racial idea is usually stronger than the political; in recent use the notion of political unity and independence is more prominent.[11]

The *OED* repeated this 1903 definition of "nation" verbatim in both its 1933 and its 1989 editions. Both later editions included the reference to "recent use."[12] Reflecting the trend in contemporary use, the online version of the *OED* by 2003 had altered the definition to read: "A large aggregate of communities and individuals united by factors such as common descent, language, culture, history, or occupation of the same territory, so as to form a distinct people. It also added: "such a people forming a political state; a polit-ical state."[13] Both "history" and "occupation of the same territory" as well as "a political state" seem to make allowance for the ever-growing number of "nations" in the civic sense of sovereign governments which are not (and very often never were) characterized properly as ethnically homogeneous.

Similar confusion has long prevailed in the use of "nationalism." Carlton J. H. Hayes, the historian who was among the first to accord scholarly atten-tion to nationalism, admitted in his *Essays on Nationalism* (1926) that "we ourselves have been using the word nationalism to indicate two quite differ-ent things." The first was "to denote ... the process of establishing nation-alities as political units." The second was "to describe ... the belief that one's own nationality ... has such intrinsic worth and excellence as to require one to be loyal to it above every other thing ... ."[14] Later, in *The Historical Evolution of Modern Nationalism*, Hayes identified a bewildering variety of forms of nationalism.[15] Toward the end of his life, he concluded that nationalism was "a religion."[16]

Hans Kohn's widely cited *The Idea of Nationalism* (1944) asserted that "nationalities defy exact definition."[17] Still later, he affirmed that "only an interdisciplinary approach would be able to cover the many facets of this complex phenomenon."[18] Kohn's contemporaries showed similar concern.

Boyd C. Shafer marveled in *Nationalism: Myth and Reality* (1955) that "A century of study of ... nationalism has produced no ... acceptable defini-tion."[19] Benjamin Akzin chose "The Terminological Jungle" as the title of the first chapter of his *State and Nation* (1964).[20] T. V. Sathyamurthy's *Nationalism in the Contemporary World* (1981) characterized the literature on the subject as "distinguished by its vagueness."[21] Harold Isaacs in *Idols of the Tribe* (1975) observed that definitions of nationality, as well as related terms, were "notably blurred to this day."[22]

More recently, Eric Hobsbawm in *Nations and Nationalism Since 1870: Programme, Myth, and Reality* (1990) considered how to define "nation." He concluded, however, that "no satisfactory criterion can be discovered for deciding which of many human collectivities should be labeled in this way." The usual criteria of "language, ethnicity, whatever" he characterized as "fuzzy, shifting and ambiguous, and ... useless." He then made an extended, historically based argument to support this conclusion.[23]

Liah Greenfeld was more sanguine, but not necessarily more convincing in *Nationalism: Five Roads to Modernity* (1992). Her book is a marvelously detailed and insightful study of the evolution of national identity in Britain, France, Russia, Germany, and the United States. "Nationalism," she affirms in begin-ning the introduction, "locates the source of individual identity within a 'people' which is seen as the bearer of sovereignty, the central object of loyalty and the basis of a collective solidarity." She then adds that 'people' is seen "always as fundamentally homogeneous."[24] That assertion seems difficult to square with Hobsbawm's position, or with Greenfeld's inclusion of the United States in particular as one of her examples. Indeed, she does confess later to being "bewildered by the complexity of the historical evidence."[25]

Four other prominent writers on nationalism require comment. Sociologist Anthony D. Smith of the London School of Economics is surely the most prolific of the innumerable writers on nationalism. His many books on the subject may well have had more readers than those of any other author. Similarly, he has almost certainly read more widely on the subject than anyone who has ever lived. Smith referred to "terminological difficul-ties" before concluding that, however desirable it might be, the aim of devising a satisfactory theory of nationalism was probably "utopian."[26]

Political scientist Benedict Anderson also found nationality, nation, and nationalism "notoriously difficult to define, let alone analyze."[27] His char-acterization of nationalities as *Imagined Communities* (1983, 1991) proved to be a very popular way of conceptualizing the issue. He is the possible excep-tion to the claim that all of these authors have expressed doubts about even their own definitions.

Philosopher and anthropologist Ernest Gellner wrote a best-selling book on *Nations and Nationalism* (1983). He defined both the words in his title in the exclusively ethnic context used by those who were targets of his criticism, but found "neither [definition] is adequate." He characterized his own *two* conceptions of "nation" as "makeshift, temporary definitions" and the concept as "elusive."[28] He might have emphasized that membership of both the League of Nations and the United Nations was not for ethnic groups, but for sovereign governments.

Historical sociologist Charles Tilly and a distinguished group of colleagues began, as he observed, "to analyze state-making and the formation of nations interdependently." They gave up on the latter effort when they found themselves unable to agree on the meaning of "nation," "one of the most puzzling and tendentious items in the political lexicon."[29]

All of the writers cited above, in addition to confessing their own uncertainty (except perhaps for Anderson), set forth their understanding of the term "nation" or one or the other of its cognates. Some, notably Anderson, found widespread scholarly acceptance for their views. Nevertheless, it remains true that no scholarly consensus has yet emerged as to how to define any one of the terms, "nation," "nationality," or even "nationalism." Definitions of all three remain disputed.

From *natio* to nation

The origin of this confusion goes back to the Romans. All three words, "nation," "nationality," and "nationalism" derive from the Latin word *natio*. Whatever the connotations it subsequently acquired, *natio* is the Latin word for "birth." The relationship is clearly evident still in cognate words such as natal, native, and nativity. Thus it would seem reasonable to assume that common ancestry was implicitly a basis for any group whose generic categorization sprang from the word *natio*. As Romans applied the term, however, *natio* seems to have had varied uses. Guido Zernatto asserted that the Romans used the term derisively to designate groups of foreigners, especially those living in ghetto-like areas of their port cities. He noted also that the similarity among members of a *natio* was assumed to derive from their having been "born in the same city or tract of land."[30] The *Oxford Latin Dictionary* affirms that Romans used *natio* also to mean "a place of origin (of natural products)."[31] Thus *natio*, even at that early time, carried some territorial connotations as well as (and more clearly) those of an ethnic, specifically a kinship, basis of group identity.

Complicating the matter still more is the relationship in Roman use between the words *gens* and *natio*. *Gens* generally meant a group of non-Romans of higher status than those in a group called a *natio*. Frequently translated as "tribe," *gens* carried, as did *natio*, the implication of common ancestry or at least of group loyalty. Romans in fact used *gens* quite loosely. Patrick J. Geary points out[32] that Romans applied the term to designate the ethnicity of the leader of a group, but that the horde which followed him was usually of quite mixed original ethnicity. Furthermore, while *natio* was usually seen as quite distinct from *gens*, the *Oxford Latin Dictionary* affirms that on some occasions it was used as if it were "identical with it."[33]

Over a considerable period the Romans then developed a body of law called *ius gentium* to regulate their dealings with non-Romans. Far more practical than the *ius civile*, the traditional law applicable to Romans, *ius gentium* became in time the principal body of Roman civil law. From the second century AD onward, new conceptions of "natural law" were added to, or confused with *ius gentium*, to produce what one authority has branded a "bewildering controversy" concerning the meaning of *ius gentium*. Similarly obscure is its bearing on the evolution of what in time would come to be called inter*national* law.[34]

How did the law of tribes, *ius gentium*, become the law of *nations*? The shift appears to have begun in the medieval era. Johan Huizinga in *Men and Ideas* (1959) asserted that in the Vulgate (long the standard translation of the Biblical writings into Latin) *natio* was used interchangeably with *gens* and *populus* in referring to groups in the Old Testament. Huizinga added that, although initially *natio* had no administrative or political connotations, it seems gradually to have acquired them.[35] Gaines Post asserted that in medieval use *natio* meant "either the locality in which one was born, or an organization of students in the university who came from the same general region."[36] Baxter's *Medieval Word List from British and Irish Sources* states that around the year 1400 *natio* had come to mean in those areas simply "territory."[37]

At the great church councils, such as at Lyon in 1274 and at Constance in 1414–17, *natio* had other connotations. According to Guido Zernatto, it meant in the context of those meetings a "representative body" whose members were in effect proxies for secular princes or universities. It was assumed, he added, that a "loose bond of territorial origin existed among the individual members of this body."[38] Amplifying Zernatto, Greenfeld points out that, in church use, the term *natio* was beginning to take on the connotations of an elite group acting in the name of the people of a particular area.[39] It is not clear whether the people of the area were presumed to be bonded by common ethnicity or by territorial interests shared by multi-ethnic residents.

Between the Reformation and the French Revolution, English use came to differ from that on most of the continent of Europe. To the English,

Greenfeld asserts, the word "nation," notably in the King James version of the Bible (1611), had become at times "a synonym of a people, a polity, and even a territory." Greenfeld also found many other meanings among the 454 uses of *nation* in the King James Bible. On most of the continent, however, the Catholic Vulgate remained the standard version of the Bible. In the Vulgate, Greenfeld found only 100 uses of *natio* – all of them indicating a group bonded by either kinship or language.[40] This helps in some measure to understand why the ethnic conception became and remains prevalent in many Catholic areas of Europe. The English, Greenfeld asserts, while retaining the meaning for *natio* long found in the Vulgate, and indeed finding other meanings as well, had come by the early seventeenth century to see *natio* in a civic as well as in an ethnic context. Such a meaning for "nation," Greenfeld insists, did not appear in any other vernacular language in Europe during this period.[41]

Furthermore, Greenfeld argues, the English began in the sixteenth century to refer to the territory associated with them as "nation" rather than "realm." The implication was that the land – and control over it – belonged to the people, not to the king. In the period of the Puritan Civil War and Commonwealth, the anti-royalist elements at times associated "nation" not only with the people but also with Parliament as the people's agent. According to Greenfeld, this tendency abated after the restoration of the Stuart monarchy in 1660, but the popular concept of "nation" came back into favor with the expulsion of the Stuart royal family in the Glorious Revolution of 1688–89.[42] This English experience, one may suspect, was in Greenfeld's mind when she wrote earlier in her book: "The location of sovereignty within the people and the recognition of the fundamental equality among its various strata, which constitute the essence of the modern national idea, are at the same time the basic tenets of democracy." "Democracy was born," she added, "with the sense of nationality."[43]

Meanwhile, in 1625, the Dutch scholar, Hugo Grotius, had produced his great treatise on *The Law of War and Peace*, which is generally considered to be the first significant work on international law. Writing in the tradition of Roman law and in Latin, Grotius used *gens* to refer to what the political scientists would later call states. However, the first English edition of his work, *The Law of Warre and Peace* (1654), used "nation" frequently, as in "that law which is between many nations, or their rulers" and "Controversies arising between Nations or Kings." A London edition of 1728 bore the title: *The Rights of War and Peace in three books wherein are explained the Law of Nature and Nations and the Principal Points relating to Government.*[44] Even more explicitly, when Emmerich Vattel's *Droit des gens* (1758) appeared in English translations in Dublin (1792) and London

(1793), each bore the title, *The Law of Nations*.[45] Thus in English legal use *gens* had come to mean nation, and to be associated not with ancestral or linguistic bases of social identity, but at least implicitly with sovereign governments.

Outside legal circles, however, English usage was more ambiguous. The *OED* cites a reference in the 1660s to the courts and counties of the nation. The context suggests that the meaning was political, but seems not to rule out an ethnic interpretation. Samuel Johnson's *Dictionary of the English Language* (1755) straddled the issue, as would so many later writers, by defining nation as "a people distinguished from another people, generally by their language … or government." He also cited the seventeenth-century author and diplomat, Sir William Temple, who asserted that a nation must have both ethnic and political unity: "A nation properly signifies a great number of families derived from the same blood, born in the same country, and living under the same government."[46] This defines, loosely, the ethnic conception of "nation state."

In France, meanwhile, "nation" was undergoing a transition somewhat similar to that in England. The *Académie française* defined it in 1694 as a collective term referring to "all the inhabitants of the same State, or of the same region (*pays*), who live under the same laws and use the same language."[47] This comes close to insisting, as Temple did, that to qualify as a nation a group must have both linguistic unity and sovereign authority. The *Encyclopédie* of 1765 defined "nation" as "a collective word which one uses to express a considerable number of people who live in a certain area (*entendue du pays*), contained within fixed borders, who obey the same government and who are distinguished from other nations by their particular character."[48] A few years later, the Jesuit *Dictionnaire de Trevous* (1771) offered a similar definition, but added that in its "primitive" sense nation had meant "a number of families sprung from the same stem or born in the same region."[49]

France's most renowned political philosophers of the eighteenth century were generally nebulous on the subject of nationality. Montesquieu, in the preface to his *Spirit of the Laws* (1748), seemed at least vaguely to equate nation and state without reference to ethnic considerations. "Every nation," he wrote, "will here find the reasons on which its maxims are founded; and this will be the natural inference, that to propose alterations belongs only to those who are so happy as to be born with a genius capable of comprehending the entire constitution of a state."[50] Rousseau was similarly vague. He dedicated his *Discourse on the Origin of Inequality* (1755) to the Republic of Geneva, the city-state in which he had been born, praising it highly as an example to other "nations."[51] His *Social Contract* (1762) with its emphasis upon the "general will" of the people as the basic source of authority seemed to view the state in a civic context, but also to see it as composed of people sharing a common culture.[52] Rousseau's writings in general, however, were clearly inspirations for the Romantic movement which would do so much in the nineteenth century to popularize the ethnic conception of nationality.[53] Voltaire's *Essay on the Customs and the Spirit of Nations* (1756) straddled ethnic and civic meanings. "Nation" in that work could mean either a "state" or groups such as the ancient Greeks, who were typically united in their ethnic identity, but not politically.[54]

Strong reassertion of the civic or political conception of nation appeared in *Droit des gens* (1758), another fundamental treatise on international law, this one by the Swiss writer, Emmerich Vattel. Vattel's subtitle was *Principles of natural law applied to the conduct and to the affairs of nations and sovereigns.* Its first sentence states bluntly: "Nations or states are bodies politic ... ."[55] Perhaps readers should be reminded also of the point made above, that both English and Irish translations of this work in the 1790s used the title, *The Law of Nations.* Thus for legal purposes both the English and the Irish followed Vattel in construing *gens* to mean a sovereign state, not an ethnic group or tribe. French political philosophers of the era, as noted, were more ambivalent.

Identifying nation with state, as eighteenth-century legal scholars were inclined to do, rather slights the distinction that "nation" may have carried greater implications of popular support than did "state." In a legal context, the existence of a sovereign government met, as it still does, the qualification for recognition as a state – whatever the degree of popular enthusiasm or lack thereof for that government. The term "nation," however, seemed to carry more of the implication than did "state" that the government belonged to the people and should serve their interests. Greenfeld, the reader may need to be reminded, insists that "nation" had taken on such connotations in England as early as the sixteenth century, but that they arose much later elsewhere.[56]

In France the Revolution of 1789 clearly made popular support vastly more important than it had been before in determining what constituted a nation. The French became almost infatuated with the term in the Revolutionary period. The explanation appears to arise at least in part from the fact that prior to the Revolution people had tended to think of the nation as consisting of the king and the aristocracy, or the king and a somewhat larger portion of the elite. Indeed, such usage, as noted above, was of long standing in Catholic ecclesiastical circles. With the Revolution, according to Zernatto, the upper portion of the Third Estate, the bourgeoisie, broadened the term "nation" to include themselves.[57] With "nation" suggesting greater popular (as opposed to elite) control of the government, people applied the term with enthusiasm to all that had been royal. The king's army became the national army; crimes against the king became crimes against the nation. A national flag, a national holiday, and a national hymn helped to commemorate the people's rise to an authority that had formerly belonged only to the king and the elite. "All that was royal," wrote Ferdinand Brunot, "became national ... ."[58] Accordingly, the nation became the people, at least the bourgeoisie, and its government became *their* government.

Overwhelming as the new national spirit appeared, it did not immediately penetrate all of the outlying regions of France. As Eugen Weber has demonstrated, patriotism was largely unknown in the Southwestern region of France well after the middle of the nineteenth century. In that area there was then still minimal involvement in the French economy, little use of the French language, and, especially among the people of lowest status, almost no sense of French identity.[59]

With the new concept of "nation" enjoying such popularity, despite the geographic and social limits of its diffusion, it was perhaps inevitable that new terms would spin off from it. Indeed they did. One was "nationalism." Its meaning was the subject of an interesting exchange in 1975 between historians Jacques Godechot and Boyd C. Shafer. Godechot argued that the first phase of the French Revolution, in which the people struggled to transfer royal authority into their own hands, should be characterized as patriotism and not nationalism. "Nationalism," Godechot held, should be reserved to characterize the attitudes of later years, when popular attention had shifted to the hostile relationship between France as a nation and foreign peoples. Shafer thought that, at least in English usage, "nationalism" applied equally well to popular feelings in both periods.[60] Notably absent from their debate was any reference to those definitions of "nationalism" that construe it as either the drive of an ethnic group to achieve its own sovereign government or the principle that each ethnic group has a moral right to its own sovereign government.

The word "nationalism" was slow to come into widespread use. It appeared in the sense of "egotism practiced by a nation" in the memoirs of an exiled French priest, Jacques Barruel, published in 1798.[61] It had appeared even earlier in the works of Johann Gottfried Herder, the Prussian scholar most responsible for popularizing the ethnic conception of nationality.[62] The first French dictionary to include it was *Larousse* in 1874. The definition there was "blind and exclusive preference for that which is properly of one's own nation." According to Sauvigny, the "derogatory tinge" connoted in this definition of nationalism may have led the French to avoid it for some time as "desecrating" the word "nation," which had become hallowed to the French by its use in the Revolution. In any case, the French decried the excesses of what they usually called "the sentiment of nationality" for some years beyond 1830, before adopting the term "nationalism" to carry that meaning. There were some early uses of the term in German and English, but in those languages, too, "nationalism" did not come into common use until late in the nineteenth century.[63]

From nation to "nation state"

Use of the term "nationality" increased following the Napoleonic wars. One of its meanings was that popularized in much of Europe by Mme de Staël in her book, *De l'Allemagne*, which was completed in 1810. Building on the earlier work of Herder, Mme de Staël saw nationality as the totality of those features which distinguished a "nation." She characterized both the French and the German people as "nations."[64] Because *the* German nation existed at that time only in ethnic and not political terms, her frame of reference for Germans was clearly ethnic. This meaning had found its way into at least two French dictionaries by 1823. In 1835 the *Académie française* defined nationality somewhat ambiguously as "State, condition of a group forming a nation distinct from others."

In Britain, as in France, "nationality" came in the nineteenth century to carry both ethnic and political connotations. The *OED* records two instances even before the French Revolution in which "nationality" was used, seemingly in a political sense, to mean "attachment to one's country." By the 1830s, however, use of the term was becoming more common and the meanings more varied. One definition that became prominent stressed the distinctive character of a group, much as in Mme de Staël's use with reference to the Germans. Another was the legal or quasi-legal sense of belonging to a particular nation, as in the nationality of a ship or person. By mid-century a further meaning had appeared: the attainment of independence or unity by a particular group. Before the end of the century there were still more references with an ethnic connotation, as, for example, to Jewish nationality.[65]

It was Germans, however, who came to use nationality almost exclusively in an ethnic sense and to popularize that usage in both Central and Eastern Europe. Why did they do so? Social psychologists have suggested that when members of a group become conscious that their group does not compare well with another group when judged by one standard, one of the actions they can take to enhance the status of their group is to change the frame of reference.[66] This is what German intellectuals of the late eighteenth and early nineteenth centuries accomplished, whether or not they consciously intended to do so. There was then little prospect of the political unification of ethnic Germans. There was also no way in which any of the many existing German states, except perhaps Austria or Prussia (neither of which was wholly German in ethnic terms), could compete effectively for status against France or Britain. Instead of aiming to create a German state that could do so, Herder and many other German intellectuals changed the frame of reference. They rejected the civic standard of national identity[67] and replaced it with an ethnic standard. The Germans would not be identified as the people of a particular sovereign territorial state, but by their ethnicity. This accorded with use in the Vulgate as well as with German mythology.

Patrick J. Geary has offered an explanation for this development. He blames German historical writers for excessive reliance upon the Roman writers, Tacitus and Pliny the Elder. Both exaggerated the enduring charac teristics of ethnic groups. Geary finds that subsequent historians of medieval Europe, following the lead of the German historians who first professionalized the writing of history, dramatically overstated the continuity of ethnic identities. Citing frequent "transformations" among medieval ethnic groups or "tribes" as they were then called, Geary asserts that the only constant relating to them was in their names.[68]

Whatever the explanation, German intellectuals of the early nineteenth century clearly took steps to raise the status of those with German ethnicity. They downplayed the Graeco-Roman heritage common to the major nations of Western Europe, which had been so exalted in the eighteenth century's Age of Reason. Instead they emphasized the new movement toward Romanticism – glorifying the heritage of German tribesmen who had defeated the Romans and avoided the Roman domination to which Western Europe had succumbed. They lauded the virility of the German peasantry. They glorified the German language and German cultural achievements. They shamed their own francophile elite for preferring the French language to German and for slavishly imitating French culture. In short, the Germans shifted the basis of comparison from the political and military power of sovereign states to the physical and cultural attributes and achievements of differing ethnic groups. They began a surge of achievement which by the end of the nineteenth century had made German culture, at least arguably, the most prestigious in Europe. Only somewhat coincidentally, by that time more pragmatic political leaders had also created a sovereign German government. Because ethnic Germans were so productive and especially because they were so numerous, far more so than the French or the British, the new German government prepared to challenge Britain's status as the world's dominant power. It did so even without encompassing all of Europe's ethnic Germans.

A number of factors help explain the growing popularity of the ethnic conception of the nation in Central and Eastern Europe in the nineteenth century. In Catholic areas the pattern of use in the Vulgate that stressed the basis of a *natio* in language or common ancestry surely helped. So did the popularity of Romanticism, which exalted emotion in contrast to the eighteenth century's preference for reason. So too did the esteem which ethnic Germans were gaining in the nineteenth century. Emphasis on common cultural identity, especially common language, had helped ambitious dynasties to achieve political unification and greatly enhanced status in both Germany and Italy. There were many other ethnic groups, notably in the old Austro-Hungarian, Russian, and Ottoman Empires, whose intellectual elites, like those of the Germans and the Italians before them, felt that identity derived primarily from ethnic considerations and not from loyalty to an existing empire or princely state. The ruling elites of the old imperial governments and smaller princely states had on the whole subjected the people of their minority ethnic groups to various forms of discrimination and thus failed notably to win their political allegiance. Such alienated minority groups drew inspiration from the example of the Germans and the Italians in creating sovereign governments to serve the interests and enhance the status of their respective ethnic groups. They embraced enthusiastically the idea that each ethnic group ought as a moral right to have its own sovereign government. Some came to call this idea "nationalism," while others called it "self-determination."

A major influence in popularizing self-determination and "nationalism" was the writing of Johann Gottfried Herder (1744–1803). A Prussian-born Protestant minister, Herder was the author of some 33 volumes. The persistent theme of his writings was that the most precious possession of any group of people is its ancestral culture, especially its language. He insisted that each homogeneous ethnic group should dwell peacefully and democratically within its own natural borders, cherishing its *Volksgeist* or spirit of the people. People identified by their "nation" (in the ethnic sense) should also resist dilution of the spirit of the people, he insisted, by intermixture with others. Governments encompassing people of different ethnicities or "nationalities," as he called them, were doomed, he wrote, as "patched up, fragile contraptions ... wholly devoid of inner life." They would have "no sentiment, no sympathy of any kind linking their component parts."[69]

To the English historian, William Stubbs, events also played a role in popularizing what in the 1880s he called not self-determination, but the idea of "nationality." In Stubbs's view, "the partition of Poland ... was the event that forced the idea of nationality upon the world ... ." The "extinction" of Polish nationality, as he saw it, "aroused a sympathy, awakened an idea of the importance of nationality as a reconstituting idea in a reformed society." Napoleon, he continued, had "carved out" nationalities "with amusing caprice." After the Napoleonic interlude, however, both the Belgians and the Greeks in their independence movements revived the ideas of self-government and of "nationality" defined primarily by ethnicity.[70]

Aided by intellectuals of the Romantic era, by the traditional use in the Vulgate, by prosaic influences such as those noted by Stubbs, and perhaps above all by the unification of both Germany and Italy, "self-determination" became enormously popular in the last decades of the nineteenth century. Its popularity, however, was distinctly greater in Central and Eastern Europe than in the West. The lesser popularity of the idea in, Spain, France, and Britain had two very practical foundations. Each of the three in its homeland was what Carlton J. H. Hayes characterized as a "small empire" rather than a "large tribe."[71] Each of the three encompassed people of different ethnicities, which partly reflected their Roman heritage. Implementing "self-determination" would have split them into several ethnic components, as indeed nationalist movements in each have sought to do since World War II. Such segmentation would have reduced dramatically the size, power, and prestige of each country. Furthermore, Spain, France, and Britain each also possessed colonial empires whose people in many instances bore an ethnic identity quite unlike any of those in the imperial homeland. Thus, in relation to their imperial status as well as to their internal unity, Spain, France, and Britain each had good reason to eschew self-determination as being decidedly disadvantageous.[72]

Self-determination, and hence also the ethnic conception of nationality, reached its peak in popularity during the period of World War I. Woodrow Wilson added greatly to its popularity by including a commitment to "national self-determination" in the Fourteen Points, in which he sought to define the war aims of the Allied powers. To him, to the millions whom he influenced, as well as to earlier converts, self-determination became almost as important a goal as democracy itself. It appealed especially to the ethnic minorities still living under the domination of either the Austro-Hungarian or the Ottoman empires, both German allies in the war and both dismembered, nominally along ethnic lines, by the peace terms.

Between the end of World War I and that of World War II, the popularity of self-determination, and of the ethnic conception of nationality, declined significantly. Wilson's Secretary of State, Robert Lansing, had denounced the idea as an impractical calamity.[73] Trying to implement it at the Versailles peace conference had proved troublesome in the extreme. It suffered also in the cynical disillusionment with all ideals which characterized the 1920s. Hitler and the Nazis, however, disgraced the concept. They used the excuse of unifying ethnic Germans to justify the annexation of Austria, the dismemberment of Czechoslovakia, and the invasion of Poland, which began World War II. Even Hitler's "final solution" to what Nazis called the "Jewish problem" was at least in some sense merely an extreme distortion of Herder's recommendation against ethnic intermixture. It is surely one of history's many ironies that Hitler's legacy to those Jews who survived the Nazi Holocaust was a deep emotional commitment to the creation of a Jewish state, a commitment which has led to the deaths of many more Jews and non-Jews since 1945.

During the period of decolonization and the Cold War following World War II, both the ethnic and the civic conceptions of nationality had successes. Pakistan and Israel were clearly formed with ethnic considerations salient. For both these new nations, religious identities clearly overrode other ethnic factors of lesser importance, such as differences of language and customs. In other areas, however, the newly independent governments kept borders which had been fixed by the European imperial powers without reference to ethnic considerations. These areas included, for example, Malaysia, Sri Lanka, and nearly all of sub-Saharan Africa. In those areas, the borders of new sovereign governments often mingled ethnic groups. In sub-Saharan Africa, the borders of new governments not only lumped ethnic groups together, but sometimes divided a single ethnic group among separate governments. Lamentably, ethnic violence has characterized nearly all of these "new nations," whether their borders were fixed by the old imperial powers or on the basis of ethnic considerations.

Since the end of the Cold War, ethnic identities have appeared paramount. The breakup of the Soviet Union, Yugoslavia, and Czechoslovakia into rival ethnic components has provided dramatic examples of the power of ethnic identities and rivalries. Ethnic separatism plagues contemporary Spain, France, and Britain. Millions have died from ethnic-related violence in Rwanda, Burundi, Sri Lanka and elsewhere in Africa and Asia. Francophone ethnic separatism has sought to dismember Canada. Several journals and an enormous body of literature focusing on ethnicity or on "nationality" conceived in ethnic terms have appeared. Most of this literature is strongly Herderian in tone. Its volume utterly dwarfs that on nationality in the civic sense.

Why, apart from its prominence in the news, has the ethnic conception of "nation" become so pervasive in recent years? The explanation probably should begin with the well established sociological finding that even random division of people into separate groups tends to produce bias in favor of the "in-group" and against the "out-group."[74] Consequently, differences in ancestry, language, religion, or in other cultural beliefs have long tended to engender rivalry among human groups which have some association with each other. Perception of ethnic differences has often led to status rivalries or to conflicts over material interests, sometimes both. Either can lead to violence. Together they are still more likely to do so. Violence tends to beget return engagements, as it did between the French and the Germans from Napoleon through Hitler. It can also lead to the domination of winners over losers. People who identify with an ethnic group which has suffered domination, discrimination, condescension, exploitation, and humiliation by people of another ethnic group almost inevitably feel a powerful desire to have their own sovereign government, their "nation state." Such groups are legion. They command widespread sympathy from others for their aspirations. Because of modern communications and other aspects of globalization, such aspirations are now more widely perceived than ever before.

But why, apart from such wider knowledge of the aspirations of ethnic groups, is world public opinion now so much more favorable to their aspirations than it has been in the past? In part the answer may be that the spread of democratic rights, education, improved transportation and communication, and the processes of globalization in general have raised standards. The internet and television continue to provide people around the world with dramatic, colorful, and nearly instantaneous images of ongoing ethnic conflict. To cite just one rather modest example, in Britain there has been in recent years an enormous outpouring of indignation by Irish, Welsh, and Scottish people expressing their resentment of English domination, discrimination, arrogance, and condescension – among other offenses.

These observations suggest that another factor helping to explain the popularity of the "nation state" is what appears to be a long-term trend in world opinion in favor of human rights. Just as world opinion in the nineteenth century turned against slavery and brought it – largely – to an end, so world opinion in recent years has turned against violations of human rights, even when perpetrated by sovereign governments. This trend is still far from bringing such abominations to an end, but world opinion shows continuing revulsion not only against Hitler's Holocaust, but against South African apartheid, Serbian "ethnic cleansing," Rwandan genocide, and, in Europe at least, even Israeli degradation of Palestinians. Ethnic groups aspiring to achieve their own "nation state" are in some measure the beneficiaries of such sentiment.

I will argue elsewhere, as I cannot in this limited context, that attempting to afford each ethnic group its own sovereign government not only misplaces priorities in an era of global crises, but is likely to produce still more, rather than less, inter-ethnic violence. The ancient Greeks, to cite one example, were highly conscious that they shared ancestry, language, religion, and customs, such as the Olympic Games. They did not unite, however, but formed competing city-states, which not only made war on one another almost incessantly, but also enslaved fellow Greeks.

A preferable solution for the future is for the international community to act, as it did belatedly in Bosnia and Kosovo, to stop "ethnic cleansing" perpetrated by any ethnic group. The international community should also encourage the formation of sovereign governments which will endeavor to serve equally the interests of all the people within the government's territory, rather than only the interests of those with a favored ethnic identity.

Criticisms of the "nation state"

One of the most telling criticisms of the concept of the "nation state" has come from one of its staunchest advocates, Walker Connor. Connor conceded long ago that very few members of the United Nations (under 10 percent in the 1970s) had ethnically homogeneous populations. Even some of those he put in the ethnically homogeneous category (e.g. Germany) were then, and still are, questionable.[75]

Anita Inder Singh has recently reaffirmed Connor's finding while identifying other problems with the concept of the nation state as well. "Ninety percent of the world's states," she maintains, "are multiethnic ... ." Echoing William H. McNeill in his insufficiently noted book, *Polyethnicity* (1986), Singh asserts that throughout history "ethnicity and territory have rarely been congruent ... ." She insists further that because the international community remains firmly committed to the territorial integrity of sovereign states, "To this day the international community has not recognized a right of secession stemming from the right to self-determination ... ." Citing the "ethnic cleansing" which followed the disintegration of Yugoslavia, she concludes that the nation state "remains one of the main threats to peace in Europe." (Some will doubt that its threat is so limited geographically, but the focus of her book was "post-communist Europe.") Another major contention of her study is that the "nation state" is "the very opposite of democracy." Inder Singh argues more specifically that "The intellectual and political pluralism inherent in democracy goes against the intolerant assimilationist and discriminatory logic of the nation state, with its built-in assumptions ... that different (ethnic) communities cannot coexist within one country."[76]

Exaltation of ethnic identities, despite its popularity in recent years, has suffered other setbacks. Edward Shils and Clifford Geertz had popularized the idea that ethnic identities should be seen as "primordial," that is, oversimplifying somewhat, that they were somehow programmed into human beings at birth and were thereafter ineradicable.[77] Indeed, that general concept appeared, and continues to appear (either implicitly or explicitly) in too much of the voluminous literature on ethnicity, despite frequent repudiation.

Several repudiations of the "primordial" nature of ethnicity stand out. In 1976 sociologist E. K. Francis asserted flatly in his widely cited volume on *Interethnic Relations* that "A nation is by no means based on shared ethnicity but on political relationships ... ."[78] Similarly, scholars focusing on African history concluded that ethnicities there were frequently quite recent creations, often resulting from European influence and urbanization.[79] Eller and Coughlan went still farther. Ethnicity, they assert, "like any emotional attachment, is born out of social interaction ... ." There are, they claim, "no circumstances in which ethnicity can be described as primordial."[80] Indeed the United States with its millions of people who have blended or abandoned earlier ethnic identities to become American can be seen as a standing refutation of primordialism.

The concept of ethnicity itself has also come under attack, especially the presumption that tribal or ethnic unity should be seen as enduring and immutable. Patrick J. Geary demonstrated that it was a "myth" to conceive of modern European ethnic nations as the literal descendants of early medieval "tribes." Such "tribes" were themselves highly fluid in membership and of very mixed ethnicity.[81] Richard White made essentially the same point about "tribal" identities among eighteenth-century American Indians of the Great Lakes region.[82] Terence Ranger, as well as René Lemarchand, demonstrated that central African tribes in the period since 1885 were similarly fluid rather than constant in their ethnic makeup.[83] Such evidence from three continents and in widely separated periods surely establishes the fluid nature of tribal and hence ethnic identities. By doing so, it also calls into question a basic assumption of those who believe that each ethnic group should control its own sovereign government – its own "nation state" in the original conception of the term.

Conclusion

For many, perhaps most people in the academic world, "nation state" appears to have become a synonym for "sovereign government." The online *OED* confirms the current equation of the two. To those who invented the term "nation state" in the nineteenth century, however, "nation" meant an ethnic group. A "nation state" was thus an ethnic group which controlled its own sovereign government and, by implication, used that control to serve the interests of the dominant ethnic group. In an earlier era, when ethnic homogeneity was presumed usual for sovereign governments, that may have been appropriate. Globalization, however, has long since made some 90 percent of the world's sovereign governments multi-ethnic. Thus, it is no longer appropriate for one ethnic group to use its prevalence within a country to serve the interests of only those who bear that ethnic identity. It is indeed a formula well calculated to produce violence, as many territories ruled by presumably once mono-ethnic sovereign governments are discovering.

The preceding pages have endeavored to support this argument by making four points. The first was that virtually all major academic writers on the subject, whether they see their subject as "nation," "nationality," or "nationalism," have expressed dissatisfaction with even their own understanding of the terms. Second, this confusion began in Roman times and has persisted into the modern era. Third, for a variety of reasons, chiefly concerning the absence of political unity then for ethnic Germans, intellectuals in the nineteenth century switched the emphasis from the civic to the ethnic basis of national identity. The online *OED* affirms that it was at the end of that century that the term "nation state" first appeared. Fourth, and perhaps most important of all, criticisms of the original "nation state" concept are both numerous and seemingly difficult to refute.

These criticisms include the following:

1   Ethnic homogeneity, which the original Herderian concept assumes, has long been evident in less than 10 percent of the world's sovereign governments.
2   Implementing the concept would increase the number of the world's sovereign governments about ten times, complicating greatly the problem of securing the concerted international action which so many problems posed by globalization seem to require.
3   Multi-ethnicity has probably been more prevalent among territories ruled by sovereign governments in world history than ethnic homogeneity.
4   In the multi-ethnic societies created by globalization the idea of the "nation state," as well as of self-determination, invite violations of human rights and by doing so encourage inter-ethnic violence.
5   The once popular idea of "primordialism" (that ethnic identities are somehow immutably programmed into people at birth) is untenable.
6   Even the enduring nature of ethnic or tribal identities appears mythical; it is repudiated by studies from at least three continents that span several centuries and show such identities to be highly fluid.
7   Globalizing tendencies have increased, and are further increasing, the well established tendency of the world's ethnic groups to migrate, intermingle, and intermarry.

For these reasons it has become almost totally impractical to define borders for sovereign governments which would encompass all the world's people of a particular ethnicity and no people whose ethnicity is different. It is even less feasible to assume that, if we could create such a government, it would remain ethnically homogeneous in perpetuity.

The ambiguity of the online *OED*'s equation of "nation state" with nation also demands attention. By using the term "nation state" without defining it, participants in the ongoing debate about whether globalization will or will not extinguish the "nation state" muddy the waters. Do they have in mind the ethnic version of the "nation state" or do they mean a multi-ethnic or civic version? The case against the ethnic version of the "nation state" seems easy to make. However, those specialists on globalization who take a long view may find that globalizing trends call into question the continued existence even of nations conceived in civic terms. This is not a theme that can be pursued here. What can be said, however, is that participants in this debate ought to know the history of the terms they use and recognize the importance of defining them – whatever the position they choose to take. Furthermore, in taking a position it is important for all parties to recognize the ethnic diversity of people in 90 percent of the world's territories ruled by sovereign governments and to tailor their judgments about the compatibility of such governments with globalization accordingly.

"Nation" ought to be construed again to mean not an ethnic group, but a sovereign government, as it did – and does – in the United Nations. Such sovereign governments ideally should be civic in character, that is, they should seek to serve equally the interests of all the people within their territory. This was a meaning which began to emerge in England centuries ago. It is the meaning hallowed to the French by their Revolution. Ethnic minorities in each country have testified at length, sometimes violently, to how far short of this ideal the practice of each nation fell. Following Herder and Mme de Staël, however, Romantic intellectuals of the nineteenth century popularized the ethnic conception of nation. They capitalized in particular on the yearning of long-subordinated ethnic groups not only for freedom from domination by another ethnic group, but for the enhanced power and status necessary for self-respect. The ethnic conception reached a peak in popularity in the era of World War I, declined significantly by the end of World War II, but has enjoyed a renewal of its popularity since the disintegration along ethnic lines of the Soviet Union, Yugoslavia, and Czechoslovakia.

Anthony D. Smith has set a good example with reference to use of the term "nation state." His early writings, especially *The Ethnic Origin of Nations*

(1986), seemed sympathetic to the concept. In 2004, however, he observed that "nation state" is "a term I try to avoid using."[84] So should we all. But those who persist in using it ought at least, in view of its original meaning, make clear not only what they mean by it but also what they do not mean. If we can use "nation" again to mean, not ethnic group, but sovereign government, we will also reduce the preoccupation of local or regional groups with their own competition against those whose ethnicity is different. We will also improve the outlook for the universal values that ought to accompany globalization: peace, democracy, and respect for human rights.

Notes

1 The author wishes to thank William H. McNeill for inspiration and encouragement, Michael L. White for invaluable aid with research and editing, and Carolyn L. White for indispensable help with computer problems.

2 E.g. Ken'ichi Ohmae, *The End of the Nation State: The Rise of Regional Economies* (New York, 1995); Robert J. Holton, *Globalization and the Nation State* (Basingstoke, 1998).

3 E.g. Anthony D. Smith, *Nationalism in a Global Era* (Cambridge, 1995), pp. 115, 160; also idem, *Nationalism: Theory, Ideology, History* (Cambridge, 2001), p. 137.

4 "Nation, *n.*" and "nation state, *n.*" *OED Online,* June 2003 (Oxford, 20 August 2004); http://dictionary.oed.com/cgi/entry/00321434, and http://dictionary. oed.com/cgi/entry/00321484.

5 "Nation state," in *Oxford English Dictionary* (Oxford, 1989).

6 Works on self-determination are legion. See, e.g. Alfred Cobban, *The Nation State and National Self-Determination,* rev. ed. (New York, 1970); for a more recent view, see Glenda Sluga, "What is National Self-Determination? Nationality and Psychology during the Apogee of Nationalism," *Nations and Nationalism,* 11 (2005), pp. 1–20; Derek Heater, *National Self-Determination: Woodrow Wilson and His Legacy* (New York, 1994); for a view fully as jaundiced as mine, see Anita Inder Singh, *Democracy, Ethnic Diversity, and Security in Post-Communist Europe* (Westport, CT, 2001), Ch. 3.

7 For a succinct exposition of the contrast between civic and ethnic conceptions, see Anthony D. Smith, *Nationalism: Theory, Ideology, and History* (Cambridge, 2001), Ch. 2; or Walker Connor, "The Timeliness of Nations," *Nations and Nationalism,* 10 (2004), pp. 35–47. For a book-length contrast, see Rogers Brubaker, *Citizenship and Nationhood in France and Germany* (Cambridge, MA, 1992).

8 David Held and Anthony McGrew (eds), *Global Transformation Reader: An Introduction to the Globalization Debate,* 2nd ed. (Cambridge, 2003).

9 Arnold van Gennep, *Traité comparatif des nationalités* (Paris, 1922), Vol. I, p. 1. This translation from French and all others which follow are mine.

10 Ernest Renan, "Qu'est-ce qu'une nation?," in Henriette Psichari (ed.), *Oeuvres complètes d'Ernest Renan, I* (Paris, 1947), p. 903.

11 James A. H. Murray, *New English Dictionary* (Oxford, 1903).

12 *Oxford English Dictionary* (Oxford, 1933 and 1989).

13 "Nation, *n.*" and "nation state, *n.*" *OED Online,* June 2003 (Oxford, 20 August 2004); http://dictionary.oed.com/cgi/entry/00321434, and http://dictionary.oed.com/cgi/entry/00321484.

14 Carlton H. Hayes, *Essays on Nationalism* (New York, 1926), p. 245.

15 Idem, *Historical Evolution of Modern Nationalism* (New York, 1931).

16 Idem, *Nationalism: A Religion* (New York, 1960).

17 Hans Kohn, *The Idea of Nationalism: A Study in its Origins and Background* (New York, 1944), p. 13.

18 Idem, "Nationalism," in *International Encyclopedia of the Social Sciences* (New York,1968), p. 64.

19 Boyd C Shafer, *Nationalism: Myth and Reality* (New York, 1955), p. 243.

20 Benjamin Akzin, *State and Nation* (London, 1964).

21 T. V. Sathyamurthy, *Nationalism in the Contemporary World* (Totowa, NJ, 1981), p. 1.

22 Harold Isaacs, *Idols of the Tribe: Group Identity and Political Change* (Cambridge, MA, 1975), p. 27.

23 Eric Hobsbawm, *Nations and Nationalism Since 1870: Programme, Myth, and Reality* (Cambridge,1990), pp. 5–6.

24 Liah Greenfeld, *Nationalism: Five Roads to Modernity* (Cambridge, MA, 1992), p. 3.

25 *Ibid.*, p. 26.

26 Anthony D Smith, *Nationalism and Modernism: A Critical Survey of Recent Theories of Nations and Nationalism* (London, 1998), p. 223.

27 Benedict Anderson, *Imagined Communities: Reflections on the Origin and Spread of Nationalism* (London, 1983), p. 12; (1991), p. 3.

28 Ernest Gellner, *Nations and Nationalism* (Oxford, 1983), p. 7.

29 Charles Tilly, *Formation of National States in Western Europe* (Princeton, NJ, 1975), p. 6.

30 Guido Zernatto, "Nation: The History of a Word," *Review of Politics*, 6 (1944), pp. 351–66.

31 *Oxford Latin Dictionary* (Oxford, 1968). See also Paul James, *Nation Formation: Towards a Theory of Abstract Community* (London, 1996), pp. 9–11.

32 Patrick J Geary, *The Myth of Nations: The Medieval Origins of Europe* (Princeton, NJ, 2002), pp. 11–13, passim.

33 *Oxford Latin Dictionary* (Oxford, 1968).

34 Arthur Nussbaum, *A Concise History of the Law of Nations* (New York, 1947), pp. 18–20.

35 Johan Huizinga, *Men and Ideas* (New York, 1960), pp. 105–7.

36 Gaines Post, "Medieval and Renaissance Ideas of Nation," in Philip Wiener (ed.), *Dictionary of the History of Ideas* (New York, 1973), p. 323.

37 James Houston Baxter and Charles Johnson, *Medieval Latin Word List from British and Irish Sources* (London, 1934).

38   Zernatto, "Nation: The History of a Word," p. 361.
39   Greenfeld, *Nationalism: Five Roads to Modernity*, p. 5.
40   *Ibid.*, p. 52.
41   *Ibid.*, pp. 51–3, 70.
42   *Ibid.*, pp. 35–42, 71–8.
43   *Ibid.*, p. 10.
44   Hugo Grotius, *The Law of Warre and Peace* (London, 1654), pp. 1–2; idem, *The Rights of War and Peace* (London, 1728).
45   Emmerich Vattel, *The Law of Nations* (Dublin, 1792); idem, *The Law of Nations* (London, 1793).
46   Samuel Johnson, *Dictionary of the English Language* (London, 1755).
47   *Dictionnaire de l'Académie française* (Paris, 1694).
48   *Encyclopédie* (Paris, 1765).
49   *Dictionnaire de Trevous* (Paris, 1771).
50   Charles de Montesquieu, *De l'esprit des lois* (Paris, 1748), p. lxviii.
51   Jean-Jacques Rousseau, *Discours sur l'inégalité des hommes* (Paris, 1755).
52   Idem, *Du contrat sociale* (Paris, 1762).
53   Marc F. Plattner, "Rousseau and the Origins of Nationalism," in Clifford Orwin and Nathan Tarco (eds), *The Legacy of Rousseau* (Chicago, 1997), pp. 183–99; Hans Kohn, *The Idea of Nationalism* (New York, 1944), pp. 23, 251; F. M. Barnard, *Self-Direction and Political Legitimacy: Rousseau and Herder* (Oxford, 1988).
54   François-Marie Arouet de Voltaire, *Essai sur les moeurs et l'esprit des nations* (Paris, 1756).
55   Emmerich Vattel, *Droit des gens* (Neuchatel, 1758).
56   Greenfeld, *Nationalism*, pp. 8, 14, 66.
57   Zernatto, "Nation: The History of a Word," pp. 361–5.
58   Ferdinand Brunot, *Histoire de la langue française des origines à nos jours: La Révolution et l'empire* (Nouvelle edition, Paris, 1967), IX, p. 638.
59   Eugen Weber, *Peasants into Frenchmen: The Modernization of Rural France, 1870–1914* (Stanford, CA, 1976).
60   Correspondence, *Annales historiques de la Révolution française*, 47 (1975), pp. 329–33.
61   Guillaume de Bertier de Sauvigny, "Liberalism, Nationalism, and Socialism: The Birth of Three Words," *Review of Politics,* 32 (1970), pp. 147–66. The quote is on p. 155.
62   Isaiah Berlin, *Vico and Herder: Two Studies in the History of Ideas* (London, 1976), p. 181. On nationalism, Berlin notes that Herder "seems to have coined the word ... ."
63   Sauvigny, "Liberalism, Nationalism, and Socialism."
64   Baroness Staël Holstein, *Germany* (3 vols, London, 1814), I, p. 4. Mme de Staël was published first in London because she ran into censorship in Napoleon's Paris.
65   Sauvigny, "Liberalism, Nationalism, and Socialism," in particular pp. 155–61.
66   F. M. van Knippenberg, "Intergroup Differences in Group Perceptions," in Henri Tajfel (ed.), *Human Groups and Social Categories* (Cambridge, 1981), pp. 560–78. Quotation from p. 564.

67 Hans Kohn, "Nationalism," in *International Encyclopedia of the Social Sciences* (New York, 1973), pp. 324–39.

68 Geary, *The Myth of Nations*, pp. 11–13, passim.

69 Quoted in F. M. Barnard, *Herder's Social and Political Thought: From Enlightenment to Nationalism* (Oxford, 1965). p. 58. See also idem, *Self-direction and Political Legitimacy: Rousseau and Herder* (Oxford, 1988); Robert R. Ergang, *Herder and the Foundations of German Nationalism* (New York, 1931); Carlton J. H. Hayes, "Contributions of Herder to the Doctrine of Nationalism," *American Historical Review*, 34 (1927), pp. 719–36; three works of Hans Kohn: *The Idea of Nationalism* (New York, 1944), pp. 427–51; *The Mind of Germany: The Education of a Nation* (New York, 1960); and *Prelude to Nation States* (Princeton, NJ, 1967); Friedrich Meinecke, *Cosmopolitanism and the National State* (Princeton, NJ, 1970); John Breuilly, "Nation and Nationalism in German History," *Historical Journal*, 33 (1990), pp. 659–75, and also "The National Idea in German History," in Breuilly (ed.), *The State of Germany: The National Idea in the Making, Unmaking, and Remaking of a Modern Nation state* (London, 1992), pp. 1–28; James J. Sheehan, *German History, 1770–1866* (Oxford, 1989).

70 William Stubbs, *Medieval and Modern History* (Oxford, 1886), pp. 236–8.

71 Carlton J. H. Hayes, *Historical Evolution of Modern Nationalism* (New York, 1931), p. 4.

72 René Johannet, *Le principe des nationalités* (Paris, 1923), p. 217.

73 Cobban, *The Nation State*, p. 62.

74 William Graham Sumner, *Folkways* (Boston, MA, 1906); Muzafer Sherif, *Intergroup Conflict and Cooperation: The Robber's Cave Experiment* (Norman, OK, 1961); Warren G. Stephen, "Intergroup Relations," in Gardner Lindzey and Elliot Aronson (eds), *Handbook of Social Psychology*, 3rd ed. (New York, 1985), III, pp. 599–658.

75 Walker Connor, "The Politics of Ethnonationalism," *Journal of International Affairs*, 27 (1973), pp. 1–21; idem, "A Nation is a Nation, Is a State, Is an Ethnic Group, Is a… ," *Ethnic and Racial Studies*, 1 (1978), pp. 377–400.

76 Singh, *Democracy*, pp. 30, 245. For her thoughts on self-determination, see Ch. 3 and pp. 10ff.

77 Edward Shils, "Primordial, Personal, Sacred and Civil Ties," *British Journal of Sociology*, 8 (1957), pp. 130–45; Clifford Geertz, *The Interpretation of Cultures* (New York, 1973).

78 E. K. Francis, *Interethnic Relations* (New York, 1976), pp. 36, 145.

79 René Lemarchand, "Ethnic Violence in Tropical Africa," in John F. Stack (ed.), *The Primordial Challenge: Ethnicity in the Contemporary World* (New York, 1986), pp. 185–205; Terence Ranger, "The Invention of Tradition in Colonial Africa," in Eric Hobsbawm and Terence Ranger (eds), *The Invention of Tradition* (Cambridge, 1983), pp. 241–62.

80 Jack David Eller and Reed M. Coughlan, "The Poverty of Primordialism: The Demystification of Ethnic Attachments," *Ethnic and Racial Studies*, 16 (1993), pp. 183–202.

81 Geary, *The Myth of Nations*, pp. 11–13, passim.

82 Richard White, *The Middle Ground: Indians, Empires, and Republics in the Great Lakes Region*, 1690–1815 (Cambridge, 1991). David R. Roediger, *Working Toward Whiteness: How America's Immigrants Became White: The Strange Journey from Ellis Island to the Suburbs* (New York, 2005) includes interesting observations on the history of the words "ethnic" and "ethnicity."

83 Lemarchand, "Ethnic Violence," pp. 185–205; Ranger, "The Invention of Tradition," pp. 241–62.

84 Anthony D. Smith, "History and National Destiny: Responses and Clarifications," *Nations and Nationalism*, 10 (2004), pp. 195–209, esp. p. 205.

10

Afterword: World History and Globalization

William H. McNeill

The global web of communication that influences everyone and every locality so strongly today is not new. Indeed, if one allows for much slower and far more sporadic communication among fewer people, themselves hemmed in by formidable and seldom crossed geographical barriers, it is nonetheless true that human societies always exchanged messages with strangers and altered behavior every so often when something new and attractive came to their attention. Even the Bering Strait and the water gap between Australia and Asia were sometimes crossed from the time human beings first showed up in Australia and America. Strangers also occasionally brought outsiders' genes to local communities along with new skills and knowledge, so despite its global dispersion, humankind remained a single biological species, shrouded in a slender but single web of communication.[1]

Yet recent concern with globalization, which A. G. Hopkins, in the first chapter of this book, dates from the 1990s, is not without basis. For the pace and volume of communication across cultural and geographical barriers intensified so markedly after about 1950 as to disrupt everyday routines and expectations almost everywhere, sometimes with satisfactory but often with painful consequences. Such a world-wide tsunami is indeed new, though the pace of social change had been building up – rather like a nuclear reaction – across millennia until in recent centuries it became unmistakable within a single generation. It started to assume run-away proportions in the nineteenth century, when daily newspapers and instantaneous telegraphic communication were followed by a cascade of new technologies for transport and communications: canals, trains, steamships, trucks, cars and airplanes, as well as photography, radio, TV, and the internet.

Such novelties were unparalleled and penetrated ever further into urban hinterlands until, by about 1950, most village communities, where the majority of humankind were then still living, began to be affected. With that development the whole of humanity began to respond to new hopes and fears, new visions of the possible, and new disappointments when wished-for change came slowly, if at all, or rewarded some while hurting others who were left behind.

Global History: Interactions between the Universal and the Local explores a wide variety of reactions to the resulting tumult across the past two centuries. These essays are unusual in two respects: the diversity of their subject matter and the cohesion of their approach, seeking always to understand what happened in terms of universal ideas and ideals, coming from afar, inter-acting with local heritages to produce something new, distinctive and intel-ligible. The resulting blend of variety and cohesion makes the book a pleasure to read and in my case brought a great deal of completely new infor-mation and understanding about Navajo weaving, the Japanese encounter with Adam Smith and Friedrich List, the Universal Races Congress of 1911, and the world-wide spread of recorded music. More familiar subjects – Hegel's philosophy of history, the breakup of the Ottoman empire, Vietnam between 1945 and 1960 and the confusion surrounding the concept of nation and nation state – attained clearer focus for me as well.

Seldom does a collection of historical essays by specialists in such diverse fields achieve so much. The authors were all recruited from the same university, and their essays show the benefits of prolonged personal inter-changes that lie behind the finished work. My experience with the fierce attachment of specialists to the established patterns of discourse that define and limit their chosen fields of history makes me wonder how Professor Hopkins, who presided over the collaboration, was able to persuade his colleagues to consider what he calls "universals." But the fertility of the result justifies their venture and puts readers in their debt.

Instead of discussing and commenting separately on each chapter, I would like to suggest another kind of universal that seems to me even more signif-icant than those considered elsewhere in *Global History*. Except for the essay on the Navajo, the writers disregard the peasant and ex-peasant majority of humankind, and focus instead on urban elites. To be sure, urban elites always attract historians' attention because they dominate political and other aspects of recorded history. Ever since the rise of urban centers and of the civilizations engendered by cities, the rural majority were largely excluded from governance and lived in semi-autonomous local village communities.

Yet villagers raised the food that kept urban folk alive, and whenever natural or man-made disaster disrupted urban food supplies, as happened often enough in early times, human biological and cultural continuity depended on the survival of villagers and of the agriculture that sustained them and everyone else. From Neolithic times, in short, agricultural villages were the cells of human society where the great majority of human beings lived and died. Cities were parasitic, drawing food and manpower from the countryside, partly by force and the threat of force but also by enticement – by offering better life prospects to immigrants than crowded, land-short villages could match, and by offering rural folk superior goods in exchange for extra food and for the various raw materials they produced.

Little by little, more or less voluntary rural–urban trade, benefiting both parties, tended to increase. Correspondingly, forcible and unrequited transfers from village to city in the form of rents and taxes became less predominant, but never disappeared. Slowly and despite innumerable local setbacks, population increased, technologies of production improved and transport and communication became more capacious. Linkages between city and villages intensified accordingly.

But until about 1950 the majority of human beings still lived in villages and raised most or all of the food they consumed. That elementary fact created a safety net for times of trouble whenever the flow of goods and services that sustained cities experienced temporary breakdown. As recently as 1920, the majority of Americans were farmers, and in times of business crisis many recent urban immigrants could return home to the farm, where they earned their keep by sharing everyday work, and waited out hard times until more attractive city jobs beckoned again. The Great Depression of 1932–38 was so serious in the United States precisely because the rural safety net had by then worn too thin to bear the strain of massive unemployment. Nation-wide relief expenditures became necessary instead, and the welfare-warfare nation state we know today was born.

The post-World War II transformation of urban–rural relationships affected far larger numbers around the globe, with long-term consequences yet to be seen. Details varied from village to village, country to country and continent to continent. I was able to watch what happened in Greece at first hand by visiting six villages at ten-year intervals between 1947 and 1976, observing some of the sudden and drastic changes that came to each community.

Two landmarks were especially significant. Village isolation withered during the civil war of 1946–49, when the American government decided to set up a radio, permanently tuned to broadcasts from Athens, in the public square of every Greek village. When peace returned, roads built during the guerrilla war to supply government troops allowed rattle-trap trucks and buses to circulate goods and persons as never before, superseding the foot-paths trodden by mule trains and humans that had previously connected hundreds of hill villages with the outside world. As a result, enhanced communication inundated every Greek village with a barrage of urban-generated words, music, and general information that soon made local ways seem old-fashioned and unacceptably restrictive, especially to the young.

This disruptive effect was reinforced in the 1960s, when the Greek govern-ment decided to create a national TV network and found it necessary (or at least convenient) to supplement programs generated in Athens by transmitting dubbed American TV sitcoms with which to fill the otherwise empty hours. The effect of exposure to American forms of TV entertainment on Greek family patterns and other folkways was profound. I well remember being asked by the president of a village in Macedonia about a character in a program called *Dallas*, which I had never watched. His surprise at my igno-rance was matched by mine at his attachment to, and concern for, a fictional character from the never-never land of American TV. Our roles were suddenly reversed: he was the up-to-date cosmopolitan and I fell behind, an old-fashioned, isolated, ivory-tower academic.

Suffice it to say that the impact of all the new communications changed Greek village life profoundly. So many of the inhabitants of poor hill-villages chose to seek their fortunes in distant cities, whether in Greece, Germany or overseas, that population shrank drastically, and one of the hill-villages I observed turned into an almost uninhabited ruin. Plains villages fared differ-ently, some adjusting successfully by improving their methods of cultivation, and finding more or less satisfactory urban markets for new, labor-intensive crops, both within Greece and abroad. Others were emptied when new machinery made farm work a part-time occupation for a few tractor drivers, supplemented by seasonal (sometimes Albanian and sometimes North African) harvest hands.

Everywhere old ways altered, and inter-generational relations were severely strained. Hollowed out by the mass emigration of vigorous young adults, the villages I studied all lost their sense of local autonomy. Cities were where everything important was concentrated. Emigrants sometimes clustered together in distant cities and sent back substantial sums to their relatives in Greece. Others simply disappeared, as far as their home village was concerned.

In the long run, both biological and cultural continuity come into ques-tion. All the villages I studied ceased to constitute tight-knit local commu-nities, where age-old custom taught everyone what to expect and how to behave, so that complex human ties made life worth living, however materially restricted or downright poverty-stricken those lives might be. That age-old local way of life disintegrated within the 40 years I was able to observe these six villages.

Profound uncertainty about the viability of emergent newly urbanized, partly nationalized, and partly cosmopolitan society prevails, for Greek birth rates, as elsewhere in Europe, have sunk below replacement levels. Unless the trend changes, soon the country as a whole will either wither or have to accept immigrants bearing different biological and cultural heritages from other parts of the world.

Moreover, when the annual food supply depends on the punctual delivery of gasoline and diesel fuel to innumerable trucks and tractors, as is now the case in Greece and most other modern countries, interruption of existing market flows for more than a few weeks raises the specter of catastrophic famine. Local self-sufficiency, the traditional safeguard against urban breakdown, is irretrievably diminished: like all the rest of us, the Greeks now depend on global markets to keep themselves alive. To be sure, global flows of goods and services sustain new wealth and permit some, but not all, to enjoy higher rates of consumption. But the risks are also greater than ever before – so much greater that long-range viability of contemporary global flows through mechanisms of interdependence seems to me to be very precarious.[2]

Other essays in this book do not touch on this intensely local yet also universal (or close to it) transformation of human society. Only the Navajo weavers can perhaps be counted as peasants, or ex-peasants, and Erika Bsumek does not discuss the communities where the weavers live. She argues that long-standing networks of meanings attached to the art of weaving remain more or less intact and interacted with new patterns of marketing to distinguish Navajo rugs and other textiles from similar woven goods coming from the looms of Zapotec Indians in Mexico. Overall, she concludes, "globalization has strengthened tribal identity by helping to codify and secure craft products to Navajo society" (p. 61).

Success in combining new dyes and designs with local tradition and inherited social discipline – exemplified by the women weavers who approached their looms armed with Spider Woman's instructions as well as with "clear and positive thoughts" (p. 48) – is unusual. I would like to know more about other segments of Navajo society. What can be said about Navajo young men – the restless social element that pioneered the disruption of Greek village society by rebelling against their fathers' often heavy-handed authority? And what is the significance of Navajo population dynamics? Population growth and decay inevitably affect all efforts to maintain traditional ways. In particular, whenever a rising generation faces local land shortages, so that young people of marriageable age cannot inherit as many acres as their parents had grazed or cultivated, drastic measures must ensue – emigration, immiseration, intensification of cultivation, and/or organized robbery and rebellion.

These stark choices confronted most Greek peasants between the late eighteenth century and 1950, for the recent collapse of birth rates reversed long-standing population growth that had strained against the limits of available cultivable land for generations. The Greek peasants whom I observed shared that problem with most of humankind in the post-war decades when run-away demographic growth altered population–land balances in innumerable localities of Asia, Africa and Latin America. And just as in Greece, intensified communications also had disruptive, though never identical, results, and provoked massive migration into cities, frequently across linguistic and cultural boundaries.

It is good to know that tradition and innovation can sometimes reinforce one another, as Erika Bsumek shows happened among Navajo weavers. It is also good to know that interplay between outside universals and local idiosyncrasies occurs in the most diverse contexts, as the other essays in this book demonstrate. But it seems to me also worth knowing that across most of the world another universal has been at work, disrupting age-old local self-sufficiency and village autonomy by folding the rural population into an urban-based, urban-managed, high-tech, flow-through society, whose potentialities for the multiplication of wealth are matched only by its potentialities for unprecedented disaster.

A. G. Hopkins has in fact already explored some instances of rural transformation and village disruption in an earlier book: *Globalization in World History*.[3] Perhaps it is time to connect all the diverse urban manifestations of modernization, as sampled in this volume, with the experience of modernity among the peasant and ex-peasant majority of humankind. Only by doing so can we come to grips with human history as it is and always has been: an interconnected whole.

Notes

1 This argument is developed in J. R. McNeill and William H. McNeill, *The Human Web: A Birdseye View of World History* (New York, 2003).

2 For a more extended discussion see William H. McNeill, *The Metamorphosis of Greece since World War II* (Chicago, 1978); and idem, *The Disruption of Traditional Forms of Nurture* (Amsterdam, 1998).

3 A. G. Hopkins, *Globalization in World History* (New York, 2002).

Index

291